Transport in
Victorian Britain

Transport in Victorian Britain

edited by
Michael J. Freeman *and* Derek H. Aldcroft

Manchester University Press
Manchester and New York
Distributed exclusively in the U.S.A. and Canada
by **St. Martin's Press**

Copyright © Manchester University Press 1988

Whilst copyright in the volume as a whole is vested in Manchester University Press, copyright in individual chapters belongs to their respective authors, and no chapter may be reproduced wholly or in part without express permission in writing of both author and publisher.

Published by Manchester University Press
Oxford Road, Manchester M13 9PL
and Room 400, 175 Fifth Avenue, New York, NY 10010, USA

Distributed exclusively in the USA and Canada
by St. Martin's Press, Inc., 175 Fifth Avenue, New York, NY 10010, USA

British Library cataloguing in publication data
Transport in Victorian Britain.
  1. Transportation – Great Britain –
History
  I. Freeman, Michael J. (Michael John)
  II. Aldcroft, Derek H.
  380'.5'0941   HE243

Library of Congress cataloging in publication data
Transport in Victorian Britain / edited by Michael J. Freeman, Derek H. Aldcroft.
  p. cm.
  Bibliography: p. 284.
  Includes index.
  ISBN 0–7190–1870–6 : $40.00 (U.S. : est.)
    1. Transportation—Great Britain—History—19th century.
  2. Transportation—Great Britain—History—20th century.
  I. Freeman, Michael J., 1950– . II. Aldcroft, Derek Howard.
  HE243.T744 1988
  380.5'0941—dc19   88–6844

ISBN 0 7190 1870 6 *hardback*

Phototypeset in Linotron Sabon
by Northern Phototypesetting Co., Bolton

Printed in Great Britain
by Anchor Brendon Ltd., Tiptree, Essex

Contents

Tables

Figures

1 *M. J. Freeman*

Introduction

The age of the railway

Western Railroad
Oh, here's a pretty row, I ween,
All through the wonders done by Steam,
You'll now not want to drag along,
    As I'll relate all in my song;
For by this wondrous mode, you see,
You'll go four hundred miles per day, –
Aye, faster than an eagle flies,
For steam all other things outvies.
You need not grieve them friends to part, –
From Falmouth you can take a start,
And be in London like a dart,
    Along the Western Railroad.

Anon. (John Johnson Collection.
Bodleian Library, Oxford)

The Victorian Age was undeniably the age of the railway. It is hard for us in the later twentieth century to register the way in which railways transformed Victorian economy and society, for there has been no parallel in later history. We may have entered the age of supersonic flight, but on land the speed of travel has not altered fundamentally in over a century. The motor vehicle is often described as having engineered a revolution in transport, but this does not bear close scrutiny. What the motor vehicle has done essentially is to allow the exercise of far greater individual freedom in transport. The organised travel of the train and the tram-car has given way to the private and highly flexible car and lorry. Even motorways are only partially *twentieth*-century counterparts of the main-line railway routes; in other ways they are simply alternatives to what is essentially a *nineteenth-century* phenomenon: high-capacity movement of people and goods along rigidly defined paths. Within urban areas, too, the tendency has been similar. The modern door-to-door delivery services of the electrical dealer and the department store are only partly new. Towards the close of the nineteenth century, for example, there evolved a remarkable range of customer services of this kind, the majority based on horse traction (see chapter 4). None of this is to say that the motor vehicle has not transformed certain dimensions of economy and society. It is simply to stress the overwhelming force and scale of the changes brought about by the railway and the steam age.

The substitution of machine for muscle power with the dawn of the railway age brought about a leap in the speed of movement which the population at large found great difficulty in absorbing. The Revd Edward Stanley, in describing the approach of trains on the new Liverpool & Manchester Railway for Blackwood's magazine, illustrated the problem in the following way: '. . . there is an optical deception worth noticing. A spectator observing their approach, when at extreme speed, can scarcely divest himself of the idea, that they are not enlarging and increasing in size rather than moving . . .'.[1] The inability to register such a rapid rate of motion became an unwillingness to do so in the face of Dr Dionysius Lardner's fearsome predictions about the effects of brake failure on a train passing through Brunel's Box Tunnel,[2] and the wider concerns over brain damage and miscarriage in pregnancy. When one examines the output of contemporary railway cartoonists and caricaturists, fantasy forms a dominant theme. The application of steam power in stationary motion was a concept which few had difficulty in accommodating. Thus the steam-powered water-sprayer for laying dust on highways which featured in Paul Pry's well-known panorama (fig. 1) was a logical and relatively easily accepted vision. But applied to motion, steam power drew responses more attuned to science fiction, witness the same cartoonist's depiction of a vacuum tube linking Greenwich and Bengal, the vacuum presumably created by the power of steam. Trial speeds of forty and fifty miles per hour achieved on some early railways diverged so sharply from the general pace of motion observed in nature that such fantastic visions were quite logical responses to what, in reality, was similarly fantastic to most popular minds.

1 The 'March of Intellect': panorama by Paul Pry, circa 1829 (Elton Collection: Ironbridge Gorge Museum Trust)

In literature we can find equivalent reactions. Dickens, perhaps the most acute observer of the railway scene and of the railway revolution especially, encapsulates the force and pace of railway motion in Carker's suicide scene in *Dombey and Son* (1846–48): 'A trembling of the ground, and quick vibration in his ears; a distant shriek; a dull light advancing, quickly changed to two red eyes, and a fierce fire, dropping glowing coals; an irresistable bearing on of a great roaring and dilating mass; a high wind, and a rattle – another come and gone . . . .'[3]

On a railway journey in *Hard Times*, Mrs Sparsit is described as 'immoveable in the air though never left behind', while through the carriage window she observed the electric wires of the telegraph which 'ruled a colossal strip of music paper out of the evening sky'.[4] Repeatedly, we are presented with imagery which evokes rapid motion and a strong sense of the lower frictional drag which characterised railroad movement alongside that by road. And in case the observations of a novelist are deemed to be unreliable, we should be reminded of Humphrey House's view that Dickens's understanding of the sensual and social effects of the whole railway revolution was deeper and wider than that of his contemporaries: 'there was never anything whimsical in his emotions about trains; they are based closely on physical experience'.[5]

In poetry, there can be few who will fail to recall R. L. Stevenson's verses 'From a Railway Carriage', in which the rhythms of the train are echoed in the rhythms of the poem and where the rapid succession of details conveys vividly the effect of speed:

> Faster than fairies, faster than witches,
> Bridges and horses, hedges and ditches;
> And charging along like troops in a battle,
> All through the meadows the horses and cattle:
> All of the sights of the hill and the plain
> Fly as thick as driving rain;
> And ever again, in the wink of an eye,
> Painted stations whistle by.[6]

In 'The lazy tour of two idle apprentices', Dickens achieves a similar effect when giving account of a journey aboard an express from Euston: 'The pastoral country darkened, became coaly, became smoky, became infernal, got better, got worse, improved again, grew rugged, turned romantic; was a wood, a stream, a chain of hills, a gorge, a moor, a cathedral town, a fortified place, a waste.'[7]

Dickens's most celebrated record of the railways' impact is, of course, his description of the making of Camden Town cutting in *Dombey and Son*. Here we are confronted with the sheer physical scale of railway technology and of its juggernaut progress through the urban fabric of London. If contemporaries found difficulty in registering the pace of railway motion, they could not fail to apprehend the colossal demands that it made in the construction of the *permanent way*. Gradients and curves commonplace on the roads were untenable in the technology of railways. Railways had to be executed on a datum and on alignments which were altogether new. Thus did their construction through areas like Camden Town give rise to such havoc. For Dickens it was as if a great earthquake had rent the whole neighbourhood:

> Traces of its course were visible on every side. Houses were knocked down; streets broken through and stopped; deep pits and trenches dug in the ground; enormous heaps of earth and clay thrown up; buildings that were undermined and shaking, propped by great beams of wood. . . . There were a hundred thousand shapes and substances of incompleteness, wildly mingled out of their places, upside down, burrowing in the earth, aspiring in the air, mouldering in the water, and unintelligible as any dream. . . . In short, the yet unfinished and unopened Railroad was in progress; and, from the very core of all this dire disorder, trailed smoothly away, upon its mighty course of civilization and improvement.[8]

Some of the social costs of railway building in London are estimated in the Demolition Statements which railway promoters were required by law to furnish before the first reading of a Railway Bill in Parliament. At least four major building schemes in London over the years from 1856 to 1897 involved the potential displacement of 4,000 to 5,000 people.[9] Outside urban areas, the lines of the railroad became notorious not for their destructive impact on the existing human fabric but for the way they thrust unimpeded through the landscape of nature. It was a development which was quickly seized upon by many contemporary artists and engravers. When J. M. W. Turner sought to evoke the pace of railway motion in his famous water-colour *Rain, Steam and Speed,* he proved to be in a minority. For most artists were content to concentrate on the static engineering feats which underpinned the new transport technology, perhaps because they sought to provide railway travellers with a pictorial record of what was often difficult to see from the vantage-point of a train window at speeds of forty or fifty miles per hour. J. C. Bourne's

now memorable volume of drawings of the London & Birmingham
Railway (1839) is absorbing for its concentration on engineering
works: on embankments, on cuttings, on tunnels and on viaducts.
Some are depicted under construction, some in finished form. In fact,
no less than twenty-eight out of the total thirty-four plates focus on
static engineering feats, sixteen of them offering records of construction scenes. Several of the representations of deep cuttings, perhaps
taking their cue from Shaw's picture of Olive Mount cutting on the
Liverpool & Manchester Railway, have qualities of the sublime
about them. The contrast of dark and light is emphasised, the sides
are made to appear almost vertical, while occasional overhanging
ledges create the impression of a cavern, not a cutting.[10] In Bourne's
subsequent volume on the Great Western Railway (1846), the
emphasis on engineering feats is reduced (presumably because the
line was by then some years old), and the focus shifts more to views
from the carriage window and the facilities provided by stations: the
wonders of construction have given way to the pleasures and con-
veniences of railway travel.

Pictures like those of J. C. Bourne were understandably seen by a
very limited stratum of society, whereas Dickens described what met
the eyes of all classes. Indeed, the broad mass of urban labourers and
artisans were soon to experience first-hand the engineering genius of
railway builders; in the massive stone and brick viaducts which
strode across working-class and factory quarters in towns like
Stockport and cities like Manchester. It was hardly the case, though,
that these were perceived as objects of admiration, for to live adjacent to or in the vicinity of one of these erections was to experience
shades of a hell on earth. Vibration, noise, smoke and soot from
passing trains were almost continuous. Night offered no respite.
Some inner areas of cities became so criss-crossed with these viaducts
that communities could become entirely surrounded, in the mould of
some primitive fortress; Manchester and Glasgow afford some
excellent examples. For vagrants and the homeless, of course, the
railway arches sometimes provided a basic form of shelter. In places
they were enclosed so as to make small workshops or other business
premises. On balance, though, railways added to the squalor,
unhealthiness and depression of the urban working classes. Price
levels severely restricted their access to railway travel until the last
decades of the nineteenth century. And as Barker writes in chapter 4,
the commonest mode of travel in towns for much of the Victorian

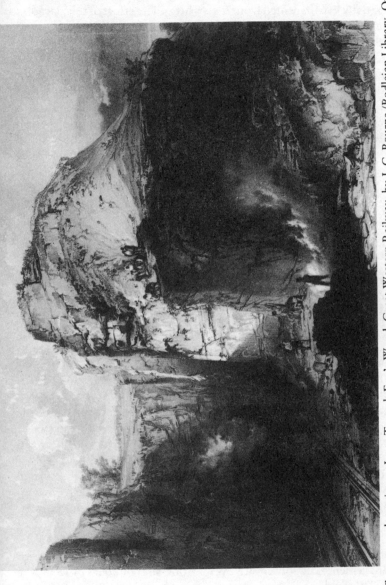

2 The approach cutting to Long Tunnel, Fox's Wood, Great Western Railway, by J. C. Bourne (Bodleian Library, Oxford, Gough Adds fol. c. 4)

Age was on foot. Thus the labouring classes may have been surrounded by the 'wonders' of the steam age as applied to traction, but
their daily lives benefited from it very little. The effect of this paradox
often served to underline the unreal image of the railway in the mind
of the common man, particularly in the first few decades of railway
extension.

In the world of business, it is true to say that railways brought
about yet another change which contemporaries sometimes found
difficulty in apprehending. In an age when the small family firm
remained a prominent feature of production organisation, British
railways were evolving under the control of an incredibly small
number of companies in a form which in the twentieth century
became labelled *managerial capitalism*. Even in 1850, over 60 per
cent of paid capital in UK railways was concentrated among fifteen
companies. Dickens registered this change in an article in *Household
Words* in 1854:

I am going to speak here of a little north-west passage which connects the
waters – not of two oceans, the Pacific and Atlantic – but, of two rivers, the
Thames and Mersey. . . . My track is on the line established by the London
and North Western Railway Company. This body is not only wealthier than
any other corporation in the world, but it is distinguished by having a larger
and more important field of operation.

The resources of the English people will be made very apparent when we
have reflected that the value of the stock-in-trade connected with this one
little home transaction is rather more than the whole capital of the East India
Company . . .; it is quite double that of the Bank of England; and it covers
very close to the total outlay upon the three thousand miles of canal now
established in Great Britain and Ireland.[11]

The London & North Western at this time was far and away the
largest of the railway companies, but in 1858 the Great Western, the
North Eastern and the Midland all had capitalisations of between
£20 and £30 million, no mean comparison against the LNW's £43.7
million.[12] The hallmark of *managerial capitalism* was the system
whereby ownership by the shareholders became divorced from control. The major companies evolved a complex managerial bureaucracy drawn largely from within the industry itself. The sheer size of
railway company operations made this division inevitable. As Gourvish writes in chapter 2, there *had* to be a professionalisation of
management functions. With over 15,000 shareholders in 1855, the
LNWR could hardly have evolved in any other way. One important
outcome was that railways in Britain were not operated with the sole

aim of maximising profits to shareholders: 'although careful to try to keep profit at a level which would prevent shareholder revolt, [railway managers] were naturally more interested in furthering company growth and extending their own power than they were in maximising returns to investors' (see chapter 3).

Steam power at sea

Steam propulsion was not only applied successfully on land. In marine transport it became a common substitute for sail after 1870, though technical and economic limitations remained in some long-distance trades until the Great War. The supreme difficulty with the early steamships was the weight and space taken up by engines and their relative inefficiency in use of fuel, necessitating the carriage of vast quantities of coal. In consequence, their earliest uses were in passenger (including the navy) rather than freight movement, and on short-sea rather than oceanic runs. Early railway locomotives were similarly inefficient in their use of fuel, but the entirely different logistics of land transport made the problem far less significant: a locomotive train could be re-coaled at any number of points along its route according to economic limits. With improvements in the construction of vessels, in particular the use of iron rather than wooden hulls, and with developments in marine engines – the increasing use of the compound engine after 1870 and the substitution of the screw propeller for the side-paddle, for instance – the steamship began steadily to oust the sailing vessel on oceanic runs. By 1883 the tonnage of steam-powered vessels in the UK shipping register exceeded that of sail.[13] By 1913, only 7 per cent of the British merchant marine was sail-powered.[14]

When Samuel Smiles wrote that the railway proved a 'magician's road', giving a 'new celerity to time'.[15] he might well have extended the same remarks to the steamship. The fastest sailing ships needed between twenty and thirty days to make the transatlantic crossing in the middle of the nineteenth century. Brunel's SS *Great Western* performed the trip in fourteen days in 1838. By the early 1870s the journey was being achieved in 9.5 days and by the early 1900s in 4.5 days,[16] a passage time which has not been improved upon in the present century. These figures were all for passenger vessels. Steam cargo vessels were slower, but the relative margins over similar sailing boats were broadly equivalent. The steamship, however, brought about some yet more subtle changes. It helped to realise fully the remarkable technical and economic properties of the sea as a transport medium: as an isotropic surface in which movement is free and easy in every direction. Using only the power of the wind, seagoing vessels were sometimes restricted and frequently retarded in their passage by the peculiar geography of the earth's air circulation. The advent of steam power more or less ended this interference. On a localised scale, it validated important estuaries like Southampton Water where sailing ships had manoeuvred always with difficulty in the face of the prevailing west winds. On an international scale it enhanced trading potential between northern and southern hemispheres: ships were no longer forced to steer a path through the succession of latitudinal wind systems at risk of penalties in time and reliability.

The 'new celerity to time' which Samuel Smiles attributed to the railroad had the logical effect, in his view, of virtually reducing England to a sixth of its size.[17] The progressive spread of oceanic steamship services performed a parallel function. The reaction of an American magazine commentator upon the arrival of one of the first emigrant steamers in Philadelphia summed up the effect: 'Time and space are annihilated . . . ten days from land to land, across that immense watery waste.'[18] The opening of the Suez Canal in 1869, which avoided the lengthy Cape route to India and the East, coupled with the United States and Royal Navy's extensive work in detailed charting of winds and currents, were important additions to the process. *The Times* referred to Suez as 'this short cut from world's end to world's end',[19] meaning the maritime worlds of Europe and Asia. Swifter and more certain sea passages obviously helped to achieve a more intensive use of vessels. According to Aldcroft, by 1911 the average steamship was making ten voyages a year, whereas a century earlier three would have been a likely figure.[20] Thus steamships were not only making faster times but sailing at far more frequent intervals.

Some freights were handled by 'liner' trades, i.e. by scheduled sailings. But many became the preserve of the 'tramp steamer' which grew to particular prominence in the last decades of the nineteenth century. It literally tramped the oceans in search of trade, *en masse* forming a great pool of world shipping capacity which could be called up almost on demand. In some ways the tramp was the supremely logical response to the isotropic transport surface which the sea presented to Western man. There was nothing like it in any other form of transport.

Within the shores of Victorian Britain, one might be forgiven for suggesting that such transformations in marine transport on a world-wide scale held limited importance. The truth was otherwise. Britain's share of the world's merchant shipping tonnage stood at around one-third throughout the later half of the nineteenth century.[21] Its share of world steam tonnage reached 50 per cent in 1880 and even by 1910 had dropped back only to 40 per cent.[22] Between 1898 and 1912, Britain built and launched, on average, 61.2 per cent of the total world tonnage of ships.[23] By 1912, according to Aldcroft, British-owned ships were carrying 92 per cent of inter-imperial trade, 55 per cent of the trade between the Empire and foreign countries and 30 per cent of the inter-foreign trade.[24] The coal necessary to fuel such an expanding fleet of steamships derived largely from Britain. In fact, just prior to the First World War, Britain supplied sixty out of the eighty million tons of bunker fuel consumed annually worldwide.[25] In 1913, some 85 per cent of Britain's total *volume* of exports consisted of cargo coal and bunker coal,[26] in turn equivalent to 8.5 per cent of exports by *value*.[27] Measured against Britain's domestic consumption these figures become yet more striking. By 1913, 14 per cent of total coal tonnage raised was going for export and bunkers, while between 1850 and 1900, when coal produced for domestic use increased fourfold, that raised for export and bunker fuel increased fifteenfold.[28] This formidable battery of statistics tell their own story in the vitality of the British metal-making, engineering, shipbuilding, shipping and coal industries in the Victorian Age.

The phenomenal role that Britain performed in world maritime transport should not be allowed to overshadow the tremendous vigour of maritime trade around the shores of the British Isles themselves. In 1850, for example, nearly 67 per cent of total tonnage entered and cleared from British ports was engaged in the coasting trade.[29] And even though the volume of foreign or overseas trade had overtaken that of coastal trade by the last years of Victoria's reign, the corresponding margin of difference was never as great, at least not up until 1914. In its exploitation of steam power, the coasting trade showed a similar advantage. Coastal steam tonnage exceeded sailing tonnage as early as 1866.[30] By 1877–81, steam tonnage was double that of sail (see chapter 5). The north-east coal trade saw the introduction of screw colliers as early as the 1850s, although it was another twenty years before these steam vessels handled the majority of the trade, the delay in some measure due to a glut in shipping capacity particularly in the traditional collier brigs (see chapter 5).

For the men of commerce, for the industrial entrepreneurs and for the statistical commentators, the impact of the steamship was plain and often of strong material advantage. For the ordinary working population and their families the position was much more ambivalent. For example, wheat and other grain imports rose from an annual average of 60.2 million cwt. in 1861–65 to 210 million by 1911–13,[31] in the process spelling depression for British arable farming, wheat especially. Between 1875 and 1894 the estimated capital value of agricultural land in Britain halved.[32] Millions of acres were converted from arable to pasture between 1875 and 1913. Indeed, in some southern and western countries of England, acreages under tillage fell by a third or more.[66] As a result, unemployment and underemployment became the lot of many farm labourers and small-time tenants.

For all the gains that accrued from the expansion of overseas trade, there were penalties. Docklands emerged to vie with Engels's horrendous descriptions of the Manchester slums. In great ports such as Liverpool, with the added dimension of a vast and too often corrupt emigrant business, the squalor, overcrowding and destitution intensified. Nathaniel Hawthorne, one-time American consul in the town, described the city's poor as 'numerous as maggots in cheese; you behold them, disgusting, and all moving about, as when you raise a plank or log that has long lain on the ground, and find many vivacious bugs and insects berneath it'.[34] In the middle decades of the nineteenth century, only the well-heeled emigrants afforded the relative comfort of passage in a steam vessel. The broad mass of emigrants voyaged by sailing packets, taking four to five weeks for the crossing. During the 1840s and 1850s, American shipowners built vessels specially for the emigrant trade, virtually all of them sail-powered and some up to 3,000 tons, an extaordinary size for a sailing ship.[35] For such 'human' cargo, the age of steam proved remote.

Transport in towns

As movement overland and overseas was progressively transformed by the application of steampower in the latter half of the nineteenth century, within the confines of Victorian towns and cities there remained a startling reliance upon human and animal power in the means of travel and of carriage. If the labouring population moved around very largely on foot, the clerks, traders and growing ranks of the middle classes continued to rely heavily on the drawing power of the horse for their means of travel. In the distribution of goods within urban areas, handcarts and horse drays dominated to an equivalent if not greater degree. The early steam engine was not well suited to road traction in urban areas. Aside from the problem of smoke, sparks and fumes, there was the difficulty of negotiating narrow and poorly aligned streets, as well as the vibration over uneven surfaces. Design improvements by the end of the nineteenth century saw both steam buses and steam lorries operating on town roads, but by the end of the Great War they had been entirely superseded by the internal combustion engine. What *was* adapted for road passenger transport in urban areas, though, was the principle of guiding wheeled vehicles along fixed tracks, and so evolved the extensive tramway systems of many Victorian towns and cities, even if horse carriage prevailed on most of them up until 1900. It was the horse tram far more than the railway that allowed London and other major cities to extend their suburban limits. It was the horse tram, too, which opened up intra-urban travel for the working man with special concessionary fares. One London commentator in the late 1850s noted how rising rents within the five-mile radial zone served by horse omnibuses made it impossible for the poorer town labourers to live outside the narrow hive in which they toiled. He saw the railways as having a social duty to rectify this.[36] In London they certainly did this to a degree (though less so in other cities – see chapter 4) and particularly among the better-off working groups. But the social obligation was otherwise performed by the horse tram. In Barker's words: 'horse power, better organised, was in this respect performing better than the latest steam' (see chapter 4).

Steam did in fact come to feature as the motive power on some tramways. Indeed, by 1894 there were over 500 steam trams in operation in England and Wales.[37] But most of these were in industrial districts, not in heavily-populated urban areas; for populations accustomed to the pyrotechnics of industry, the smoke and fumes from steam trams signified relatively little. The change that was to eclipse the muscle power of the horse was the electric motor. However, as Barker indicates in chapter 4, Britain proved something of a laggard in adopting electric traction. Not only was the USA almost a decade ahead in tramway electrification, but it established itself as the leading manufacturer of electric tramway equipment. Leeds was one of the first major sites of electrified tramways in Britain, in 1891, but it was another ten years before electric operation was widespread in major British cities. The delay was explained partly by a legislative framework which discouraged new investment and partly by the success of horse tramway operations. In the mid-1880s, the Glasgow Tramway Corporation was earning a net profit of 9.5 per cent per annum,[38] that is, relying solely on the tractive power of the horse. Full electrification there did not come until after the death of Victoria in 1901.

Beyond the steam age

Electrification, of course, was not confined to the street tramway. In London it became a *sine qua non* of the deep tube railways. Underground railways nearer the surface, previously reliant on steam traction, were soon converted to electricity. Beyond this, however, there was remarkably little utilisation of electric power by the leading railway companies. The large amounts of capital tied up in steam traction, allied to the increasingly unattractive character of the railway investment market after 1900 (see chapter 3), severely dampened the enthusiasm for innovation; this applied especially outside the area of London. Thus, for those who saw in electric traction the dawn of a powerful successor to the steam engine, at least on land, the event was to prove otherwise. Conversion of both main-line and suburban lines was painfully slow, although much less so on the European Continent than in Britain. Ebenezer Howard's 'Garden City' ideal, in which municipally-operated electrified railways formed the centrepiece of transport organisation,[39] was largely lost on later generations. Deficiencies in the capital market, especially in the inter-war years, were partly to blame. There was also an innate conservatism among managers and a willingness to rest complacently on former achievements. But above all, electric traction began to be exposed to the competition of the internal combustion engine and in a form which placed emphasis upon the individual as operator, in contrast to the collective operation which, of necessity, characterised the railway or tramway principle. From John Davidson's *Testament of Sir Simon Simplex* concerning *Automobilism*, the motor car revealed 'ineptitude in railway-trains', exposing them as 'democratic and vulgar':

> Class, mass and mob for fifty years and more
> Had all to travel in the jangling roar
> Of railways, the nomadic caravan
> That stifled individual mind in man,
> Till automobilism arose at last!
> Now with the splendid periods of the past
> Our youthful century is proudly linked;
> And things that socialism supposed extinct,
> Degree, nobility, and noble strife,
> A form, a style, a privacy in life
> Will re-appear. . . .[40]

In the penultimate decade of the twentieth century, most of us will have no hesitation in saying that, in the Western world at large, the age of the railway has indeed given way to the age of the automobile; certainly, anyone who is familiar, for example, with the geography of modern North-American cities would be exceptionally hard-pressed to argue otherwise. But in Europe, where rates of land occupancy are very much higher and collective responsibility has a far firmer tradition, the claim cannot be so wholeheartedly supported. In cities across the European Continent, tramways still carry millions of passengers daily, and most of these transit systems receive continuing investment. In France, inter-urban railways operations have become a focus for massive new capital investment and innovation. Beyond the Iron Curtain, moreover, the role of public transport, including railways and tramways, is underpinned in political ideology. In other words, it is much less easy to say that the motor age has supplanted the railway age, perhaps in much the same way that the age of steam cannot easily be seen as heralding the demise of horse traction: the British horse population was never greater than in the age of the railway.

The economic and social context

It is easy and also quite common to think of the railway specifically and the era of steam propulsion generally as principal constituents of the Industrial Revolution. But closer examination reveals that this view requires substantial qualification. Notwithstanding the difficulties of establishing as well as justifying start and end points to the Industrial Revolution, it is impossible to escape the fact that a number of major producing sectors of the economy had undergone

extensive technological and organisational transformation well
before railway transport had become widespread, and before steam
power was the primary means of propulsion at sea. As has been
argued elsewhere, the extending system of transport provision
associated with the decades from 1780 to 1830 saw no fundamental
revolution in transport technology.[41] What essentially prevailed was
a constant process of adjustment and improvement to pre-existing
transport technologies. Why *did* steam propulsion on land and at sea
come late to British industrialisation? Was it a function of technical
barriers? Were there deficiencies of capital accumulation? Were the
existing conditions of transport demand and supply relatively well
adjusted?

The technical realm
The eighteenth-century steam engine was heavy and cumbersome in
nature. It required the inventive genius of the Cornish engineer,
Trevithick, before it could be adapted for motion. This was first
achieved only in the opening years of the nineteenth century when he
demonstrated both a steam road carriage and a steam railway locomotive. Even then, certain technical problems remained, and, with
Trevithick's attentions attracted to other projects, developments did
not proceed until the work of George Stephenson in the 1820s which
was eventually to produce the prototype of the modern steam locomotive, the now famous *Rocket*. A second factor in the steam
railway's relatively slow progress was the difficulty of providing
sufficiently durable rails for locomotive running. Trevithick
encountered this problem. Indeed, the breaking of the cast-iron rails
under intensive use may conceivably have been the major reason why
he neglected to pursue the commercial potential of his locomotive
design. The substitution of wrought iron for cast iron was part of the
solution; the other was an improved design of rail. The penalty in
this, of course, was that steam locomotion required the laying of an
entirely new permanent way; making do with an existing plateway,
for instance, was not adequate. The implications of this for capital
demands are self-evident and may explain why it took strong
commercial pressure, of the kind exerted for the Liverpool &
Manchester scheme, to set up the steam railway as a clear alternative
mode of transport. The application of steam power in marine propulsion met with similar difficulties, as we have already seen; indeed,
the particular logistics of marine transport served to enhance the

impact of the major technical weaknesses, especially in the bunker-
ing problem.

Deficiencies of capital
The railways absorbed some £240 million of accumulated capital up
to 1850.[42] This was a vast sum. By the mid-1820s canal companies
had taken up only £12.2 million and all other private companies only
around £38 million.[43] It is true that a large proportion of railway
investment was wasted, much of it committed in the speculative
manias of the later 1830s and 1840s and altogether without
economic rationality. But the productive proportion that remained
still represented a massive, single investment sector; moreover, it is
impossible to view the profitable portion outside the speculative
context in which it was generated. There can be little doubt that this
scale of railway investment would have been impossible to stage in
earlier decades. Not only was gross capital formation much more
restricted – at the beginning of the nineteenth century it may have
been no more than 7 per cent of national income,[44] whereas by the
railway manias it had reached 10 per cent[45] – but the habit of private
company investment was then ill-formed. The major outlet for
accumulated capital had traditionally been in government stocks
and, short of a state programme of railway-building, the capacity for
large-scale capital initiatives of the kind necessary in railway construction was limited. Furthermore, the early industrialists had
generally been compelled to put the bulk of their accumulated profits
back into their mills and factories, so that an otherwise highly logical
constituency of transport investment had in fact figured relatively
little up to the 1830s. A final dimension of the railway investment
boom which again made it very much a product of its times lay in the
role performed by provincial money markets. After half a century of
industrialisation, areas such as South Lancashire were beginning to
become major reservoirs of capital. All the time that government
stocks formed the standard mode of investment, there could be little
localised take-up of these reserves because London brokers dominated the market in such securities. With the emergence of the
railway as the investment focus, the way was suddenly opened for
provincial broking, since railway securities were not a field in which
London could have any prior claim. The results were spectacular,
aided by a mushroom growth in the investment press, including
journals like the *Railway Times* of 1837. Lancashire capital,

chanelled through newly-established stock exchanges in Liverpool
and Manchester, was soon underwriting not just local railway
schemes but a major part of English railway development generally.
The London & Birmingham Railway had almost half its total £2.5
million supplied by Liverpool, for example.[46] The dominance of the
provincial stock exchanges in the railway securities market proved a
short-lived one and London soon re-established its hold. But their
part in mobilising the accumulated profits of northern manufacturers and merchants was a vital step in the evolution of Victorian
company finance.

The inadequacies of the capital market which retarded an earlier
development of the steam railway were no less significant in the
expansion of steam power at sea. In the marine sector, though, a
number of more specific factors acted as brakes upon development.
In one case they derived from mercantile interests and practices. In
another they sprang from trade fluctuations, particularly from the
depression in the mercantile marine which followed in the aftermath
of the Napoleonic Wars. The mercantile world survived in such
legislation as the Navigation Laws and in monopolies like those of
the East India Company; neither provided particularly conducive
conditions for 'entrepreneurial innovation'. But an equally serious
difficulty was the way shipowning, as Jackson reminds us in chapter
7 was largely an ancillary of merchanting: 'merchants for whom
ships were a necessity rather than an investment usually spread their
risks by owning shares in various vessels which carried their goods'.
The trading opportunities of the Napoleonic Wars saw the beginnings of shipping as a capitalist industry *per se,* but it was several
more decades before *active* shipowning became typical (see also
chapter 5).

The balance of transport demand and supply
There must be few writers who would deny that there were not
transport bottlenecks prior to the advent of the railways. Some of the
later canal schemes were direct responses to these, the Birmingham
and Liverpool Junction scheme among them. But as Hobsbawm has
remarked, there is no evidence that transport difficulties crippled
industrial development in general.[47] The Liverpool–Manchester line
may have been nurtured within a climate of intense dissatisfaction
with the existing canal links. Beyond such single instances, though,
road, water and waggonway transport appear to have been servicing

the needs of the industrialising economy without undue difficulty. The relatively slow growth of railway freight traffic relative to that carried by inland water and by coasters testifies to this.[48] Indeed, the twelve most important canals in the country increased their tonnage from 10.5 to 14.0 million between 1838 and 1848.[49] Apart from railway lines like the Stockton & Darlington, which were built specifically for heavy mineral carriage, much early rail freight was opportunist in nature. Traffic managers were slow to perceive the potential scale of railway usage beyond the realm of passenger carriage. This was apparent in the desultory provisions that some companies made for the supply of rolling stock for freight conveyance. In the mid-1840s, the LSWR was reported to have carried coal only when they had no other traffic.[50] Indeed, coal did not become a universal item of railway traffic until after 1850. Many companies are said to have been shy of carrying coal, in the case of the LNWR even contending that it was not respectable to have coal trains running alongside trains carrying passengers.[51] There were also a series of much more practical barriers to the growth of railway freight traffic. A central problem here was trans-shipment between different company lines. Canal and waggon proprietors had had decades in which to perfect such arrangements. Railway managers were forced into rapid improvisation. In 1842 the Railway Clearing House was founded to try to facilitate the *accounting* of through traffic, but as Bagwell has shown, it made a poor showing in its early years; even by 1857 only about one-third of all goods traffic receipts went through the Clearing House, while coal traffic more or less fell outside its control altogether.[52] Railway managers also faced novel difficulties over the integration of passenger and freight traffic. The very nature of railway technology is not conducive to the frequent running of traffics of different operational types. For example, without very elaborate provision of passing loops, a line with an intensive traffic in fast passenger trains is hardly able to accommodate an equivalent traffic in stopping freight trains. The mix of traffic types, operating to different time schedules and varied stopping cycles, was never a problem in road or coastwise movement and only rarely so on canals. With railways, though, the matter became progressively more acute over the course of the nineteenth century. In some cases it could be resolved through traffic pooling agreements between adjacent companies. In other cases it was resolved only by discriminating in favour of one kind of traffic over another: the companies with prestige long-distance passenger operations, for example, became less and less willing to have their main lines cluttered up with slow/moving goods traffic, and ultimately there evolved certain pricing policies which favoured one sort of freight traffic over another, especially import/export commodities.[53]

A further singular disadvantage of railway technology was the relative difficulty with which continuing changes in the geographical bases of transport demand could be accommodated. Coastal brigs could vary their ports of call with comparative ease; carrier operators could modify or extend their routes. In the pre-rail era, only the waterways were restricted in this respect – through the penalty of a fixed track. And the railways naturally laboured under the same constraint, even given the aid of elaborate webs of horse-drawn road services around stations.

When one focuses specifically on marine transport, the picture of demand/suppy conditions is not altogether dissimilar. Steam power was more readily adopted at sea in the sense that steam vessels required no special track in the way that a steam railroad did; and as Jackson writes, other capital expenditures associated with steamship operation (e.g. piers) could be readily shifted on to the public purse. Not surprisingly, therefore, the steamship emerged before the steam train. Indeed, by the time the Liverpool–Manchester railway was under construction there were well over 300 steamers plying Britain's coastal waters and estuaries[54] (see chapter 5). Most of these vessels, however, were passenger-carrying. Steam-driven cargo vessels were a much rarer phenomenon: as previously indicated, screw colliers, for instance, were not properly established in the coastal trade until the 1870s. Steam cargo vessels offered speed but not necessarily cheapness. And coupled with the depression in British maritime trade during the 1820s and 1830s, the picture was one of surplus, not deficit shipping capacity. During the French Wars, traders undoubtledly met growing problems of deficient shipping capacity, as Jackson describes in chapter 7. But this need was mostly met by foreign vessels, so that the energies of British inventors missed out on what might otherwise have been an impor-tant trial-ground. It remains true, however, that the speed which the steam railway eventually conferred upon inland freight movement found no direct parallel in coastal and overseas freight carriage. The survival of the ocean clipper until the turn of the century is obvious demonstration of this.

Although one can identify a whole set of impediments to an earlier utilisation of steam power, it is essential also to consider the possibility of more clearly positive dimensions to the timing of the steam age in transport. It is possible, for instance, to see railway development as related to the burgeoning interest in scientific knowledge which characterised the decades from Waterloo, sometimes rather cynically described as the 'March of Intellect'.[55] Another interpretation would be one which considers railway expansion in combination with the growth of steam power at sea: they formed part of a continuously widening search for materials and markets in Europe and beyond as prospects in the domestic sphere were exhausted or became uncompetitive.[56] In the broad terms of Marxist analysts, they provided means towards a resolution of the growing crisis of capitalist accumulation in early Victorian Britain. A third, not unrelated, view is that suggested by Langton and Morris. It is that railway development in particular was part of a process of reassertion by the metropolitan economy.[57] During the Industrial Revolution, London's powerful dominance of national economy and society had been diminished by the rapid growth of resource-based regional systems in the Midlands, the North, South Wales and central Scotland.[58] Railway development, with London as an undisputed focus in network and later in financial terms, helped rectify this, even if certain latent forces of regionalism were carried over in powerful railway company organisations such as the North Eastern. The following discussion examines each of these dimensions in turn.

The 'March of Intellect'
It was Klingender in 1947 who argued that so broad a section of the English middle class had never been so genuinely interested in science as in the early nineteenth century. And although Victorians (of all classes) had initial difficulties in registering the true nature of steam-powered transport, faith in science encouraged their investment in it.[59] There were certainly many reasons for contemporaries to doubt the success of railway technology. Inadequate and unreliable motive power, boiler explosions, minor collisions and operating disorganisation were common enough on most early lines. And the fact that it took until the early 1850s before the volume of goods carried by rail first exceeded that carried by canal once again testifies to the railways' somewhat shaky entry. But would-be investors were clearly unruffled by such questions – as one sceptical observer put it

in 1848: they were dazzled and deceived by the 'air of assumption and parade about a railway' . . . it was 'the very type of enterprise, energy and efficiency'.[60] The railway engineers and builders themselves were by no means certain of their ground: witness the reliance on stationary engines and cable traction in the approaches to the stations at Liverpool Wapping and London Euston Square, and, even more seriously in hindsight, the elaborate and expensive measures to restrict gradients on account of doubts over hauling power and adhesion. As Gourvish points out in chapter 2, Britain's railway costs per route mile were eight times higher than those in the United States, nearly two-thirds of the extra expenditure being attributable to more lavish engineering standards. Popular interest and investment in railways was thus not exactly in accord either with their performance or with scientific and engineering confidence. The appeal, therefore, of a deeper, pseudo-religious faith in science has obvious merits in our appreciation of the railway age.

Such considerations exercised less force in the adoption of steam power at sea, and this was reflected in the way the marine sector saw little of the speculative mania which prevailed in railway development. Notwithstanding the Promethean enterprises of engineers like Brunel, the shipping realm was, partly by definition, much less exposed to the public gaze and, by the same token, impinged upon their daily lives of citizens in equivalently reduced measure. The maritime world perhaps received its most public exposure through the agency of the Royal Navy.

The outward drive of capital
The view that the age of steam on land and at sea can be viewed as allied and integral components of a stage in the evolution of British capitalism has obvious attraction. The special commitment of many nineteenth-century railway companies to the handling of foreign trade became a source of increasing antagonism among home traders. The scale of railway company investment in ports and in 'short-sea' shipping brought forth equivalent reactions. In terms of the national exchequer, the invisible earnings which flowed from British shipping concerns in their multifarious activities across the world's seas have long been a standard feature of the textbooks; and such income became a vital part of the balance of payments in the middle decades of the nineteenth century.[61] But these clips of evidence, of course, engage theory with reality in only the loosest and

most superficial of ways, notwithstanding the conceptual barriers to any conventional empirical testing of Marxist theory. To begin to claim a consistency of empirical and theoretical realms, we need to answer many more basic questions. Ideally, for instance, it would be advantageous to establish the proportion of railway tonnage which was import/export trade. However, this not only involves fundamental problems of definition and delineation, but it also imposes data demands that are not capable of realisation without much juggling of statistics in the fashion of the cliometricians, with all the attendant perils.

In 1913 the total tonnage of imports and exports has been estimated as around 150 million.[62] For the years 1908–13 the average tonnage carried on the railways, allowing for double counting, was 329 million.[63] The resulting, albeit crude, ratio is clearly an impressive one, especially when it is borne in mind that most overseas trade was handled at a small number of major ports which drew upon a limited number of regional railway systems. The difficulty here, of course, is that one cannot assume that the entire import/export trades were handled by the railways. Some imported goods and some exported goods were consumed or produced in the immediate vicinity of the ports themselves and thus incurred no inland carriage at all. Moreover, the coasting trade undoubtedly handled some of the business of internal collection and delivery; excluding the coastal *coal* trade, most of which was for domestic use, some 50 million tons were handled by coasters in 1910 (see chapter 5). There is also, by contrast, the question that some part of British exports consisted of manufactures. Railway carriage was used extensively in the assemblage of raw and semi-finished materials for the making of such goods, so that there was an indirect although no less important contribution to the export trade. This trade in manufactures was obviously small, since by 1913 the coal export trade alone accounted for 85 per cent of total export volume (including re-exports).[64] However, the aggregate tonnage involved in the assembly of materials would have been many times greater than in the movement of finished products, particularly given the extensive weight loss in manufacturing processes such as iron and steel. In 1879 the making of pig-iron alone involved carriage charges on material inputs, which represented some 32 per cent of the total sums received by the railways for mineral traffic.[65]

It is clear from this discussion that the more one attempts to probe the scale of the railways' reliance upon overseas trade, the more difficult does any answer become. Above all, perhaps, one has to confront the distinction between value and volume which can yield very different outcomes. Inevitably, then, one falls back upon the statistics quoted at the outset: railway tonnage was not of such a scale as to dwarf the tonnage of overseas trade. And one finds some confirmation of the significance of this observation in railway companies' attitudes to the import/export business.

The policies of the railways towards the import/export trades became a bone of contention among many members of the British business and industrial community in the last three decades of the nineteenth century. Their central complaint was that foreign commerce was given undue preference in pricing and the issue eventually became part of a wider enquiry into railway charging policy undertaken by a Parliamentary Select Committee in 1881. The proceedings of this committee make illuminating reading as regards the place of import/export trades in railway traffic and, more widely, in the railways' economic management. Some of the most glaring differentials in charging occurred in food imports. American meat and cheese, for example, could be brought into Liverpool and then despatched by rail to London at roughly half the charge for which Irish meat or Cheshire cheese were similarly conveyed.[66] In textile manufacture, worsted merchants in Bradford could bring in foreign wool from London at a charge of 2.25d per mile, but for wool from Banbury, Oxon, they paid 3.5d per mile.[67] In Birmingham's iron and steel wire trade, meanwhile, firms complained how Antwerp wire could be delivered to Birmingham via London at 16s 8d per ton, whereas Birmingham wire delivered in London cost 28s 4d per ton.[68] There was little uniformity to the size of the differentials, either in the import or in the export business. Some ports were 'nursed' by railway companies which meant that they got more favourable rates than some others (see later). Those regions which were unlucky enough to be in particularly disadvantaged locations relative to these ports found much to complain of: Birmingham was among them.[69]

The explanations for the favour accorded foreign trade were various and not always very clear. The Select Committee inquiry rarely got fully to grips with the matter: lines of questioning, as well as answers, were sometimes confused and occasionally even obscure. The railway companies certainly discovered in the growing import/export trades a source of volume traffic which could usually be very simply trans-shipped over their respective networks. For example, to carry 1,000 tons a year from producing centre A to outport B was infinitely preferable to carrying 1,000 tons from A to markets at D, E, F . . . Z. This was just the traffic to offset the fairly heavy fixed costs that most companies had to support. It was also the traffic manager's dream. As a result, companies actively sought out such trades and, in order to secure them, agreed special rates. In some cases, reductions were enhanced by inter-company competition for import or export traffics. In other cases, the low levels of rates were simple functions of the need to ensure a delivery price that realised a market. The very low rates on American meat and cheese imports into London through Liverpool appear to have been in this category. A more precise illustration has been quoted by Cain in respect of the NER.[70] In 1903 the company handled 561.7 thousand tons of grain. Some 295.8 thousand tons of this (53 per cent) were carried away from the ports, most from Newcastle and Hull. The remainder was carried from 467 different stations at an average of 569 tons per station per year. The grain imports at Hull and Newcastle cost much less to move than the grain traffic orginating from a multiplicity of local stations, the product of home agriculture. Some railway managers went so far as to claim that the volume traffics of the import/export business were vital to supporting the rates that prevailed on home goods. The fact that many companies also granted concessionary rates on *volume domestic* traffics adds credence to this, even though the position was frequently cast simply as the outcome of the power of bigger businesses against small-scale dealers and producers. The merits to the companies of a regular volume trade along a few select routes were often not enunciated.

It was perfectly logical that in their concern to handle foreign trade railway companies would eventually be led into the acquisition of port facilities. As trade volumes expanded, ports increasingly became the Achilles' heel of the import/export operation. Investment in new docks was an expensive enterprise, particularly given the scale of the increase in the average size of vessels in the Victorian era. Private and corporation-owned dock or port authorities encountered steadily greater difficulties in responding to new capacity demands, and, with a number of them, fragmentation of control (as in London) or simple conservatism (as at Hull) exacerbated the incongruencies arising from deficient capital input and the basic lumpiness of new capital investment when it eventually came. As some of the most highly capitalised organisations in the land, the major railway companies were often much better placed to undertake port and dock investment. And this was quite apart from the altogether separate incentives which inevitably flowed from control over the break-of-bulk operation. Thus the North Eastern Railway built a major coal dock at Jarrow on Tyneside in the late 1850s, and developed Hartlepool as a prime competitor to Hull with its complacent and, in some eyes, incompetent port management. On the Humber, the Manchester, Sheffied & Lincolnshire Railway (later the Great Central) played a major role in developing the new port of Grimsby; in the later 1860s it was briefly the fifth port in the land, by value of trade (see chapter 6). By the 1890s the great packet port of Southampton lay in railway hands, while dotted around the entire country's coastline were dock enterprises, of various forms and sizes, which owed their existence to railway managers. Immingham on Humberside was one of the outstanding later successes (Great Central Railway). By contrast, the Furness Railway's £2 million investment in Barrow never really paid off.[71] But this was not very different from some *public* dock enterprises: there were few certainties in seaborne trade, especially against the onward march of technology, economic fluctuations and a competitive spatial system in almost continuous flux. By the later 1930s, railway companies had sunk approximately £66 million into Britain's ports.[72] Alongside the Mersey Docks and Harbour Board which had invested some £45 million, this appears small, except that Liverpool was a giant among ports.[73]

Railway investment in ports was accompanied by a growing interest in 'short-sea' passenger ferries. By the end of the nineteenth century most of the larger companies had built up fleets of passenger boats to service traffic across the Channel, over to Ireland, across the North Sea and to the Scottish archipelago. The cross-channel sector undoubtedly held the greatest traffic potential, and to have railway and steamer operations under unified control and ownership was clearly advantageous in realising this. But because the cross-channel sector was also exposed to strong competitiveness (central southern and south-east England were served by no less than five different companies), the returns upon investment were equivocal. The greatest beneficiary of this investment, in fact, was probably the travelling public, who benefited from steadily rising standards of service, in much the same mould as occurred on long-distance railway routes. In cargo carriage, railway companies were also active participants, particularly on runs like those from the Humber to the southern shores of the North Sea. Much less is known of these activities, but competition undoubtedly yielded its penalties, even if some services were first conceived as 'loss leaders', anyway.[74] In the oceanic shipping sector, direct railway participation was by and large negligible. It was left rather to private shareholders to register the interconnectedness of inland and overseas transport provision and to invest accordingly, although the aggregate constituencies of railway shipping investment remain to be identified.

The wider forces which underlay the behaviour of the railway interest in the later nineteenth century undeniably bear a certain labyrinthine character: the debate about the companies' poor profitability, as examined by Cain in chapter 3, is evidence enough of this, as were the difficulties experienced by the Select Committee when enquiring into railway charges. However, the inexorable workings of capital are not hard to seek, either within the confines of the 'performance' debate or within the wider realm that this discussion primarily addresses. The facility for private individuals to own freight waggons, for example, provided the *petit-bourgeois* business community with a lucrative long-term capital investment, but at great penalty to the railway companies in terms of operational and economic efficiency.[75] Such waggons could not be moved around and utilised at will. They also represented a form of institutionalised obsolescence in terms of the pressure on companies to introduce waggons of larger and more efficient capacity. It is difficult to conceive of a more inappropriate context for enactment of the principle of private property, but for anyone with a few hundred pounds to spare it proved a highly attractive proposition: once the initial capital outlay had been made, a *private-owner* waggon required little attention or management. The wider issue of shareholders' profits presents a slightly more ambivalent picture. The great initial waves of railway investment were of course fired by the spectacular returns which ventures like the Liverpool and Manchester yielded. And the traffic policies of many companies up to about 1850/1860 laid stress on high cost/price margins. But two factors contributed to a shift in this position. Increased competition and increasingly high fixed costs prompted companies to seek out volume but low-margin traffics – in freight especially, but also in passenger movement.

Secondly, the shareholders and the interest that they represented were pushed more and more into the background as railway companies developed characteristics of corporatism, as previously described. The objectives of the managerial bureaucracy were often somewhat at variance with those of the shareholders. Railway managers, as Cain reminds us in chapter 3, were invariably more concerned to further company growth and extend their own power than simply to maximise dividends. However, where a company was so geographically delineated as to identify with a discrete set of business interests (e.g. in the case of the NER), the argument clearly becomes more a question of profitability to a defined constituency of interest (see chapter 3). The interests of capital were also reflected in the determination of companies to avoid intervention by the state. As the earlier discussion of the 1881 Parliamentary Committee on rates indicated, public disquiet about railway management grew considerably in the later decades of the nineteenth century and railway managers ended up trying to sustain a delicate balance between public demands and company interests so as to stave off major state intervention. When intervention became a reality in the 1890s, the companies embarked upon a path which began to look to the state as a possible protector of their interests; but, as Cain writes, the results were relatively fruitless, in part because of the growing radicalisation of railway labour.

The pull of the metropolitan economy

One of the most remarkable contrasts between the canal era in transport and the age of the railway was the dominance of London. In the two and a half centuries from the Tudor accession until the beginnings of industrialisation in the mid-eighteenth century, London exerted an exceptional power over the provinces.[76] It was, for instance, a prime focus of migration and soon became the largest city of Europe. In trading terms, it was the undisputed centre of mercantile capital and control. In particular, London merchant houses held a virtual monopoly in a great many sectors of British foreign trade dealing. Early transport improvement by and large reflected London's dominance. The turnpike road system initially evolved very much as a polar network, with London as its focus.[77] The road carriage trade echoed the pattern.[78] Only after almost a century of turnpike development did the increasing economic significance of the Midland and Northern provinces begin to reveal itself –

seen, for example, in the startling densities of turnpikes in parts of the Severn Valley and in the belt from the Black Country north towards Sheffield.[79] River improvement and, later, canal construction reinforced this trend. Indeed, Langton has even gone so far as to say that canals represented a fundamental building block in the emergence of the regional (i.e. provincial) industrial economies,[80] although this obviously could not have applied to the North-East where there were no canals. A variety of technological, operational and investment factors affecting canals made canal-based economies, according to Langton, 'more specialised, more differentiated from each other and more internally unified'.[81] Tertiary functions which had previously been performed only by London were now undertaken at centres like Manchester and Liverpool. The latter's eclipse of London as the country's cotton-broking capital is perhaps one of the most singular examples of this. And one previously unrecognised adjunct to this decentralisation process lay in the cost–space divergence which flowed from Pitt's raising of mail charges on a distance rating over the period 1784 to 1814. Commercial intercourse between the provinces and London became steadily disadvantaged, notwithstanding a growth in various extra-legal channels of mail distribution.[82]

Although it was in the industrial provinces that the seats of the railway revolution were to be found and although, for a time, it was the desire to link major industrial metropoli with outports and each other that fuelled development, it was soon to London that most company sights became ultimately directed. By mid-century, the railway network had evolved into one showing clear radial characteristics, focused on London, rather in the fashion of the early turnpike system over a century before. The division of Britain's railway network among a large number of private companies actually enhanced London's simple network polarity. The companies competed with each other in the range and standard of service provision, so that the many routes into the metropolis acquired facilities which they would never have possessed under national control or under conditions of combination. The Great Exhibition in London provided the setting for perhaps the starkest demonstration of the change which was being effected. No less than six million people, or a third of the English and Welsh populations, were conveyed to the exhibition by rail.[83] Such an enterprise could never have been mounted before the railway era; equally, it could not have been realised if London had not possessed so pivotal a position in the nation's railway network. Railway carriage of the Post Office's mail traffic likewise enhanced London's position as the national centre of economic and social intercourse. Railways had contracted to carry mail from the opening of the Liverpool & Manchester in 1830 and the facility of rail carriage was vital to Rowland Hill's securing of Parliamentary approval for the universal *Penny Post* from 1840. The cost-space divergence of the existing postal system was transformed overnight under the Penny Post. Distance, as far as mail carriage went, was annihilated.[84] It was changes of this sort which enabled the London stock market to gain control over the bulk of dealings in railway securities by the 1850s, at the expense of the early markets in the North and the Midlands. How far railway companies were *active* cultivators of metropolitan dominance is, of course, exceptionally hard to assess. Distinctions between demand and supply-led change are not readily elucidated; and competition provided a case apart. What is indisputable is that, by the later nineteenth century, the capital, with its increasing concentration of wealth, services and professions, had become a 'shop-window' in which the principal companies displayed their 'wares'. Thus arose such edifices as Scott's St Pancras for the Midland Railway Company. The profusion of luxury train services in and out of London repeated the pattern.

The context in view

From this survey of the economic and social context, it is hard to avoid coming to the conclusion that railways, together with steam-powered transport generally, developed much less as specified responses to the evolving transport demands of an industrial society, but rather as *manifestations* and *agencies* of much more fundamental social transformations, using the word *social* in its widest possible meaning. One might well caricature railway magnates as having hijacked the country's internal transport system, especially when one registers the continuing *capabilities* of waterway and coastal carriage in the Victorian Age and the public dissatisfaction with railway freight carriage almost intermittently throughout the Victorian Age. Reservoirs of capital, accumulated from the first phases of industrialism, literally flooded in the wake of railway promotions. This was partly because of the spectacular economic success of early railway ventures which, rather untypically, *did* spring from transport bottlenecks, but partly because they fired imaginations: the steam railway was an early and major representative of Victorian society's increasing fascination with mechanical contraptions. Once established, the railway became an agent of its own success. To the surprise of many, it transformed travel into a consumer good in a way never known before. In alliance with steam power at sea, it opened wide the capacity for the growth of exchange economies. And in their notional annihilation of space, overland and across the oceans, both railway and steamship played up to the symbol of progress that their intrinsic forms expressed. In a sense, the railway and the steamship were creating a world after their own image, as A. H. Clough implied in a lament entitled 'The Effect of the Great Engine' written about 1850:

> The age of instinct has, it seems, gone by,
> And will not be forced back . . . The modern Hotspur
> Shrills not his trumpet of 'To Horse, To Horse!'
> But consults columns in a railway guide;
> A demigod of figures; an Achilles
> Of computation; . . . [85]

There was, however, a dimension of Britain's railways which lent a somewhat peculiar character to certain aspects of the economic structure of which they formed part. It related to the division of railway operation among some dozen or so private companies. It was not, though a question of competition, at least not in any direct sense: indeed, it is justifiable to argue that, under forces of competition, Britain acquired a railway network and railway services which were second to none. The question, instead, was over the particular geographical division of territory. There was often very limited economic–geographic rationale for the way in which the many spheres of company influence evolved. And when this was coupled with the desires of most companies to maximise their traffic through variable commodity and distance pricing, the results were highly confusing. In certain respects, the effect was tantamount to imprinting a novel set of geographical relations upon the face of the country. Given that railway communication was otherwise a great annihilator of space (i.e. reducing the 'drag' or 'tyranny' of distance) it was somewhat paradoxical that, at the same time, it came to compartmentalise it, almost in the fashion of ancient fiefdoms. It is largely this question that forms the subject of the next section.

Railways and the Victorian space–economy

Improved transport performs the notional function of bringing places and areas closer together. Although no transport form is ubiquitous in geographical space, the benefits conferred might be expected to be generally uniform within the specific geographical confines of the mode being considered. This would be making the assumption, however, that the transport rates broadly conformed to a uniform mileage base. In the case of road and waterway carriage, and even early railway conveyance, this assumption generally holds good. But as the railway system matured, and in freight movement especially, it became more and more an abstract datum, even if disgruntled traders repeatedly cited it in their complaints about railway pricing. The freight charging policies of companies meant that some centres and some regions benefited more from railways than others.

One component in the deviation from a uniform mileage base was the need to levy terminal charges. The very nature of railway tech-nology made handling costs a factor in pricing in a way that was hardly ever so in the road-carrying industry and only to a limited degree with waterways. The levying of 'terminals' is normally associated with the appearance of the 'tapering' transport rate whereby progressively longer line-hauls become steadily cheaper on a unit cost basis. Hawke was not convinced that this was the mechanism that explained tapering rate structures during the period up to 1870 that he examined.[86] But it must remain a possibility that permitted or declared 'terminals' became in the nature of *nominal* charges, still leaving some parts of the handling costs to be reflected in the basic point-to-point quotations made by companies. As Hawke himself reminds us, the extreme reluctance of some railway company managers to accept that rates were in fact an amalgam of two separate charges, one for handling and one for haulage, underline this.[87]

Whatever the underlying cause, the tapering rate (fig. 3) has a geographical or, more precisely, a spatial impact in so far as places further distant are notionally brought closer together than places less distant. In the specific geographical context of later Victorian Britain, this was frequently enhanced through competition from coasting vessels. On a short haul such as London–Ipswich, coasters were only marginally a competitive threat – assuming that there

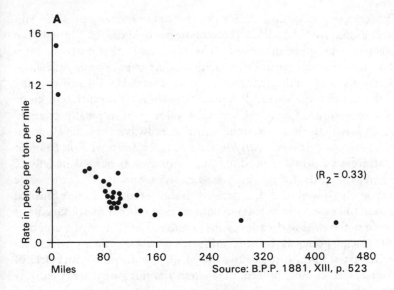

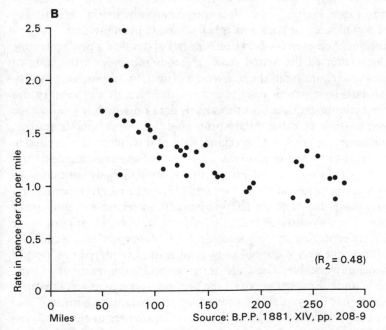

3 Tapering freight rates: A: Birmingham hardware rates, *c.* 1881 (including terminals); B: London sugar rates, *c.* 1881 (excluding terminals)

existed a clear logistical choice in commodity movement. On a run such as that from London to Newcastle or to Aberdeen, though, the position was quite otherwise. The result was that railway rates described an even greater exponential effect over certain pathways. A second factor in the unequal benefits conferred by the railways lay in the way that there were different classes of rates for different kinds of commodities. Goods of low unit value were typically charged much less than those of high.[88] British railways thus developed a policy which involved *charging rates that the traffic would bear,* so that areas of *primary* production like mining benefited heavily,[89] whereas manufacturing districts (i.e. *secondary* production) were not nearly so well served, especially in the despatch of their finished goods and especially as foreign competition eroded their margins of profit in the closing decades of the century. The justice of a commodity pricing policy of this sort is difficult to assess. The injustices that it conferred upon British railways in the twentieth century are, of course, well known. Indeed, the system was not swept away entirely until the early 1950s, when charges became based on the costs of conveyance. In the nineteenth century, it was an obvious reflection of the significance of coal and other minerals in many early railway ventures. And even if it had been desired to develop a pricing regime which reflected the actual costs of goods movement, the state of railway accounting in the nineteenth century made such a proposition largely impracticable. Not until the turn of the century did companies begin to collect the sort of data on which it would have been possible to differentiate profitable from unprofitable traffics. The contrast in this pricing regime with that which had prevailed in the canal and waggon eras was a sharp one. For example, the nature of the road-carrying industry with its small, largely autonomous units of operation, much less inextricably tied to a given permanent way, made it easy to fix charges broadly in relation to movement costs. The way carriage rates altered in relation to the price of horse provender during the Napoleonic Wars illustrates this well.[90] By contrast, the very nature of railway operation rendered this kind of model unworkable. The scale, intensity and complexity of railway traffic and the exchanges of traffic between companies were features which made any real monitoring of the balance of income and expenditure exceptionally difficult. As Cain writes in chapter 3, the railway companies were way ahead of their time as business organisations, and it must come as no surprise that as late as 1900 they were still learning the arts of profit or efficiency accounting.

It remained the case, of course, that within any one commodity grouping, rates were generally lower on a long haul and higher on a short one. Likewise, volume traffics generally attracted lower rates and ephemeral traffics higher ones. But to assume that this reflected any well-founded system of accounting is to invite immediate suspicion. The problems of equifinality are everywhere present here: the quotation of lower rates on traffics to and from distant ports might as easily have been for reasons of inter-company rivalry, as for the perceived efficiency gains from handling volume traffics along single paths, or the ability to spread loading costs over a greater number of line-haul units. Figure 4A shows how much the North Eastern Railway's rates on raw cotton imported through Hull varied not only from a uniform mileage base but also from any clear semblance of a tapering rate.[91] For Liverpool, in particular, the effect was notionally to reconstruct entirely one dimension of the map of northern England (fig. 4B). When presented in these terms, it is small wonder that cotton manufacturers at places like Preston complained so bitterly about railway pricing. Even set alongside Manchester, they might as well have been at the bottom of the Irish Sea! A not dissimilar pattern can be observed in figure 5 which shows comparative rates on refined sugar despatched from Greenock and from London to thirty-nine towns in the eastern half of England. The figures derive from a table compiled by an aggrieved London refiner who pointed to the way Greenock refiners were able to sell sugar almost in his own backyard. The table was part of a presentation made to the 1881 Select Committee on Railways.[92] It is clear, of course, that the supposed unfair treatment of London refiners, which the diagrams at first sight depict, is in greater part a result of failing to compare like with like: the two scattergrams, for instance, might well be amalgamated – as they stand, they largely represent mutually exclusive distance bands. London certainly operated under the penalty of higher terminals (excluded here) and the scattergrams do reveal a clear margin in favour of Greenock where the distance bands actually coincide. But what the data show, above all, is the stimulus which existed for long-haul commodity movement and also the way places at identical distances could be accorded quite widely different rates. Northampton, St Ives and Newmarket, for instance, were all roughly seventy miles from London and yet the quoted rates (exclusive of terminals) were 1.0*d*, 1.62*d* and 2.48*d* per ton mile

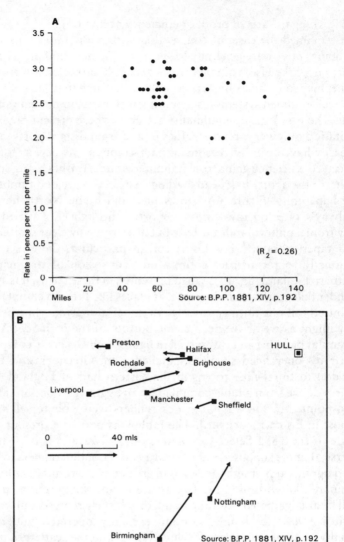

4 A: North Eastern Railway rates on cotton from Hull, *c.* 1881;
   B: North Eastern Railway rates on cotton from Hull: sample
deviations from a uniform mileage base (Note: directional arrows indicate
mileage scale by which receiving centres were further from or closer to Hull
as a result of the differential pricing policy of the NER. Liverpool, the highest
positive outlier, was advantaged by fifty-six miles. Brighouse, the second
highest negative outlier, was disadvantaged by eleven miles)

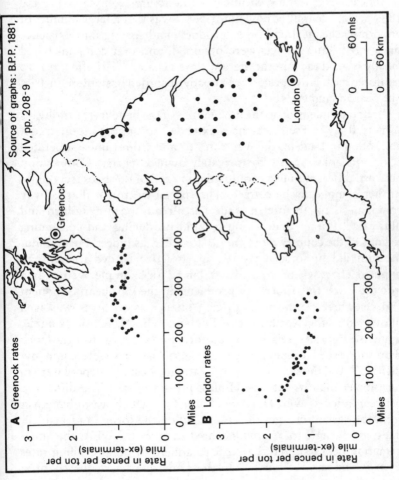

5 Sugar rates from Greenock and from London to thirty-nine towns in Eastern England

respectively. In other words, sugar carriage, like cotton, revealed a similar contempt for the cardinal geographical relations.

Another criticism about charging policy was that as new manufacturing products or materials appeared over the course of the later nineteenth century, there was little attempt to systematise their rate classification. A leading chemical manufacturer complained to the 1881 Select Committee how notorious it was that a large number of important chemical and other products had sprung into existence since most Railway Acts were obtained, and that companies had mostly ranked them in the highest class of rate.[93] The effect was to reinforce the relative preference already accorded to staple industries like coal and minerals.

A related dimension to the inequalities of the benefits that railways conferred lay in the preferences extended to import/export trades and, often in tandem, the way rates to and from railway-operated ports undercut those to privately-owned ports. Competition between different railway companies in each of these respects could further complicate the pattern. The special treatment that railway companies gave to foreign trade has already been examined and illustrated. Rather than acting to bind producing and consuming regions of the country more closely together, as indeed rail communication did in some measure, this practice tended towards an opposite effect whereby port hinterlands, for example, were drawn into the marketing spheres of producers in the European Continent and elsewhere. Differential pricing on routes to ports was well illustrated in the North-East of England. The NER, for example, granted lesser rates (relative to a uniform mileage base) to Tyne Dock than to West Hartlepool, even though both ports were company-owned.[94] And the same company's rates to West Hartlepool were in turn lower than its rates to Hull, a private port.[95] The difference between rates to West Hartlepool and Tyne Dock was a hangover from the variant charges that prevailed on the former independent lines which came to be amalgamated to form the NER; the amalgamation deal required the NER to adhere to the prevailing rates from inland sites to ports.[96] In the same quarter of the country, inter-company cleavages were largely responsible for South Yorkshire coalowners paying 7*d* to 10*d* per ton more to Hull by the MSLR than their fellow West Riding owners did by the NER.[97]

For most companies, of course, competing for traffic was a double-edged sword; and the more so given the relatively poor knowledge of the financial efficiency of operations. Some rate concessions damaged not only the company whose traffic was the target but also the company which offered them in the first place. It is hardly surprising, then, that pooling agreements were made from time to time by companies in more or less direct competition for defined groups of traffic. In the case of the ports of the north-east coast from Grimsby to Tyne Dock, one such series of pooling arrangements were the Humber, Hartlepool and Midland agreements of 1855–56.[98] These sought to restrict competition to facilities and accommodation for passengers and goods, and to mineral rates. The participant companies were the NER, MSLR, LNWR and L&YR and the agreements related specifically to traffics to and from Liverpool, Manchester, Ashton and Stalybridge, and, later, centres in South Yorkshire and the Midlands. The outcome was that companies could rely on a certain predictable volume of receipts, and within the scope of their knowledge, channel traffics over the most profitable routes. The exclusion of coal traffic clearly placed a formidable brake upon the impact of the agreements, but beyond this the effect was generally to spread trade around the north-east ports such that no single centre was able to draw on an unduly disproportionate share. For railway-owned ports, there was much to be recommended in this. For the private port of Hull, though, the traffic pool was seen as depriving it of the true advantages of its geographical position relative to the industrial regions of Lancashire, Yorkshire and the Midlands. Set alongside the price discrimination which the NER appeared to exert against Hull from within its own operating domain, the merchants and businessmen of Hull responded with an independent line of railway, the Hull & Barnsley, in the process fuelling competition yet further.

Certain of the kinds of discriminatory pricing outlined above came to contribute to, or were specifically formulated parts of, *regional* policies pursued by railway companies. Predictably, these found clearest expression in the case of those companies whose lines were broadly coincident with economic regions, or else where the network of lines described a discrete area. The NER provides one of the clearest examples of the former (see chapter 3); the LBSCR of the latter. Hawke saw this aspect as the most controversial part of the railways pricing policy;[99] and he further observed that 'as the railway companies were approximately divided into geographical regions, a policy of regional development was easily made compatible with pursuing the companies' interests'.[100] It would probably have been more correct to say 'areas' rather than 'regions', for some company networks had the most tenuous of coincidences with regions as uniquely interwoven population/resource groupings. The MSLR (later the Great Central) had the strangest of network configurations, for example. Even a giant among companies like the LNWR had only limited regional identity in the true geographical sense. And the Great Western was actually splayed out across a whole series of geographical regions. Linear network configurations were in fact almost as numerous as web or polar ones if the national railway map as it existed by 1900 is scrutinised carefully enough (fig. 6). This is actually a dimension of British railways which has received remarkably little attention. In what ways, for instance, did the particular geographical division of companies, especially those characterised by linear network configurations, institute novel economic–geographic patterns? Given that, as Hawke has remarked, another aspect of railway pricing was to bring different supply areas into competition at a given market,[101] it is clear that railway networks like those of the LNWR or the Midland, notwith-standing pooling agreements, were likely to orchestrate commodity flows along paths which a more unified railway system would likely not have done. In other words, the spatial divisions of railway ownership and operation conferred upon the evolving economic geography of Victorian Britain a series of configurations somewhat similar to those which Langton has described for the fragmented canal system.[102]

The relationship of the railways to the coalfields provides an especially interesting illustration of this feature. A coalfield which was served by a single company (ignoring the existence of any highly-localised company lines, e.g. mineral railways), whose lines also extended into land areas which were bereft of coal, was more likely, for example, to generate long-range coal flows than the coalfield served by a company whose network was broadly coinci-dent with it and which relied on transmissions via other companies for a deeper market penetration. In 1866 the Great Western Railway, for instance, carried away some 2.3 million tons of coal from the South Wales field,[103] involving, according to Hawke, an average lead (haul) of 76.2 miles.[104] This contrasts with the NER which handled upwards of 7.5 million tons mined in the north-eas-tern coalfield[105] with an average lead of only 32.6 miles.[106] The

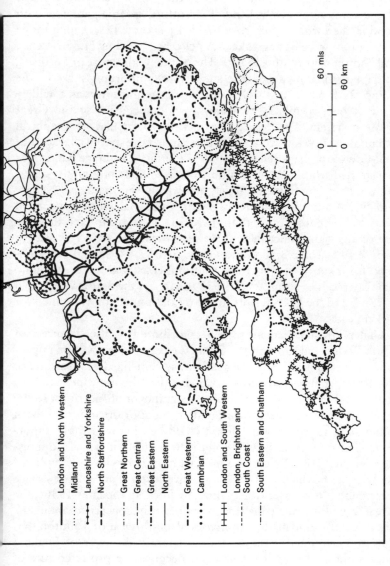

	London and North Western
	Midland
	Lancashire and Yorkshire
	North Staffordshire
	Great Northern
	Great Central
	Great Eastern
	North Eastern
	Great Western
	Cambrian
	London and South Western
	London, Brighton and South Coast
	South Eastern and Chatham

6   Railway company organisation, c. 1900

pattern of GWR coal-flows (excluding those under 5,000 tons) is illustrated in figure 7. Among the long-range flows, London and Birkenhead were predominant, accounting for 7.1 and 8.6 per cent of the total respectively. And if Brentford is amalgamated with London the former figure rose to 11.4 per cent. Lesser long-range destinations were Basingstoke (1.5 per cent), Reading (1.3 per cent), and Tipton near Stafford (1.5). The South Wales port of Swansea, perhaps predictably, took the single most important share of the traffic (27.9 per cent).[107] But otherwise the pattern was a widely diffused one, seemingly realising a wide spectrum of the Great Western system. The degree to which the particular geographical extent of the GW system actively determined the spatial character of coal-flows is perhaps reflected in the diminutive tonnage which was transmitted from GW metals on to contiguous company systems. Only 4.2 per cent of the total was involved in this manner.[108] There remains, of course, the matter of South Wales coal which was carried away by companies other than the Great Western. In fact, the only line of any significance in tonnage terms was the Taff Vale, which carried away some 3.38 million tons in 1867,[109] the bulk presumably for export or for redistribution coastwise. The Midland Railway received a miniscule 1,637 tons from the South Wales field in 1867, and the LNWR only about 57,000, much of it destined for Birkenhead.[110]

One particular element which contributed to the diffusion of South Wales coal through the Great Western system was its importance in locomotive firing. On a railway system like the Lancashire & Yorkshire, coal was so widely available that the movement of loco coal would rarely have assumed very significant proportions. In the case of the GWR, and, for that matter, most of the other southern and eastern railway companies, it could be of considerable importance. The returns of the GWR in the Report of the Royal Commission on Coal (1871) contain a number of very obvious examples of coal despatch which was for locomotive firing – notably to service through workings over other company lines. In the later 1930s, the Great Western management were sufficiently concerned about the high cost of supplying locomotive coal south-west of Taunton that they commissioned a survey for electrifying the west of England lines. Nothing in fact became of it, because the projected rate of return was less than one per cent.[111] But the episode is highly instructive of the problems faced by companies which had lines far

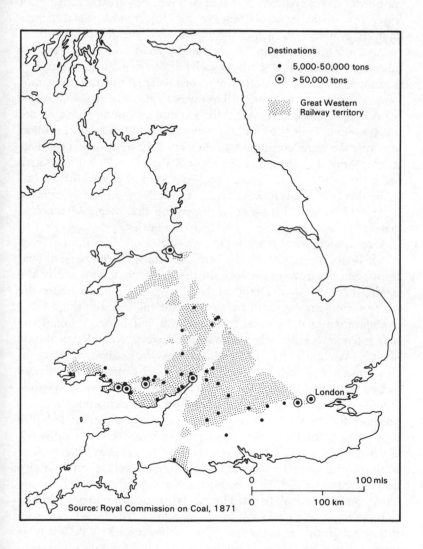

7 Great Western Railway distribution of coal from the South Wales coalfield, 1866

removed from coal supplies. Moreover, locomotive firing was vastly less efficient in the nineteenth century than in the twentieth, so that the burden of supplying loco coal must have been greater rather than lesser. Hawke makes no reference to the subject in his social savings analysis, even though such coal-flows would have inflated the social savings attributable to the railways (the road and canal-carrying businesses, for instance, made no such parallel demands). In part this is probably because the statistical record is largely silent on locomotive coal movement. The GWR returns to the Royal Commission contain no explicit references, for example. Among those of the NER, though, some 0.19 million tons of coal and some 0.22 million tons of coke were 'consumed by the North Eastern's own engines, etc.'[112] And in chapter 3, Cain records that, in 1903, locomotive firing consumed 5.5 per cent of total coal output, probably no mean figure if it could be translated into a ton-mileage format. Gourvish (chapter 2) echoes this point in suggesting that steam locomotive demand boosted output in high-quality collieries.

A somewhat parallel example to GWR coal distribution from South Wales is provided by the Midland Railway's carriage of coal from collieries in Leicestershire, in the Erewash Valley and in the mining area north of Derby in 1856 (fig. 8).[113] Once more the railway company appears to have made full use of its network configuration, in this case a highly linear, bi-axial one. Although the date is ten years earlier than the Great Western example, an almost identical volume of coal (2.2 million tons) was conveyed away. In clear contrast to this, however, some 29 per cent of the coal was passed on for transmission over alternative company systems, including almost a quarter of a million tons delivered to Peterborough for the Eastern Counties Railway and a further 108,000 tons to Kew for the South Western and South Eastern railways. Given the MR's wide national penetration, it comes as little surprise to find it supplying non-mining areas. Remarkably, though, it also despatched some 108,000 tons for the North Staffordshire Railway, hardly an area of coal deficit. The available statistics do not allow us to establish how far other railway companies distributed coal from the same group of collieries. The GNR and the LNWR were potential participants, but generally the Midland enjoyed a considerable areal monopoly here.

Even as late as 1911, one could find examples of coal movement which bore the imprint of company territorialism. Figure 9 shows

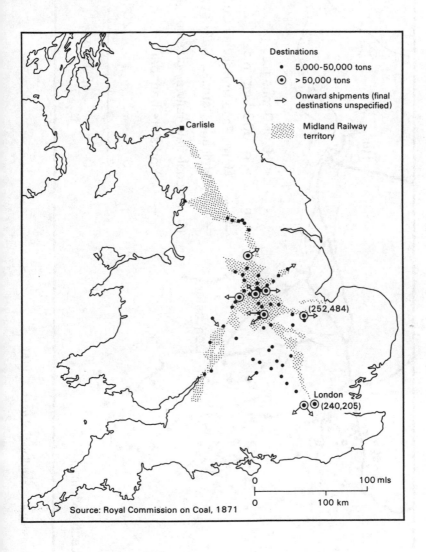

8 Midland Railway distribution of coal from Leicestershire collieries, from collieries in the Erewash Valley and from those north of Derby, 1856

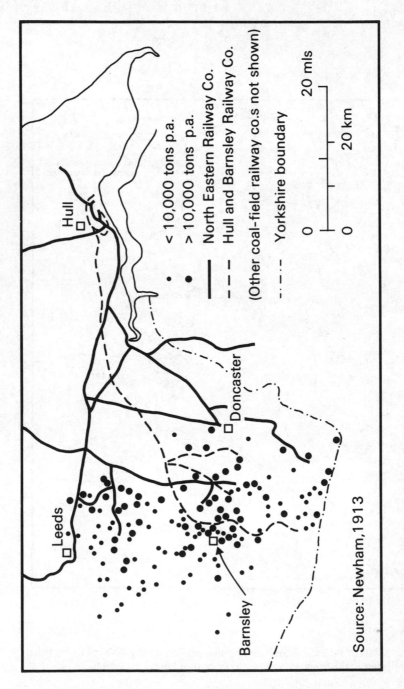

Key:
- • <10,000 tons p.a.
- ● >10,000 tons p.a.
- —— North Eastern Railway Co.
- – – – Hull and Barnsley Railway Co.
- (Other coal-field railway co.s not shown)
- –·–·– Yorkshire boundary

20 mls

20 km

Source: Newham, 1913

9 Yorkshire collieries sending coal to Hull, 1911

the Yorkshire collieries which supplied the bulk of coal arriving in Hull that year.[114] The port in fact drew upon a wide expanse of the York, Derby and Nottinghamshire field, in other words extending at least another thirty miles south from the Yorkshire boundary. The pits of Derbyshire and Nottinghamshire, however, contributed only 8.7 per cent of the 6.46 million tons sent to Hull. It was the Yorkshire pits which supplied the lion's share, a massive 5.9 million tons, most of it, of course, for export. As the map depicts, the only railway companies with access to Hull were the North Eastern and the Hull & Barnsley. It can be no coincidence that the coalfield area which supplied most of Hull's export coal was broadly consistent with the domains of the North Eastern and the Hull & Barnsley.

In railway passenger traffic, there was no counterpart to the spatially discriminatory pricing which pertained in freight operations. The uniform mileage base was by no means universally held, but, as Hawke has stated, rates were close to a mileage rate, modified in the few cases where alternative transport services existed or where competing railways with longer lines had to take lower fares per mile carried.[115] There was, of course, a hierarchy of train services, based partly on distinctions of social class and partly on the speed at which it was desired to travel. In very clear contrast to the freight sector, though, the force of these distinctions waned over the course of the nineteenth century, those of class especially. Whereas much of the railways' freight traffic had been there for the taking, the bulk of rail passenger traffic was in fact generated anew. From the 1850s, companies were substituting a low-margin, high-volume policy for the initial practice of catering mainly for the coaching clientele: numerically small but providing lucrative margins. By 1865 almost two-thirds of total passenger journeys (excluding season tickets) were third-class.[116] The Midland Railway Company, in particular, became a pace-setter in courting the custom of the lower socio-economic groups. After 1872, for example, it provided third-class carriages on all of its trains; the existing practice had been for selective provision only. Then, in 1875, it abolished the second-class altogether, opening its doors wide to a much broader mass of the population. Other companies soon followed and, with the help of such statutory mechanisms as the regular provision of workmens' trains at very cheap fares (1883), the pattern was finally sealed. By the early twentieth century, according to Aldcroft, nearly 95 per cent of all railway passengers were travelling third-class.[117]

The railway passenger business was also distinguished from that of freight in being much less of an aid to the expansion of direct productive activities. Hawke described railway passenger travel as having introduced an almost entirely new commodity into the economy; in effect, railways offered a consumer service.[118] It is admitted, nevertheless, that the broad division of passenger traffic, as between business and leisure travel, is exceedingly hard to demarcate.[119] Nor is it easy to evaluate the savings in journey times from which the business community undeniably benefited in some measure. The adjacent isochrone maps (fig. 10) which document travel in and out of London from the stage-coach era to the peak of the railway age illustrate perhaps the maximum range of time-savings: London's focal position on the railway network largely secured this.[120] But it is a complex task to try to translate these into production gains, particularly at times when the Penny Post and the Electric Telegraph were revolutionising business communication, so lessening the need for armies of commercial men to roam the country. The facility of speed which the railways offered was, of course, a vital facet in the expansion of the Post Office's mail service. The Penny Post did not in itself hinge on the railways, but without them, it would have soon ground to a halt under the sheer volume of correspondence which it generated. And to the extent that a vastly improved mail system facilitated the pace of capital circulation, the railways also had a part in that process.[121]

The emergence of the railways as a consumer good was undoubtedly the dimension of passenger traffic that yielded some of the most sharply defined results for the Victorian space–economy. Assisted by such statutory mechanisms as holidays with pay, the passenger business acted as a catalyst for the emergence of coastal resorts, particularly those for popular mass consumption. The cheap excursion fares which brought some six million people to the Great Exhibition in London in 1851 were to form a landmark in the railway companies' pursuit of high-volume/low-margin traffic. In seeking to estimate railway passenger receipts for his social savings analysis, Hawke concluded that by the later nineteenth century the returns from excursion traffic and workmens' trains approximately balanced those from first and second-class traffic.[122] Perkin considers that many of the resort settlements can be seen as industrial towns, but with a very specialised product: recreation and recuperation.[123] They in fact became among the fastest-growing

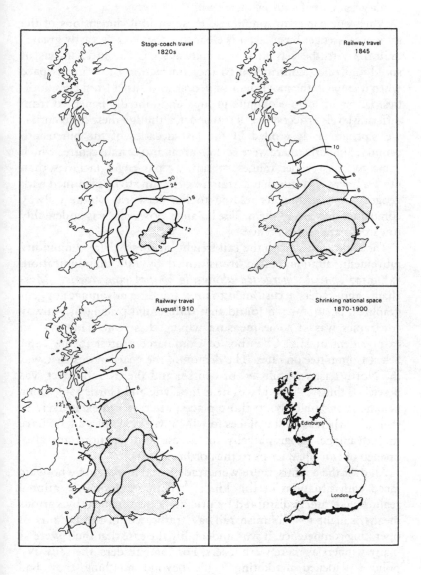

10 Travel times (hours) from London, 1820–1910 (from M. Freeman in J. Langton and R. J. Morris (eds.), *Atlas of Industrializing Britain*, Methuen, 1986, p. 90)

centres in the country, in some instances eclipsing the rates of growth of the great manufacturing metropoli.

When one comes to summarise these various dimensions of the railway passenger business, it is clear that there was a vastly greater uniformity to the way in which railways, via the mechanisms of speed and price, contributed to the contraction of national space when it came to the movement of people as distinct from commodities. Different socio-economic groups undoubtedly benefited from differing levels of access to rail transport, although these differentials were progressively eroded in the last decades of the nineteenth century. Similarly, there were certain areas and certain centres which came to boast wider ranges of railway passenger facilities than others. It was also true that certain resorts came to be identified with geographical catchments related to the networks of the railway companies that served them. The balance, however, was undeniably towards spatial convergence.

The contrast was with the rail freight business where commodity movement, although often transformed by rail communication, exhibited *spatial divergence alongside spatial convergence*. Merchants and traders accustomed to long-standing advantages of geographical position soon found that differential pricing by railway companies was in some measure wiping these out. Thus did an ex-president of Hull Chamber of Commerce protest to the 1881 Select Committee on rates. The demon of the peace in this case was the North Eastern Railway, of course, and the overall effect was described thus: 'All the places near the Tyne and Hartlepool which belong, geographically, to those places, are reserved exclusively to them . . . whereas all the places to which we (i.e. Hull traders) have the advantage, geographically, of access and position, are also, opened out on equal terms to the northern ports.'[124]

All over the country there were traders and merchants who were faced with situations of this kind.[125] Thus traditional locational realms were rudely disrupted by pricing policies which, by various means, sought to maximise railway traffic within the bounds of operating competence. It was undeniably the case that there were as many winners as there were losers. For some traders, the railways' policies widened marketing fields beyond anything they had dreamed of. The mayor of Grimsby, in giving evidence alongside the ex-president of the Hull Chamber of Commerce, had nothing but praise for the facilities provided for the port by the MSLR.[126] In this particular instance, the port was more or less the creation of the railway company. It is undeniable that much benefit was realised even amongst those traders who complained so vigorously about railway pricing. The problem as far as they were concerned was that others had benefited much more: in too many cases, the accidents of geography were being neutralised.

One is presented, then, with a rather strange paradox. On the one hand, railways contributed greatly to socio-geographic convergence, whether one thinks of this in terms of the extending distances between marriage partners, the imposition of national entertainment fads, or the success with which central government was able to foil the Chartists through rapid deployment of troops by train.[127] But on the other, one sees a railway system which, in economic terms, appeared to be sharpening geographical divides. Companies like the North Eastern forged even stronger regional identities for the traditional geographical regions they grew up to serve (see chapter 3). Already vigorous seats of cotton manufacture like Manchester had their economic advantages reinforced by pricing policies like that of the NER, which enabled them to import cotton through Hull at vastly lesser rates than nearby competitors such as Preston. The favours granted to import/export trades contributed in similar manner: areas of economic production became tied more and more to external markets. This last aspect was often at its sharpest in coal-mining: extractive industry generated none of the common reciprocal relations with other regions which even a manufacturing sector producing mainly for export would have done.

Naturally this is a heavily schematised view. The reality would have displayed many cross-currents, not least those which flowed from the peculiar spatial configurations of railway companies such as the Midland, the Great Western and the LNWR. But one does not have to look far for corroboration of the general tendency towards spatial economic divergence. As Alderman has noted, most manufacturing and trade associations were regionally or locally entrenched, sometimes up to as late as 1900.[128] Local Chambers of Commerce, for instance, remained for much of the nineteenth century 'narrow-minded and inward-looking'.[129] The British Iron Trade Association was not set up until 1876.[130] According to Alderman, only where *whole* industries were threatened by falling profits or higher costs did national organisations emerge with any degree of force or permanency.[131] And part of the reason why the evidence presented by traders to the 1881 Select Committee on Railways was sometimes confused and often sectionalist was because they had mostly failed to evolve co-ordinated national bodies to represent them.[132]

The territorial characteristics of the railway companies in some measure evolved directly out of these regional economic interest groups; and what subsequently happened was that, through various forms of discriminatory pricing by companies, these groups were cemented and in cases enhanced. Indeed, the pattern could not fail to sharpen, given the increasing inland transport monopoly enjoyed by railways generally. Thus it is a short-sighted view which has led some commentators to look at the national railway system of the 1870s onwards and talk in terms of rising currents of national economic integration. Of course, there were instances of commodity flows which appeared to reflect this. But the Victorian space–economy, at large, was fragmented and regionalised, the legacies of which have survived well into the twentieth century in, for example, the divided nature of modern trade unionism and the diverse problems of the many 'depressed areas'. The fortunes of the railway system in the same century have been closely intertwined with these legacies.

Notes

1   Quoted in F. D. Klingender, *Art and the Industrial Revolution*, Paladin, 1972, p. 129.

2   E. T. Macdermot, *History of the Great Western Railway, 1833–1863*, rev. edn, Newton Abbot, 1964, pp. 6, 13.

3   C. Dickens, *Dombey and Son*, World's Classics, Oxford, 1982, p. 651.

4   C. Dickens, *Hard Times*, Penguin Classics, Harmondsworth, 1985, p. 233.

5   H. House, *The Dickens World*, 2nd edn, Oxford, 1942, p. 145.

6   Quoted in J. Warburg (ed.), *The Industrial Muse*, Oxford, 1958, p. 79.

7   C. Dickens, 'The lazy tour of two idle apprentices', *Household Words*, 16, 1857–58, p. 314.

8   C. Dickens, Dombey and Son, *op. cit.*, pp. 52–3.

9   H. J. Dyos, 'Some social costs of railway building in London', *Journal of Transport History*, III, 1957–58, pp. 23–31.

10   An excellent selection of railway prints can be found reproduced in G. Rees, *Early Railway Prints: a Social History of the Railways from 1825 to 1850*, Oxford, 1980.

11   C. Dickens, 'Iron incidents', *Household Words*, 8, 1853–54, p. 412.

12   M. Freeman and D. Aldcroft, *The Atlas of British Railway History*, Beckenham, 1985, p. 33.

13   H. J. Dyos and D. H. Aldcroft, *British Transport: an Economic Survey from the Seventeenth Century to the Twentieth*, Leicester, 1969, p. 241.

14   R. Tames, *The Transport Revolution in the 19th Century: 3: Shipping*, Oxford, 1971, p. 24.

15   Quoted in Klingender, *op. cit.*, p. 122.

16   See Tames, *op. cit.*, pp. 5 ff; Dyos and Aldcroft, *op. cit.*, p. 244; T. Coleman, *Passage to America*, 1972, pp. 236 ff.

17   Klingender, *op. cit.*

18   Coleman, *op. cit.*, p. 237.

19   Tames, *op. cit.*, p. 50.

20   Dyos and Aldcroft, *op. cit.*

21   *Ibid.*, p. 232.

22   *Ibid.*

23   *Chambers Encyclopaedia*, 12, 1959, p. 491.

24   Dyos and Aldcroft, *op. cit.*, p. 234.

25   M. E. Fletcher, 'From coal to oil in British shipping', *Journal of Transport History*, new ser., III, 1975, p. 3.

26   *Ibid.*, p. 2.

27   W. H. B. Court (ed.), *British Economic History, 1870–1914*, Cambridge, 1965, p. 95.

28   Fletcher, *op. cit.*

29   T. Baines, *History of Liverpool*, 1852, p. 743.

30   P. S. Bagwell, *The Transport Revolution from 1770*, 1974, p. 64.

31   Tames, *op. cit.*, p. 59.

32   C. R. Fay, *Great Britain from Adam Smith to the Present Day*, 5th edn, 1950, p. 244.

33   J. T. Coppock, 'The changing face of England: 1850–circa 1900', in H. C. Darby (ed.), *A New Historical Geography of England after 1600*, Cambridge, 1976, p. 313.

34   Quoted in Coleman, *op. cit.*, p. 66.

35   *Ibid.*, pp. 88–91.

36   See *Household Words*, 19, 1858–59, p. 13.

37   Bagwell, *op. cit.*, p. 154.

38   M. Simpson, 'Urban transport and the development of Glasgow's West End, 1830–1914', *Journal of Transport History*, new ser., I, 1971–72, pp. 150–1.

39   E. Howard, *Garden Cities of Tomorrow*, rev. edn, Eastbourne, 1985.

40   Warburg, *op. cit.*, p. 99.

41   M. J. Freeman, 'Introduction', in D. H. Aldcroft and M. J. Freeman, (eds.), *Transport in the Industrial Revolution*, Manchester, 1983, pp. 1–4.

42   E. J. Hobsbawm, *Industry and Empire*, Harmondsworth, 1968, p. 112.

43   M. C. Reed, 'Railways and the growth of the capital market', in M. C. Reed (ed.), *Railways and the Victorian Economy*, Newton Abbot, 1969,

p. 162.
44   Hobsbawm, *op. cit.*, p. 75.
45   *Ibid.*
46   Reed, *op. cit.*, p. 174.
47   Hobsbawm, *op. cit.*, p. 111.
48   Bagwell, *op. cit.*, pp. 113–14.
49   P. S. Bagwell, *The Railway Clearing House in the British Economy, 1842–1922*, 1968, p. 64.
50   M. Freeman, 'The industrial revolution and the regional geography of England: a comment', *Transactions of the Institute of British Geographers*, new ser., 9, 1984, pp. 507–12.
51   See *British Parliamentary Papers (B.P.P.)*, Report from the Select Committee on Railways, XIII, 1881, p. 408.
52   Bagwell, Railway Clearing House, *op. cit.*, pp. 78–9.
53   For the effects on the Black Country iron trade, see M. le Guillou, 'Freight rates and their influence on the Black Country iron trade in a period of growing domestic and foreign competition, 1850–1914', *Journal of Transport History*, new ser., III, 1975, p. 109.
54   J. Armstrong and P. S. Bagwell, 'Coastal shipping', in Aldcroft and Freeman, *op. cit.*, p. 163.
55   See, for example, Klingender, *op. cit.*, pp. 94–5.
56   See, for example, Hobsbawm, *op. cit.*, chs. 6, 7.
57   J. Langton and R. L. Morris (eds.), *Atlas of Industrializing Britain, 1780–1914*, 1986, pp. xxviii–xxix.
58   See J. Langton, 'The industrial revolution and the regional geography of England', *Transactions of the Institute of British Geographers*, new ser., 9, 1984, pp. 145–67.
59   Klingender, *op. cit.*, p. 94.
60   Bagwell, *Transport Revolution, op. cit.*, p. 156.
61   See Hobsbawm, *op. cit.*, p. 145.
62   *The Economist*, 21 February 1925.
63   J. Armstrong, 'The role of coastal shipping in UK transport: an estimate of comparative traffic movements in 1910', *Journal of Transport History*, 3rd ser., VIII, 1987.
64   Fletcher, *op. cit.*, p. 2.
65   *B.P.P.*, Report from the Select Committee on Railways, *op. cit.*, pp. 390.
66   *Ibid.*, pp. 341ff.
67   *Ibid.*, pp. 68ff.
68   *Ibid.*, pp. 527ff.
69   See le Guillou, *op. cit.*; see also K. Warren, *The British Iron and Steel Sheet Industry since 1840*, 1970, pp. 57–60.
70   P. J. Cain, 'Railways and price discrimination: the case of agriculture, 1880–1914', *Business History*, XVIII, 1976, p. 198.
71   *B.P.P.*, Report from the Select Committee on Railways, *op. cit.*, p. 81.
72   Dyos and Aldcroft, *op. cit.*, p. 256.
73   *Ibid.*

74   *Ibid.*, p. 156.
75   Bagwell, *Railway Clearing House, op. cit.*, p. 84.
76   E. A. Wrigley, 'A simple model of London's importance in changing English society and economy, 1650–1750', *Past and Present*, XXXVII, 1967, pp. 44–70.
77   See E. Pawson, *Transport and Economy: the turnpike roads of eighteenth-century Britain*, 1977.
78   See J. A. Chartres, 'Road carrying in England in the seventeenth century: myth and reality', *Economic History Review*, 2nd ser., XXX, 1977, pp. 73–94.
79   See Pawson, *op. cit.*
80   Langton, 'The industrial revolution and the regional geography of England', *op. cit.*, p. 162.
81   *Ibid.*, pp. 162–3.
82   See D. Gregory, 'The friction of distance? Information circulation and the mails in early nineteenth-century England', *Journal of Historical Georgraphy*, 13, 1987, pp. 130–54.
83   H. Perkin, *The Age of the Railway*, London, 1970, p. 99.
84   See Gregory, *op. cit.*
85   Warburg, *op. cit.*, p. 54.
86   G. R. Hawke, *Railways and Economic Growth in England and Wales*, 1840–1870, Oxford, 1970, p. 345.
87   *Ibid.*, p. 344.
88   The Clearing House classification of 1847 stipulated five classes of rates in ascending order of cost. Class I rates included very low-value goods like chalk, bones, potatoes, timber and turnips; Class V rates included very high-value goods like china, silks, clocks and plate glass. See Bagwell, *Railway Clearing House, op. cit.*, p. 74.
89   This was enhanced by the way railway companies do not appear to have raised their rates in periods of high coal prices. See Hawke, *op. cit.*, pp. 322–3.
90   See W. Albert, *The Turnpike Road System in England, 1663–1840*, Cambridge, 1972, ch. 8.
91   *B.P.P.*, Appendix to Report from the Select Committee on Railways, XIV, 1881, p. 192.
92   *B.P.P.*, Report from the Select Committee on Railways, *op. cit.*, pp. 208–9.
93   *Ibid.*, p. 472.
94   *Ibid.*, p. 430.
95   *Ibid.*
96   *Ibid.*, p. 436.
97   *Ibid.*, p. 410.
98   D. Brooke, 'The struggle between Hull and the North Eastern Railway', *Journal of Transport History*, new ser., I, pp. 220–37.
99   Hawke, *op. cit.*, p. 325.
100   *Ibid.*, p. 326.
101   *Ibid.*
102   Langton, 'The industrial revolution and the regional geography of

England', *op. cit.*, pp. 162–3.

103   B.P.P., Royal Commission on Coal, XVIII, 1871, Report of Committee E, pp. 139–40.

104   Hawke, *op. cit.*, p. 182.

105   B.P.P., Royal Commission on Coal, *op. cit.*, p. 70. The appendix to the report of committee E gives much higher figures: 9.9 million tons of coal; 2.6 million tons of coke (p. 85).

106   Hawke, *op. cit.*, p. 184.

107   All data on South Wales coal-flows from *B.P.P.*, Royal Commission on Coal, *op. cit.*, p. 139ff.

108   *Ibid.*

109   *Ibid.*

110   *Ibid.*

111   O. S. Nock, *History of the Great Western Railway, 1923–47*, pp. 152–5.

112   B.P.P., Royal Commission on Coal, *op. cit.*, see note 20.

113   *Ibid.*, appendix pp. 91ff.

114   H. E. C. Newham, *Hull as a Coal Port*, Hull, 1913; see G. Jackson, 'Sea trade', in Langton and Morris, *op. cit.*, p. 105.

115   Hawke, *op. cit.*, p. 358.

116   M. Freeman and D. Aldcroft, 'The Atlas of British Railway History, *op. cit.*, p. 36.

117   Dyos and Aldcroft, *op. cit.*, p. 149.

118   Hawke, *op. cit.*, p. 54.

119   *Ibid.*, p. 51.

120   From M. Freeman, 'Transport', in Langton and Morris, *op. cit.*, p. 90.

121   See D. Gregory, *op. cit.*

122   Hawke, *op. cit.*, p. 47.

123   Perkin, *op. cit.*, pp. 224–5.

124   B.P.P., Report from the Select Committee on Railways, *op. cit.*, p. 430.

125   The 1881 Select Committee is replete with examples, although witnesses were frequently guilty of presenting incomplete evidence in order to enhance the merit of their case.

126   B.P.P., Report from the Select Committee on Railways, *op. cit.*, p. 453.

127   See F. C. Mather, 'The railways and the electric telegraph, and public order during the Chartist period, 1837–48', *History*, XXXVIII, 1953, pp. 40–53.

128   G. J. Alderman, *The Railway Interest*, Leicester, 1973, p. 13.

129   *Ibid.*

130   *Ibid.*

131   *Ibid.*

132   *Ibid.*, p. 99.

Railways 1830–70:
the formative years

The foundation of the network

When did the railway age begin? A case might be made for the year 1805, with the opening of the Wandsworth–Merstham route by the Surrey Iron and Croydon, Merstham & Godstone railways, both public, horse-drawn plateways intended for freight traffic; or for 1807, when the 'first passenger railway', The Oystermouth, saw regular services provided by a local contractor; or for 1825, when the Stockton & Darlington opened as a line with mixed horse and steam-power. But the conventional choice is 1830. *All* the basic ingredients of a modern railway were included in the inter-urban Liverpool & Manchester Railway, opened on 15 September 1830: a reserved track, public traffic facilities, provision for passengers, and mechanical power. The new company, which had been promoted as a freight line to carry cotton, gave a great stimulus to passenger travel after its Rainhill Locomotive Trials of 1829. In the first full year of working, 1831, revenue from passenger traffic made up 65 per cent of total gross revenue. In the country as a whole, passenger traffic then dominated company balance sheets for the next twenty years.[1]

The opening of the Liverpool & Manchester Railway also marks the beginning of a forty-year period in which the core of the United Kingdom's rail network was constructed. Only fifty-one miles (82 km) of route had been opened by the end of 1829. At the end of 1871 the figure was 15,736 miles (24,800 km). This represented about two-thirds of the ultimate network, or about the same route-mileage that British Rail was operating in 1965, nearly a century later.[2] Although the data imply an average construction rate of about 365 miles a year, a considerable portion of the total was built in the wake of the great investment 'manias' of 1837–40, 1845–47, and 1862–65. At the end of 1836 only 400 miles of route had been opened, but four years later the total amounted to 1,500 miles, including completion of several important lines – the London & Birmingham, Grand Junction (Birmingham to Newton-le-Willows on the Liverpool & Manchester), London & Southampton (quickly renamed the London & South Western) and Midland Counties (Rugby–Nottingham/Derby). Trunk lines connecting London with Bristol (Great Western) and Brighton (London & Brighton) were completed in the following year. By 1850, after the second invest-ment 'mania' had been reflected in construction, 6,600 route-miles had been opened. Not only had companies such as the South Eastern, Manchester, Sheffield & Lincolnshire (later the Great Central), North British and Great Northern emerged, but significant company mer-gers had produced the Midland (Midland Counties, Birmingham & Derby Jnc., North Midland) in 1844, the London & North Western (London & Birmingham, Grand Junction [which included the Manchester & Birmingham and Liverpool & Manchester]) in 1846, and the Lancashire & Yorkshire (Manchester & Leeds and smaller railways) in 1847. Rail travel was now available between London and Plymouth, Holyhead, Glasgow, Edinburgh and Aberdeen. The pace was slower in the 1850s, but a significant landmark was the amalgamation of the York & North Midland, Leeds Northern and York, Newcastle & Berwick railways to form the North Eastern Railway in 1854. By the end of the decade there were 10,400 miles of route open, and the railway had penetrated such outposts as Haver-fordwest, Nairn, and Wells-next-the-sea. The third 'mania' in the 1860s produced many a duplicate, subsidiary, and rural branch line. It was also accompanied by the opening of the world's first urban underground railway, the Metropolitan, in London, in 1863; the formation of the Great Eastern, a merger of the Eastern Counties and four other ailing companies in East Anglia, also in 1863; and the establishment of the Midland's independent access to London with its station at St Pancras, opened in 1868. The story was very much one of fits and starts. In fact, some 7,800 miles of route, about half of the 1871 network, were opened in only two periods, 1846–50 and 1860–66. The late 1840s and the first half of the 1860s thus emerge as the decisive years in the history of UK railway-building.[3]

Railway investment

One of the most obvious elements in the railway-building process

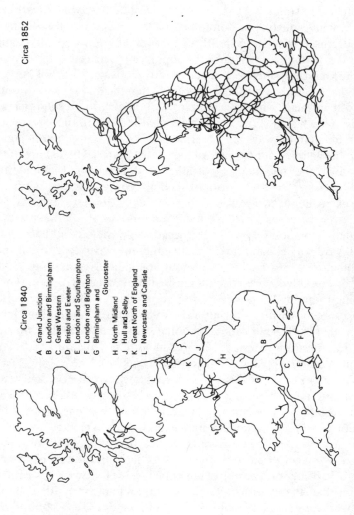

Circa 1840

A Grand Junction
B London and Birmingham
C Great Western
D Bristol and Exeter
E London and Southampton
F London and Brighton
G Birmingham and
     Gloucester
H North Midland
J Hull and Selby
K Great North of England
L Newcastle and Carlisle

Circa 1852

11 The early development of the railway system (from M. Freeman in J. Langton and R. J. Morris (eds.), *Atlas of Industrializing Britain*, Methuen, 1986, p. 89

was its considerable cost. Railways consumed capital in large measure, rapidly establishing themselves as a giant new industry in the Victorian economy. By 1870 the several companies had raised a total of £530 million, and five years later this sum had increased by another £100 million.[4] In Figure 12 the available series indicate that railway investment was dominated by 'cycles' of activity, the most important peaking in 1839/40, 1847, and 1865/66. The significance of this expenditure in macro-economic terms has been duly recorded in the literature, of course. Over twenty years ago Mitchell pointed out that the railways quickly became a significant element in domestic investment, with their gross capital formation (*excluding* land) consuming nearly 2 per cent of national income in the late 1830s. Investment in railways in the period 1837–42 was apparently higher than the value of our exports to the United States. Their share of the national cake then increased dramatically, reaching at its height in 1847 6.7 per cent of national income, equivalent, in Mitchell's words, to 'about two-thirds of the value of all domestic exports, and ... over twice as great as the maximum level of the Bank of England's bullion reserve in the decade'.[5] In the second half of the 1840s railway expenditure consumed about 5 per cent of national income, or about half of total domestic capital formation. In the 1850s the railway presence diminished somewhat, with investment falling to about 1.5 per cent of national income. But in the period 1862–66 a further boom saw expenditure (excluding land) equivalent to 2.5 per cent of national income and about a third of total domestic investment. Figures including expenditure on land would naturally produce higher percentages.[6]

The importance of this scale of investment in the UK has rarely been questioned by economic historians. However, the recent work of Feinstein on investment and Crafts on output has raised a few doubts, and their findings require examination. Feinstein suggested that gross investment ratios of Lewis-Rostovian proportions, that is 10–15 per cent of national income, occurred in the late eighteenth century, *before* the coming of the railways. He followed this with the claim that 'the investment ratio was not significantly lifted by the railway construction boom of the 1840s and 1850s'.[7] But all this rested on output estimates which Feinstein conceded were 'very uncertain throughout', and his hypothesis has never seemed very convincing, given the quality of much of the investment data and the contentious nature of many of the assumptions employed. It has

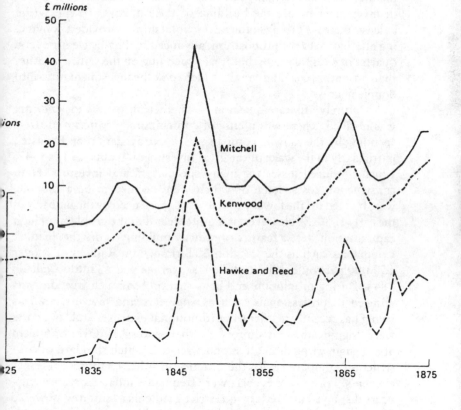

12   UK railway investment, 1825–75
Source. T. R. Gourvish, 'Railway enterprise', in Roy Church (ed.), *The Dynamics of Victorian Business*, 1980, p. 131. The series are: Mitchell: UK gross capital formation (including land), 1831–1919 (data excluding land also available); Kenwood: British gross investment (excluding land, legal and parliamentary costs), 1825–75; Hawke and Reed: UK paid-up capital and loans, 1825–1912

recently been challenged by Crafts, who argues that by using Deane and Cole's data to construct output estimates in constant prices, Feinstein has underestimated output levels in the second half of the eighteenth century and therefore overestimated the investment ratio. His revised calculation indicates double-figure ratios in 1821 and 1831, on the eve of the railway age.[8] All this has complicated the picture, but it has certainly not resolved the debate about the extent of investment before the building of the railways. To this writer at least, there is nothing in the new scholarship to provide a convincing alternative to the proposition, advanced by Phyllis Deane over a quarter of a century ago, that it was spending on the railways rather than on cotton, coal and canals, which took the investment ratio into double figures.[9]

An entirely separate question is whether all of this expenditure was justified. There was plenty of contemporary criticism of overspending by the railway companies, of 'extravagance' and 'waste', particularly in the wake of the great investment 'mania' of 1845–47, which produced losses for many speculators and investors. High construction costs, some of which were deemed to be avoidable, were blamed for the lower profit levels experienced by the industry in the early 1850s.[10] However, it is quite clear that the problems of high capitalisation were a feature of railway building *before* the 'mania'. Companies such as the London & Birmingham Railway cost over £50,000 per route-mile, and the UK average was £33,000 a mile in 1844. During promotion and construction too much freedom was allowed to professionals such as engineers and lawyers, and, as Irving has recently reaffirmed, promotional expenses and land costs were 'significant contributors to the process'.[11] Over-optimism about engineering difficulties and a relatively high standard of construction compared with the practice in other countries were key elements. For example, costs were frequently inflated because engineers displayed an anxiety to restrict gradients to suit low-powered locomotives which were quickly superseded by improved designs.[12] As Irving points out, a Board of Trade submission to the Select Committee on Railways of 1844 contended that Britain's railway costs per route-mile were eight times higher than those in the USA and three to four times higher than in Germany. The data supporting this proposition indicated that the 'excess spending' amounted to about £8,000 per mile, 35 per cent of which was due to the extra costs associated with the process of obtaining a Private Act of

Parliament and with the regulations governing the compulsory purchase of land. The remaining excess was explained by more lavish
engineering standards.[13] Thus, it is possible to argue that about 25
per cent or £130 million of the £530 million spent on UK railways by
1870 might have been avoided, had we pursued less expensive
procedures with regard to the planning and promotion of lines, and
contented ourselves with a much more basic infrastructure.

In fact, then, high capitalisation, with its implications for earning
power, was a problem established in the first two decades of railway
building, and there was no sharp increase in capital costs after the
great 'mania' of the 1840s, despite the losses on uncompleted lines
and the need to provide more facilities for increased traffic flows.
Over half of the capital raised in the period 1825–70 was found after
1850, but the average capitalisation per route-mile rose by only
£3,000 to just under £36,000.[14] Nevertheless, spending on this scale,
whether deemed extravagant or not, must have had an effect on
investment opportunities elsewhere in the economy. Feinstein, for
example, has suggested that in the period 1841–60 railway investment produced a redirection of resources from housebuilding. In the
peak years it is also likely that consumption was affected.[15]

The effects of railway investment were not only negative, of
course. If railway expenditure was far from parsimonious, there is no
doubt that the results proved beneficial to customers in terms of
improved operating standards and higher levels of competition. But
heavy capitalisation may have constrained rates of return for private
investors. The average dividends (on ordinary shares) of the leading
companies fell from over 6 per cent in the first half of the 1840s to
under 3 per cent in the worst years, 1849 and 1850. Although there
was a subsequent recovery, dividends remained below 5 per cent
until the early 1870s.[16] As yet, no-one has really challenged Hawke's
assertion that the *social* rate of return on railway investment was
impressively and consistently high. His calculation for England and
Wales, speculative as it may be, suggests that net social returns (net
revenue plus social savings minus expenditure on reproducible capital) were of the order of 15–20 per cent in the period 1830–70, with
no sign of deterioration after 1840. He also claims that this is an
underestimate of the true return. If shareholders had to suffer lower
profits, then on Hawke's evidence the economy certainly appears to
have gained substantially from the investment process.[17]

One of the commonly accepted ways in which railways supported economic activity lay in the contra-cyclical behaviour of railway expenditure itself. Railway companies made their greatest demands for capital in the upswing of each trade cycle, but the lag between promotion and actual construction ensured that the companies spread these funds well beyond the cycle peaks. Thus the industry played a supporting, rather than a leading role in the growth process. This hypothesis has a long and respectable pedigree, stretching from Matthews and Hughes to Mitchell and Hawke (the latter with some reservations).[18] The case is not without its critics, however. In the first place, the strength of the lag factor appears to have weakened with time, and in particular after 1850. In the 1860s, for example, it is much more difficult to find clear evidence of an interval between the peak of output and the peak of railway expenditure. Why is this? The imprecision of the existing data may be one element. More importantly, the researches of Broadbridge and Reed have pointed to the complexity of factors governing decisions to invest and spend, and it is clear that at times railways both led and followed changes in direction in the economy. Promoters obviously reacted favourably to a general climate of optimism, but they were also influenced by factors endogenous to the railway industry, such as technological development, the progress made by the successful pioneer companies, and changes in Parliamentary procedures and statute law. Reed may have exaggerated the case when he argued that for the period to 1844 railway 'manias' were in large measure self-generating phenomena induced by 'rational' elements internal to the railways, such as the geographical logic of network expansion and the impact of new technology on costs. However, he is on much firmer ground when asserting that the railway investment process combined 'rationality' and 'risk'. All this should serve to warn us against following simple prescriptions when assessing the role of the railways in the growth process.[19]

After 1850, it does seem that endogenous factors lost some of their force, and railway investment activity became increasingly dependent upon the state of the UK capital market. In the 1860s, railway investment peaks tended to *coincide* with the peaks of economic booms, and the industry's contra-cyclical function virtually disappeared. The industry was by this time more mature, of course. Many of the new additions to the network took the form of either risky ventures in Greater London or extensions with dubious prospects in the remoter rural areas. Since speculative interest in railways was increasingly focused on foreign companies, domestic promoters of what were essentially second-class ventures found difficulty in attracting funds and were driven into the arms of the railway contractors and finance companies, a feature particularly evident in the boom of 1863–66. Such bodies not only participated in company flotations but were also involved in attempts to sustain the financing of construction. It was the fragility of many of the arrangements made with financial intermediaries which helps to explain why the railway boom collapsed immediately after the failure of the bankers, Overend, Gurney & Company, in 1866.[20] Some examples will clarify what was happening. Many of the contractors' lines of the 1860s were small: they included the Neath & Brecon, Northampton & Banbury Junction, and Kettering, Thrapston & Huntingdon railways.[21] But two of the larger companies which experienced difficulties were the Great Eastern and the London Chatham & Dover, both forced into bankruptcy in the wake of the 1866 'crash'. The Great Eastern had not only committed itself to a heavy £3 million investment in 'metropolitan extensions' (inner-city and suburban lines in the East End of London) without making provision for the placing of capital, but had also taken on operating responsibility for several loss-making rural railways, including the West Norfolk, Tendring Hundred, and Ware Hadham & Buntingford. Over 40 per cent of the company's paid-up capital was committed to geared stocks paying 5 per cent or more. The average dividends enjoyed by ordinary shareholders amounted to a mere 0.67 per cent in the decade 1863–73.[22] The London Chatham & Dover was in an even more precarious position. Ordinary shareholders gained nothing from an expansion programme which trebled the capital account in only four years (£5 to £15 million, 1862–66) and increased the capitalisation to £120,000 per route-mile, three times the national average. The cost of London extensions included £1.9 million through issuing shares at a discount to the contractors, Peto & Betts, and a further £1.1 million was lost as a bad debt due from the same firm. After a painful reconstruction the company ledgers revealed that the full cost of issuing capital at a discount was £4.2 million by June 1870, or 24 per cent of the total nominal capital of £17.5 million.[23] In the 1860s, then, the climate in which railway investment took place was quite different from that before 1850. Because companies experienced difficulties in attracting capital without the help of external bodies, their independent role in a contra-cyclical movement was severely weakened.

Other effects of the railway investment process had a more enduring impact. There is no doubt at all that the scale of railway company
business provided a tremendous boost to the London capital market,
helping to widen the investing base for joint stock securities. Provincial stock exchanges were established specifically to handle railway
paper: Liverpool and Manchester in 1836; Leeds, Glasgow and
Edinburgh, among others, in 1844–45. However, initial support for
railway companies usually originated outside the formal capital
market. Although a core of local supporters could be found in any
list of subscribers, the leading commercial interests of London and
Lancashire dominated promotional activity in the first two decades
of the 'railway age'. Railways really made their impact on the capital
market by stimulating the market which developed subsequently for
partly-paid and fully-paid shares and, in particular, for fixed interest
securities such as preference shares and debenture stock. It was the
trading in railway shares which extended the occupational and
geographical basis of shareholding in the UK.[24]

The railways did not stimulate change only because they were
regarded as a safe and positive investment. There was much contemporary concern in political and financial circles about the implications of company failures and frauds, notably the undignified down-
fall of George Hudson, the 'Railway King' and chairman of four
major companies, in 1849.[25] Anxiety was sustained by further
scandals, including that surrounding Leopold Redpath, who made
over £250,000 by issuing fictitious Great Northern Railway shares
before he was exposed in 1856, and the 'Turner–Pepper defal-
cations' of 1869, where C. H. Turner, the Great Eastern's deputy
chairman, used company funds improperly and unsuccessfully to
speculate in the company's stock.[26] A desire to protect the interests
of the small investor against losses arising from such depredations
was as important in stimulating the legislation extending joint-stock
financing with limited liability status in 1855–62 as any positive
demonstration of the soundness and worth of the British railway
company. Half a century ago Shannon claimed that the railways
'won the acceptance of general limited liability'. This now seems
unlikely. Railways were merely one of a number of influences encouraging changes in company law and the financing of business enterprises, and their impact most probably resulted from the murkier
aspects of railway management.[27] The difficulties of sustaining

railway investment after 1850 also worked in the same direction. Problems surfaced whenever interest rates rose or attractive alternative investments (e.g. foreign railways) appeared. The financial embarrassment of large companies such as the Great Eastern and London Chatham & Dover and the cash-flow problems of the smaller, more marginal railways encouraged bankers, stockbrokers and other financial intermediaries to play a more active part in the industry's management. Leading stockbroking firms such as Foster & Braithwaite, Heseltine Powell and Henry Cazenove were often called in by railway directors to advise on the state of the money market, and they sometimes assumed an underwriting function. By 1870 they represented a substantial interest in their own right. For example, they can be found pressing for a merger of the South Eastern and London Chatham & Dover companies in the mid-1870s. The role of contractors may have faded after the 1866 'crash' but bankers and brokers continued to influence the financial strategies of railway companies. Direct institutional investment in railways also increased, and the process was encouraged by a growing emphasis on geared stocks. By 1870 just under half of UK railway capital (excluding loans) bore a fixed rate of interest.[28]

Railway construction

Railway construction stimulated much more than the capital market and financial institutions, of course. Orders for equipment proved to be a potent influence upon a number of supplying industries, notably iron, engineering, coal, timber, and building materials generally. These 'backward-linkage' effects are difficult to quantify with precision but historians are agreed that they were considerable, particularly during the railway-building booms. Most research has focused on the railways' relationship with the iron industry, where the impact was probably greatest. Mitchell's estimate of the pig-iron requirements of UK railways shows that in the period 1844–51 about 18 per cent of pig-iron output was used in constructing the permanent way, equivalent to about 29 per cent of domestic consumption. The railways' dominance was at its height in the year 1848, when about 30 per cent of total output and 40 per cent of domestic consumption was used.[29] This is not to say that the relationship was always either dominant or positive. Mitchell points out that the railways' share of iron output fell to only 8.2 per cent in the period 1852–69. Furthermore, the disruptive effect of the 'manias' on iron company stability should not be discounted, notably in 1841–43 but also in the late 1840s, when demand fell away. Hawke has gone even further. He suggests that railways 'were not essential to the existence of an iron industry . . . nor were they responsible for technical advances and external economies in the finishing processes and rolling mills'. The decisive influences in shaping the expansion of the industry are to be found, it seems, in Neilson's hot-blast technique in the 1830s and the surge of export growth in the following decade.[30]

There are a number of reasons for suspecting that the Mitchell–Hawke assessment is too bleak. Most of the available studies concentrate on the iron needed for the railways' permanent way. But the metal required for locomotives, rolling stock and other equipment amounted to another 25 per cent on top of this. In addition, a good case could be made for the proposition that railway demand encouraged technological developments in iron. In the blast furnace sector, for example, scale economies in association with the hot-blast may well have been stimulated, and in South Wales there seems little doubt that growth of iron output was dependent upon railway company orders for rails, particularly in the period to 1850.[31] Finally, if we accept the notion that the *full* effects of railway demand for iron should include the demand from foreign railways, then the dependence of the iron industry on its new customer becomes very clear indeed. In the peak years, 1844–51, well over a third of UK iron production went into railways, home and overseas, and in 1852–69 the proportion, though lower, was still as high as a quarter.[32] Mitchell's more cautious assessment limits the argument to domestic railways and permanent-way building. Here, railway companies took under 10 per cent of pig-iron production in 1835–69 and the 'dominant' phase was limited to the 1840s. But the full impact of railways on the iron industry was much greater than his figures imply.

The substitution of steel for iron rails began tentatively in the late 1850s, encouraged by the heavy maintenance costs associated with increased traffic volumes and higher speeds. Experimentation was led by the Midland (1857), London & North Western (1861) and Great Northern companies. The London & North Western erected a Bessemer steel plant at Crewe in 1863–64 and began the production of a compound rail, where a steel surface was welded on to an iron base. Solid steel rails were not favoured for another decade. The reason was simple. Despite their much greater durability, steel rails cost 2½ times more than iron, and doubts about the quality of rails made with early Bessemer steel were slow to disperse. The close links between railway boards and the ironmasters dampened the enthusiasm of companies such as the North Eastern. When steel prices fell sharply in the 1870s the decisive shift to steel occurred. By 1878, for example, most of the tracks of the London & North Western and Midland companies were made of steel. Railway demand, if not crucial, was an important element in the home market for steel in that decade.[33]

For other industries, the evidence on backward linkages is far from abundant. The railways' *direct* demand for coal was not particularly large – about 3 per cent of total UK production in 1855 and 1869, for example. On the other hand, it is clear that the search for the good quality coal suitable for use in steam locomotives gave a boost to high-quality collieries in the North-East, such as those in south Durham.[34] More importantly for the present discussion, coal was also required in the production of iron-made railway equipment. It seems that at the peak of railway demand for iron, viz. 1844–51, about 5 per cent of total UK coal output went into the iron industry in order to satisfy railway company orders. After domestic heating and iron and steel, railway construction was one of the coal industry's major customers, if only for a short time.[35] For engineering, it is now something of a cliché to point out that the railways created an entirely new sector of the industry – mechanical engineering, symbolised by the establishment of the Institution of Mechanical Engineers in 1847. But we must also remember that railway orders were a sizeable proportion of the demand for *all* engineering products in the late 1830s and 1840s, perhaps some 20 per cent of the total. Brick-making received a similar stimulus, with about 25–30 per cent of output going into railways in the 1840s. In both areas, however, further research would be welcome to refine these tentative generalisations.[36]

Railway construction was essentially a labour-intensive activity, and the impact of this new industry on the labour market was enormous. In most years before 1850 the employment generated by the building of new railways dwarfed the more permanent employment of staff to operate completed lines, just as the annual gross capital formation exceeded gross turnover.[37] In the four decades to 1870, about 30,000 miles of track were laid to form 15,500 miles of route, providing work for about 60,000 men a year, or about one per cent of the male labour force. Lest this be judged to represent a rather modest addition to UK employment as a whole, it should be pointed out once again that railway building took place in concentrated bursts of activity, and at these times the impact on employment was much larger than that suggested by the forty-year average. In 1845–49, for example, annual employment was of the order of 172,000, with 257,000 (about 4 per cent of the male labour force) in May 1847, the peak year, and in 1862–66 106,000 per annum. About 80–85 per cent of those recruited were unskilled manual labourers, and, notwithstanding the presence of large numbers of Irish navvies on projects in the Scottish borders, Lancashire, the North Midlands, and South Wales, recruitment was predominantly local. It is therefore logical to hypothesise that railway wages provided a substantial impetus to effective demand across the country, particularly in times of depression. Thus, in the second half of the 1840s the wages paid were probably of the order of £11 million per annum, or about 2 per cent of GNP, and in 1847 £16 million, or about 3 per cent of GNP. The multiplier effects of these payments, though obviously difficult to pin down with accuracy, must have helped to cushion the effects of depression at a critical stage of Britain's economic development.[38]

Our view of the longer-term effects should be more temperate. In the next boom, 1862–66, for example, wage costs amounted to about £7 million per annum, but the cushioning effects of railway building work on the ensuing recession were rather limited, since demand for labour coincided with the upswing in economic activity and employment dwindled rapidly after the 1866 'crash'. It is not easy to find out what happened to the navvies and other construction workers who were displaced when construction was cut back in the early 1850s and late 1860s. The 257,000 workers employed in 1847 had been reduced to under 36,000 by 1852. Some may have worked on foreign railways with the larger contracting firms, others may have found jobs in railway operating. However, we must assume that most of them were returned to the pool of underemployed, unskilled labour. Thus, the benefits to labour of railway construction were large in certain years, but in the long run more modest. Railway operation was to offer more permanent employment opportunities on a large scale, with 60,000 working on UK lines open for traffic in

1850, 127,500 ten years later, and 274, 500 by the end of 1873.[39]

Railway construction provided work for other, more highly-paid staff. There were sudden demands for professional expertise in areas such as engineering, law, accountancy and surveying. In engineering, the railways were particularly important in the 1840s and 1860s. In the first of these decades there was a threefold increase in the numbers engaged in civil engineering in Britain, 3,000 being listed in the 1851 census. In addition, the railways acted as a training ground for the development of engineering generally, attracting pupils to their large workshops, and encouraging the differentiation between civil and mechanical engineering.[40] Elsewhere, it is more difficult to detach the railways' constructional from their operational needs, but it is certainly true that the railway 'manias' provided lucrative employment for specialist lawyers such as the Parliamentary agent (who handled private bill submissions), of whom there were twenty-nine in 1841 but 141 in 1851, and for firms of solicitors specialising in railway work, such as Baxter Rose Norton.[41] The accounting profession also received a considerable stimulus from the railway 'mania' of the 1840s, developing from broking and auctioneering into an interest in monitoring the financial progress of large-scale businesses. The legislation of the mid-1840s required the railways to keep detailed accounts and provide a system of audit, and the industry's difficulties once the 'mania' collapsed produced numerous demands for accountants to assist shareholders' or directors' committees of inquiry. Leading accounting firms such as Deloitte, Coleman, Quilter Ball, and Price Holyland & Waterhouse owned their rise to such work, and it was Deloitte's which was given the task of unravelling the mess left by Redpath in the Great Northern share registers in 1856. But it was the regular half-yearly auditing of railway accounts which helped to establish accountancy as a legitimate profession. The railway companies also employed their own accountants. In June 1860, for example, there were as many accountants and cashiers as engineers working directly for the railways.[42] Finally, it is no exaggeration to assert that surveying was transformed by the railways, turning away from its land-measuring roots to specialise in valuation and arbitration. As with the navvies, the numbers engaged in some of these new 'professions' fell back in the 1850s after the 'mania' subsided. But the railways' sudden demand for services had a more lasting impact in that, by attracting incompetent or unscrupulous persons into

activities such as surveying, they encouraged the process of professionalisation, with attempts to control entry, protect standards, and
establish the ground-rules for specialisation and differentiation. For
example, fifteen of the twenty founding fathers of the Institute of
Surveyors of 1868 were railway surveyors.[43]

One last point should be made about the effects of the railway-
building process. The construction of the rail network in a comparatively densely populated and increasingly urbanised country, where
the popularity of passenger travel was quickly established, had
obvious implications for the urban landscape. As John Kellett has
noted, the building of the large London termini, such as Euston,
King's Cross, St Pancras and Liverpool Street, together with major
stations in the other leading cities, including Birmingham (New
Street), Liverpool (Lime Street), Manchester (Victoria) and Glasgow
(Buchanan Street), had powerful repercussions in the city centres and
the inner districts immediately adjacent to them. He has estimated
that in the five major cities the railways had consumed between 5.2
and 9.0 per cent of the 1840 built-up area by 1900 and acquired
much larger acreages in the peripheral areas beyond. Of course, the
process of urban change was complex, embracing the interconnected
factors of landownership patterns, autonomous market growth, and
the contribution of road transport. Nevertheless, the railways were
one of the most important single influences, encouraging commercial
and industrial development, increasing land values and providing
opportunities for commuting to work (only for the wealthy before
the 1870s). At the same time they added to traffic congestion and the
overcrowding of working-class housing. The railways' impact on the
urban working class was mixed. The companies required a labour
force for their inter- and intra-urban business in passengers and
freight, but they also stimulated industrial relocation, while the
demolition of the cheapest properties in the city centres displaced the
casual, unskilled workers, producing a social cost to be set alongside
the railways' obvious social benefits. In all this, there was an important difference from the other effects of railway construction which
we have described. The railways' urban impact was *not* at its height
in the 1840s. Major changes to stations and other facilities and the
building of new stations and yards took place from the late 1860s, as
a response to inter-company competition and the growth of traffic.
The effect was aggregative, gathering pace in response to industrial
and urban development.[44]

Railway traffic

It is in operation that the railways' enduring impact on the British economy is to be assessed. As table 1 shows, there was a steady growth of railway traffic, both in passengers and freight, from the early 1840s, when the first reliable statistics were collected. In the short space of eight years, 1842–50, the number of passengers carried trebled and freight tonnage increased sevenfold. Traffic volumes then roughly doubled in the 1850s and again in the 1860s. The growth of gross revenue was more modest. Passenger receipts doubled between 1842 and 1850, freight receipts quadrupled over the same period, and the sectors experienced a 70–150 per cent increase in the 1850s followed by a 45–75 per cent increase in the 1860s (table 1). The explanation for these trends is now clearly understood. Although many coalfields received a direct stimulus from the coming of rail transport, the railways established themselves in the market for transport by offering improved facilities for *existing* users. The trunk-line companies of the 1830s and early 1840s specialised in high-tariff business. They defeated the stage coaches and took high-value merchandise traffic from road and canal carriers by virtue of a much superior quality of service. However, as the railway industry expanded and the level of competition within it increased, encouraged by government intervention, the companies were forced to move down market and charges fell. This produced two major changes in traffic composition: a greater emphasis on freight traffic from *c.* 1845; and a switch to low fare-paying, i.e. third-class passengers. The first of these changes was rapid indeed. In only five years, 1845–50, the revenue breakdown of the major British railway companies shifted from 74 per cent passenger/26 per cent freight to 49 per cent passenger/51 per cent freight (44/56 by 1870).[45] The composition of the passenger business changed more gradually, but was nevertheless significant. In 1845–46, the major companies derived only 20 per cent of their passenger receipts from third class; by 1870 the figure had risen to 44 per cent, and five years later it had climbed to 61 per cent. The effect of all this was that traffic volume growth outpaced revenue growth, and the industry experienced reduced profit margins. The experience of the London & North Western Railway may serve as an illustration. The company's revenue composition (passenger/freight) moved from 62/38 in 1846 to 45/55 in 1859, by which time 56 per cent of

Table 1 UK railway operating statistics, 1842–70 (millions)

| Year | Traffic volume | | Gross traffic revenue (£) | | | Total revenue (£) | |
	Passengers (numbers)	Freight (tons)	Passenger	Freight		Gross	Net
1842	24·7	c. 5·0–6·0	3·1	1·7		4·8	–
1850	72·9	38·0[a]	6·8	6·4		13·2	–
1860	163·4	89·9	11·6	16·2		27·8	14·6
1870	336·5	169·4[b]	17·0	28·1		45·1	23·4

Notes:
Data attribute mails and parcels traffic to freight throughout, and season ticket-holders are excluded from passenger numbers.
[a] Estimate.
[b] 1871 figure.
Sources: Railway Returns. 1842 data from Select Committee on Railways, 1844, B.P.P. 1844, XI, appendix 2 (= data collected on UK railways [cf. Gourvish, 1980, p. 26] plus Laing's estimate for companies omitted).

its passengers were third or parliamentary class. Its net revenue margin, or total gross revenue minus total costs expressed as a percentage of total gross revenue, fell from 56 in 1846 to 42 in 1851 and 29 in 1859.[46] There was a sharp contraction in returns to shareholders in 1846–50, followed by a slow recovery. However, ordinary dividends remained low, those of the leading fifteen companies averaging only 3.65 per cent over the quarter-century from 1850, compared with over 6 per cent before 1846.[47]

The railways' impact on the economy through their transport services has been subjected to critical scrutiny by Mitchell. Following a theme first pursued by Clapham, he suggests that the railways' freight operations produced little in the way of market-widening effects before the 1850s. The railways' slow penetration of the London coal trade, where coastal shipping retained a predominance until the 1860s, is cited in support of the view that the companies were slow to exploit their inherent advantages. Only with the company amalgamations of the mid-late 1840s, and the use of the Railway Clearing House (established in 1842) to facilitate inter-company exchanges of traffic did the railways, in Mitchell's view, offer a real challenge to road and canal transport and coastal shipping.[48] This thesis is pessimistic and, in some ways, even misleading. The emphasis placed on the importance of amalgamations and inter-company exchange is rather overdone. Average freight hauls for most companies were about 20–30 miles, about double that suggested for the canals.[49] Mergers encouraged the growth of longer-distance traffic, of course, but the stimulus given to longer hauls was not dependent upon such developments. It is also difficult to accept that the railway companies missed opportunities to capture freight traffic, since they profited so well from exploiting the quality end of the market. In any case, railways were scarcely equipped to deal with freight flows in bulk before locomotive technology had developed sufficiently and the administrative arrangements for handling freight had been developed. As late as 1840 Parliament was debating whether to allow private operators to run railway services (it decided against), and it took another decade for the railway companies' relations with the established carrying firms, such as Pickfords, to be worked out.[50] If there was a 'lag' in the railways' response, then it could only have occurred in the second half of the 1840s, when investment 'mania' was the preoccupation. But even at this time managerial preferences were the main determinant of traffic composition. A recent examination of the coal industry has not only upheld the view that the railways were critical for the development of inland coal markets but has also pointed out that the apparent 'failure' to carry South Yorkshire coal was as much a matter of deliberate management choice (on the part of the Great Northern Railway directors) as anything else.[51]

To conclude. It is true that in the period 1830–45 the railway companies were interested primarily in the affluent passenger traffic and high-value freight, though some owed their rationale to the coal trade, as the canals had done. However, once the industry had been encouraged to go for higher traffic volumes, by a government keen on combining tighter pricing controls with higher levels of competition, it did so with alacrity. The emphasis should really be placed on the speed with which the railways responded to post-'mania' conditions. Here the market could be, and often was, widened even where hauls were relatively short, as in the case of inland coal. After 1850 most if not all the companies had accepted the opinion of Mark Huish, General Manager of the London & North Western, that given burgeoning capital accounts quantity was essential to successful trading. And over the next quarter-century the excess capacity in the rail network created by the 'mania' of the 1840s was gradually eliminated.[52]

There is more agreement about the impact of the railways in reducing transport costs, although it is difficult to be precise. Jackman's long-standing approximation may be taken as a basis for discussion: he suggested that in the period to the mid-1840s the railways undercut the stage coaches by about 15–20 per cent and the canals by a larger margin of 30–50 per cent.[53] In fact, there is every reason to challenge both estimates. In the passenger market the railways quickly ousted the coaches on the longer routes, and were then able to maintain high fares of up to $3\frac{1}{2}d$ a mile first class and $2\frac{1}{2}d$ second class, little lower than the road fares for inside and outside travel. However, since the quality of rail services was markedly higher, even second class was superior to travel inside the coach. Thus, rail fares of 2–$2\frac{1}{2}d$ a mile were substantially cheaper than the $3\frac{1}{2}$–$4\frac{1}{2}d$ commonly charged by road. With regard to freight, it is clear that the railways' impact came earlier than Mitchell implies, if only because canals and coastal shipping frequently cut their rates in anticipation of railway competition. And Hawke has given Jackman's proposition some support, favouring a figure of $3d$

a ton-mile for canal transport charges and accepting Lardner's mid-1840s estimate of average railway rates of 1.67*d*. This indicates a reduction of 44 per cent, though we are not necessarily comparing like with like.[54] However, given the lack of data for non-rail freight movements and the complexities of the market it would be foolish to fix upon precise percentage reductions.

We know more about the movement of rail charges. After the mid-1840s both passenger fares and freight rates came down. By 1870 the former were something like 40 per cent lower than they had been three decades before, while freight rates also fell, probably by around 30 per cent, if Hawke and Lardner are to be believed. All this occurred in spite of collusive traffic-sharing and price-fixing agreements involving several railway companies or railway companies and their competitors. Undoubtedly, a fair proportion of the fall in tariffs was the result of changes in traffic composition – the dependence on third-class passengers already mentioned, and, in the freight sector, the increasing dominance of the low-tariff heavy mineral traffic, and coal in particular, which by 1870 made up 60 per cent of the total tonnage carried. Nevertheless, we must conclude that notwithstanding the lack of precise information, the railways contributed to a sizeable reduction in transport costs by 1870 as well as producing a clear improvement in the quality of transport services.[55]

The railways were also a force for change in British markets. Once again Mitchell has cast a sceptical eye over events, observing that since 'British railways were built with existing traffics very much in mind' they did not create new industries and new towns in 'virgin territory'.[56] Much of this is true, but we should not underestimate the railways' ability to promote change, as the canals had done, by eroding the position of regional and intra-regional monopolies. In any case, Mitchell exempts coal from his generalisation, pointing out how the possibilities of rail transport encouraged the exploitation of new pits in the remoter parts of coalfields. Church shows how the railways brought 'competition into markets hitherto monopolized by intra-regional supplies' and thereby 'stimulated further interest in railway provision'. The result was an increasingly complex market for the mineral, with the railways at the centre of the exploitation of key inland fields such as Derbyshire, Leicestershire, and South Yorkshire.[57] Indeed, the railways did much more than transform the coal market. Many new traffics were essentially railway traffics, for example, perishable foods such as fresh fish, milk and vegetables. And the railways did open up some new locations, in South Wales (iron, anthracite), Northamptonshire (iron ore), South Yorkshire and the North-East (coal). The 'railway town' was a not inconsiderable addition to the industrial townscape, with the manufacturing and repair activities at places such as Crewe (London & North Western), Swindon (Great Western) and Darlington (North Eastern) representing large-scale production at a time when the small family firm was the characteristic form in the British economy.[58] With improved transport services went improvements in communications – the telegraph, the post, and national newspapers. The number of letters delivered by the Post Office increased from 76 million in 1839 to 863 million in 1870, boosted on the one hand by the Penny Post of 1840 and on the other by the railways, which charged £463,000 for conveyance in 1854, and only £587,000 for a much expanded traffic in 1870.[59] The railways' own ancillary activities in hotels, tourism, food and franchising were important. For example, the rise to prominence of the firm of W. H. Smith was dependent upon its bookstall and advertising contracts with the railway companies, starting with agreements in 1848 and 1851 with the London & North Western Railway.[60] Many of these changes took time to develop. The rise of a *mass* market in seaside resorts such as Brighton and Blackpool was a post-1870 phenomenon, and the same is true of perishable foods. But railways did have an impact on a wide range of activities, both manufacturing and service, and it is hoped that further research will illuminate this. The linkage effects of railway operation deserve as much attention as those arising from railway construction, as the UK economy moved into a mature stage.

The railways' contribution to economic growth

Can we be more exact in our estimate of the contribution of the railways to economic growth? Stimulated by the pioneering work of Fogel and Fishlow in the USA over twenty years ago, a 'social savings' approach has been applied to the question, and calculations have been produced for several countries with the intention of focusing our minds more sharply on the scale of this contribution. For the UK economy, the path-breaking work was Hawke's estimate of the saving produced by railways in England and Wales in the year 1865 (although we should not neglect Vamplew's more sceptical research on railways in the Scottish economy). Written in 1970, this wide-ranging evaluation of the available evidence was packed with pertinent if often contentious results. And although a veritable artillery of criticism has been thrown up at Hawke's findings, both in terms of the theoretical assumptions employed and the strength of the empirical evidence, there is no sign of his 'social savings road-show' coming to a stop. Far from it, the basic findings have reappeared recently, with little or no amendment, in books edited by Floud and McCloskey in 1981 and Patrick O'Brien in 1983.[61]

What did Hawke argue? It should be noted at the outset that he did *not* claim to be providing a comprehensive measurement of the railways' contribution to economic development. His inquiry was limited to the question: 'to what extent did the economy depend on railways in 1865?', which could be quantified if presented in the form 'to what extent could the national income of 1865 have been attained without the innovation of railways?' Here, 'social saving' is 'measured as the difference between the actual cost of the transportation services of a given year provided by the railways and the hypothetical cost of those same services in the absence of the railways using the best alternative source of transport services'.[62] Hawke found that railways produced a saving over the non-rail alternatives – coaches for passenger travel and canals for freight – of between 6 and 11 per cent of the national income of England and Wales (5–9 per cent of the UK national income), the variation depending, in the main, on the value placed on the quality of passenger travel (see table 2 for a synopsis of the calculation).

Hawke indicated a preference for the upper-bound, 11 per cent figure, and although recognising that social savings were lower in years prior to 1865 – perhaps 2.5–6.5 per cent of national income in 1850, 6.5–8.5 per cent in 1855 – concluded that 'the innovation of the railway within England and Wales did have a considerable impact on the growth of that economy'.[63] The author's preference has been taken by some critics to demonstrate that the railways made a significantly high contribution to economic growth in the mid-1860s. Patrick O'Brien, for example, used Hawke's findings to assert that in order to have made up the saving in a five-year period, 1865–70, the economy would have to have experienced a 40 per cent increase in its growth rate, a similar rise in investment, and a cut in consumption of 5 per cent per annum.[64] On the other hand, Church and, more recently, Crouzet have suggested that the contribution to

Table 2 *Hawke's social saving calculation for railways in England and Wales, 1865*

1. Saving on passenger traffic (2,228·45m. passenger-miles):
   Calculation (1) [a]   £17·5m.   2·6% nat. inc. (E. & W.)
   Calculation (1)
   error corrected [b]:   £13·1m.   2·0% nat. inc. (E. & W.)
   Calculation (2) [c]:   £47·9m.   7·2% nat. inc. (E. & W.)
2. Saving on freight traffic (3,120m. ton-miles):
   Basic calculation: £14·0m.   2·1% nat. inc. (E. & W.)
   Additional savings [d]:   £11·0–£14·1m.   1·7–2·1% nat. inc. (E. & W.)
3. Total savings:
   With passenger (1):   £42·5–£45·6m.   6·4–6·8% nat. inc. (E. & W.)
   With passenger (1)
   amended: £38·1–£41·2m.   5·8–6·2% nat. inc. (E. & W.)
   With passenger (2):   £72·9–£76·0m.   10·9–11·4% nat. inc. (E. & W.)

Notes:
[a] Unintentionally compares 1st and 2nd-class rail with inside coach travel, 3rd-class with outside travel.
[b] Compares 1st-class rail with inside coach travel, other classes with outside travel. This error, pointed out in Gourvish, 1980, *op. cit.*, p. 34, appears to have been picked up by Hawke in recent synopses. Cf. Hawke and Higgins, in Floud and McCloskey, *op. cit.*, I, p. 242.
[c] Compares 1st-class rail with 'posting' (special coach hire), 2nd-class with inside coach travel, 3rd-class with outside travel.
[d] Livestock and meat traffic (£0·–£2·5m), supplementary wagon haulage (£10·6m), inventory adjustments (£0·0–£1·0m).
Sources: Hawke, 1970, *op. cit.*, pp. 43, 48–9, 62, 88–9, 188, and see also commentary and table in Gourvish, 1980, *op. cit.*, pp.34–7.

economic growth was more modest than had earlier been assumed. Crouzet takes the saving to confirm the proposition that 'the economy did not receive any decisive boost from the railways'.[65]

Before contributing to this debate, two things must be done. The first is to establish whether Hawke's calculation is soundly based; the second is to interpret his findings in light of the railways' broader role in the growth process. Dealing with the first of these, it is clear that most critics have isolated both methodological and empirical problems in his social saving analysis, although all concede the practical difficulties in attempting such an exercise when data relating to key parts of the calculation are scarce. The technique used is essentially a social cost benefit analysis carried out in a partial equilibrium framework, and is therefore more useful for the assessment of individual investment projects in the present than for measuring the impact of an entire industry in the past. Thus, most of the theoretical objections to Hawke hinge upon the *ceteris paribus* assumptions: an inelastic demand for transport in 1865; an inelastic demand for quality of service in passenger travel; no technical change in the non-rail alternatives; constant real canal costs over time; rail and coach charges equal to resource costs (perfect competition).[66]

There are also several criticisms of Hawke's empirical approach. A great deal of scepticism has been directed at the comparison of rail and non-rail alternatives. In passenger traffic, some confusion was caused by Hawke's first calculation, which compared first- and second-class rail with inside coach travel, and third-class with outside travel, and not, as intended, first with inside, and second and third with outside (see table 2 above).[67] More important, however, is the validity of the second calculation, which produces a much higher social saving. Here, Hawke took up a suggestion made by the Royal Commission on Railways of 1865 and compared first-class rail with 'posting', special coach hire with horses changed en route (second class was then compared with inside coach travel, and third with outside). Since posting was taken to cost 2*s* a mile, compared with only 2.11*d* for first-class rail, this single comparison produced a social saving of £33.6 million, 5 per cent of the national income of England and Wales and 44–46 per cent of the entire upper-bound savings total. Whether the comparison is sound is open to question. But in any case there are reasons to challenge all of the road–rail calculations, since the data on coach charges are particularly fragile.[68]

Turning to freight, it is a great pity that information on coastal shipping is so limited, since that mode was clearly the best alternative to rail for a number of key traffics, for example the transport of coal from the North-East to London. But the canal data are not very abundant either, and critical attention has been focused on Hawke's canal resource cost estimate of 2.3*d* a ton-mile, which when compared with 1.21*d* for rail produces the initial freight savings figure of £14.1 million (table 2). Evidence for canal costs is rather weak, and Hawke is forced to rely on data for two canals, the Leeds and Liverpool (1820–40) and the Kennet and Avon (1812–24), both of which experienced difficulties in construction and operation and lay outside the major trunk routes. However, these canals provide only 0.4*d* of the 2.3*d*, the *direct* canal cost element. The remaining 1.9*d*, 1.5*d* for shipping costs and 0.4*d* for the canals' extra journey lengths compared with rail (held to be about 20 per cent), is justified on the flimsiest of evidence. Other crucial calculations, for example the length of haul of rail freight, are similarly based on scraps of information found in secondary sources such as Dionysius Lardner's *Railway Economy* of 1850, or in evidence given to Parliamentary select committees. The list of quibbles is a long one.[69]

Recently, I tried to illustrate the practical difficulties of all this by providing alternative upper and lower-bound savings figures, 'without challenging [Hawke's] theoretical base or resorting to extravagant flights of fancy'. Supportable estimates of under 3 per cent of national income and 23 per cent were the outcome, and this without criticising Hawke's view that additional savings via linkage effects and external economies (iron industry, labour, mobility, managerial skills, location, and investment) could be safely dismissed.[70] This leads us to the second major question, the interpretation of Hawke's findings in the context of the railways' overall contribution to the UK economy. The conclusion must be that while Hawke has extended our understanding of the impact of the railways, his social savings arithmetic is difficult to use. Supported on rather insecure foundations, it is too speculative to either support or refute the hypothesis that railways were vital to Britain's growth after 1830. A hundred years before Hawke, Dudley Baxter offered Victorians a similar assessment, produced with less intellectual effort. He suggested that 'had the railway traffic of 1865 been conveyed by canal and road at the pre-railway rates, it would have cost three times as much'. A saving of £72 million in the UK economy was thus obtained, equal to about 9 per cent of net national income. This may be as useful a guide to historians looking for precision, where precision is elusive, as Hawke's more sophisticated, and much longer, work.[71] Otherwise, to look for the relationship between railways and economic growth requires a variety of approaches in addition to the rather limited conclusions which can be drawn from a social savings approach. Hawke recognises this when he states in a recent summary that 'it is . . . true that one can never hope to make definitive statements about counterfactual situations'.[72]

We must conclude by noting that any assessment of the railways' impact on the economy must look at factors which defy precise measurement. To be fair to Hawke, he did much in his book to illuminate some of the broader aspects of railway construction and operation, though his conclusions were more often negative than positive. For example, he was rather sceptical of the external econ-omies which the new form of transport was held to have produced, in the labour market, in business management, and the capital market. However, more recently he has conceded that 'the difficulty with such external economies is simply that they must be identified and measured',[73] and further research may provide fresh insights. This writer at least has argued that the railways' contribution to modern corporate forms, management hierarchies, the separation of ownership and control, in short to the transition to managerial capitalism, should not be discounted, despite the persistence of the family firm in British industry. The railway companies, public joint-stock concerns with limited liability and a dispersed ownership, were pioneers of the modern business organisation. The large-scale pro-duction and distribution activities of the leading railways ensured the separation and professionalisation of management functions. For example, the ten largest companies had an average of 7,700 shareholders each on the last day of 1855, the highest recorded figure being 15,115 for the London & North Western Railway.[74] The industry's work-force of 275,000 (in 1873) was also concentrated in the larger business units, as was turnover and investment. Moreover, such features were established at an early stage in the railways' history. By 1850, for example, the top fifteen companies controlled 61 per cent of UK paid-up capital and 75 per cent of the industry's turnover. Twenty years later the percentages controlled by the same companies had risen to 80 and 83 respectively. The leading railways were giant enterprises by British standards which not only provided and sold transport services but also manufactured a wide range of products. As we have already noted, the railway workshops were substantial manufacturing units in their own right.[75] The dispersion of ownership led inevitably to the creation of complex organi-sational systems. These were usually departmental, i.e. 'functional' in nature, with specialist departmental managers responsible for engineering, operating, accounts, legal affairs, and so on, and a chief exective, the general manager, at the top. The leading companies also introduced schemes for staff development, and were particularly interested in attracting potential general managers. The relevance of the railways' example for the development of more sophisticated management systems elsewhere in the economy may be challenged, but it remains true that managerial capitalism was established in the railway industry and from an early date.[76]

Railways were also distinguished by the degree of government control which they attracted in the 'Age of *Laissez-faire*'. Although the promotion and construction of the UK network was very much a matter for private enterprise, the state built up a considerable body of interventionist legislation affecting the financing, organisation and operating of the railway companies, while retaining the private company structure. Control was exercised in two ways: through the private bill procedures of Parliament; and by resort to the general statute law. Each new railway company (or each addition to an existing company) which sought powers to raise capital under conditions of limited liability and to acquire land compulsorily had to obtain a Private Act of Parliament. After 1836 the Parliamentary rules or standing orders governing the consideration of such applications were fairly stringent, covering the subscribing of capital, borrowing powers, and the depositing of plans. Parliamentary committees inserted maximum rate-clauses in each Act and often added further restrictions to protect the interests of landowners, local authorities and institutions. In addition to, and more important than this, there was the substantial body of statute law established from the 1840s. The legislation of 1840–70 was in the main permissive rather than compulsory in nature, and state supervision was not entirely consistent. Many of the major elements of interference with the railways' managerial freedom came in the late nineteenth century. Nevertheless, as early as 1840 Parliament accepted that for safety reasons railways would have to possess an operating monopoly, and therefore the legislature had a duty to ensure that competitive levels were maintained in the 'public interest'. An Act of 1840 created a government department – the Railway Department of the Board of Trade – to supervise and monitor aspects of railway operating, and in 1844 Gladstone's famous measure imposed the first general requirement about passenger trains – the obligation to provide a basic third-class service at fixed fares. The same Act also set a precedent by giving the state an option to purchase new lines after twenty-one years if profits remained high. An Act of 1868 required the companies to publish a standardised set of annual accounts. Thus, by 1870, the railway industry was quite clearly characterised by large oligopolistic businesses operating under a considerable measure of state control.[77]

Railways may not have been essential to Britain's economic growth in the nineteenth century, nor did they in Rostovian terms produce a 'take-off', which was already under way by 1830. But they were of enormous significance in the 1840s and 1860s, and throughout the period had a considerable impact upon the capital market, supplying industries, and transport services generally. There is no doubt that railways had a greater influence than any other single innovation before the age of oil and electricity. The 'social savings' approach may be frustratingly difficult to interpret, but it is quite clear that much of the scholarly work involved has demonstrated the range of the industry's impact. Some of these wider ramifications, embracing managerial change in business and the presence of the state in industrial decision-making, should not be discounted in any assessment of the importance of the 'railway age'.

Notes

1   T. J. Donaghy, *Liverpool & Manchester Railway Operations 1831–1845,* Newton Abbot, 1972, p. 173; T. R. Gourvish, *Railways and the British Economy 1830–1914,* 1980, pp. 26–7.

2   15,991 miles, end of 1964, 14,920 miles, end of 1965: British Railways Board, *Report and Accounts, 1965,* II, 1966, p. 43.

3   Data for UK taken from B. R. Mitchell and P. Deane, *Abstract of British Historical Statistics,* Cambridge, 1962, pp. 225, 228, and H. G. Lewin, *Early British Railways. A Short History of Their Origin and Development 1801–1844,* 1925, p. 186.

4   G. R. Hawke and M. C. Reed, 'Railway capital in the United Kingdom in the nineteenth century', *Economic History Review,* 2nd ser., XXII, 1969, p. 270.

5   B. R. Mitchell, 'The coming of the railway and United Kingdom economic growth', *Journal of Economic History,* XXIV, 1964, p. 322, reprinted in M. C. Reed (ed.), *Railways in the Victorian Economy,* Newton Abbot, 1969, p. 18.

6   E.g. 1845–49: 4.5 per cent GNP without land, 5.5 per cent with land. Note that railway investment's share of gross domestic fixed capital formation is based on Mitchell's railway investment estimates and Deane's revised (1968) estimates of investment. Feinstein contends that Deane's estimates are too low. If this is correct then the railways' share of domestic investment in 1845–49 was nearer to 35–40 per cent, instead of the 54 per cent indicated by Deane's data (excluding land), or 63 per cent (with land). See Gourvish, *Railways in the British Economy,* pp. 13, 60; P, Deane, 'New estimates of gross national product for the United Kingdom 1830–1914', *Review of Income and Wealth,* XIV, June 1968, p. 104; C. H. Feinstein, 'Capital formation in Great Britain', in P. Mathias and M. M. Postan (eds.), *The Cambridge Economic History of Europe,* VII, Pt. 1, Cambridge, 1978, pp. 41, 58–9.

7   Feinstein, *loc. cit.,* pp. 90–1, repeated in his 'Capital accumulation and the industrial revolution', in R. Floud and D. McCloskey (eds.), *The*

Economic History of Britain Since 1700. I: 1700–1860, Cambridge, 1981, pp. 131–2, 134–5.

8   N. F. R. Crafts, 'British economic growth, 1700–1831: a review of the evidence', *Economic History Review*, 2nd ser., XXXVI, May 1983, pp. 194–5, repeated in N. F. R. Crafts, *British Economic Growth during the Industrial Revolution*, Oxford, 1985, pp. 71–3.

9   P. Deane, 'Capital formation in Britain before the railway age', *Economic Development and Cultural Change*, IX, 1961, reprinted in F. Crouzet (ed.), *Capital Formation in the Industrial Revolution*, 1972, p. 117.

10   T. R. Gourvish, 'Railway enterprise', in R. A. Church (ed.), *The Dynamics of Victorian Business. Problems and Perspectives to the 1870s*, 1980, p. 135.

11   R. J. Irving, 'The capitalisation of Britain's railways, 1830–1914', *Journal of Transport History*, 3rd ser., V, March 1984, p. 8.

12   Cf. C. J. A. Robertson, *The Origins of the Scottish Railway System 1722–1844*, Edinburgh, 1983, pp. 202–3.

13   Irving, *loc. cit.*, pp. 13–16. Ths submission was drawn up by Samuel Laing, Chief Law and Corresponding Clerk to the Board of Trade. There is some ambiguity in Laing's account. He calculated that excess spending amounted to £700 a route–mile in Parliamentary costs, £500 in legal and incidental expenses, £1,500 for land and compensation, and £5,000 for the extra cost of construction. It is not clear from his text whether the last item (£5,000) included £500 a route–mile for heavier rails and £2,000 for superior railway stations. If, as Irving suggests, the £5,000 item referred only to 'earthworks, bridges &c.' then the total excess spending would rise from the £7,700 shown by Laing to £10,200 per route–mile. Unfortunately, the submission lacks unambiguous support for such an interpretation. The data relate to UK railways in June 1843, and to foreign railways in 1840 or 1841. See *Select Committee on Railways*, 1844, *B.P.P.* 1844, XI, appendix 2.

14   £35,944 per UK route–mile, 1871 (paid-up capital £552.669 million, route–miles 15,376, from Hawke and Reed, *loc. cit.*, p. 270, Mitchell and Deane, *op. cit.*, pp. 225, 228). Irving has argued that Hawke and Reed fail to allow for the importance of nominal additions to capital *before* 1890. This is quite true, but the sums involved before the mid-1870s were small. Only £2.3 million in nominal additions was identified by 1871 (for Great Britain, excluding Ireland). If this is deducted from the paid-up capital figure shown by Hawke and Reed, then the estimate of real capital per route–mile falls by only a negligible amount, to £35,794. Cf. Irving, *loc. cit.*, pp. 21–2.

15   Feinstein, in Floud and McCloskey, *op. cit.*, I, p. 134; G. R. Hawke, *Railways and Economic Growth in England and Wales 1840–1870*, Oxford, 1970, p. 210.

16   Gourvish, in Church, *op. cit.*, pp. 127–9.

17   Hawke, *op. cit.*, pp. 405–8, and see also G. R. Hawke and J. P. P. Higgins, 'Transport and social overhead capital', in Floud and McCloskey, *op. cit.*, I, p. 247.

18   R. C. O. Matthews, *A Study in Trade Cycle History: Economic Fluctuations in Great Britain 1833–1842*, Cambridge, 1954, pp. 202 ff.; J. R. T. Hughes, *Fluctuations in Trade, Industry and Finance: A Study of*

British Economic Development 1850–1860, Oxford, 1960, pp. 184, 206; Mitchell, *loc. cit.,* pp. 329–30; Hawke, *op. cit.,* pp. 363–79.

19 S. Broadbridge, *Studies in Railway Expansion and the Capital Market in England 1825–1873,* 1970, pp. 168–75; M. C. Reed, *Investment in Railways in Britain 1820–1844,* Oxford, 1975, pp. 1–31; and cf. also B. L. Anderson and R. F. Wynn, 'The equity market and UK railway investment 1831–1850', *Recherches Economiques de Louvain,* XLI, September 1975, pp. 230–1.

20 H. Pollins, 'Railway contractors and the finance of railway development in Britain', *Journal of Transport History,* III, 1957–58, pp. 41–51, 103–10 (reprinted in Reed, 1969, *op. cit.,* pp. 212–28); P. L. Cottrell, 'Railway finance and the crisis of 1866: contractors' bills of exchange, and the finance companies', *Journal of Transport History,* new ser., III, 1976, pp. 20–40.

21 All mentioned by Cottrell, *loc. cit.*

22 P.R.O., Great Eastern Railway, 'Report of the Directors on the Financial Position of the Company', printed report, 22 April 1868, Great Eastern Board Minutes, same date, RAIL227/6; Gourvish, in Church, *op. cit.,* p. 130.

23 P.R.O., London Chatham & Dover Railway Reports and Accounts, RAIL1110/293; London Chatham & Dover Capital Expenditure ledger, No. 1, 1853–70, RAIL415/139; Keith Lampard, 'The promotion and performance of the London Chatham & Dover Railway', *Journal of Transport History,* 3rd ser., VI, September 1985, pp. 56–9.

24 M. C. Reed, 'Railways and the growth of the capital market', in Reed, 1969, *op. cit.,* pp. 174–9; Reed, 1975, *op. cit.,* p. 96; J. R. Killick and W. A. Thomas, 'The Provincial Stock Exchanges, 1830–1870', *Economic History Review,* 2nd ser., XXIII, April 1970, pp. 96–112, and W. A. Thomas, *The Provincial Stock Exchanges,* 1973, pp. 3–71, 283 ff.; R. C. Michie, *Money, Mania and Markets. Investment, Company Formation and the Stock Exchange in Nineteenth-Century Scotland,* Edinburgh, 1981, esp. part III.

25 Hudson was Chairman of the Midland, Eastern Counties, York & North Midland, and York, Newcastle & Berwick railways. See R. S. Lambert, *The Railway King. 1800–1871,* 1934.

26 D. Morier Evans, *Facts, Failures and Frauds,* 1859; M. Robbins, *Points and Signals,* 1967, pp. 139–43; P.R.O., Great Eastern Board Minutes, 20 August 1869–6 May 1870, Annual General Meeting Proceedings, 16 February 1870, RAIL227/6–7, RAIL1110/158.

27 H. A. Shannon, 'The coming of general limited liability', *Economic History,* II, 1931, and J. B. Jeffreys, 'The denomination and character of shares, 1855–1885', *Economic History Review,* 1st ser., XVI, 1946, both reprinted in E. M. Carus-Wilson (ed.), *Essays in Economic History,* I, 1954, pp. 376, 347; J. Saville, 'Sleeping partnerships and limited liability, 1850–1856', *Economic History Review,* 2nd ser., VIII, 1956, p. 425; Hawke, *op. cit.,* pp. 390–2; H. Pollins, *Britain's Railways,* Newton Abbot, 1971, p. 44. It should be noted that recent work largely ignores the railways' influence in limited liability legislation. Cf. P. L. Cottrell, *Industrial Finance*

1830–1914, 1980, pp. 39–54, and P. W. Ireland, 'The rise of the limited liability company', *International Journal of the Sociology of Law*, XII, 1984, pp. 241–4.

28 T. R. Gourvish, 'The performance of British railway management after 1860: the railways of Watkin and Forbes', *Business History*, XX, July 1978, p. 190; Gourvish, 1980, *op. cit.*, pp. 18–19. W. J. Reader, *A House in the City*, 1979, notes that Foster & Braithwaite dealt in the securities of nearly sixty UK railway companies between 1857 and the early 1880s (p. 57).

29 Mitchell, 1964, *loc. cit.*, p. 325.

30 Hawke, *op. cit.*, p. 245, cit. in Gourvish, 1980, p. 23; A. Birch, *The Economic History of the British Iron and Steel Industry 1784–1879*, 1967, pp. 126, 222–4; and see also C. K. Hyde, *Technological Change and the British Iron Industry 1700–1870*, Princeton, New Jersey, 1977.

31 Hawke, *op. cit.*, pp. 241–5; P. O'Brien, *The New Economic History of the Railways*, 1977, pp. 65–7.

32 Gourvish, 1980, pp. 24–5, and see also P. J. Riden, 'The iron industry', in Church, 1980, *op. cit.*, pp. 82–4.

33 T. R. Gourvish, *Mark Huish and the London & North Western Railway*, Leicester, 1972, p. 241; Jack Simmons, *The Railway in England and Wales 1830–1914. Volume 1. The System and its Working*, Leicester, 1978, pp. 148–9; R. J. Irving, *The North Eastern Railway Company 1870–1914*, Leicester, 1976, pp. 132–4; B. Reed, *Crewe Locomotive Works and its Men*, Newton Abbot, 1982, pp. 63–6; D. Brooke, 'The advent of the steel rail, 1857–1914', *Journal of Transport History*, 3rd ser., VII, March 1986, pp. 21–4.

34 B. R. Mitchell, *Economic Development of the British Coal Industry 1800–1914*, Cambridge, 1984, pp. 12, 18; R. A. Church, *The History of the British Coal Industry. Volume 3. 1830–1913. Victorian Pre-Eminence*, Oxford, 1986, pp. 19, 30. Both writers produce similar data for selected years, 1830–1913, the only divergence coming in 1855, where Mitchell has railway consumption as 1.4 million tons (2 per cent) and Church 2.4 million tons (3.1 per cent).

35 Calculation based on estimated tonnage of iron products for railways in Gourvish, 1980, pp. 25, 60 and new estimate of UK coal output in Church, 1986, *op. cit.*, p. 86. The percentage given is lower than that shown in Gourvish, 1980, p. 25. Church has increased his estimate of coal output for 1844–51 from *c.* 250–380 million tons to 449.4 million tons, and he also points out that the railways bought a great deal of their iron from South Wales, where coal was used more efficiently. Thus, a figure for coal usage of six tons for each ton of finished iron is to be preferred to the seven tons used in the 1980 estimate.

36 Mitchell, 1964, *loc. cit.*, pp. 327–9, and see also R. A. Buchanan, 'Gentlemen engineers: the making of a profession', *Victorian Studies*, XXVI, Summer 1983, pp. 415–16, and his 'Institutional proliferation in the British engineering profession, 1847–1914', *Economic History Review*, 2nd ser., XXXVIII, 1985, pp. 47–8.

37 Gourvish, 1980, p. 20. The exceptions were 1843 and 1844 for

employment, and 1844 for turnover.
    38   *Ibid.*, pp. 20–1, 60; D. Brooke, *The Railway Navvy*, Newton Abbot, 1983, pp. 10–32.
    39   Gourvish, 1980, p. 21; *Parliamentary Papers (P.P.)*, 1851, LI, 1860, LXI and 1874 (H.L.), XIII. Hawke's UK figures, *op. cit.*, p. 262, are in error both for 1850 and 1860, the latter arising from an error made by Hughes, *op. cit.*, p. 197.
    40   Gourvish, *op. cit.*, pp. 21–2; T. R. Gourvish, 'Professionalisation and railway management', unpublished paper, summarised in *Social History Society Newsletter*, III, Spring 1978; T. R. Gourvish, 'The rise of the professions', in T. R. Gourvish and A. O'Day (eds.), *Later Victorian Britain, 1867–1900*, 1988, pp. 30–3; W. J. Reader, *Professional Men*, 1966.
    41   Philip Rose joined the London, Brighton & South Coast Railway as an 'advising solicitor' in the wake of the 1866 'crash': P.R.O., London, Brighton & South Coast Board Minutes, 2 July 1867, RAIL414/74.
    42   *Railway Returns, B.P.P.*, 1860, LXI; Gourvish, 'Rise of the professions', *op. cit.*, p. 31; N. A. H. Stacey, *English Accountancy*, 1954, p. 13; Sir Russell Kettle, *Deloitte & Co. 1845–1956*, Oxford, 1958, pp. 1, 7, 17, 22–4, 27–30; E. Jones, *Accountancy and the British Economy 1840–1980. The Evolution of Ernst & Whinney*, 1981, pp. 29–33, 61; H. Pollins, 'Aspects of railway accounting before 1868', in Reed, 1969, *op. cit.*, pp. 138–46; J. R. Edwards, 'The origin and evolution of the double account system: an example of accounting innovation', *Abacus*, XXI, March 1985, pp. 37–9.
    43   F. M. L. Thompson, *Chartered Surveyors*, 1968, pp. 14–15, 108, 131.
    44   J. R. Kellett, *The Impact of Railways on Victorian Cities*, 1969, and esp. pp. 15–17, 289–95, 324–36, 346–53, 365; H. J. Dyos, 'Railways and housing in Victorian London', *Journal of Transport History*, 1st ser., II, May 1955, pp. 11–21, November 1955, pp. 90–100, and the same author's 'Some social costs of railway building in London', 1st ser., III, *Journal of Transport History*, May 1957, pp. 23–30.
    45   Gourvish, in Church, 1980, *op. cit.*, pp. 136–7.
    46   Gourvish, 1972, *op. cit.*, pp. 273–4, 280–1. Note that here passenger traffic includes mails but excludes parcels, and total costs includes substantial sums set aside for track maintenance and renewals. There are no adequate data on UK railway costs before 1854–55.
    47   Gourvish, in Church, 1980, *op. cit.*, pp. 128–30.
    48   Mitchell, 1964, *loc. cit.*, pp. 319–20; Gourvish, 1980, *op. cit.*, p. 27.
    49   Hawke, 1970, *op. cit.*, p. 64; G. Turnbull, 'Canals, coal and regional growth during the industrial revolution', *Economic History Review*, 2nd ser., XL, 1987, p. 543.
    50   Cf. G. L. Turnbull, *Traffic and Transport. An Economic History of Pickfords*, 1979, pp. 106–20.
    51   Church, 1986, *op. cit.*, pp. 41–7 and cf. Mitchell, 1984, *op. cit.*, pp. 24–5.
    52   Gourvish, 1972, *op. cit.*, pp. 134–5; Gourvish, 1980, *op. cit.*, pp. 28–9.

53   W. T. Jackman, *The Development of Transportation in Modern England*, II, 1916, pp. 605, 635 (see also 1962 edn).

54   Hawke, 1970, *op. cit.*, pp. 64, 86. Note a distinction should be made between transport resource costs and charges (i.e. rates). Here Hawke assumes that rail costs and charges could be equated, while canal resource costs were 2.3*d* per ton–mile, cf. 3.0*d* for canal charges.

55   Gourvish, 1980, *op. cit.*, p. 30.

56   Mitchell, 1964, *loc. cit.*, p. 316.

57   Church, 1986, *op. cit.*, p. 43.

58   Cf. P. J. Atkins, 'The growth of London's milk trade, *c.* 1845–1914', *Journal of Transport History*, new ser., IV, September 1978, pp. 208–26; Robb Robinson, 'The evolution of railway fish traffic policies, 1840–66', *Journal of Transport History*, 3rd ser., VII, March 1986, 32–44; Gourvish, 1980, *op. cit.*, p. 31.

59   M. J. Daunton, *Royal Mail. The Post Office since 1840*, 1985, pp. 80, 122–32.

60   Gourvish, 1972, *op. cit.*, pp. 154, 241; Charles Wilson, *First With the News. The History of W. H. Smith 1792–1972*, 1985, pp. 88–154.

61   Hawke and Higgins, in Floud and McCloskey, *op. cit.*, I, pp. 235–48, reproduced with only minor textual changes in Patrick O'Brien (ed.), *Railways and the Economic Development of Western Europe 1830–1914*, 1983, pp. 181–96.

62   Hawke and Higgins, in Floud and McCloskey, *op. cit.*, I, p. 237.

63   Hawke, 1970, *op. cit.*, p. 410. For the pre-1865 calculations see Gourvish, 1980, *op. cit.*, pp. 35, 60.

64   O'Brien, 1977, *op. cit.*, pp. 27–8.

65   R. A. Church, *The Great Victorian Boom, 1850–1873*, 1975, p. 31; François Crouzet, *The Victorian Economy* (translated by A. S. Forster), 1982, p. 303.

66   See for example Gourvish, 1980, *op. cit.*, p. 38.

67   *Ibid.*, pp. 34, 36–7.

68   *Ibid.*, p. 34, and cf. review of Hawke, 1970, in *History*, LVII, 1972 by R. Floud.

69   Gourvish, 1980, *op. cit.*, pp. 38–9. Note that Fogel has recently taken up Hawke's estimate that canal shipping rates would have exceeded marginal costs by about a third in the absence of railways to suggest that the social saving calculation should thus be lower. R. W. Fogel, 'Notes on the social saving controversy', *Journal of Economic History*, XXXIX, March 1979, pp. 22–3.

70   Gourvish, 1980, *op. cit.*, pp. 39, 58–9.

71   R. D. Baxter, 'Railway expansion and its results', *Journal of the Statistical Society*, XXIX, 1866, reprinted in E. M. Carus-Wilson (ed.), *Essays in Economic History*, III, 1962, p. 41.

72   Hawke and Higgins, in Floud and McCloskey, *op. cit.*, I, pp. 240–1.

73   *Ibid.*, p. 240.

74   *Return of the Number of Proprietors in each Railway Company in the U.K. . . . on the 31st day of December 1855, B.P.P.,* 1856, LIV.

75   T. R. Gourvish, 'The railways and the development of managerial

enterprise in Britain, 1850–1939', in Kesaji Kobayashi and Hidemasa Morikawa (eds.), *Development of Managerial Enterprise,* Tokyo, 1986, pp.
187–8.

76 *Ibid.,* pp. 188–90.
77 Gourvish, 1980, *op. cit.,* pp. 49–51, and T. R. Gourvish,
'Government, nationalisation and business performance: the nationalised
transport enterprises in the UK, 1830–1980', in Vera Zamagni (ed.), *Origins
and Development of Publicly Owned Enterprises,* Ninth International
Economic History Congress, Berne, 1986, Section B11, pp. 40–1.

Railways 1870–1914: the maturity of the private system

For the railway companies of Britain, the years 1870 to 1914 encapsulate both the zenith of their achievement and the beginnings of economic troubles which threatened the future of the system of private operation. The system was at its maximum extent when war broke out; the companies moved more tons of goods in 1913 than was ever to be the case again (passenger journeys peaked just after the First World War); and the overall impact of the railways on both economy and society was greater between 1870 and 1914 than it was either before or after. At the same time, the novelty of steam had worn off by 1870. Railways were no longer regarded as technological marvels but merely as an everyday part of business life. Public attitudes to railway services became steadily more critical and, in some circles, the companies became deeply unpopular. And, partly as a result of attempts to overcome the hostility of their customers, the companies ran into financial difficulties at the turn of the century which threatened the future of the private system and entailed a wholesale reappraisal of working methods, organisation and the relations between the industry and the State which was still under way in 1914, and was only resolved by the Big Four groupings set up under the Railways Act of 1921.

The network matures

If the heroic age of construction was largely over by 1870, the system nonetheless underwent considerable extension before 1914. Line mileage in Great Britain was 13,562 in 1870 and had reached 20,266 by 1913 and, if total track and sidings mileage is included, there were 50,000 miles of railway in the latter year. Some of these later extensions are well known: the Settle–Carlisle line, opened by the Midland in 1876, gave the company an independent line to Scotland;[1] in the later 1890s, spurred on by Sir Edward Watkin's ferocious determination, the Manchester, Sheffied & Lincoln transformed itself into the Great Central whilst opening the last, and least necessary, major trunk route to London.[2] The age could also boast some spectacular engineering feats including the Great Western's Severn Tunnel in 1886, the Tay (1887)[3] and Forth (1890) bridges which gave Aberdeen and Dundee better access to the South, and the creation, and eventual electrification of the London underground network. Nonetheless most of the improvements were of a less spectacular nature. The famous 'cuts' through which the Great Western Railway shed its title as the 'Great Way Round' and shortened distances between London, South Wales and the West, are good examples of this.[4] It was in this period, also, that the railway reached out into many rural areas, hitherto untouched by steam, and penetrated such 'fringe' areas as the Highlands of Scotland and Cornwall. Another marked feature of the times was the extension of railway facilities to the suburbs which sprouted up around the main cities, especially London. On the freight side, the most remarkable feature was how often mileage and facilities were extended to accommodate the rapidly growing coalmining industry, with the greatest concentration of effort being put into the opening and extension of the coalfield area of South Wales.[5]

A proportion of this mileage, widening, station and warehouse building and related activities, was provided by existing companies with great reluctance because they feared that Parliament might otherwise sanction further competition within their territory. Much of the Great Western's work on shortening its major routes was undertaken with the threat of an independent South Wales Railway in the background.[6] The force behind the extension of colliery lines at Cannock in Staffordshire where 'independent lines were promoted in the hope that the London and North Western would undertake their construction, thereby solving the transport problems of individual pits without incurring any expense to the colliery owners'[7] was both successful and typical. But established companies did not always respond to these pressures and new companies sometimes resulted. The Hull & Barnsley was built by aggrieved businessmen who felt the North Eastern was not meeting their needs in the 1880s,[8] and the boom in the coal industry in South Wales

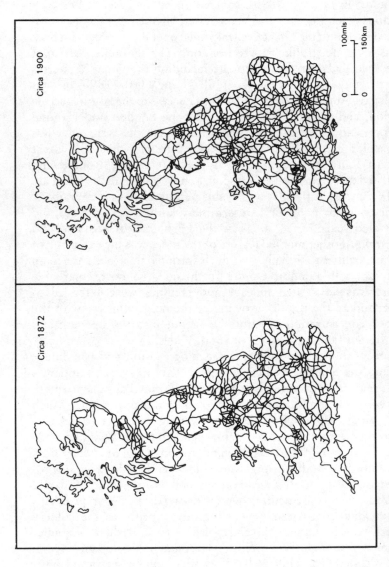

Circa 1872

Circa 1900

0   100mls
0   150km

13 The railway network in the later Victorian age (from M. Freeman in J. Langton and R. J. Morris (eds.), *Atlas of Industrializing Britain*, Methuen, 1986, p. 89)

produced the Barry company in the same decade.[9] The Barry was a dock company as well as a railway and railways were sometimes built to extend or link with competing forms of transport. The Manchester Ship Canal Company, for example, constructed 154 miles of railway to act as feeders to its canal.[10]

Most of the extensions of mileage were modest ones, designed to accommodate steady traffic growth rather than to open up new areas. In 1889 – to take a typical year – thirteen different companies opened twenty-four different sections of line, totalling 136 miles of track. The longest was the Great Eastern's 16.5 mile stretch between Wickham, Woodham Ferrers and Southend, a part of their growing suburban network.[11] In so far as new territory was opened up it was in more sparsely populated rural areas where the potential traffic was never very large; and, but for competition, spurred on by Parliament, the railway would often never have reached them.[12] In fact, most of the new building was in urban areas: the companies owned between 7 and 10 per cent of the land in major cities[13] whereas they occupied only about 0.25 per cent of the land of the main agricultural counties of England and Wales.[14] This 'land hunger'[15] in the cities and towns of Britain, spurred on by a need to furnish not only lines but also to provide sidings, marshalling yards, shunting sheds, warehouses and storage depots, meant constant land purchase in areas where land, already highly priced, was made yet more expensive by the tortuous legal procedures which surrounded property ownership in Britain.[16] In the circumstances, it is not surprising that railway capital should double between 1870 and the Great War or that the capital cost of British railways per mile of single track should have risen from around £37,000 to £52,000 in the same period.

Railway investment

The total paid-up capital of all the railways in Great Britain is given in the *Railway Returns* as £502.6 million in 1870 and £1,256.2 million in 1912; but this is a gross figure, inflated by nominal additions to the companies' stocks. Net paid-up capital actually rose from £500.3 million to £1,074 million over the period (table 3 below). The amount invested was a sizeable chunk of the nation's capital stock – roughly one-seventh in 1870, falling to one-tenth just before the First World War.[17] But as the latter figures suggest, railway investment was becoming less important as an element in the nation's capital spending. The companies' share of gross capital expenditure of the UK fell from nearly 14 per cent in 1882–89 to 6 per cent by 1907–13; and their share of all transport investment shrunk similarly from 35 per cent in the 1880s to just over one-fifth in 1907–13.[18]

Although the railway system as a whole remained profitable before 1914, many smaller companies failed to pay dividends not only on their ordinary stocks but upon some of their preference and debenture stocks also: the Cambrian, despite its 241 miles of track in 1913, suffered this fate throughout the period. The largest companies, such as the GWR, the L&NWR and the Midland were, however, a different proposition and before 1900 both their equity and their loan stocks were widely regarded as excellent investments, not much inferior to government paper, at a time when 'safe' outlets for savings were few. T. H. Green, the Oxford philosopher, was given railway stock as a wedding gift in 1871;[19] and, amongst that 'aristocracy of investments' which Anna Tellwright of the Potteries inherited on her twenty-first birthday were £10,000 worth of North Staffordshire Railway ordinary shares.[20] Railway paper also loomed large in the portfolios of the established wealthy after 1870. Apart from the land he owned, the banker Lord Overstone had £2 million worth of investment properties in 1881, of which nearly one-fifth was placed in the debenture and preference stocks of a number of leading companies.[21] Even aristocratic fortunes were sometimes tied to railway investment. As his rents fell in the depression, the Earl of Leicester put about £170,000 in home railways between 1870 and 1891, or about half of all his non-landed investments.[22]

The appeal of railways as investments began to fade in the late 1890s for a complex of reasons, which included declining company profitability (see table 4), fear of labour troubles and their consequences and the widening of investment opportunities, especially overseas.[23] As a result the stocks of the leading companies fell by about 30 per cent in price between 1896 and 1911.[24] A sign of the times was that insurance companies, always on the look-out for safe havens, began to shed their railway stocks at this time. The Union Marine, for example, had 34 per cent of its funds in home railways in 1896 but this had fallen to 17 per cent by 1913.[25] By the latter date, middle-class families like the Schlegels were buying 'Foreign Things', whilst the companies' stocks 'declined with the steady dignity of which only Home Rails are capable'.[26]

Railways and the economy

The tonnage carried by the railways grew from 166.5 million tons in 1871 to 513 million tons in 1912 (appendix I) or at an average rate of 2.8 per cent per annum but, measured from peak to cyclical peak, the growth was most rapid between 1873 and 1882 and 1889 and 1899 (3.4 per cent per annum) and slowest between 1907 and 1913. These fluctuations reflect fairly accurately the changing fortunes of manufacturing industry in Britain over the period. Coal and coke were the outstanding commodities carried. Consistent figures are hard to come by for the whole period, but just before the war coal and coke provided three-fifths of total freight tonnage, other minerals one-fifth and 'general merchandise' the rest,[27] and there is no reason to believe that the proportions had changed fundamentally over the previous forty years. Some idea of the importance of the rail freight network at this time can be grasped by considering that the canals carried only about eighty million tons of freight at their peak in the late 1880s, or less than one-third of that carried by the railways at that time.[28]

The official statistics of tonnages are not much help to the historians trying to assess how much work the companies actually performed because they do not show how far freight was carried. Average haul figures were not collected officially, save by the North Eastern company after 1900, and without them the ton–mileage carried by railways cannot be known. Tentative recent estimates of average hauls (see appendix II) suggest that ton–mileage in England and Wales increased from about 4,200 million in 1871 to 12,500 million in 1912 and coal ton–mileage probably accounted for about half of this.[29]

Despite their importance as carriers of coal and minerals, the railways' direct impact upon those industries in the form of its own demands was not great. In 1903, at its peak, railway consumption of coal was only 5.5 per cent of total output, and this was despite the fact that coal consumption per locomotive was rising rapidly after 1870 as speeds improved.[30] Also, despite the rapid replacement of iron rails by steel after 1870, railway demand was never a very significant factor in the development of the British steel industry.[31] The railways' contribution to the electricity industry, via the growth of the London electric system, was rather more significant. In 1904, one third of all capital formation in the electrical trades was concentrated on the underground system and this was about 4 per cent of gross domestic investment in that year. Nonetheless, in the twenty years before the war, the growth of the tramway networks of the major towns was a far more important stimulus to the growth of the electrical industry.[32]

The industry most significantly affected by railway development was mechanical engineering. The value of locomotives produced in Great Britain in 1907 was £12.4 million and two-thirds of this came from the companies' own workshops. Within the engineering sector itself, only the manufacture of textile machinery produced a larger gross output than locomotive building.[33] Over forty years, technical improvements in locomotive building and performance were numerous and the increases in the speed and pulling power of engines were impressive. But the companies' domination of the industry had its drawbacks for the nation. Company workshops were shielded from competition, forcing the private builders to find markets overseas, and no doubt costs were higher than they would have been in competitive conditions. Company building also meant lack of standardisation and left lines at the mercy of idiosyncratic or overbearing chief engineers.[34]

Just before the war the companies were employing 50,000 men in engineering works around Britain.[35] The greatest concentration was at Swindon, where the Great Western employed 4,000 men in 1875 and 14,000 thirty years later.[36] The two other outstanding 'railway towns' were Crewe, where employment in the L&NW's shops increased from 4,000 to 7,000 between 1870 and 1900,[37] and Stratford in East London, where the Great Eastern employed 3,000 in 1872 and 6,500 in 1906.[38] A number of new, if significantly smaller, railway towns appeared after 1870. The most important of these was Eastleigh, a junction on the London and South Western, where engineering works were sited in 1891. Eastleigh's 1871 population of 515 had risen to 15,217 by 1911 and, in that year, 14 per cent of the work-force were in railway employment.[39] The growth of Horwich in Lancashire was almost as rapid after the Lancashire and Yorkshire opened a locomotive works there in 1886;[40] and the development of Neasden in north London after 1880 owed much to the establishment of the Metropolitan Company's locomotive-building sheds.[41] The biggest new development was at Doncaster, where the Great Northern's locomotive-building and repair sheds, opened in 1867, were employing 3,000 people by 1911. But Doncaster, like

Derby and Darlington, was too large and complex to be called simply a railway town.[42] On the other hand, some towns which never possessed railway workshops were practically railway creations. Willesden, for example, owed a great deal to its role as junction and interchange point between the L&NW and the North London after 1866, and had a population of 115,000 by 1901.[43]

In the main, the influence of rail transport on British industry and commerce was indirect rather than direct, subtle rather than obvious. In Adam Smith's famous words, railways played a primary role in furthering the division of labour by widening the extent of the market. They created new demand sources and cheapened supply and, in so doing, both increased the degrees of competition and helped to concentrate particular trades and industries in favoured locations. Rail connections played a significant, though not overwhelmingly important role in concentrating the brewing industry in Burton,[44] Alloa and Glasgow.[45] Generous railway provision also contributed to the establishment and rapid development of large firms in the food-processing industry such as Huntley and Palmers, the biscuit makers, at Reading, Cadbury's chocolate in Birmingham and Chivers jams in Cambridgeshire.[46] And without the facilities provided by the railways and the Manchester Ship Canal, it is unlikely that the Co-operative Wholesale Society would have concentrated its activities in Manchester or employed 13,000 people there before the war.[47] Increasingly speedy services also helped to turn the London dailies such as *The Times* into national newspapers after 1870:[48] and the rail network also helped to make the fortunes of the great retail distributors of newsprint, W. H. Smith, who for many years used rented stalls on railway station platforms as their chief outlet.[49]

If railways aided specialisation and growth, they also intensified competition. The effect of both was felt in the agricultural industry. As ocean-going and coastal shipping rates fell after 1870, and imports of foodstuffs rose, the companies became involved in a battle to divert the traffic to ports connecting with their systems rather than those of rivals. In the process, they created new docks – as the Great Central did at Immingham – or bought up ailing concerns, like those at Hull and Southampton.[50] They also cut their rates on imported commodities to much lower levels than were generally accorded to agriculturalists at home, much to the distress of farming interests in Britain.[51] But at the same time as they brought cheap imports of meat and wheat, they were also encouraging the growth of new sources of income in rural areas. In Wensleydale, where the NER opened a branch in 1879, the competition of cheap imported produce was met by increased specialisation in liquid milk as well as by the development of slate-quarrying and the growth of tourism.[52] Wensleydale added its small stream to the flood of rail milk entering London, which rose from 9.3 million gallons in 1870 to 93.2 million in 1914, when it accounted for about four-fifths of London's consumption[53] and was coming from as far away as Cornwall.[54] Cheap and rapid transport also encouraged fruit-growing in Evesham and in Hampshire where there was a well-established seasonal strawberry trade to London by the end of the century.[55] In mid-Wales, and in the south-west of the principality, the railways' arrival opened up the possibilities of transporting cattle, and encouraged milk production. Here, as elsewhere, railways were probably the chief force behind the concentration of marketing on the larger towns with the better transport facilities.[56] Outside agriculture, however, the railways did little to change the location of industry or of population; 'their substantial contribution was to strengthen connections between existing towns and make continued modernization feasible'.[57] The facilties provided for the carriage of passengers aided this process. The official figures for passengers journeys in appendix I are a significant underestimate, since they do not include season ticket-holders. Estimates of contract journeys are unreliable, but Munby's figures suggest that total passenger journeys were 1,427 million in 1900 and 1,729 million in 1912.[58] Growth was most rapid in the 1890s, at about 3.5 per cent. Estimates of passenger-mileage are even cruder than for ton-mileage but, for what they are worth, the estimates in appendix III indicate growth from 2.8 billion in 1870 rising to about 13 billion by 1912. What none of the statistics can show is that in terms of speed, comfort and frequency, the passenger service in 1913 was greatly superior to that of 1870.

Even before the Midland's historic decision in 1872 to put third-class carriages on every train, the predominance of third-class travel on the railway was assured, since it already accounted for about three-quarters of all passenger journeys. By 1912, and including contract passengers, 90 per cent of all travel was third-class. The period also saw the beginnings of substantial amounts of surburban commuter traffic, with the construction of the inner London lines and the growth of the underground network.[59]

It would however be a grave exaggeration to believe that the railway 'created' the suburbs. In Thompson's words, the railway was a 'necessary' though not a 'sufficient' cause of suburban growth.[60] The pace and the character of development were chiefly dependent upon the will of local landlords and ratepayers and the housing and amenities they were willing to tolerate. Indeed, companies were often reluctant to build suburban lines, given the price of land and the weight of local rates, and because they were forbidden to develop the land they acquired except for railway purposes. Railways usually followed, somewhat reluctantly, in the wake of suburban development, fitting in with local social aspirations and setting fares and services accordingly.[61] The only important instance of the character of an area being transformed by railway policy is in the case of Walthamstow and Edmonton in North-East London, where the Great Eastern was obliged by special Acts of Parliament in the 1860s to provide cheap fares for workmen who could henceforth live in the suburbs and commute into the City. Even here, cheap fares would have been unavailing if local landlords had not been eager to provide cheap housing.[62] In 1883 the Cheap Trains Act gave the Board of Trade powers to compel the provision of workmen's trains. But the powers were used sparingly, and the companies were often reluctant to provide those services, because of the loading problems they entailed and because they felt that extending facilities for workmen might drive away more profitable traffic at higher fares.[63] In 1913, only 17 per cent of all passenger journeys were on workmen's tickets[64] and that traffic was heavily concentrated in a few areas, as on the Great Eastern lines.[65] On the whole the companies reinforced the 'natural' tendency to suburban zoning by class, rather than counteracted it, as their more radical critics insisted they should.[66]

By 1914, middle-class commuting by train was well-established, sometimes over long distances; as early as the 1880s there was a steady stream of daily business traffic between Manchester and the Lake District.[67] The growth of Brighton and Southend was partly dependent on their status as 'dormitories' for London commuters, and Southport had the same role in relation to Liverpool.[68] The age of mass commuting had not, however, dawned in 1914. In South London, to take one example, only one person in twelve actually used transport for work purposes in 1900.[69] And, where business traffic was heavy, the railways were usually not the chief means of locomotion. In London in 1914, trams and buses carried twice the daily load of passengers as railways, despite the creation of the tube network.[70] In the Glasgow area, trams carried two and half times as many passengers as railways in 1913.[71] Overall, the bulk of the working class still walked to work or travelled by tram by the end of the period, their train trips 'reserved for holidays or the occasional excursion'.[72]

Another marked feature of Victorian and Edwardian life was the growth of holiday traffic. As in the case of suburban development, railway services were important in the growth of seaside resorts and spas, but the character of these places was largely determined by the structure of local property ownership and landlord responses to demand. Blackpool had three million visitors a year by 1900, the result of high wages amongst Lancashire cotton operatives, the establishment of regular summer holidays and the provision of cheap hotel accommodation. The railways' own response to Blackpool's growth was slow and hesitant.[73] Bournemouth – whose populations rose from 6,000 to 78,000 between 1871 and 1911 – and Eastbourne, thrived on a middle-class clientele drawn from all parts of the country and the railway, in response to local wishes, kept excursions and other cheap travel to a minimum.[74] Occasionally, railways did play a crucial part in resort development. Malvern and Buxton were revived, and Llandridnodd Wells practically created, as spas by rail connection.[75] Also, some companies actually invested in seaside development, as did the Great Central at Cleethorpes. Skegness, on the same coast, is another good example of a resort which arose from collaboration between a railway company prepared to invest heavily in ample accommodation ahead of demand and a dominant local landowner keen to finance holiday amenities in the town.[76] By and large, however, the railways provided, with greater or lesser enthusiasm, the services which confirmed, or accentuated, the already established ambience of the resort concerned.[77]

What in general was the railways' overall contribution to the economy in this period? One way of approaching this is to give an estimate of the 'social savings' brought by railways after 1870.[78] No systematic attempt to assess social savings has yet been made, but there are some rough estimates worth considering here. Using Hawke's figures,[79] Gourvish has suggested that the contribution of the railways to the economy of England and Wales was greater after 1870 than before[80] and that, in 1890, social savings could have been as high as three-tenths of the national income. This breaks down roughly into £130 million of savings on freight and £190 million on passengers at a time when the national income was £1,122 million.[81]

Hawke's estimates on passenger-mileage for 1870–90 blend in reasonably well with the new figures for 1900 and 1912 presented in appendix III. This, together with the fact that competition for passenger traffic, actual and potential, was extremely limited, makes a high social savings figure for passengers in 1890 look reasonable. Estimates for social savings on freight made from Hawke's data are rather more questionable. Hawke gives a figure of 10.5 billion ton-miles for 1890 but more recent work suggests that about 8 billion ton-miles is nearer the mark (see appendix II). On this criterion, social savings on freight would be about a fifth less than implied by Gourvish's use of Hawke's figures. Besides this, it is probable that Hawke has overestimated non-rail costs after 1870 since, in a non-rail world, the chances of significant improvement in other forms of freight transport must have been high. The Royal Commission on Canals and Waterways may have exaggerated the possible benefits from its proposed refurbishment of the canal system of England, but there is a strong probability that canals, freed from railway company ownership, would have been cheaper and more efficient competitors for bulk freight.[82] Also, social savings estimates based on Hawke's data take no account of coastal shipping competition, which increased considerably after 1870 as costs fell. Overall, it seems likely that the railway system produced social savings after 1870 considerably in excess of those achieved before 1870 and that, as in the earlier period, the bulk of these savings arose from the passenger traffic rather than freight.

Railways as business organisations

If the amount of capital invested in the railway system was enormous, so was the size of the major companies which dominated it. The £120 million of capital invested in the Midland in 1911, for example, made it roughly six or seven times as large as the biggest firm outside the industry.[83] The degree of concentration within the industry was also high. There were well over one hundred companies open for traffic in Great Britain in 1874, but the four largest owned 39 per cent of the track mileage and earned 47 per cent of the gross receipts; and the top ten companies accounted for nearly 70 per cent of the mileage and took three-quarters of the gross receipts. Concentration was also a great deal higher in England and Wales, and in Scotland, than it was in Great Britain as a whole: the top four companies in England and Wales absorbed 53 per cent of the gross receipts in 1874 and the two leading Scottish companies accounted for three-quarters of the total.

Concentration does not appear to have increased over the next forty years: the top four companies owned a slightly higher proportion of the line mileage in 1913 (43 per cent) but their share of gross receipts was practically the same. The figures for 1913 are misleading to some degree since they give no indication of the extent to which the great companies may have increased their control over small, but only nominally independent, companies; nor do they indicate how far traffic and receipts were tied up via pooling agreements or other restrictive practices. The latter certainly increased in importance after 1900, as we shall see. On the other hand, the degree of concentration in 1874 is understated in that the revenues of companies jointly owned by the industry's leaders are included in the statistics for the biggest companies in 1913 but are listed separately in the *Returns* for the earlier date.

The fact that the structure of the industry did not change dramatically over forty years owes something to the determination of Parliament, egged on by a vociferous and suspicious trading public, to enforce competition on the railways as far as possible. Left entirely to market forces, the natural tendency of the industry, where size and profitability went together, would have been towards steadily greater concentration. Parliamentary hostility stood in the way of unions between large companies after 1870, though small companies were steadily swallowed up by their larger neighbours. Also, as we have seen, although costs of entry were high after 1870, the creation of new companies did occur and this offset, to some extent, the absorption of small companies by the great.

Throughout the period, in fact, the market for railway services remained oligopolistic or duopolistic. There were only a few substantial centres of population not served by two or more competing companies, though small intermediate points were often not so lucky.[84] Competition from outside agencies was also considerable. Canals, though largely ineffective and often controlled by the companies themselves, were still a potent force in a few regions such as the West Riding of Yorkshire and South Lancashire, where the

Manchester Ship Canal was designed as a direct rival to the railways. By 1914, too, motor vehicles were just beginning to make an impact upon the companies' short-distance traffic in the towns.[85] By far the most important source of competition for the companies was coastal shipping, which was a force of great importance in a country where so many major centres of population were either ports or had easy access to a port, and where imports played such an important role in consumption. In 1872 it was claimed that about three-fifths of all the companies' freight rates were influenced by competition from the sea,[86] and competition clearly intensified after that date, when shipping rates fell, and the companies became involved in battles to capture imported traffic and send it to its destination through their ports rather than see it pass on to the system of a rival. Some idea of the intensity of the competition with coastal shipping can be given by looking at the London coal trade. The companies pushed up their share of the trade from mid-century until the late 1870s, when they accounted for about 63 per cent of London's imports. As coastal freights fell, their share then declined steadily, and was only about 45 per cent by 1905. The tonnage carried by rail fluctuated around 7 or 8 million tons from 1890 onwards, while the amount carried coastwise increased from about 5.6 million tons in 1890 to 9 million by 1910.[87]

Passenger traffic was, of course, less liable to outside competition than freight but, even here, the spread of the municipal electric tram after the mid-1890s made inroads into the short-distance traffic of the companies in large towns and cities. If London electric railway traffic is excluded, non-contract passenger journeys on British railways actually fell from 1,100 million in 1903 to under 900 million in 1900; and some leading companies, like the London, Brighton and South Coast and the L&NW, were badly affected.[88] It is also worth noting here that passenger traffic was less dominated by the great companies than was freight. In 1913, the top four companies carried half of all the goods traffic but only two-fifths of the passengers. The chief reason for this was the vast amount of passenger traffic on short suburban and electric lines, especially in London. Three London suburban and commuter lines – the Metropolitan, the London Electric and the Metropolitan District – carried 16 per cent of the passenger traffic of Great Britain in 1913, although they owned only 130 miles of track or 0.6 per cent of the total.

Rail pricing

There is little doubt that the price of rail transport was falling after 1870. Freight rates were roughly $1.33d$ per ton per mile in 1870 and fell steadily, except in the 1890s, to around $1d$ per ton per mile at the outbreak of war (appendix II). Inter-company competition over pricing was dead by 1870 and local rates probably changed little over the period.[89] Competition from coastal shipping, on the other hand, pushed down the rates on long-distance and through traffic substantially.[90] Although evidence about fares is harder to come by, there is little doubt that they, too, fell steadily over forty years. Average fares in 1913 were probably around $0.6d$ per mile and many have been double that in 1870 (see appendix III). The fall in fares was probably greater than in rates, despite the fact that traders were more effective lobbyists than passengers.

After 1870, rates fell less than did prices in general and the real cost of freight transport began to rise amidst a chorus of complaints from the companies' customers. They constantly compared British rates unfavourably with those available on the Continent or in the USA. However, as appendix II shows, short journeys were the norm in Britain as were small loads and, as the companies insisted, the latter often reflected the 'retail' nature of business in a country where the small firm was dominant and where speedy delivery was at a premium. The traders, naturally enough, were not convinced by the companies' claim that 'for the quantities in which English traders consign their traffic and for the usual English distances', rates were comparable with, if not better than, those obtainable elsewhere.[91] They were disturbed by the fact that the maximum rate schedules originally given to companies in their Special Acts were too high to be effective and by the evidence that, by 1870, the companies had ceased to compete over prices and decided upon changes in through rates at meetings in the Clearing House.[92]

Nonetheless, the central matter of dispute between the companies and their customers was not usually the level of rates – although the companies' determination in the 1870s to charge for 'terminal' expenses caused uproar[93] – but the practice of charging differential rates. Railway companies, as oligopolists, could practice price discrimination and, in so far as discrimination helped distant suppliers to reach markets from which they would otherwise be excluded, it brought widespread economic benefits.[94] However, under the terms of the Railway and Canal Traffic Act of 1854, the companies were only allowed to discriminate on the basis of differences in costs whereas, naturally enough, most of the companies' decisions on pricing were based on competition with shipping companies. There were many bitter complaints from traders in the Midlands, for example, that they suffered higher carriage rates than their competitors fortunate enough to live near a port.[95] Some companies also gave cheap rates on imported traffic, especially agricultural imports, in order to attract it to a port served by themselves, rather than see it travel directly to London or to rival ports. Under scrutiny, the companies did make a case for lower rates on imported traffic in terms of distances travelled and size of loads, but no one doubted that the crucial determinant was shipping competition and inter-company rivalry.[96]

In their customers' eyes the companies were merely 'monopolies', a perception heightened by their size and their increasingly bureaucratic methods. As monopolists it was assumed they were open to interference by the state, and the remedies proposed by the traders for higher rates, and what was called at the time 'undue preference', were charges based on cost of service and equal mileage rates, irrespective of length of haul. The response, by the companies and their supporters, that these prescriptions were both contradictory and impossible to apply without drastically reducing the amount of traffic carried,[97] cut little ice. The traders were organised in Chambers of Commerce and well-represented in Parliament,[98] where they clashed with the powerful 'railway interest'[99] over the fate of the companies. This epic battle between rival vested interests began in the late 1870s, led to a long and exhaustive enquiry into railways' charging powers in 1881/82 and, eventually, to the Railway and Canal Traffic Act of 1888, which gave rise to a detailed revision of the companies' maximum rating powers. The enquiry took nearly five years and at the end of it the companies were told to adopt new rate schedules, which would have lowered some of their maximum charges while making little difference to actual rates.[100] The companies' response – based partly on bureaucratic confusion, partly on a greedy determination to maintain rates and wreck the revision – was to raise their rates to the new maxima at the beginning of 1893. As a result, the Liberal Government, hurried along by a furious Parliament, passed the Railway and Canal Traffic Act of 1894, which gave the Railway and Canal Commissioners, created in the 1888 Act to supervise the new leglislation, the right to peg rates at the levels pertaining in 1892, unless there were proven increases in costs.[101] By 1900, however, a famous legal case had made it plain that the companies could not raise their rates at all while the 1894 Act remained in force and, since prices were rising from the late 1890s, and some rates were falling under the stress of competition, the real cost of transport fell substantially in the Edwardian period.[102] Business complaints about the level of rates fell away somewhat after 1900, though the question of discrimination remained a constant irritant in the relationship between the companies and their customers until the war.

Earnings, costs and profitability

The companies' gross receipts increased by nearly three times over the whole period, with growth much more rapid after 1895. The best way of evaluating this performance is to look at the ratio between the receipts and the growth of the companies' net paid-up capital, which we can call the 'earnings ratio'. This gives a rough indication of the fruitfulness of the companies' investment and is summarised in table 3. It is clear from this that, after the earnings ratio had reached new heights in the early 1870s, it fell away until the late 1880s, before

Table 3   *Earnings ratio: British railways, 1870–1912 (five-yearly averages)*

Years	1 Gross receipts (£m)	2 Net paid-up capital (£m)	3 Earnings ratio (%) (1÷2)
1870–74	50·4	538·5	9·36
1875–79	59·5	628·4	9·47
1880–84	66·0	700·5	9·42
1885–89	69·1	761·6	9·07
1890–94	78·5	821·6	9·56
1895–99	90·0	883·1	10·19
1900–04	104·7	976·2	10·73
1905–09	114·2	1,042·0	10·96
1910–12	122·1	1,065·9	11·46

Sources: Col. 1: Mitchell and Deane, *Abstract*, pp. 225–6; Col. 2: G. R. Hawke and M. C. Reed, 'Railway capital in the United Kingdom in the nineteenth century', *Economic History Review*, 2nd Ser., XXII (1969), table 1, pp. 270–2 and table 2, pp. 284–5; R. J. Irving, 'The capitalization of British railways, 1830–1914', *Journal of Transport History*, 3rd Ser., V (1984), appendices 1 and 2, pp. 19, 22.

rising steadily to previously unrecorded levels by 1912. Capital expenditure was heavy in the late 1870s, when the growth of gross receipts slowed down, and continued to outpace receipts in the 1880s; the growth of the latter in the late 1880s was particularly slow. The result was that the peak earnings ratio of 1873 (9.94) was not achieved again until 1896.

The overall improvement in the companies' earnings ratio was countered, however, by the deterioration in the cost position. The two key periods here were the early 1870s and the 1890s. In both cases rapid increases in gross receipts were matched by sharp increases in working expenditure, and the working expenditure/ gross receipts ratio, or the 'operating ratio' as it was known, rose from 48 per cent to 54 per cent between 1870 and 1875 and from 54 per cent to 62 per cent between 1890 and 1900.

Rising working expenditure and a worsening operating ratio were closely associated with declining labour productivity on the railways after 1870.[103] A detailed study of the North Eastern[104] has shown that it was in the labour-intensive operating sectors, particularly the Traffic Department, that productivity declined, mainly because of high labour costs, while output per man in engineering and maintenance rose because labour-saving techniques could be introduced. Labour costs rose partly because of union pressure, partly because of government limitations on hours of work as in the Railway Regulation Act of 1893.[105] But the chief reason for escalating costs was the companies' practice, for reasons to be discussed presently, of providing increasingly elaborate services for both freight and passengers. While rates were declining, albeit slowly, the companies introduced a 24-hour goods delivery service throughout Great Britain and provided traders with a range of services, such as warehousing facilities, and use of wagons and sidings, cheaply or at no cost.[106] In the meantime, goods train loads, which were already low by Continental or American standards in 1870, grew hardly at all between 1880 and 1900 (appendix II). On the passenger side, improved comfort increased the weight of carriages; and this, plus the ever higher speeds on inter-city services, led to demands for increasingly heavy and expensive locomotives.[107]

Rising labour costs before 1890 were offset to some degree by falling raw material prices after 1875. After 1890, raw material prices were moving in the opposite direction, and the pressure on wages was also significant. Services also increased rapidly in the

1890s: the increase in train mileage of nearly 20 per cent between 1895 and 1900 was more rapid than at any time since the early 1870s (appendix I). The result was that working expenditure rose very rapidly in the 1890s and, although gross receipts went up sharply, no less than 85 per cent of the increase in receipts in that decade was absorbed by rising costs.

As a result of the deteriorating cost position, the growth in the companies' net receipts over the forty-year period was slow (negative in the early 1900s), and the profitability of the industry in decline.

Conventionally, the 'profit ratio' – the ratio of net receipts to paid-up capital – was derived by using figures for gross paid-up capital. On this basis, the ratio declined steadily from 4.61 in 1870–74 to 3.60 until just before the First World War. Using the net capital figure, however, gives a different picture, with the profit ratio showing only a slow decline up to 1900, followed by a sharp fall up to 1910 and an equally sharp recovery in the few years before the war (table 4).

Table 4 *Net receipts and profit ratios: Great Britain, 1870–1912 (five-yearly averages)*

Years	Net receipts	Profit ratio
1870–74	24·8	4·61
1875–79	27·8	4·43
1880–84	31·6	4·52
1885–89	33·0	4·34
1890–94	34·9	4·26
1895–99	38·5	4·36
1900–04	37·6	4·06
1905–09	42·7	4·09
1910–12	46·0	4·32

Sources: Railway Returns and table 3.

After 1875, and until about 1890, the declining earnings ratio brought about by sluggish gross receipts and high capital expenditure was the chief influence upon profits. After that date, although gross receipts were more buoyant and the earnings ratio rose steadily, the rise was offset by high working costs and profit continued to decline. It was only in the few years before the war, when the companies had cut down new capital expenditure to very low levels indeed, that the profits ratio made a significant recovery.[108]

The decline in the profits ratio was not great and table 4 gives some credence to the view that the 'profit crisis' was largely a passing phenomenon, resulting from rapidly rising labour and raw material costs in the 1890s, and quickly corrected through the practice of economy in the Edwardian period.[109] But this interpretation of events rather glosses over the accumulating problems of falling labour productivity and poor loading after 1870; and, given the potential for economies of large-scale operation, it makes sense to ask why the companies did not do their work more efficiently and why profits did not *rise* in the late nineteenth century.

Some historians have argued that the railways' plight in the late nineteenth century was mainly the result of capital overspending. Those who see the Great Central's extension to London as typical tend to argue that this overspending was largely a product of reckless empire-building: but Professor Aldcroft argues not only for the creation of unnecessary capacity but also lays the blame for low productivity on poor management.[110] The L&NW's decision not to electrify some of its main lines after 1900[111] and the companies' stubborn refusal to adopt ton-mileage statistics as a check on per-formance[112] are two good examples of this failure to adopt 'best practice techniques'.[113] On the other hand, supposedly badly man-aged companies, like the London Chatham and Dover and the South Eastern, produced results, in terms of capital expenditure and earnings and profit ratios after 1870, which were roughly compara-ble to those achieved by companies universally acknowledged to be well managed, such as the North Eastern.[114] This suggests that the companies' problems were often beyond their control: Ashworth argued, many years ago, that although there was excess capacity on the system after 1870, this was due to competitive pressures which forced reluctant companies into heavy outlays on unremunerative rural and suburban services.[115] More recently, Irving has given a subtle twist to this line of thinking. He dismisses the idea of excess capacity by pointing to the rise in the earnings ratio between 1870 and the Great War. Profits suffered not because of capital overspend-ing but because of rising costs; and costs were pushed up because services had to be continually extended and improved in order to meet public and Parliamentary demands and to stave off interference in the companies' affairs.[116]

In practice, it is probably unwise to make such sharp distinction between problems arising from high capital expenditure and those stemming from rising working expenditure. Improving services without improving loading often put pressure on facilities at key points, particularly in busy urban areas, forced increased capital spending to keep traffic flowing smoothly, and kept the earnings ratio at a lower level than would otherwise have been the case. On comparative criteria, moreover, British railways do appear to have been over-capitalised after 1870, as well as suffering from high operating ratios.[117]

If the British problem was the result of both the relatively low earning power of capital and high operating costs, to what extent can this be attributed to political pressures? Both railway capital expenditure and running costs were raised substantially by legislation covering safety and hours and conditions of labour and, especially in the 1880s when they were trying to fight off revision of their maximum rates, the companies probably did respond by providing some uneconomic services. Heavy falls in receipts per train-mile for both freight and passengers were recorded between 1875 and 1890 and the earnings ratio declined substantially after 1875 (table 3 and appendix I). The latter was due, initially, to the heavy capital expenditure needed after bottlenecks appeared in the system at the height of the early 1870s boom,[118] but capital outlay also ran well ahead of demand in the 1880s.[119]

The political element in company strategy can, however, be over-estimated. It is going too far to suggest, as some historians have done, that the companies were beginning to act like 'public utilities' in the late nineteenth century.[120] Frequently, however, railway policy was influenced by what we might call 'managerial' motives as well as by the drive to maximise profit. These managerial strategies arose from the fact that the companies, as large organisations, developed what has become known in the twentieth century as a 'corporate structure', one where ownership (by the shareholders) was divorced from control which fell into the hands of directors and managers.[121] By the late nineteenth century the latter had developed into a powerful bureaucratic elite recruited from within the industry itself; and the chief executives of the great companies, the general managers, were the single most important decision makers in the industry in this period.[122] They, and the traffic managers, line superintendents, engineers and other leading officers of the companies, although careful to try to keep profit at a level which would prevent shareholder revolt, were naturally more interested in furthering company growth and extending their own power than they were in maximising returns to the investors.[123]

One striking case in which 'managerial' motives played a predominant part in the investment planning is on the Great Western between the late 1870s and the early 1890s. In this case, the managing director, Gooch, was an engineer, and engineering and allied concerns were given high priority by the company. Revenue on the Great Western, as on the rest of the railway system, grew very sluggishly after 1875 and through the 1880s. Investment was high in the late 1870s because the company was still implementing decisions made in the 1870–73 boom. But in the 1880s, investment on lines and rolling stock was kept at a much higher level than some directors, with an eye to the dividend, thought wise because Gooch and his supporters were determined to keep the engineering work-force together in hard times.[124]

In addition to this, it must be remembered that when company officials or other interested parties spoke of the power of 'public opinion' in influencing policy, they were not necessarily referring to the direct political pressures which could be brought to bear on them. The use of such phraseology might also mean that the companies were shaping policy to reflect the needs of the businesses and the communities they served in ways which sometimes cut across the demand for maximum profit; or they could also mean that given the high degree of competition which still existed after 1870, both within the industry and from shipping, each company could only maintain or increase its share of the traffic by constantly outbidding its rivals in the provision of services and facilities. On the whole, reference to 'public needs' or similar phrases were more likely to relate to these factors than to Parliamentary pressure. Both need to be examined separately although, as we shall see, they were interrelated.

As for 'business' motives influencing policy, Herbert Spencer was clear about their importance as early as the 1850s. The boards of railways companies, he claimed, were largely composed

of gentlemen residing at different points throughout the tract of country traversed by the railways they control; some of them landowners; some merchants or manufacturers; some owners of mines and shipping. Almost always they are advantaged by a new branch or feeder. Those in close proximity to it, gain either by the enhanced value of their lands or by increased facilities of transit for their commodities. Those at more remote parts of the main line, through less directly interested, are still frequently interested to some degree: for every extension opens up a new market for either produce or raw materials.[125]

Spencer accused boards of directors of conspiring against shareholders by promoting less profitable extensions: but a more charitable interpretation must stress that one outstanding feature of railways was the production of externalities, or economic benefits which could not be captured by the companies themselves in terms of revenue but which accrued to the communities they served. It was well known at the time that the railway could enrich a whole area 'though the shareholders who made the line never received, and never will receive, a penny of dividend'.[126] How large 'business' motives loomed in company strategy would require extensive research, but their influence in some cases is beyond doubt. The North Eastern had a board of directors carefully composed of representatives of all the principal industries in the region it served.[127] The company's investment policy was sometimes directly influenced by industrial need[128] and similar accommodations were made over prices, including the famous agreement to introduce a sliding scale of rates which would move according to the market price of iron and steel products.[129] Irving's conclusion is that 'such policies cannot simply be looked at in terms of long run profit alone';[130] and given the interests represented on its board, the 'North Eastern might be regarded as a sort of holding company for the region as a whole . . . [and] may have been attempting to maximise not just company profit but also the profits of local industry'.[131] In other words, the North Eastern was a businessman's line and its directors and managers had a clear perception of the externalities generated by the system. No doubt the strategy, especially in the 1880s, had a political element within it, since taking care to meet the needs of its chief customers was one way of damping down demands for rate revision and greater state control of railways; but it was nonetheless a reflection of the unique importance of rail transport to the prosperity of business at the time. How far this 'business' motive was active elsewhere requires greater knowledge than is at present available, but the projection of some new lines after 1870 can be explained better in terms of the desire for greater regional competitiveness than the pursuit of railway dividends. The Hull & Barnsley is one example, some of the remoter Scottish lines another – though, in the latter case, the landowners who played such a prominent role in encouraging new lines did so to protect their prestige and authority as well as to enhance the region's trade.[132] Also, although the Golden Valley railway is best remembered for the wild over-optimism of its original projectors, it was also regarded as a social asset in the wider sense. When the company failed to pay, one modest shareholder consoled himself for his losses by claiming that he had made 'a subscription towards the trade of Hay',[133] the principal town on the line.

'Managerial' and 'business' motives for unprofitable expenditure are important but, over the railway system as a whole, it is likely that neither had quite the impact of competition, the force of which has, perhaps, been rather underrated by historians in recent years. Walter Bagehot, the famous editor of the *Economist,* was the person who probably saw most clearly the potency of competition. Bagehot understood the oligopolistic structure of railway enterprise in Britain – he called the companies 'competing monopolies' – and how, 'given our instincts for freedom and our Parliament', the creation of such a system had been inevitable. He also saw that as long as it was allowed to flourish, 'directors are in truth helpless: they *must* quarrel fight and spend', in order to protect their traffic from rivals.[134] Bagehot was writing in the 1860s when competitive building was still the central feature of railway rivalry. This was less pronounced in our period, though building still took place and small, unprofitable companies were swallowed up by larger ones for 'strategic reasons' or 'to occupy ground that might otherwise fall to a rival'.[135] The extension of the network into the extreme south-west of England, for example, cannot be properly understood without appreciating the continuous rivalry between the Great Western and the London & South Western.[136] By the 1870s the competitive emphasis was shifting from line-building and rate-cutting, 'that disastrous struggle without finality',[137] to competition in services and facilities.[138] There is little doubt that the companies felt they were replacing an expensive form of rivalry with a cheaper one, but here they were badly mistaken. In recent years economists have demonstrated that, in oligopolistic markets with high barriers to the entry of new firms, non-price competition will continuously raise marginal costs until all profits above the competitive norm have been eliminated and that, on balance, the costs of price competition to the industry concerned are likely to be less than those of competition in services.[139] In other words, service competition alone would have been sufficient to promote levels of capital spending and methods of

operation which continuously eroded profitability in the late nineteenth century, irrespective of any public burdens placed upon the
railways or any sense the companies might have had of their role as
public servants. Indeed, company chairmen often rationalised
competitive behaviour by referring it to 'public' pressures and,
whether intentionally or not, found a convenient excuse for disap-
pointing dividends.

The classic example of widespread competition was in the 1890s
when, with receipts rising very rapidly, the companies responded
with a huge increase in services and train-mileage and pushed up
capital expenditure and operating costs in what one manager later
called a 'wave of extravagance'.[140] The earnings ratio increased
steadily from an average of 9.08 in 1885–89 to 10.73 in 1900–04;
but the profit ratio declined from 4.43 to 4.06 in the same period and
actually fell below 4 per cent in 1901 (tables 3 and 4).

Another, less obvious, form of service competition involved the
buying-up or establishment of ancillary businesses. Companies
bought up docks linked with their systems after 1870 because the
latter were in danger of collapsing under the stress of competition
with the port of London, and because in taking them over the
companies could use them to attract import traffic from their
rivals.[141] They also bought into steamboats for similar reasons;[142]
and their hotel enterprises were, like their other businesses, designed
to feed traffic on to their lines rather than make a profit.[143] Figures
collected for the first time in 1913 suggest that the companies had
spent about £61.5 million of capital on hotels, steamboats and docks
or about 6 per cent of net paid-up capital. Earnings at £9.4 million
were high, but the expenses were also high at £7.5 million, so the
operating ratio was roughly 80 per cent. Only the docks appear to
have made a reasonable profit.[144]

The Midland, which straddled England 'like some huge letter "X"
... deeply embedded in Lancashire, Yorkshire, Bristol and
London',[145] is the extreme case where competitive pressures was
all-encompassing, the company's role throughout being that of
intruder upon the territory of others. The London & North Western
also suffered heavily from competition, but the Great Western was
less affected by it and the North Eastern less influenced by it than any
other leading line. The latter was, however, by no means immune.
Parliament's willingness to sanction new lines even after 1870 meant
that there was a permanent threat hanging over the company's

district monopoly, and policies were therefore based on 'an acceptance of the fact that it would retain possession of its monopoly only as long as the most important persons in the district believed it was serving them adequately' and that the company 'would have to provide the benefits traditionally supposed to flow from competition'.[146] The company was also subject to what was called at the time 'the competition of districts'. As its officials were only too well aware, if the North Eastern had attempted to charge its customers higher rates than other companies charged to the traders on their lines, or if it gave them poorer facilities than were available elsewhere, the region's industries would suffer or move away from the North-East and the company's earning power would decline.[147]

Competition, combination and the state

Laying stress upon competition rather than public pressure as the key to understanding company behaviour also makes it easier to explain the major changes which took place in the running of the railway system after 1900. Management structures were completely overhauled,[148] capital expenditure cut, facilities once granted free or below cost withdrawn, loading of goods trains dramatically improved (appendix II) and a sustained effort made to reduce competition permanently through combination and agreement.[149] If fear of public opinion as expressed in Parliament had been the guiding force behind company policy it is difficult to understand what happened after 1900, since the business community was thoroughly alarmed by the new trends, the strength of the railway interest in Parliament declining rapidly and the companies' ability to resist political pressure falling accordingly.[150] At the centre of the dramatic changes in strategy which were introduced in the Edwardian period was the simple fact that the non-price competition pursued over the previous thirty years had finally reduced profitability to the point where, given the increasing attractiveness of overseas investments (many of them safe railway stocks), the companies found it difficult to raise money at remunerative rates for the first time since the 1866 financial crisis.[151] Reform was now imperative to allay shareholder anxiety, encourage new investment and reverse the steady decline in profits. To achieve this required not only internal reform but a new, collective definition of the limits within which competition would be allowed to act, similar to that which had taken place around 1870.

Between 1871 and 1873, in the wake of the profits crisis of 1866–68, the Midland attempted an amalgamation with the Glasgow and South Western and had plans for closer links with other English companies. Partly in retaliation, the London & North Western proposed a merger with the Lancashire & Yorkshire. Both projects were killed off by trader and Parliamentary fear of monopoly:[152] but if the overall structure of the industry remained the same, the crisis also led to the final elimination of price competition, the ending of competitive line and station-building and the substitution for these of service competition. In the second great combination movement between 1906 and 1910 the front-runners were the Great Central, the Great Northern and the Great Eastern – collectively known as the 'Three Greats' – who proposed a 'working union' which would have merged together practically everything except the capital stocks of the three companies. Their move then triggered off a similar, if less comprehensive, merger proposal between the London & North Western, the Lancashire & Yorkshire and the Midland, which followed a close agreement, in 1904, between the first two companies mentioned. Other great companies, including the North British and Caledonian in Scotland, and the Great Western and London & South Western, also came much closer together over policy at this time.[153] These moves to suppress and limit service competition were justified as necessary to maintain a reasonable degree of profitability. State interference with labour costs after 1906 and the fact that, after 1900, the 1894 Railway and Canal Traffic Act worked to prevent companies from raising rates even though working expenses were high and rising, served only to confirm the railway companies in their opinion that fundamental changes in the structure of the industry were necessary.

The struggle to dampen the force of competition, and to win economies of scale by reducing the number of large companies, involved a change in the relations between government and the railway companies. Before 1900, the companies had tended to see the state as a dangerous force likely to be captured by their aggrieved customers or the railway trade unions and used to reduce their freedom and their profits. When intent on combination and reducing competition, however, the companies began to see the possibilities of using the power of Parliament and the state to authorise a new structure within the industry. Between 1907 and 1911 an elaborate game of diplomacy was played out between the companies, the Board of Trade and its successive presidents (including Lloyd-George and Churchill), designed to launch the companies on a new course. The companies wanted combination in order to improve efficiency, cut out competitive waste, increase profitability and improve their ability to borrow. In return, state control would be extended, in order to ensure that services would not fall below a specified level.[154] Initially, at any rate, far from being forced on a reluctant industry, increased state control was welcomed by the companies if it encouraged the elimination of competition and raised profits, while the quid pro quo for the state and its officials was an extension of regulatory authority.[155]

This attempt to create a code of practice under which close combination would be allowed was eventually stymied, between 1911 and 1913, not because the principal parties in the exchange failed to agree on the need for restructuring but because trader hostility forced the Board of Trade and the Government to try to exact terms which the companies felt entirely eroded the benefits of closer co-operation between themselves. The traders still insisted on the need to maintain a high degree of competition, oblivious of the fact that competition had played the principal part in bringing about the combination movement they so bitterly deplored. They also demanded the maintenance of a level of service provision which had already proved insupportable.[156] In addition to this, any chance of agreement was blown away by the effects of the 1911 railway strike. The Government's response was to urge the companies to be more generous over pay, something the latter refused until the Government agreed to modify the 1894 Act. The Act was duly amended in 1913 to allow the companies to raise rates where wages could be shown to have risen, but the concession so offended the trading community that any possibility of an accommodation on the combination question ceased to be practical politics for a time.[157] The companies' response was to form looser, more secretive, agreements amongst themselves which brought less benefit to them than more open agreements would have done, while damping down competition and increasing the traders' sense of alienation from the industry.

Despite the apparent impasse, by 1913 the industry was clearly entering a new era in its fortunes, one in which its structure and its relationship with the state were bound to undergo fundamental revision. Even the companies' most ardent champions, such as the economist William Acworth, felt that a re-examination of the whole question of transport provision was now required. Competition, he wrote in 1912,

is dying when it is not already dead. And although its efforts still persist, and will persist for some years to come, they must ere long die out too. Now if our railways have not been more than adequately controlled by the joint force of state regulation and competition, the conclusion is inevitable that, in future, competition being withdrawn, further state regulation must be introduced to take its place.[158]

In the light of this, and in view of the failure of the combination movement to resolve itself satisfactorily, it is not surprising that the debate over nationalisation was revived on a scale not seen since the 1865–73 period. In 1914, faced with a industry which had a mutinous work-force, a discontented and suspicious bunch of customers and a precarious profitability, Sydney Buxton, now President of the Board of Trade, set up a Royal Commission with a remit to discuss the possibilities of nationalisation, which even some shareholders had begun to feel might be the best answer to their own problems if compensation were pitched high enough. The war broke out before the Commission had time to collect much evidence.[159]

The railways were at the peak of their influence and achievement in Britain between 1870 and 1914, whether measured by social savings or by more informal criteria. At the same time, the system of private management began to run into serious difficulties. There was waste and inefficiency on the railway system of Great Britain between 1870 and 1914, and this was registered in declining labour productivity before 1900, a relatively low earnings ratio and a tendency for profits to fall. Some of this can be traced to bad management or errors of foresight, some to the effects of political pressure. What we have called 'managerial' and 'business' motives for building and running railways also militated against a strategy of profit maximisation. Nonetheless, the chief influence upon the companies' behaviour was probably non-price competition, and this was linked with both managerial and business motives and with the public pressures faced by railways, in the sense that these forces were often shaped and directed by the unavoidability of inter-company rivalry. What competition meant as regards the freight traffic was that the railways were forced to accommodate themselves to the needs of an economy of small firms in relative decline *vis-à-vis*

Continental and American rivals, and, as it were, share their inefficiencies. Despite this, the area in which competition had freest play and proved most expensive was passenger traffic, especially long-distance through traffic. This was also the competition which proved most difficult to eliminate after 1900 as the passenger train-mile figures show (see appendix I). By 1900, the public had grown used to luxury, high speeds and great frequency and, as with modern taxi services, excess capacity was an unavoidable feature of the business.[160]

Between 1900 and 1913, the railways staved off a profit crisis which might have put the whole private system in question through a mixture of internal reforms and informal collaboration which had, roughly speaking, divided Britain between half a dozen railway groupings. By the time war broke out, the companies were reaching the limits of the possibilities opened up by these means. If they were to continue to provide the services the public expected and, at the same time, pay their men a reasonable living wage, further concentration and greater changing flexibility were essential. This in turn meant a new phase in the complex relations between the railways and the state; but it took the upheaval of war to bring fundamental change in the form of the Railways Act of 1921 and the creation of the 'Big Four'.

Appendix I Railway traffic, train mileage and receipts, Great Britain, 1870–1912

Year	1 Freight tonnage conveyed (millions)	2 Freight train mileage (millions)	3 Freight receipts (£m)	4 Receipts per freight train-mile (d)	5 Passenger journeys (millions)	6 Passenger journey mileage (millions)	7 Passenger receipts (£m)	8 Receipts per passenger train-mile (d)
1870	166·5[a]	86·6[a]	25·5[a]	71·3[a]	322·2	80·8	18·1	53·5
1880	231·7	112·1	34·5	73·7	596·6	115·7	25·8	52·6
1890	298·8	139·4	40·8	70·1	796·3	158·2	32·7	48·9
1900	419·8	174·8	51·8	71·1	1114·6	209·5	43·3	49·1
1912	513·6	146·5	61·9	101·1	1265·2	247·3	52·0	50·3

Note:
[a] These figures are for 1871.
Sources: Cols. 1–3 and 5–7, B. R. Mitchell and P. Deane, *Abstracts of British Historical Statistics*, Cambridge, 1962, pp. 225–6. Cols. 4 and 8 are from the *Railway Returns* and are for the UK. The figures here exclude mileage by mixed trains. Figures in Col. 5 exclude all journeys by season ticket-holders.

Appendix II *Ton-mile estimates, England and Wales, 1871–1911*

	1	*2*	*3*	*4*	*5*	*6*
Year	*Ton miles (billions)*	*Average haul (miles)*	*Freight receipts (£m)*	*Rate per ton per mile (d) (3 ÷ 1)*	*Train mileage (millions)*	*Train load (tons) (1 ÷ 5)*
1871	4·2	30	22·4	1·28	74·0	56·9
1880	6·0	30	30·5	1·22	97·9	61·4
1890	7·8	30	36·0	1·11	122·3	63·6
1900	9·7	27	45·3	1·12	153·3	63·3
1911	12·6	28	52·3	1·00	130·9	95·9

Note: Train mileage excludes mileage by mixed trains.
Source: P. J. Cain, 'Private enterprise or public utility? Capital, output and pricing on English and Welsh railways, 1870–1914', *Journal of Transport History*, 3rd ser., 1 (1980), table 5. The table is slightly amended from the original.

Appendix III *Passenger mileage estimates, England and Wales, 1870–1912*

Year	1 Passenger miles (billions)	2 Passenger journeys (millions)	3 Average journey (miles) (1÷2)	4 Passenger receipts (£m)	5 Fare per passenger mile (d) (4÷1)	6 Train mileage (million)	7 Train load (1÷6)
1870	2·8	332	8·4	14·5	1·24	71	39
1890	6·5	865	7·5	25·1	0·93	140	47
1900	10·3	1283	8·0	32·7	0·75	183	56
1912	13·1	1580	8·0	38·3	0·6	220	60

Note: Passenger train mileage excludes mileage by mixed trains. All the figures in col. 4 are net of receipt for parcels, mails, dogs, horses, etc.

Sources:

(a) For 1870 and 1890 figures in col. 1 are taken from G. R. Hawke, *Railways and Economic Growth in England and Wales 1840–1870*, Oxford, 1970, pp. 48, 301. (On p. 301 Hawke gives 2·66m. passenger miles for 1870.) Passenger journeys are from the *Railway Returns*, with a 5 per cent and 10 per cent addition to the figures for 1870 and 1890 respectively to allow for journeys by periodical tickets, as are cols. 4 and 6.

(b) For 1900 and 1912, passenger mileage had to be estimated independently, starting with the fact that in 1921, the average fare in Great Britain was 1·04d per mile and that fares had risen 75 per cent in wartime (D. L. Munby and D. K. Watson, *Inland Transport Statistics. Great Britain 1900–70*, Vol. I, Oxford, 1978, pp. 113, 115). This suggests an average fare of 0·6d per mile for 1912 for which the figure in col. 1 is derived. This gives an average journey of eight miles in 1912 and, assuming that it was the same in 1900, makes it possible to devise col. 1 by multiplying col. 2 and col. 3. Col. 2 figures for 1900 and 1912 are from Munby and Watson, *op. cit.*, p. 101, and reduced on the assumption that passenger journeys in Scotland were 10 per cent of the total for Great Britain. Cols. 4 and 6 are from the *Railway Returns*.

Notes

1 P. E. Baughan, *North of Leeds. The Leeds–Settle–Carlisle Line and its Branches,* 1966.
2 H. Pollins, 'The last main line to London', *Journal of Transport History,* IV, 1959–60; G. Dow, *The Great Central,* 1962, II, pp. 236 ff.
3 The first Tay Bridge, completed in 1878, had collapsed within two years of opening.
4 E. T. McDermott, *History of the Great Western Railway II 1863–1921,* 1964 edn, rev. C. R. Clinker, ch. XI.
5 D. S. M. Barrie, *South Wales,* A Regional History of the Railways of Great Britain, Vol. XII, Newton Abbot, 1980. There is an excellent pull-out map in J. Simmons, *The Railways of England and Wales 1830–1914,* Leicester, 1978, which illustrates the development of the system in this period.
6 *Victoria County History (V.C.H.) of Wiltshire,* Vol. IV, Oxford, 1959, p. 289.
7 P. L. Clark, 'Railways', *V.C.H. Staffordshire,* Vol. II, Oxford, 1967, p. 326.
8 D. Brooke, 'Struggle between Hull and the North Eastern Railway 1854–1880', *Journal of Transport History,* new ser., I, 1971–72; R. J. Irving, *The North Eastern Railway Company 1870–1914 An Economic History,* Leicester, 1976, pp. 118–21.
9 Barrie, *South Wales,* pp. 125–7; M. J. Daunton, *Coal Metropolis: Cardiff 1870–1914,* Leicester, 1977, pp. 33–6; J. Rimell, J. Davis and J. Hailey, *History of the Barry Railway Company 1884–1921,* Cardiff, 1923.
10 D. Farnie, *The Manchester Ship Canal and the Rise of the Port of Manchester,* Manchester, 1980.
11 E. Carter, *An Historical Geography of the Railways of the British Isles,* 1959, pp. 470–1.
12 Preservationist sentiment ensured that the railways, which got as far as Ambleside, never penetrated further into the Lake District. See L. A. Williams, *Road Transport in Cumbria in the Nineteenth Century,* 1975, pp. 155–60. For other substantial settlements which never received the benefits of rail communication see J. Simmons, *The Railway in Town and Country 1830–1914,* Newton Abbot, 1986, pp. 291–3.
13 J. R. Kellett, *Railways and Victorian Cities,* 1969, p. 2.
14 Simmons, *The Railway in Town and Country,* table 20, p. 302.
15 Kellett, *Railways and Victorian Cities,* p. 289.
16 *Ibid.,* pp. 391 ff.
17 P. Deane and W. A. Cole, *British Economic Growth 1688–1959,* Cambridge, 1964, table 81, p. 306.
18 C. H. Feinstein, *Statistical Tables of National Income, Expenditure and Output of the U.K., 1855–1965,* Cambridge, 1976, Vol. I, p. 91.
19 P. Bagwell, *The Transport Revolution From 1770,* 1974, p. 123.
20 See Arnold Bennett's *Anna of the Five Towns,* ch. 3.
21 R. C. Michie, 'Income, expenditure and investment of a Victorian millionaire: Lord Overstone, 1823–83', *Bulletin of the Institute of*

Historical Research, LVIII, No. 137, 1985, pp. 73–4.

22   S. W. Martins, *A Great Estate at Work. The Holkham Estate and Its Inhabitants in the 19th Century*, 1980, pp. 59, 267–9.

23   R. J. Irving, 'British railway investment and innovation 1900–1914. An analysis with special reference to the North Eastern and London and North Western companies', *Business History*, XIII, 1971, pp. 51–3.

24   A. Stockbroker, 'The depreciation of British home investments', *Economic Journal*, XXII, 1912, p. 223.

25   B. L. Anderson, 'The Union Marine Insurance Company 1897–1915', in S. Marriner (ed.), *Business and Businessmen. Studies in Business, Economic and Accounting History*, 1978, table 3, pp. 50–1.

26   E. M. Forster, *Howards End*. The quotations are from p. 11 of the first edition of 1910.

27   D. L. Munby and A. H. Watson, *Inland Transport Statistics. Great Britain 1900–1970*, Vol. I, Oxford, 1978, table A10, p. 83.

28   Bagwell, *The Transport Revolution*, p. 156.

29   This is based on the crude assumption that the average haul for coal and other minerals was twenty miles, and for general merchandise fifty. See J. S. Jeans, *Railway Problems*, 1887, pp. 485, 497.

30   B. R. Mitchell, *Economic Development of the British Coal Industry 1800–1914*, Cambridge, 1984, pp. 12, 32–3.

31   D. Brooke, 'The advent of the steel rail, 1857–1914', *Journal of Transport History*, 3rd ser., VII, 1986.

32   I. C. R. Byatt, *The British Electrical Industry 1875–1914. The Economic Returns to a New Technology*, Oxford, 1978, esp. pp. 67–74.

33   S. B. Saul, 'The market and the development of mechanical engineering industries in Britain 1870–1914', *Economic History Review*, 2nd ser., XX, 1967, p. 112.

34   *Ibid.*, pp. 114–17.

35   *Ibid.*, p. 115.

36   D. E. C. Eversley, 'Engineering and railway works', *V.C.H. Wilts.*, Vol. 4, pp. 213–18.

37   On Crewe see the famous work by W. H. Chaloner, *The Social and Economic Development of Crewe, 1780–1923*, Manchester, 1950.

38   Simmons, *The Railway in Town and Country*, p. 36.

39   B. J. Turton, 'The railway towns of southern England', *Transport History*, 2, 1969, pp. 111–15.

40   Simmons, *The Railway in Town and Country*, pp. 190–1.

41   R. Barker, 'The metropolitan railway and the making of Neasden', *Transport History*, 12, 1981.

42   Simmons, *The Railway in Town and Country*, pp. 182–3.

42   *Ibid.*, p. 68.

44   *Ibid.*, pp. 151–2.

45   J. R. Hume, 'Transport and towns in Victorian Scotland', in G. Gordon and B. Dicks (eds.), *Scottish Urban History*, Aberdeen, 1983, pp. 212–14.

46   J. Richards and J. M. MacKenzie, *The Railway Station. A Social History*, 1986, p. 193; Simmons, *Railway in Town and Country*, p. 329.

47   Simmons, *Railway in Town and Country*, p. 128.
48   A. J. Lee, *The Origins of the Popular Press in England, 1855–1914*, 1976, pp. 59–60, 64–5, 73.
49   In 1904–05, the turnover on railway stalls was £1.4 million and rent paid to railway companies £192,000. In 1905, attempts to force up the rents persuaded Smith's to abandon their stalls and to concentrate upon high-street selling. C. Wilson, *First With the News. The History of W. H. Smith, 1792–1972*, 1985, esp. pp. 182–3, 200–10, 235–42, 257–61.
50   P. J. Waller, *Town, City and Nation. England 1850–1914*, 1983, p. 97; Simmons, *Railway in Town and Country*, p. 219.
51   Simmons, *Railway in Town and Country*, pp. 204–07, 211–13.
52   C. Hallas, 'The social and economic impact of a rural railway: the Wensleydale line', *Agricultural History Review*, 34, 1986.
53   P. J. Atkins, 'The growth of London's milk trade, *c.* 1845–1914', *Journal of Transport History*, new ser., 1977–78, esp. tables 1 and 2, pp. 209–10.
54   Richards and MacKenzie, *The Railway Station*, p. 194.
55   *Ibid.*, p. 195.
56   D. W. Howell, *Land and People in Nineteenth-Century Wales*, 1977, pp. 121–7; Simmons, *Railway in Town and Country*, p. 326.
57   Waller, *Town, City and Nation*, p. 17.
58   *Inland Transport Statistics*, table A17, p. 101.
59   T. C. Barker and M. Robbins, *A History of London Transport. Passenger Travel and the Development of the Metropolis. Vol I. The Nineteenth Century*, 2nd edn, 1975, chs. IV, V and VII. J. Simmons, 'The power of the railway', in H. J. Dyos and M. Wolff, *The Victorian City. Images and Reality*, vol. I, 1973, pp. 277–310; Simmons, *The Railways of England and Wales;* pp. 131–6; Simmons, *Railways in Town and Country*, pp. 59–85.
60   Thompson, *The Rise of Suburbia*, Leicester, 1982, p. 19.
61   Kellett, *The Impact of Railways on Victorian Cities*, chs. XI, XII.
62   *Ibid.*, pp. 376–7.
63   *Ibid.*, pp. 371–6.
64   Munby, *Inland Transport Statistics*, p. 101.
65   H. J. Dyos, 'Workmen's fares in South London', *Journal of Transport History*, I, 1953.
66   See H. Perkin, *The Age of the Railway*, Newton Abbot, 1971, ch. 9.
67   Simmons, *Railway in Town and Country*, pp. 119–20.
68   *Ibid.*, pp. 114, 244.
69   Waller, *Town, City and Nation*, p. 159.
70   Simmons, *Railway in Town and Country*, p. 58.
71   Hume, 'Transport and towns in Victorian Scotland', pp. 210–12.
72   Kellett, *Impact of Railways on Victorian Cities*, p. 358. Traffic increased, as Kellett says, because of 'the widening of effective demand and the growth of a larger class who could afford to pay the railways' charges rather than to the revolutionary expansion of popular suburban travel by active promotion or cost reductions' (p. 380).
73   J. K. Walton, *The Blackpool Landlady*, Manchester, 1978; Simmons, *Railway in Town and Country*, pp. 248–50.

74   Waller, *Town, City and Nation*, p. 135; Simmons, *Railway in Town and Country*, pp. 245–7; Bagwell, *The Transport Revolution*, p. 127.
75   Waller, *Town, City and Nation*, pp. 133–5.
76   Simmons, *Railway in Town and Country*, p. 256.
77   Apart from the works already cited there are good accounts of resort development in Perkin, *Age of the Railway*, ch. 8; J. A. R. Pimlott, *The Englishman's Holiday*, 1947; J. K. Walton, *The English Seaside Resort: A Social History 1750–1914*, Leicester, 1983 and H. J. Perkin, 'The social tone of Victorian seaside resorts in the North-West', *Northern History*, XI, 1976. See also S. Farrant, 'London by the sea: resort development on the south coast of England, 1880–1939', *Journal of Contemporary History*, 22 (1), 1987.
78   For a discussion of the concept of social saving see Gourvish's article in this book, and G. Hawke and J. Higgins, 'Britain', in P. O'Brien (ed.), *Railways and the Economic Development of Western Europe, 1830–1914*, 1983, pp. 184–8.
79   G. R. Hawke, *Railways and Economic Growth in England and Wales 1840–1870*, Oxford, 1970, pp. 48, 89, 301.
80   T. R. Gourvish, *Railways and the British Economy 1830–1914*, 1980, p. 41.
81   *Ibid.*, p. 61, n. 11. O'Brien's estimate of the social savings on freight in 1890 is similar to that of Gourvish's. See P. K. O'Brien, 'Transport and economic growth in Western Europe 1830–1914', *Journal of European Economic History*, XI, 1982, table 2, p. 347.
82   On the Royal Commission's proposals see Bagwell, *The Transport Revolution*, pp. 156–68; for arguments for and against the possibilities of substantial cuts in canal costs see J. E. Palmer, *British Canals. Problems and Possibilities*, 1910 and E. A. Pratt, *Canals and Traders*, 1910.
83   The total capital invested in the largest non-rail company, Imperial Tobacco, was £17.5 million in 1905. P. L. Payne, 'The emergence of the large-scale company in Great Britain, 1870–1914', *Economic History Review*, 2nd ser., XX, 1967, pp. 539–40.
84   The most important towns 'monopolised' by railway companies before 1914 were Northampton, Southampton, Coventry and Ipswich. Simmons, *Railway in Town and Country*, pp. 153–8.
85   E. A. Pratt, *A History of Inland Transport and Communication in England*, 1912, pp. 482, 499.
86   *Report of the Joint Select Committee on Railway Companies' Amalgamations*, P.P., 1872, XIII, Pt. I (364), xix–xx.
87   Figures are taken from P. J. Cain, 'Private enterprise or public utility? Output, pricing and investment on English and Welsh railways, 1870–1914', *Journal of Transport History*, 3rd ser., I, 1980, appendix 2, pp. 25–6, where a list of sources is given. On this subject see also R. Smith, *Sea-Coal For London. History of the Coal Factors in the London Market*, 1961, ch. 27.
88   In 1910, the General Manager of the L&NW claimed that tram competition cost his company £100,000 per annum in revenue. *Departmental Committee on Railways Agreement on Amalgamations. Minutes of*

Evidence, P.P., 1911 XXIX (Cd 5927), Pt. II. Q 15556. For a good example of the effects of tramway competition in the West Midlands see *V.C.H. Staffs.*, Vol. II, p. 329.

89 W. M. Acworth, 'The theory of railway rates', *Economic Journal,* VII, 1897, p. 329.

90 P. J. Cain, 'The British railway rates problem 1894–1913', *Business History*, XX, 1978, pp. 89–92, gives a review of the evidence available.

91 George Gibb, quoted in the *Department Committee on Railway Accounts and Statistics, P.P.*, 1910 LVI (Cd 5052), p. 704. See also Cain, 'The British railway rates problem', pp. 93–4; and E. A. Pratt, *German v. British Railways*, 1907, pp. 21–48.

92 *Report of the JSC on Railway Companies Amalgamations*, 1872, p. xxiv and P. Bagwell, *The Railway Clearing House in the British Economy 1842–1922*, 1968, p. 263.

93 Bagwell, *The Railway Clearing House*, pp. 85–9.

94 Hawke, *Railways and Economic Growth*, p. 334.

95 Cain, 'The British railway rates problem', pp. 92–3; M. Le Guillou, 'Freight rates and their influence on the Black Country iron trade in a period of growing foreign competition, 1850–1914', *Journal of Transport History,* new ser., III, 1975, pp. 108–18. The evidence presented by Le Guillou is interesting but his analysis is suspect.

96 P. J. Cain, 'Railways and price discrimination. The case of agriculture 1880–1914', *Business History*, XVIII, 1976, pp. 90–104; R. Perren, *The Meat Trade in Britain*, 1978, pp. 145–8.

97 For a lively defence of the companies' pricing policies see W. M. Acworth's books, *The Railways and the Traders*, 1891 and *Introduction to Railway Economics*, 1905.

98 For a good example of the traders' attitudes to railway companies in general see A. R. Ilersic and P. F. B. Liddle, *Parliament of Commerce. The Story of the Association of British Chambers of Commerce*, 1960, ch. 10.

99 G. J. Alderman, *The Railway Interest*, Leicester, 1973.

100 Alderman, *The Railway Interest*, chs. 6, 7; J. Mavor, 'The English railway rate question', *Quarterly Journal of Economics*, VIII, 1893–94.

101 P. J. Cain, 'Traders versus railways. The genesis of the Railway and Canal Traffic Act of 1894', *Journal of Transport History*, new ser., II, 1973.

102 Cain, 'The British railway rates problem', pp. 87–9. As an example it is worth noting that the companies in 1903 failed to persuade the Commissioners of their right to raise the rates for the carriage of mail despite rising costs. M. J. Daunton, *Royal Mail. The Post Office Since 1840*, 1985, pp. 135–8.

103 D. H. Aldcroft, 'The efficiency and enterprise of British railways, 1870–1914', in *Studies in British Transport History*, 1974, table 2, p. 33. This article was originally published in *Explorations in Enterpreneurial History* in 1968.

104 Irving, *The North Eastern Railway Company*, ch. 4.

105 *Ibid.*, ch. 3.

106 E. A. Platt, *Railways and their Rates*, 1905, pp. 91–7.

107 Simmons, *The Railways of England and Wales*, esp. pp. 194–200.

If the figures in appendix III are at all accurate, loading of passenger trains did improve after 1870 from very low levels indeed, but a much greater improvement would have been needed to justify the cost of new facilities.

108   Irving, *North Eastern Railway Company,* pp. 279–82; H. Pollins, *Britain's Railways. An Industrial History,* 1971, pp. 99–100.

109   For the movement of profits on one major company over the whole period see Irving, *The North Eastern Railway Company,* chs. 8, 10. Pollins, *Britain's Railways,* pp. 87–106.

110   D. H. Aldcroft, 'The efficiency and enterprise of British railways'. See also D. H. Aldcroft, *British Railways in Transition,* 1968, ch. I; and an interesting contemporary work with the same message, G. Paish, *The British Railway Position,* 1902.

111   R. J. Irving, 'British railway investment and innovation 1900–1914'. He concludes that 'the reluctance of the two companies discussed to press forward with apparently viable projects seems to have been due to more to a lack of appreciation of the widespread benefit to be gained than to the adverse state of the capital market, unfavourable though that was' (p. 63).

112   Aldcroft, 'The efficiency and enterprise of British railways', p. 48. For their adoption by the North Eastern see Irving, *The North Eastern Railway Company,* pp. 218–24. The companies' statistics were described by an informed critic in 1902 as 'a tribute to the wisdom of our ancestors and the ancestor worship of their descendants'. W. M. Acworth, 'English railway statistics', *Journal of the Royal Statistical Society,* LXV, 1902, p. 613.

113   Aldcroft, 'The efficiency and enterprise of British Railways', p. 44. As one example of 'empire building' see P. R. Reynolds, 'Watkin's invasion of Wales: the Welsh Union scheme of 1889', *Transport History,* 11, 1980.

114   T. R. Gourvish, 'The performance of railway management after 1860: the railways of Watkin and Forbes', *Business History,* XX, 1978. It is clear, however, that the rivalry between the two men did prevent the union of the South Eastern and the London Chatham & Dover until 1899. P. Bagwell, 'The rivalry and working union of the South Eastern and London Chatham and Dover Railways', *Journal of Transport History,* 2, 1955–56.

115   W. Ashworth, *An Economic History of England 1870–1939* (1960), pp. 118–26. Professor Ashworth put this argument in a more general context in his article 'The late Victorian economy', *Economica,* new ser., 33, 1966.

116   R. J. Irving, 'The profitability and performance of British railways 1870–1914', *Economic History Review,* 2nd ser., XXXI, 1978. See also his article 'The capitalisation of British railways 1830–1914', *Journal of Transport History,* 3rd ser., 5, 1984, pp. 6–19; and *The North Eastern Railway Company,* ch. 12.

117   For a rough comparison on these lines between Britain and Prussia see Cain, 'Private enterprise or public utility?', table 6, p. 20. It is also worth noting that the ratio of gross operating revenue to net capitalisation on railways in the United States moved from 13.9 to 19.9 between 1890 and 1906. *Historical Statistics of the United States. Colonial Times to 1957,* Washington, 1960, pp. 433–4.

118 Irving, *The North Eastern Railway Company*, p. 165.

119 See the views of the North Eastern General Manager, Henry Tennent, quoted in Irving, 'The profitability and performance of British railways', p. 55, and in *The North Eastern Railway Company*, pp. 195–6.

120 'If railways were not made a state concern, as a whole or in part, as in most European countries, it was simply because they acted for the most part as if they were public utilities.' D. E. C. Eversley, 'The Great Western Railway and the Swindon Works in the Great Depression', in M. C. Reed (ed.), *Railways in the Victorian Economy*, 1969, p. 134. Of course, some people at the time thought the companies *ought* to act in this way. See Alderman, *The Railway Interest*, pp. 109, 112; and T. R. Gourvish, *Railways and the British Economy*, pp. 47–8.

121 On this question see G. Channon, 'A. D. Chandler's 'visible hand', in transport history', *Journal of Transport History*, 3rd ser., 2, 1981, pp. 53–64.

122 T. R. Gourvish, 'The British business elite. The chief executive managers of the railway industry, 1850–1922', *Business History Review*, XLVIII, 1973. See also Gourvish's article, 'The railways and the development of managerial enterprise in Britain, 1850–1939', in K. Kubayashi, *Proceedings of the Fuji Conference*, Tokyo, 1986, pp. 185–205.

123 See the perceptive comments of Lord Salisbury in this context quoted in T. C. Barker, 'Lord Salisbury, Chairman of the Great Eastern Railway, 1868–72' in S. Marriner (ed.), *Business and Businessmen. Studies in Business, Economic and Accounting History*, Liverpool, 1978, p. 91.

124 Eversley, 'The Great Western Railway and the Swindon Works in the Great Depression', *passim*.

125 H. Spencer, 'Railway morals and railway policy', in *Essays: Scientific, Political and Speculative*, Vol. II, 1868, pp. 286–7.

126 *Economist*, 1 December 1866, quoted in J. Simmons, *The Railways of England and Wales*, p. 13.

127 Irving, *The North Eastern Railway Company*, pp. 131–2.

128 *Ibid.*, pp. 132–4.

129 *Ibid.*, pp. 32–3, 130–1.

130 *Ibid.*, p. 134.

131 *Ibid.*, p. 138.

132 N. T. Sinclair, 'The Aviemore Line. Railway politics in the Highlands, 1882–1898', *Transport History*, 2, 1969.

133 R. C. Mowat, *The Golden Valley Railway*, Cardiff, 1964, p. 84.

134 W. Bagehot, 'The true remedy for the evils of railway competition', *Economist*, 28 February 1863, reprinted in N. St. J. Stevas, *Collected Works of Walter Bagehot*, Vol. X, 1978, pp. 443–6.

135 J. Simmons, *The Railways of England and Wales*, p. 103.

136 J. Simmons, 'Great Western versus South Western – railway competition in Cornwall and Devon', *Journal of Transport History*, 1959–60.

137 *Report of the Departmental Committee on Railways Agreements and Amalgamations*, P.P., 1911 XXIX (Cd 5631) Pt. II, Para. 13.

138 Kellett, *Railway and Victorian Cities*, p. 67.

139 G. J. Stigler, 'Price and non-price competition', *Journal of Political*

Economy, 76, 1968. This has been demonstrated in the case of modern American aircraft companies. See G. W. Douglas and James C. Miller III, 'Quality competition, industry equilibrium and efficiency in the price-contrained airline market', *American Economic Review*, 64, 1974. I am grateful to Rosemary Clarke for drawing my attention to this literature.

140 Guy Granet, General Manager of the Midland before the *D.C. on Railways Agreements and Amalgamations, Minutes of Evidence*, 1911, Q 18755.

141 Cain, 'Railways and price discrimination', pp. 191, 197. There is a list of docks owned by railway companies in appendix XXX of the *D.C. on Railways Agreements and Amalgamations 1911* (Cd 5927).

142 B. F. Duckham, 'The railway steamship enterprise – the Lancashire and Yorkshire's east coast fleet 1904–14', *Business History*, X, 1968.

143 J. Simmons, 'Railways, hotels and tourism in Great Britain, 1839–1914', *Journal of Contemporary History*, 19, 1984.

144 Figures are from the *Railway Returns* for 1913. The figure for railway expenditure on docks, harbours, wharves, and steamships in 1913 are in Simmons, *Railways in Town and Country*, table 15, p. 234.

145 E. G. Barnes, *The Midland Main Line 1875–1922*, 1969, p. 40.

146 Irving, *The North Eastern Railway Company*, p. 17.

147 *Report of the Board of Trade Railway Conference*, App. 2, No. 2, pp. 163–4; See also Irving, *The North Eastern Railway Company*, pp. 116–17.

148 Irving, *The North Eastern Railway Company*, chs. 9, 11. There is a brief and incomplete look at the Midland reorganisation after 1900 in Barnes, *The Midland Main Line*, pp. 223 ff.

149 P. J. Cain, 'Railway combination and government 1900–1914', *Economic History Review*, 2nd ser., XXV, 1972.

150 See Alderman, *The Railway Interest*, chs. 11–13.

151 Cain, 'Railway combination and government', pp. 628–9.

152 E. Cleveland Stevens, *English Railways. Their Development and their Relationship to the State*, 1915, pp. 232 ff.

153 P. J. Cain, 'Railway combination and government', pp. 630–3.

154 *Ibid.*, pp. 631–2, 633–7.

155 This paragraph has been influenced by the assumptions made by modern economists interested in the theory of regulation and the economic implications of state interference in private business. For an excellent introduction to the literature see R. B. Ekelund and R. F. Hébert, *A History of Economic Theory and Method*, 2nd edn, 1983, pp. 529–35.

156 Cain, 'Railway combination and government', p. 635.

157 *Ibid.*, p. 637; G. Alderman, 'The railway companies and the growth of trades unionism in the late nineteenth and early twentieth centuries', *Historical Journal*, XIV, 1971.

158 W. M. Acworth, 'The State in relation to railways in England', in Royal Economic Society, *The State in Relation to Railways*, 1912, p. 7.

159 The best introduction to the nationalisation debate over the whole period is E. Eldon Barry, *Nationalization in British Politics. The Historical Background*, 1965.

160 Irving's argument that the failure to improve efficiency in the passenger sector on the North Eastern after 1900 indicates that the company's officials had a 'blind spot' is something which needs further investigation in regard to that company and to the other large enterprises. Irving, *The North Eastern Railway*, pp. 245–9.

Urban transport

Introduction

Steam railways, by encouraging national economic growth, also stimulated urbanisation; but they were relatively little concerned with urban transport itself, where distances were short, or with the outward growth of built-up areas, where they were usually not much longer. In all these busy, bustling, rapidly growing places, apart from the very largest of them, traditional methods of getting about, or moving goods, were still the norm until the very end of the nineteenth century. For short-distance transport, which included almost all movement in towns, human and animal power continued to be used. Most journeys or errands by men and women were still made on foot. Much shifting of goods also depended on human energy whether these goods were pushed (or pulled) on barrows or carts, or carried by hand or on the back.

The major development in urban transport in the Victorian Age was not the introduction of mechanical traction but the greater supplementation of human by animal power. The number of horses used in passenger and freight transport in Britain during the Railway Age quadrupled, from about 250,000 to a little over a million at the peak in 1901.[1] This was in the country as a whole; but since short journeys were being made increasingly in growing towns, the urban share of this total was certainly increasing. To this extent, historians now see changes in urban transport in very much the same light as they have come to see the growth of manufacturing industry during the nineteenth century: much additional output was achieved not by power-driven, labour-saving machinery but by adapting traditional labour-intensive methods, taking advantage of the continuously increasing, vigorous young labour force resulting from rapidly grow-ing population. The mechanisation of urban transport, like the spread of factories, was a much slower process than once supposed. Urban and suburban railway traffic began the process, especially in London, from the middle of the nineteenth century; but it was much less important elsewhere. The tramway was a significant innovation in most towns from the 1870s, but it depended upon horse haulage until electric power was introduced. In British towns this did not occur until around 1900. The mechanisation of the less important horse bus came a decade later. Almost all freight haulage by road was still by horse on the eve of the First World War.

Consideration of this subject must begin by stressing how geographically confined most towns still were in the 1830s. Even London, far and away the largest of them at the beginning of the Victorian period when about two million people lived there, was spatially still relatively small. In the 1830s the central built-up area stretched only for about four miles north to south and six miles east to west;[2] that is to say two to three miles at most from perimeter to centre. Beyond the built-up area lay more habitations scattered along the roads leading outwards for another mile or two. Glasgow and Edinburgh and the largest English provincial towns, with populations little more than a tenth of London's, were even more limited in area. Manchester and Salford, taken together, then numbered only about 250,000 people. It stretched at most for little more than a mile either from north to south or from east to west. Both the capital and the larger towns elsewhere were places where most of the inhabitants could, and did, easily walk from the outskirts to the central business areas. Those already living in the centre had no difficulty in getting to work on foot or in running errands; and the local hostelry then, as now, was close at hand. Victorian towns were predominantly places for walking, not for riding, for legs not for wheels.

Goods transport

Human energy was still used to a considerable extent in the movement of goods. A visitor to the Liverpool docks in the 1830s, for instance, observed labourers carrying sacks of oats 'at a uniform, unremitting pace, a trot of at least five miles an hour' from warehouse to vessel fifty yards away. He estimated that they made 750 trips a day and walked nearly forty-three miles, half of them heavily loaded.[3] Within towns goods of all sorts were still carried or hawked for considerable distances. Many uptown street porters (ticket porters) in the City of London, for instance, continued to carry on their heads or backs loads of from ½–3 cwt. for distances up to three miles. In 1841 they still had their authorised pitching places where they could rest their loads for a minute or two before continuing on their journey.[4] Henry Mayhew, writing of London in the middle of the nineteenth century, refers to the packmen and their bales of software. Coal was carried round the streets in small quantity for delivery to the poor, or carried home by the poor themselves from the local coal-shed men, 'a very numerous class'. Coke, too, collected from the gasworks for delivery to those who could not even afford coal, was often moved by 'itinerant vendors who carry one, and in some cases two, sacks lashed together on their backs . . .'.[5] Teenage coster girls carried baskets of apples or other produce weighing nearly 2 cwt. on their heads for eight to ten miles, selling in the streets from central London as far out as Woolwich.[6] Other street vendors conveyed their wares in large baskets or in trays suspended round their necks and strapped behind their backs. 'Door mats, baskets and "duffer's packs", wood pails, brushes, brooms, clothes-props, clothes-lines and string, and grid-irons, Dutch ovens, skewers and fore shovels' were carried across the shoulders.[7] Provincial towns lacked their Mayhew; but it is reasonable to suppose that there, too, much depended upon 'fortunate possessors of an athletic frame'.[8]

As the country became richer, more wheeled vehicles came increasingly to replace these human beasts of burden. Long in use in towns for freight transport, they ranged from the splendid horse-drawn wagons which supplied well-to-do areas to the humble barrows, pushed (or drawn) by the poor to supply the even poorer. Even the human coke transporters, just referred to, represented only about a third of the total labour force involved in these deliveries.[9] Those who had a little money behind them could start with a horse, or at least a donkey; others moved up to them from hand barrows, to which the human carriers graduated. An estimated 161,000 horses pulled freight vehicles in various parts of Britain in 1851, 500,000 in 1891, 702,000 in 1901 and 832,000 in 1911.[10] How many of these worked in towns is not known, though the fact that 80 per cent of the country's population was urban by the end of the century, and most economic activity occurred in towns, suggests that most of the horse-drawn goods traffic was to be found there. A writer in the early 1890s estimated that the railway companies used 6,000 horses to draw their collection and delivery vans in London alone. Other carriers employed 19,000 more. The larger London brewers kept 3,000 horses to pull their heavy drays, the local authorities 1,500 to clear refuse, and post office contractors 600 to horse their mail vans.[11] By 1901 over 6,500,000 people lived in the London area. Other larger towns, like Manchester, Liverpool or Birmingham, still had only about one-tenth of that total; Glasgow rather more. Presumably the number of horses involved in freight transport in these places was proportionately lower.

In his well-documented account of Pickfords, cartage agents to the London & North Western Railway, Dr Turnbull has drawn attention not only to the huge trade in shop goods which developed during the Victorian period – in about 1880, one London drapery firm alone reckoned to send 200,000 bales and parcels every year to 12,000 outlets throughout the country – but also, as a result of better communucation by post, telegraph and, eventually, telephone, to an increasing tendency for goods to be ordered one day for delivery the next. 'Two or three delivery rounds each morning, afternoon and evening . . . inevitably meant more horses, more carts, more men.'[12] Better service, that is to say, meant more vehicles on the road for a given volume of traffic; and total traffic, especially parcels traffic from the 1860s, was itself on the increase.

It would obviously be wrong to suppose that there were as many horse-drawn vehicles as horses to pull them, for heavier vehicles required more than one horse, not to mention spares in case of accident or illness. We do not have any fiscal help here, however, for horse-drawn commercial vehicles ceased to be taxed in 1825; but Goschen's abortive attempt to tax commercial vehicles again in 1888 yielded the estimate that there were then 300,000 trade carts (two-wheelers) and 150,000 wagons.[13] Whether 80 per cent of this vast total was to be found in urban areas, it is impossible to say, though if we add the regular carrier services from surrounding villages into market towns, studied by Professor Everitt,[14] it seems likely that this percentage is not an underestimate. The whole subject of nineteenth-century freight transport by road still awaits much further investigation, as do the widening geographical origins of these draught animals, their price and the new breeds produced for particular haulage purposes. Their very large numbers have been recorded visually in Victorian and Edwardian street scenes. The abundant, slow-moving (or stationary) horse-drawn freight traffic, with the horses taking street space ahead of the vehicles (not, as with motors, forming part of the vehicles themselves), is a major feature of the severe congestion in urban centres. All these carts and wagons employed a vast army of men to service them. And, by 1901, there were another 450,000 horses throughout the country engaged in passenger transport,[15] the overwhelming majority engaged in urban service. Their numbers had grown much more rapidly than those in freight transport, though, with mechanisation, the total was to fall, while the number of freight horses went on growing for a little longer.

The role of horse-drawn coaches and omnibuses in urban growth

So long as towns were small and compact, proprietors lived at, or close to, their businesses, and their employees within walking distance, if not even on the spot. With economic growth, the central sites were devoted more exclusively to business purposes which paid higher rents. Those who could afford to do so moved to residences on the fringes of the built-up area or, as we have seen, down roads leading out of it. The rest remained, as one mid-nineteenth-century commentator put it, 'chained to the spot',[16] unable to escape from the centre which was becoming increasingly congested as sites there were switched from domestic to business use. More people worked in urban centres but fewer people lived there. Only when cheaper transport allowed the better-off workers to follow the middle classes into new suburbs was the central congestion eventually eased. New methods of passenger transport held the key to this outward urban growth.

The beginnings of this process were first to be seen in London, the population of which already exceeded one million by 1800. The movement of the privileged into the splendid houses and spacious squares of the West End has been described in Sir John Summerson's notable book, *Georgian London*.[17] Low-density building then moved northwards. Lord's cricket ground was moved to its present site, and round the edge of Regent's Park appeared pairs of semi-detached houses, 'the first part of London, and indeed any other town', Summerson observes, 'to abandon the terrace house for the semi-detached villa – a revolution of striking and far-reaching effect'.[18] The built-up area was enlarged in other directions, too, and from it, there was ribbon development down all the roads radiating outwards, to link up with local communities at places like Camberwell, Peckham and Dulwich.[19] Unlike Continental cities, London grew outwards rather than upwards; and other English towns followed London's example, but the Scottish, less so.

The really well-to-do had their own private carriages which they kept in mews behind their houses. Others could afford to take hackney coaches or the smaller or faster two-wheeler, the cabriolet (or cab), introduced from Paris in the 1820s. Both types of vehicle became more plentiful after the hackney coach monopoly in central London was abolished in 1832. Improved cabs , hansoms, coaches and broughams came into use.

Other riders took advantage of the short-distance stage-coaches (or short stages) which ran from central London to the outskirts. These had been running regular services to places such as Islington or Kensington even in the 1760s.[20] By 1825, 418 of them were already making a total of 1,190 journeys in and out of the City every day. These vehicles, however, were not suited to urban service, for they were difficult to mount, especially to the roof, or to alight from. When the omnibus (basically a box on wheels) was introduced, also from Paris, in 1829, it soon began to replace the short stages, especially after the abolition of the hackney coach monopoly allowed these vehicles to pick up and set down in the crowded central streets. By the end of the 1830s, 620 omnibuses (and 225 short stages) were licensed in London.[21]

The cost of operating omnibuses, however, was high. The London bus of the 1830s was usually pulled by two horses and carried fifteen passengers, twelve inside and three sitting on the edge of the roof by the coachman. To keep one of these vehicles on the road for fourteen hours a day for seven days a week required a stud of eleven horses, for apart from allowing for illness of the horses, omnibus work was so exacting that each pair of animals needed a rest for part of the day and a complete rest for one day in four. Although at £20 per horse and £100 per vehicle, the fixed capital cost was not great (£320), the operating cost was far higher. Feed in the early Victorian period could amount to about 15s per horse per week (£429 per bus per year). The animals also had to be housed and looked after. There were veterinary bills and the cost of horseshoeing. The vehicles needed frequent attention and repair. There was also at that time a heavy mileage duty (3d per mile for every mile the vehicle travelled in service, whether it was full or empty).[22] If sixty miles were run every day, that meant 15*s* per day (or over £270 per year) duty; to which were to be added the wages of the coachman and conductor (about £160 per year for both of them). Turnpike tolls had also to be paid on some routes. With such high operating costs, fares, though lower than those on the short stages, remained high: 1*s* single to the outskirts and 6*d* to hop on and off in the central streets. At a time when a skilled man's wage rarely reached 30*s* per week and most workers earned 20*s* or less, riding by bus, unless it was a special treat, was not for them. Indeed, horse buses only started to run at 7.30 in the morning, when most wage-earners were already at work. These vehicles did, however, enable clerks and others in the lower reaches of the middle classes to move out from the most congested central area. A London eye-witness summed up the position well in 1837:

In the mornings from the hours of eight to ten, the various short-stages and omnibuses are pouring in, bearing with them the merchant to his business, the clerk to his bank or counting house, the subordinate official functionaries to the Post Office, Somerset House, the Excise or the Mint, the Custom House or Whitehall. An immense number of individuals, whose incomes vary from £150 to £400 or £600 and whose business does not require their presence till nine or ten in the mornings, and who can leave it at five or six in the evenings; persons with limited independent means of living, such as legacies or life-rents, or small amounts of property; literary individuals; merchants and traders small and great; all, in fact, who can endeavour to live some distance from London . . .'.[23]

Omnibuses had replaced short stages in London by the mid 1840s. Their numbers grew to about 1,000 in the early 1850s. Together they brought to work about 20,000 commuters every day.[24]

This tidal flow each weekday was caused by only a small minority of those who lived in the new suburban areas. In 1851, for instance, perhaps only about 750 men and thirty women travelled in daily from the area north-west of Regent's Park in what came to be the borough of Hampstead (population then about 12,000). This, however, represented nearly one-third of the employed males living there.[25] They were the main breadwinners whose earnings kept many others employed in the district, mainly to serve them and their families. These other 'locals' presumably moved about mainly on foot. A similar picture emerges from the south London suburb of Camberwell. Because it lay nearer to the centre, however, and within walking distance of work there, its population was more variegated; but the minority of the better-off travelled to work by horse bus and Thomas Tilling built up a thriving omnibus service in the 1850s and

1860s.[26]

The halving of the mileage duty (from 3*d* to 1½*d* per mile) in 1842 reduced operating costs; and the basis upon which it was levied, by the vehicle and not by the number of seats, encouraged omnibus operators to carry more passengers without increasing the vehicle's size. Two seats began to be placed lengthwise on the open roof – knifeboard seats, they came to be called – access to which was obtained by vertical ladder at the back of the vehicle. Its carrying capacity was thereby increased from fifteen to twenty-five. With the cut in duty and the advent of these double-deckers, we hear of 3*d*, 2*d*, and even 1*d* fares over very short distances (or stages, the old name, still used to this day). The mileage duty was later further reduced, to 1*d* in 1855 and ½*d* in 1866; it was abolished altogether in 1870. Omnibus design was improved later in the century in emulation of new competitors, the horse trams, which we shall consider later. The vertical ladder was replaced bx a more negotiable and (in view of the amount of horse manure which clung to passengers' footwear) more sanitary, winding staircase; knifeboards were replaced by garden seats facing the direction of travel; larger, plate-glass windows were introduced so that inside passengers on the lower deck had a better view out. Horse feed became cheaper as a result of greater international competition in grain. But the fares by horse-bus never became low enough to allow the working classes to use them as a matter of course. They had to await other forms of transport before they could escape from fairly close proximity to their work – or walk the longer distances.

The horse-bus nevertheless facilitated London's growth by maintaining good and frequent communication with its outward-moving building frontier, enabling that middle-class frontier to keep moving outwards for up to four or five miles or an hour's journey; and operators on the various routes very soon joined together in associations to allocate 'times' on each of those routes. In 1856 most of these omnibus proprietors were absorbed in a combine, the London General Omnibus Company (LGOC), with which the remaining independents worked in concert.[27] Within the central streets, busier than ever in daytime, these still rather crude, bone-shaking vehicles did a brisk business, picking up and setting down at will. There were no bus stops. They often ran to the opposite side of the road to collect a fare, for, before the 1880s and winding staircases, the entrances was at the back and there was no need to pick up on the nearside.

The LGOC and its associates shared with the faster hansom cab the growing number of better-off passengers who needed to ride to business, for pleasure, for shopping or to visit friends or relatives. The more cumbersome, four-wheel hackney coaches were used when more than two people needed to travel or when luggage was carried. They were also hired for special occasions such as weddings or funerals, on such occasions perhaps by people of more modest means. By the 1850s, 3,000 cabs and coaches were licensed in London. Together with the horse buses and privately-owned carriages, and added to the vast numbers of barrows, carts and wagons already mentioned, they greatly increased traffic congestion as they endeavoured to travel at different speeds in the central streets. Jams became severe. By the 1850s it was quicker to go on foot down some streets at busy times than to ride.[28]

Before long, urban congestion had become so bad that it deterred some of the better-off from keeping their own carriages in towns. There were also parking problems, for horses (unlike cars) could not be left for long unattended in the street. Carriage ownership throughout the country, which grew rapidly from four per 1,000 inhabitants in 1840 to 14 per 1,000 in 1870, failed to go on rising faster than population.[29] Since carriage ownership outside towns seems to have increased apace, it was obviously within towns that private carriages were becoming less popular at a time when public transport of various sorts was improving; and those who did, in fact, continue to run their own vehicles in towns increasingly hired their horses from jobmasters.[30] Mews quarters are missing from speculative builders' plans in the 1860s and 1870s.[31] Yet despite this arrested growth after about 1870, there were still over 23,000 private carriage licences issued for the administrative county of London at the end of 1891, twice the number of hackney cabs and coaches.[32] There were then 1,600 omnibuses licensed to run regularly through London's streets.[33]

The Builder in 1844 hazarded the guess that 'in a very short time it seems certain that all England will be a London'.[34] So far as the spatial growth of these other places was concerned, and the development of horse-drawn transport to make such growth possible, the time-span was to prove much greater. Settlements down main roads certainly appeared, as did the growth of villages just outside; but, as was emphasised at the outset, much smaller populations required much smaller built-up areas. Walking distances survived for much longer, even to better-off residences on the outskirts. The need for wheeled vehicles to carry people, as distinct from goods, was far less. According to a map of 1875, for instance, which shows the three largest English provincial towns on a scale of three inches to a mile, the built-up areas of Manchester and Salford still extended only for about two miles from east to west and about the same distance from north to south on its western side, though a little farther on its eastern flank; Liverpool for about a mile inland from the river and about two miles north to south; Birmingham for about two miles by two miles.[35]

All these larger places had their quota of hackneys and private carriages by the 1830s. Stage-coaches connected them with neighbouring towns as well as with places farther afield. Short stages began to appear. One ran from Manchester to Pendleton, for instance, in 1824, and a coach-builder was trying to construct an omnibus in 1830. (We known about this because it fell through the floor of his workshop and injured some of his craftsmen.[36]) A new eight-inside omnibus was reported from Manchester in 1835 and, a few years later, Engels was to comment upon the omnibuses, running every fifteen or thirty minutes, which brought in the upper classes from their villas 'surrounded by gardens . . . in the higher and remoter parts of Chorlton and Ardwick or on the breezier heights of Cheetham Hill, Broughton or Pendleton'.[37] By the middle of the century sixty-four of these Manchester vehicles were running out along all the main roads. This was quite an impressive number but still only about one-fourteenth of London's total at that time. Two-wheelers (hansoms) were replacing the old, four-wheel coaches in Manchester by 1840. By 1861, 200 hackneys were licensed in the borough, seventy-five of them hansoms.[38]

Much the same story emerges from Birmingham. First, the beginnings of omnibuses in 1834 which, with private carriages, explain early residential development about a mile from the centre, at New Hall (just south of Snow Hill) and Edgbaston. Then Small Heath and Sparkbrook, two miles out, were connected by omnibus and, by the 1840s, Saltley, Handsworth and Smethwick. Services were very limited, however; even when the frequency to Handsworth was improved in the 1860s, for instance, there were still only two omnibuses an hour. Fares were high: 6*d* single, raised to 8*d* or 9*d* if the weather was bad.[39] Glasgow by then had a good, 2½-minute omnibus service in the centre and plenty of cabs; but the development of the Second City's West End was a slow and laborious process. Landowners had great difficulty in selling building plots, had to put up money to complete the Great Western Road and, from 1847, subsidise a bus service on it. This was still running only half-hourly in the 1850s. Not until the later 1860s did Kelvinside grow with any rapidity.[40] Leeds, like Manchester, had acquired some omnibuses by the 1840s; but even in the 1860s there were only thirteen a day to Headingley.[41] Horse-drawn vehicles were enabling the better-off to live outside town centres as in London, but on a proportionately smaller scale.

The limited importance of railways

Only in the much more extensive London area did railways play any notable part in passenger transport and urban growth, and even there it was a much smaller part than that of horse-drawn vehicles until the 1860s.[42] Most lines were halted south of the river or, by Parliamentary edict, north of Euston Road. Only two of them penetrated the City itself: the Eastern Counties Railway to Shoreditch in 1840 (the extension to Liverpool Street had to wait until the 1870s) and the London & Blackwall Railway to Fenchurch Street in 1841. The London & Greenwich Railway's terminus at London Bridge (1836) was also conveniently situated, just a short walk from the City, and Waterloo (1848) was also not too far away. Other railways were soon built which also ran into these termini, and built up a local traffic at middle-class fares to stations not only out to Bow or Greenwich but also to the village of Blackheath, to the market town of Croydon or, on the main line to Southampton, to a new estate near Kingston-on-Thames which a guidebook of 1856 called 'Kingston on Railway'. (It was later called Surbiton.)[43]

More interesting for our present purposes was the East and West India Docks and Birmingham Junction Railway, never originally intended for passengers but as freight line to carry the London & North Western's heavy goods traffic to the Thames. Built in the later 1840s from Camden Town on the main line to Euston, through the fields of Canonbury, Kingsland, Homerton and Bow, that is to say round the perimeter of the built-up area of that time, it very soon attracted commuters already living to the south of it and encouraged building to the north and east, for it connected via the Blackwall line into Fenchurch Street. At fares of 6*d* single first-class and 4*d* single second (there was no third), this roundabout, but relatively quick, route to work soon attracted a considerably better-off clientèle. During the first six months of 1851, when a fifteen-minute service was provided from a middle-class starting time of 8.30 a.m. to 10 p.m., when such respectable people were supposed to be at home again, more than 1,750,000 passengers were carried on the new railway, nearly half of them to and from Fenchurch Street. Trains were soon extended westwards along the main line from Camden Town to Willesden Junction and thence by a new railway to Kew. The venture was renamed the North London Railway in 1853.

Even with this attractive addition to suburban railway capacity, a count made by a Select Committee on London Termini in 1854 indicates that the numbers passing through London Bridge, Fenchurch Street and the other London termini were probably well below 10,000 a day , considerably below the 20,000 or so then coming in every morning by horse-bus; and, of course, the railways never carried all the traffic within the built-up area which the horse-buses did throughout the day. Nevertheless, as the building frontier was moved farther out, the railways' greater speed gave them an increasing advantage. At four or five miles distance, an hour's travelling time, the horse-bus reached its limit. New houses down the line near railway stations proved increasingly attractive to commuters and, when these comfortable residences were occupied, their inhabitants used the railways for other journeys, too.

The peripheral North London's success encouraged others to promote another line farther in. Little vacant land remained upon which to build it. So this Metropolitan Railway was laid partly in open cuttings or immediately under the streets, the surfaces of which were removed while the cuttings were made and then replaced. Thus was built the world's first underground, opened from the City to Paddington in 1863. It connected directly with the main lines at King's Cross and Paddington (and at St Pancras when the Midland Railway main line was opened there in 1868); suburban trains on those railways had direct access to the City. The underground was quickly extended westwards, by another company (the Metropolitan District Railway) through Kensington and round via Victoria and under the Victoria Embankment (then being built) to a terminus rather optimistically called Mansion House, reached in 1871. (The final section of what was to be known as the Inner Circle (later the Circle Line) was completed through the City in 1884.)

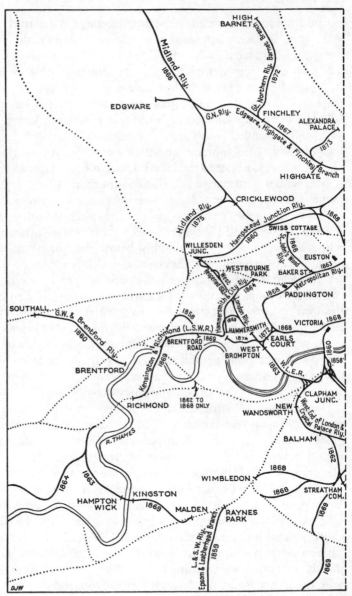

14 London's railways in 1855 and 1875: dotted lines indicate railways previously opened (from T. C. Barker and M. Robbins, *A History of London Transport, Vol. 1, the Nineteenth Century*, Allen & Unwin, 1975, pp. 136–7; London Transport Museum.

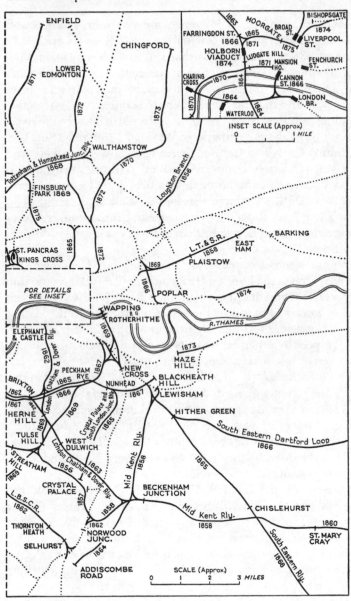

Offshoots were sprouted to Hammersmith, St John's Wood and West Brompton soon after the original stretch of line was opened.

During the 1860s, when all this urban railway-building was taking place, increasing carrying capacity in the centre and encouraging building activity near the offshoots, the main-line companies from the south were also making their suburban services more attractive by extending their lines to new termini on the north bank of the river, nearer their passengers' destinations. Between 1860 and 1866 Victoria, Charing Cross and Cannon Street termini were opened; and Ludgate Hill (and later Holborn Viaduct) stations were built to provide city accommodation for a new railway from Kent via Bromley and West Dulwich which also had a West End terminus at Victoria. These lines, and most of those feeding into London's other main-line termini, built new suburban branches to create additional local traffic.

Even more significant, perhaps, than this great extension of railway provision in the London area was the railways' introduction of cheaper fares. These at last enabled some better-paid working men to travel to work and to follow the better-off, if not into the leafiest suburbs, at least into less densely-packed housing and fresher air. Railways, especially urban railways, were costly to build and needed to be worked as intensively as possible to justify such heavy capital expenditure. Packed, early-morning trains would help to attain this objective. The recently-opened underground showed the way when, in May 1864, two trains began to run from Hammersmith to the City at 5.30 and 5.40 every weekday morning at a fare of 3*d* return. A glimpse of the new traffic has been captured in a well-known illustration by Gustave Doré. By the end of 1865 between 1,800 and 2,000 workmen were using the new service every day.

Soon afterwards the London, Chatham & Dover Railway into Ludgate Hill and Victoria also began to run cheap trains at 2*d* per day return. Before this time railways had deprived the working classes (usually the poorest members) by knocking down cheap housing in order to extend their lines into the central area;[44] now they were starting to redress the balance by enabling the working classes (though usually the skilled and better-off) to find accommodation elsewhere. It soon became usual for all railways which promoted new stretches of line through built-up areas to provide workmen's trains. By the early 1870s these were bringing in traffic from as far away as Enfield Town, 10¼ miles, for 2*d* return, quite exceptional value. The new service changed the character of the neighbourhood round Stamford Hill, Tottenham and Edmonton, and to Walthamstow on a branch. Houses in their own grounds and open fields gave place to rows of terrace housing. By 1875 the company concerned, the Great Eastern, was issuing about 9,000 workmen's tickets per day and the London, Chatham & Dover about half that number. For all London's railways the total reached 25,000 a day by 1882.[45]

At first tickets were issued only to artisans, mechanics and daily labourers who had to give the names and addresses of their employers; but these restrictions were in due course relaxed. By 1883, when the Cheap Trains Act was passed, giving the Board of Trade powers to oblige railway companies to introduce workmen's fares, over 100 workmen's trains were already running daily in the London area. By the early 1890s they started from as far away as Penge (7¼ miles), South Croydon (11½ miles) and even Weybridge (19 miles). Only to the inner suburbs, however, were fares so low as 2*d* return. They extended to such places as Clapham Junction or Herne Hill. Fourpenny returns would bring in passengers from Crystal Palace or Greenwich.[46] Nevertheless, by the end of the nineteenth century, London's railways were enabling an increasing number of the working classes to emulate the better-off.

Outside London, railways siphoned many fewer people from the densely settled urban centres to the outskirts, even in the largest towns, i.e. Glasgow, Manchester, Liverpool and Birmingham. Their populations in 1881 were still only between about 500,000 and 600,000, the size London had reached in 1700. Even in 1901 the largest of them, the Glasgow conurbation, had reached only about 900,000 and in 1911 roughly 1,000,000 (London's population in 1800). Birmingham was then about 850,000 and Manchester and Liverpool each about 750,000. In all these places, as has been seen, horse-drawn transport was already enabling the middle classes to start moving out, and the railways continued this process on a modest scale, as has been shown by Dr Kellett in his detailed study, *The Impact of Railways on Victorian Cities,* and, more recently, by Professor Simmons.[47] New suburban lines were built, for instance, from central Manchester to Altrincham at the end of the 1840s, from central Birmingham to middle-class Selly Oak and King's Norton in the 1870s and their equivalents in other conurbations. Sometimes, as with Cadbury's move to Bournville in 1879, factories moved out, taking advantage of the railway and transferring their work-force to new estates. (Port Sunlight on the Wirral, dating from the end of the 1880s, is another good example.) The even better-off commuted longer distances from their large houses farther afield: from Alderley Edge, for instance, where the businessmen caught the 8.25, 8.50 or 9.18 into Manchester. 'Anyone out early would see them hurrying to the station . . . Dr Hopkinson from Ferns, Mr Schill from Croston Towers, Mr Bles from Underwood, Mr Lees from St Mary's Cliffe . . .'[48] A daily express even rought some very rich people into Manchester from Windermere.

Workmen's fares by rail, as Professor Simmons has observed, 'were essentially London devices'[49] which failed to produce large traffics elsewhere. The Liverpool Overhead Railway, however, was an exception; it catered for dock workers and derived nearly a quarter of its revenue from workmen's tickets;[50] but perhaps only about 1,500 workmen's ticket-holders commuted *into* Liverpool in the 1890s and perhaps about 8,000 into Manchester. In Glasgow, where local rail travel was unusually cheap, working-class commuters travelled outwards from the city centre to Singer's at Clydebank or to the steelworkers at Newton or Coatbridge. There was some outward commuting from Manchester, too. Taking this into account, and also daytime travel by those on shift, Professor Simmons has estimated that the total volume of workmen's travel in the Manchester area may have reached 30,000 per day by 1913. It was then probably at the top of that particular league.[51]

The greater importance of horse tramways

The modest, uninspiring and essentially utilitarian horse tramway was far more important outside London than the railways and has received less credit than it deserves. It involved no major technology and, therefore, has not attracted the attention of the technically-minded; and, because it could be laid along public thoroughfares by arrangement with the local authorities and the 'frontagers' who lived there, no large land purchases or heavy capital expenditure were involved either. By many the horse tram is dismissed as a variant of the horse bus: lumbering, dirty and slow. In economic terms, however, it was a major innovation, for it greatly reduced operating costs per passenger carried.

The rolling resistance of iron wheels on metal rails was much lower than that of omnibus wheels on (usually rough) road surfaces. The same number of horses could, therefore, pull a much heavier vehicle on a tramway and many more fares could be taken. The typical horse tram could seat up to fifty passengers, the horse omnibus, as has been seen, only half that number. Interest on capital invested in the track had to be taken into account and the cars themselves cost more than omnibuses; but the potential increase in revenue was considerably greater than the extra expenditure. There was considerable scope to offer lower fares in order to fill the additional seats and, therefore, to maximise income. Early-morning workmen's trams at very low fares were a feature from the outset, and normal fares were considerably cheaper than those on the horse-omnibuses. The tramcar, as the *Cornhill Magazine* noted in 1890, had become the working man's favourite vehicle. 'He can enscounce himself there in his mortar-splashed clothes without restraint.'[52]

The tramcar also catered for the better-off who patronised the horse bus, not only because of the lower tramway fares but also because of the greater comfort. The larger, new cars had spiral staircases to the top deck and large glass windows below. The ride was smoother, and because the cars ran on smaller wheels, tucked in underneath the lower deck, there was added width and spaciousness inside and a lower loading platform, making it easier to get on and off. The horse trams were, in fact, the first form of public road transport which catered for people of all classes.

Tramways had originated in the United States in the 1830s and had become increasingly popular there from the mid-1850s.[53] George Francis Train's attempts in the early 1860s to introduce them to England in Birkenhead, London, Darlington and the Potteries proved generally unsuccessful, because he used step rails which protruded above the road surface and interfered with all other traffic. Although the Birkenhead venture continued and also that in the Potteries (with a less objectionable form of rail), Train's three 'street railways' in London were soon ordered to be removed.[54] Uninterrupted tramway building dates only from 1868, when the Liverpool Tramways Company obtained a local Act to lay rails there of a type which did not interfere with other traffic. Similar separate Acts were obtained in the following years by three companies to build tramways in different parts of London, all also using grooved rails laid flush with the road.[55] These were acceptable to the public but much harder work for the horses, for they easily became clogged

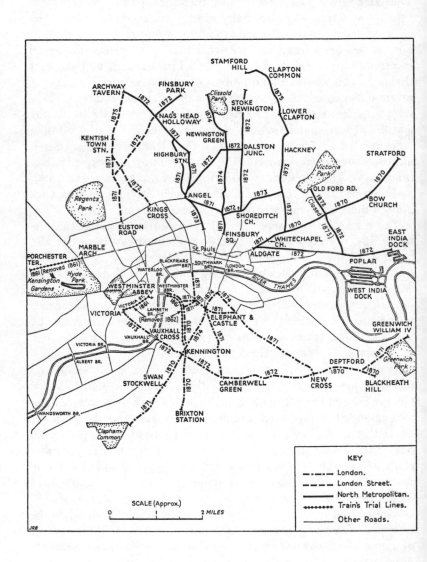

15 London's tramways in 1875 (from T. C. Barker and M. Robbins, *A History of London Transport, Vol. 1, the Nineteenth Century*, Allen & Unwin, 1975, p. 185; London Transport Museum.

by dirt. In 1870 a general Tramways Act was passed which made promotion much easier elsewhere.

Local authorities owned the track which they leased to the operating companies, usually for twenty-one years. They had powers to veto tramways and some kept the newcomers out of residential areas. The City of London banned them altogether, as did some of the West End vestries. In 1872 Parliament itself legislated against all tramway building in central London. This prolonged the life of the horse buses, which were allowed to continue running in the forbidden central streets. But fares on the trams were so reasonable – by 1872 69 per cent of all fares in London were 2*d* and the ride all the way from Westminster Bridge to Greenwich, 6¼ miles, at the normal fare cost only 4*d* – that a large traffic was soon built up. By 1875 nearly 50,000,000 passengers were being carried by horse tram, nearly as many as by the London General's omnibuses; and the tramway system was still incomplete.[56]

As the London system was extended farther outwards, the horse tram served more suburbs previously catered for mainly by the horse bus. More people travelled by day to multiple stores which were then opening in the high streets served by these tramways, by night to places of entertainment, which were also multiplying, and on Saturday afternoons, a half-holiday for an increasing number, to sporting events. By 1896 the horse trams were carrying 280,000,000 passengers in London and the omnibuses, spurred on by the new competition, about 300,000. Average tram fares had by then fallen to just over 1*d*. Two to three-minute frequencies were common. By comparison, London's railway service, much extended both geographically and socially, accounted for considerably fewer journeys than those by road, though each was, on average, longer. Indeed, between 1875 and 1896, London's railway traffic grew only from 170,000,000 to 400,000,000 passengers a year. The combined omnibus and tramway traffic, as has been seen, had grown at a faster rate, from 120,000,000 to 580,000,000.[57] Old horsepower, better organised, was in this respect performing better than the latest steam.

Outside London, where suburban railways were far less important and where horse tramways were usually allowed into busy city centres, their impact was all the greater and horse buses lost passengers. By 1890 the Liverpool United Tramways and Omnibus Company owned 225 trams and only 134 omnibuses (of much smaller capacity).[58] Glasgow, Edinburgh and Aberdeen all had horse trams

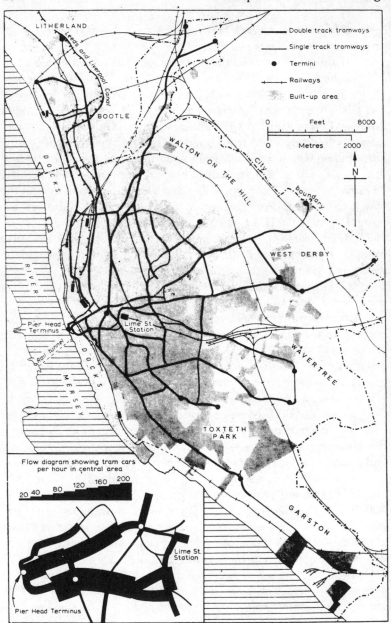

16   Liverpool tramways, 1905 (from H. J. Dyos and D. H. Aldcroft, *British Transport*, Leicester University Press, 1969, p. 221)

running in the early 1870s; the busy routes out of Birmingham to Handsworth and Edgbaston were served, from 1873 and 1876 respectively; Manchester, though cautious at the outset, also soon had horse trams running through the centre from all quarters, and Bristol even created its own Tramway Centre.[59] By the 1880s, towns even of 50,000 population possessed tramcars.[60]

By the 1880s attempts were made to mechanise these tramways. Cable traction was successful on a few hilly routes such as those up Highgate Hill in north London or over the steep ridge between Princes Street and Queen Street in Edinburgh. The latter tramway was extended and became eventually the fourth largest cable system in the world, thirty-six track miles. When Glasgow's subway was opened in 1896, it was cable-hauled.[61] Steam was inevitably tried in many places but usually not for long; sparks can be dangerous in busy thoroughfares and smoke was most unwelcome to passengers on the top deck, fumes from coke little less so. Nevertheless, steam traction was adopted on less densely settled routes, for instance in the Rossendale Valley, or out of Wednesbury in Staffordshire, carefully avoiding Wednesbury High Street and Market Place.[62] Over 500 steam trams were operating in various parts of Britain in the mid-1890s.[63] though in lightly-populated industrial, rather than specifically urban, areas.

Electrification

Electricity for lighting purposes spread from the later 1870s and the new means of transmitting energy was soon used to drive motors. For traction purposes a number of problems had to be solved. After various experiments in different parts of the world, in 1888 an able American, Frank J. Sprague, managed to provide all the answers at Richmond, Virginia. He demonstrated successfully the overhead trolley, the series/parallel controller and a method of mounting each motor, 'wheelbarrow fashion', partly on the axle and partly by springs to the tramcar frame. The early motors were of low horsepower but they made possible speeds twice as fast as were possible using horses, capable of serving longer routes; and much faster tramcars were later developed. More important, operating costs were much lower than with teams of horses. When interest on the larger amounts of fixed capital was taken into account, the savings were very considerable. Lower fares, as well as better

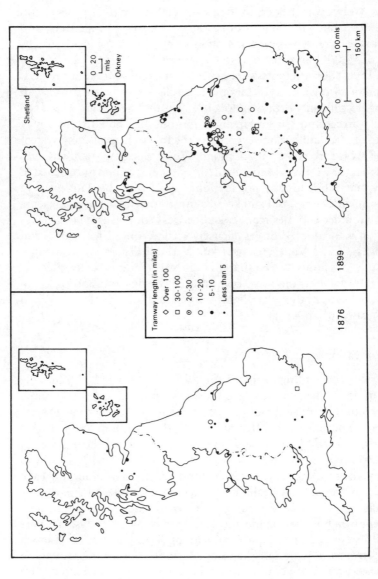

17 Trams, 1876–99 (from R. J. Morris in J. Langton and R. J. Morris (eds.), *Atlas of Industrializing Britain*, Methuen, 1986, p. 175)

Tramway length (in miles)

◇ Over 100
□ 30–100
⊙ 20–30
○ 10–20
● 5–10
· Less than 5

Shetland

Orkney

0   20
mls

1876   1899

100mls
150 km

0
0

services, could be offered. The already popular tramcar became even more popular.

Electrification of the tramcars, and the greater profits they offered, attracted American capital, and two large manufacturers eventually emerged, General Electric and Westinghouse, to mass-produce standardised equipment at low cost. Cuts in journey times and lowering of fares encouraged further outward growth, as electric tramways were built beyond the existing limits of Boston and other American cities.[64] 'Electric traction in the United States', remarked a British tramway specialist in 1893, 'is encouraged primarily by estate agents and speculators. . . . The estates were worth very little – probably they were only agricultural or waste land – but they have been developed by those means. The profit derived by the speculation has in many instances more than paid for the electrical street railway.'[65] By 1890, one-fifth of the total length of tramway in the United States was already being operated electrically, and by 1895 nearly 12,600 miles had been built there; only 1,250 miles of horse-drawn line remained.[66]

The British were slow to follow America's example partly because many companies, whose 21-year leases from local authorities were about to end, were reluctant to indulge in capital expenditure of any sort and partly because, in that era of gas-and-water socialism (also extended to embrace electricity works), many local authorities were keen to acquire, electrify and work the tramways themselves. These authorities worked through committees of elected representatives who, not well versed in the new technology, had to seek outside advice and took time to make up their minds, appreciating that, in a period of technical development, delay probably meant a better product in the long run.

After a few isolated ventures, on the promenade at Blackpool, at Bradford, Leeds and elsewhere, the opening of electric tramways started in earnest in Britain in 1895, in Bristol, using American equipment. (The Americans, having saturated their home market by then, were pressing harder for orders abroad.[67]) Other towns soon followed suit. Liverpool Corporation, for instance, which acquired seventy-five track miles from the private horse tramway company when its lease ended in September 1897, had its first stretch of electrified line open in November of the following year and the whole system converted and extended into the newer suburbs by 1902. Glasgow Corporation, too, had replaced all its horse trams by then and suburban railways soon lost traffic.[68] Manchester Corporation, which owned its electricity works, took its tramways into public ownership as soon as the private company's lease ran out in 1901. The Corporation Tramways Committee adopted a policy of reducing ordinary fares as much as possible and making everyone pay alike. Traffic there grew impressively, from 23.6 million passengers in 1902, when electric trams started running, to 206 million in 1913/14. The undertaking not only paid for itself but was soon contributing over £50,000 per year in support of the rates.[69]

In London the County Council took this policy of municipal control even further. The Progressive Party saw that really low fares were the best means of relieving overcrowded accommodation in the centre, which still persisted despite the transport improvements already described. When electric trams began to run south from the river to Clapham and Tooting, therefore, in 1903, it introduced ordinary ½d fares to stages up to 1,600 yards, 1d fares up to 2½ miles, 2d up to 5 miles and 3d for all longer distances. Workmen's tickets, available on all journeys ending before 8 a.m. (and on those trams which ran all night) cost 2d return to the terminus at Tooting, six miles away, near where the LCC began to lay out a Council estate. The cottages, with sculleries and small gardens, were self-supporting at rents of 7s or 7s 6d per week, considerably less than anything of similar standard in smoky central London, even after a shilling a week had been added for tram fares.[70] Such rents could be afforded only by better-off skilled workers; but there were other less expensive dwellings to be had elsewhere along the tram route. As in Manchester, a vast new traffic was created which was further increased when the LCC acquired the tramways north of the river (and connected them to its southern system via the Victoria Embankment and a tunnel under the new thoroughfare, Kingsway). LCC tramway traffic increased from 117 million journeys in 1903 to 505 million in 1910 (42 million of the latter workmen's).[71] Charles Masterman, the Liberal politician and writer, who moved to Camberwell just before the arrival of the electric tramway, compared it most favourably with the 'few erratic horse omnibuses and lines of slow-moving, two-horse trams'. How different were the 'fast lines of electric trams, brilliantly lighted, in which reading is a pleasure, hurrying us down from over the bridges at half the time expended under the old conditions. Each workman . . . has had an hour added to his life – half an hour actually saved from the transit and half an hour given back to him in the transit.'[72] Sir Robert Ensor, the journalist and historian, who lived in Poplar from 1904 to 1910, likened this London exodus to 'the draining of the marshes'. He added:

It is true that the movement went by layers, and when Poplar transferred to East Ham, Walworth to Wandsworth, or North Camberwell to Lewisham, the places left vacant might be filled from more central and crowded areas; true also, that the new houses . . . took the best-off and not the neediest workers. Nevertheless, especially between 1905 and 1910, the net social gain was great . . .'.

The same effect was felt elsewhere. Tramway traffic throughout Britain grew threefold, from about 1,000,000 passengers to 3,300,000 per year between 1900 and 1913. Trolley-buses came into service in Leeds and Bradford in 1911 and in Dundee in 1912; but this form of electric traction was as yet of only nascent importance.[73]

Electric traction also began to be applied to some urban railways, especially in London. It made possible the construction of the capital's deep tubes. The first of these, the City & South London, was opened to Stockwell in 1890 and extended to Clapham in the south and the Angel in the north in 1901. In the previous year the Central London Railway (now the Central Line), which ran under the main thoroughfare from Shepherd's Bush to the Bank, came into service and compensated to some extent for the ban on tramways in the heart of London. By 1907 all the tubes within London itself (apart from the relatively recently built Victoria and Jubilee Lines) were open for traffic, although most of them originally stopped within the outer limits of the existing built-up area and were extended only after the First World War. Even so, they greatly supplemented the passenger-carrying capacity of the existing underground and stimulated urban development, especially in the Golder's Green/Hampstead Garden Suburb area which all railways had until then passed by. By 1914 the new tubes were carrying about 200 million passengers a year.

By then the steam underground had also been electrified (1905), not only in the middle of London but also as far out as Wimbledon, Hounslow, South Harrow and Uxbridge. Because of their greater speed and acceleration, up to forty trains per hour could be run on the busiest part of the system from the City via Charing Cross to South Kensington. Despite the big improvement in service, however,

mechanised road transport proved a strong competitor. The Metropolitan was hard put to maintain its traffic at about 100 million
passengers a year. The Metropolitan District, however, catering for
the new western suburbs and those living out towards East Ham as
well as the very busy urban stretch, increased its carryings from
about 50 million to about 75 million between 1906 and 1910.[74]

London's main-line suburban services were also improved, and
some electrification was embarked upon south of the river in order to
win back traffic lost to the new electric trams. The South London
Loop, from London Bridge to Victoria via Peckham Rye and Brix-
ton, was electrified in 1909, and the line from Victoria to Crystal
Palace in 1911. These and the other main-line services accounted for
about 250 million journeys just before 1914, bringing the total
traffic on London's railways, tube, underground and main-line
suburban, to just over 700 million by that time,[75] 75 per cent greater
than it had been little more than a decade before at the end of the
nineteenth century. But even in London, with a population of over
seven million, sprawling over a huge area then stretching from Ealing
to Woolwich and from Enfield to Croydon and therefore depending
heavily on rail travel, all these lines were carrying fewer passengers
than the 800 million who then travelled by the more accessible tram
car.[76]

In the provinces, where railways were relatively less important
because towns were much smaller, there was much less railway
electrification to combat tramway competition. Notable exceptions
were three lines in Liverpool (the Overhead, electric from the start in
1893; the Mersey Railway, electrified in 1903; and the railway to
Aintree and Ormskirk, electrified between 1906 and 1913) and,
most important of all and much referred to, the Newcastle, Tyne-
mouth and Whitley Bay loop which served sixty stations within ten
miles of Newcastle Central. Professor Simmons has shown that it
increased its traffic from 6.9 million per year to nearly 8.5 million per
year between the 1890s and 1900–07, though the total fell a little
after that.[77]

Motorisation

The internal combustion engine, first applied to very light moving
vehicles in Germany in the mid-1880s, took longer to be developed
commercially than the electric tramcar because more complex, and

more numerous, technical problems confronted the engineers involved.[78] Motor cars, tricycles, and, later, bicycles, remained rudimentary and few in number until the early years of the twentieth century, and heavier motor vehicles took longer to develop. The first experimental motor buses, which came on to Britain's roads at the very end of the nineteenth century, were commercially unsuccessful;[79] but early in the twentieth century a few of them managed to maintain a service on lightly-trafficked routes either outside towns (the Great Western Railway, for instance, from 1903, used them to save building new branch lines in Cornwall), and in places with little traffic such as Eastbourne, also from 1903.[80] Motor buses, however, were not robust enough to operate in heavy urban traffic, and a number of companies which were floated in 1905 to run them in London, where they still had a monopoly in central streets, soon went out of business after the vibrating vehicles kept breaking down and eventually shook themselves to pieces. Some existing London horse bus operators also lost money by moving prematurely to motors. The London General, however, wisely held back. Not until 1909 did it develop a satisfactory motor bus and not until 1910 did this start to run in service, along with an improved model, the 'B' type. Motors were, however, then rapidly adopted; the General operated no horse buses after October 1911 and it soon bought out other motor bus competitors. Just under 2,000 were licensed in London in 1911: in 1913 this total had been increased to over 3,500. Most of them seated thirty-five passengers, ten more than the displaced horse bus.[81]

These vehicles not only had greater carrying capacity but they also ran at greater speeds and operated at lower cost. They were more manoeuvrable than the electric trams and could traverse busy thoroughfares more readily. They could also open new routes and extend existing ones up to fifteen miles or more. Whereas only twelve horse bus services had run out of Victoria, for instance, covering in all ninety-three miles, motor buses were soon operating on forty routes, covering 371 miles. Many new services were started in the suburbs where new garages were opened. By 1914 these services stretched from Golder's Green station, terminus of one of the new tube lines, to St Albans and from Stockwell to Reigate. Equally important, lower operating costs made possible lower fares. The new motor buses were never exclusively middle-class vehicles starting at middle-class times as their horse-drawn predecessors had been. The number of bus journeys in the London area shot up from 401 million in 1911 to 757 million in 1914, within fifty million of the electric tramways' impressive total.[82]

Outside London, where electric tramways penetrated town centres and played a relatively greater role, and where the municipalities, often their operators, were reluctant to encourage competition, motor buses made much less headway. Their main field of activity, with a subsidiary of British Electric Traction very much to the fore, seems to have been outside towns in areas where the electric tramways had not penetrated or beyond the tramways' outer termini.[83] In Manchester the motor buses carried only about one million passengers per year just before 1914; Manchester tramways were then carrying 206 million.[84] Even after the war, Manchester Corporation Tramways Committee short-sightedly believed that, because so many of its tram routes connected with those of other authorities, the scope for motor buses even beyond its boundaries was strictly limited.[85] In Birmingham, where the Birmingham & Midland Omnibus Co. Ltd (Midland Red) had, in 1905, acquired twenty-seven undependable motor and 119 horse buses, it soon abandoned the former and continued to work with horses until more serviceable motor vehicles became available in 1912. Birmingham Corporation started to run motor buses in 1913 and in the following year acquired all other motor buses then running within its boundaries.[86] No statistics have so far been collected in any systematic way for motor bus operations outside London before 1914 and Dr Hibbs, the authority on this subject, contents himself with the ultra-cautious conclusion that 'most of the larger towns and cities had services of some kind'.[87] Munby estimated a total of 6,000 motor buses licensed throughout Britain in 1914.[88] We know that 3,500 of these were licensed in the London area, a much larger proportion to the rest of the country than of trams (about 2,800 in London and 13,000 throughout the country). As we also know that, unlike the tramways, the motor buses served lightly-trafficked routes, often outside towns, it is clear that even in 1914 the impact of motor buses in towns outside London was strictly limited and of relatively recent date.

There were also more smaller motorised passenger vehicles on urban roads. Private motoring was costly and much of it, by car or motor cycle, was described as 'pleasure motoring', presumably to get out of towns; but doctors, commercial travellers and others soon found it paid to become mechanised. By April 1904 about 30,000 motor cars and cycles had been licensed in Britain; 4,600 of them were in the London area, 700 in Birmingham, 560 in Manchester, 390 in Liverpool, 220 in Glasgow and about the same number in Edinburgh.[89] The total for the whole of Britain grew eightfold between then and 1914, to about 250,000, half of them motor bikes.[90] Motor cabs also spread quickly. The first appeared on London's streets, for instance, in 1903. Equipped with taximeters from 1907, the total grew to 8,400 by 1913. Under 2,000 horse-drawn hackney cabs and coaches then remained in the capital.[91] A traffic census carried out in the London area in that year showed that only 6 per cent of all passenger vehicles were then horse drawn.[92] Presumably horses involved with passenger transport were disappearing at roughly the same rate in other British towns.

Most goods traffic, however, remained unmechanised. The census of 1913, just mentioned, revealed that 88 per cent of London's road goods vehicles were still horse drawn. Carts and wagons were much less intensively used. Relays of horses were not required and speed was much less important. There was much standing about collecting and delivering. Small, horse-drawn delivery areas were still common in busy urban centres. Carter Paterson, for instance, in 1914, still had 800 such districts in central London, each of them only half a mile square.[93] Under these circumstances the motor vehicles of those days were more costly to own and operate, though motor vans did come into increasing use where fast delivery was an advantage and where the incidental advertisement of the shop, store or newspaper on the vehicle's side as it sped through the streets was an added gain. And, as more reliable heavier petrol vehicles became available to supplement, and later replace, steam lorries, these were increasingly used for larger loads over distances greater than those which could be served by horse, thus avoiding the need for crating or more careful packing and the transfer to and from railway goods wagons. Pickford's, for instance, used motors for transfer work between City Basin and in Brentford, Fulham and Kingston from 1904. The operational range was speedily pushed out to thirty or forty miles.[94]

There is evidence that the railways were beginning to suffer from such motor transport competition in the years before 1914, for railway merchandise traffic, 114 million tons for the whole country in 1900, fell below that figure during the Edwardian period, when total traffic growth was not arrested, and returned to it only during the very prosperous boom years just before 1914.[95] The total number of goods vehicles of all sorts in Britain, many of them small delivery vans, grew from 4,000 in 1904 to 64,000 in 1913.[96] Many of these were running from, in or through towns. As Edwin Pratt noted, in a book published in 1912:

In almost every class of trade or business, the commercial motor is being steadily substituted for horse vehicles. There are large retail houses in London which have each their 'fleets' of up to fifty or sixty motor-vans or lorries. The carrying companies would hardly be able to provide their extensive suburban services today without road motors. Fishmongers, ice merchants and fruit salesmen, who especially require to have a speedy means of distributing their wares, favour the commercial motor no less than do the managers of evening newspapers. Laundry companies – to whose business great impetus has been given of late years by the increasing resort to residential flats – find commercial motors of great service in the collections that have been made on Mondays and Tuesdays and the deliveries effected on Fridays and Saturdays . . . Brewers, mineral water manufacturers, oil companies, coal merchants, pianoforte makers, brick makers and scores of other traders besides, are all taking to the new form of street or road transport.[97]

Growing complaints of traffic congestion were heard from all city centres. A major cause was the surviving, slow-moving horse-drawn freight traffic taking up more than its fair share of road space as the horses moved, or stood, in their shafts well ahead of the vehicles behind them. As faster motor vehicles replaced these slow movers, the position improved; but this lay in the future. It was not until the 1920s and 1930s that most horse-drawn freight traffic was replaced. Street scenes of that period show – for a short spell – much freer movement, at least in the main thoroughfares.

The early motor vehicles created much new pollution of various sorts. Oil dripped on to the roads in quantities nowadays unknown. Clouds of smoke resulted from imperfect combustion and loud bangs from ill-timed engines. The early machines vibrated a great deal and were very noisy. But each horse deposited up to 7½ tons of manure per year somewhere or other, much of it on urban streets.[98] This extremely unhealthy, fly-ridden nuisance, having grown during the nineteenth century, had been substantially reduced by motor competition by 1914. Were not oil drippings and the rest preferable to horse droppings?

The bicycle, the form of transport generally welcomed without reserve by all environmentalists, became more widely used in these

Edwardian years. Safety bicycles had been available from the 1880s but at a price so high (about £20) that only well-to-do young swells could afford them. The mid-1890s had seen a boom in the industry, largely caused by a new demand for bicycles from middle-class women. After the boom, prices had fallen and had reached just under £5 by 1908. There was also a thriving second-hand market.[99] Many of those who had been obliged to walk considerable distances were able to buy bikes. Shops used them for delivering goods. There were obviously many more machines on urban roads as the years passed but we have no official statistics; the pedal cycle was seen as of such general utility that it was never taxed in Britain.

Retrospect

The growth of passenger transport in Britain's towns was a function of urban size, purchasing power and transport cost. During the nineteenth century most journeys were short and most people walked. As towns grew outwards and journeys became longer, however, those who wished to ride, and could afford to do so, could take advantage of the short-stage coach and, from about 1830, the horse omnibus. Railways soon provided suburban services in London and, in a much more limited way, in some of the largest cities elsewhere; but for many years the fares were such that, as with the horse buses, the majority of people could not afford to use them. Yet these facilities by road and, to a much smaller extent, by rail, enabled the middle classes to move out of city centres to the more salubrious suburbs as the centres themselves became more commercialised and congested. Hackney carriages, long available in these places, could still be hired and greater competition brought improved vehicles on to the roads and a completely new type, the two-horse cab. The really wealthy rode in their own private carriages.

The most significant development of the century occurred in 1864, when the new London underground railway started to provide cheap early-morning workmen's trains. Other companies in the ever-expanding London area followed suit. So, a few years later, did the new horse tramways, which had lower operating costs per passenger seat. In the other main towns, where journey distances were not usually long enough to encourage much local rail travel, horse trams were of paramount importance; and in London itself, despite their banning from the City and West End, they were soon carrying as many passengers as the more expensive and exclusive horse buses, even though the latter had been building up traffic for forty years and more. A new trend was established as, during the last quarter of the nineteenth century, real earnings rose and public transport fares fell. The mechanisation of road transport after the later 1890s hastened this process; it did not start it.

In the 1830s much movement of goods in towns depended on human energy either by direct bodily carriage or aided by a barrow or handcart. In subsequent years horses increasingly supplemented these human efforts, the number of horses used to move freight throughout Britain probably increasing fivefold between 1851 and 1911. Mechanisation, in the form of the motor van or motor lorry, only began to have a very limited impact in the years just before 1914.

Urban transport remains a rather neglected aspect of transport history. Further investigation is needed on a town-by-town basis to discover to what extent the social composition of these places or major physical barriers, such as a coastal zone, wide rivers or steep hills, may have affected the broad pattern here outlined. This chapter has attempted to indicate the present state of knowledge about a broad, fascinating subject which, as an interdisciplinary study concerning changes in the various transport modes, demographic and spatial growth of towns and growing purchasing power, is still in its infancy. The greatest rewards, however, await those who are prepared to mine new seams of scholarship.

Notes

1   F. M. L. Thompson, 'Nineteenth-century horse sense', *Economic History Review*, XXIX, 1976, p. 80.

2   See detail from Froggett's *Survey of the County Thirty Miles Round London* (GLC Collection), reproduced in Francis Sheppard, *London 1808–1870: The Infernal Wen*, 1971, between pp. 84 and 85.

3   Sir George Head, *A Home Tour Through the Manufacturing Districts of England in the Summer of 1835*, 1836.

4   Walter M. Stern, *The Porters of London*, 1960, pp. 56–9.

5   Henry Mayhew, *London Labour and the London Poor*, 1851, reprinted Cass, 1967, Vol. II, pp. 1, 82, 85.

6   *Ibid.*, I, p. 44.

7   *Ibid.*, I, p. 27.

8   *Ibid.*, II, p. 86.

9   *Ibid.*

10 Thompson, p. 80.

11 W. J. Gordon, *The Horse World of London*, 1893, pp. 49, 67, 69, 74, 84.

12 Gerard L. Turnbull, *Traffic and Transport*, 1979, p. 136.

13 Thompson, p. 69.

14 Alan Everitt, 'Town and country in Victorian Leicestershire: the role of the village carrier', in Alan Everitt (ed.), *Perspectives in English Urban History*, 1973, pp. 213–40; *id.*, 'Country carriers in the nineteenth century', *Journal of Transport History*, III, 3, February 1976, pp. 179–202.

15 Thompson, p. 80.

16 Evidence of Charles Pearson to the Royal Commission on Metropolitan Termini, 1846 [91] XVII, question 375.

17 John Summerson, *Georgian London*, 1945.

18 *Ibid.*, p. 159.

19 H. J. Dyos, *Victorian Suburb*, Leicester, 1961, p. 38.

20 *Baldwin's New Complete Guide to all Persons who have any Trade or Concern with the City of London and Parts Adjacent*, 11th edn, 1768.

21 For these beginnings, see T. C. Barker and Michael Robbins, *A History of London Transport*, 1963, I, chs. 1, 2.

22 *Ibid.*, p. 39.

23 *The Penny Magazine*, 31 March 1837.

24 Barker and Robbins, I, pp. 26, 37, 57–8.

25 F. M. L. Thompson, *Hampstead. Building of a Borough, 1650–1964*, 1974, p. 55. For the built-up area at various dates in the nineteenth century, see map, *ibid.*, pp. 42–3.

26 Dyos, pp. 67–9.

27 Barker and Robbins, I, ch. 3.

28 *Ibid.*, p. 66.

29 F. M. L. Thompson, *Victorian England: The Horse-drawn Society*, 1970, p. 16.

30 Gordon, pp. 101–5.

31 Thompson, *Victorian England*, p. 17.

32 Gordon, p. 102.

33 Barker and Robbins, I, pp. 251–2.

34 Quoted in Donald J. Olsen, *The Growth of Victorian London*, 1976, p. 19.

35 Brunel University, David Garnett Collection. Insets in Map of Railways in England, Wales and Scotland by Kell Brothers, 1875.

36 *The Times*, 9 September 1830.

37 W. O. Henderson and W. H. Chaloner (trans. and eds.), *Engels' Conditions of the Working Class in England*, Oxford, 1971, p. 55.

38 Arthur Redford, *The History of Local Government in Manchester*, II, 1940, pp. 19, 85–6.

39 John R. Kellett, *The Impact of Railways on Victorian Cities*, 1969, pp. 139, 360–2; Alec G. Jenson, 'Early omnibus services in Birmingham, 1834–1905', in John Hibbs (ed.), *The Omnibus*, Newton Abbot, 1971, pp. 113 ff.

40 *Ibid.*, pp. 315, 354; Michael Simpson, 'Urban transport and the development of Glasgow's West End, 1830–1914', *Journal of Transport*

History, new ser., I, 3, February 1972, pp. 147–50.

41 G. C. Dickinson, 'The development of suburban road passenger transport in Leeds, 1840–1895', *Journal of Transport History,* IV, 4, November 1960, p. 217.

42 This paragraph and the next two are based upon Barker and Robbins, I, ch. 2. See also Michael Robbins, *The North London Railway,* 1937, and subsequent editions.

43 Jack Simmons, *The Railway in Town and Country 1830–1914,* Newton Abbot, 1986, p. 64. Ch. 3 of this book is concerned with the suburban expansion of London. For the Greenwich line, see R. H. G. Thomas, *London's First Railway,* London, 1972; paperback reprint 1986.

44 H. J. Dyos, 'Railways and housing in Victorian London', *Journal of Transport History,* II, 1, May 1955, pp. 11–21; II, 2, November 1955, pp. 90–100; 'Some social costs of railway building in London', *Journal of Transport History,* III, 1, May 1957, pp. 23–30.

45 Simmons, p. 83.

46 H. J. Dyos, 'Workmen's fares in South London, 1860–1914', *Journal of Transport History,* I, 1, May 1953, pp. 3–19.

47 Kellett, 87–99; Simmons, ch. 4, which also provides maps of railways in six provincial cities and a table (p. 116) of passenger journeys, 1890–99, 1900–07, and 1908–13 in five of them.

48 Katharine Chorley, *Manchester Made Them,* 1960, p. 114. For Alderley Edge, see also Simmons, p. 113.

49 Simmons, p. 120.

50 *Ibid.,* p. 121.

51 Kellett, pp. 93–4, 355; Simmons, pp. 120–3. A good summary of the position in Glasgow will be found in Colin Johnstone and John R. Hume, *Glasgow Stations,* Newton Abbot, 1979, ch. 6.

52 *The Cornhill Magazine,* March 1890, pp. 303–4.

53 John Anderson Miller, *Fares, Please!,* New York, 1960, ch. 2.

54 Charles E. Lee, 'The English street tramways of George Francis Train', *Journal of Transport History,* I, 1 & 2, May and November 1953.

55 Charles Klapper, *The Golden Age of Tramways,* 1961, pp. 31–2, 85–6; Barker and Robbins, I, pp. 183–97.

56 *Ibid.,* p. 196.

57 *Ibid.,* p. 263.

58 Klapper, pp. 86–7.

59 *Ibid.,* ch. xiv, pp. 133, 149, 176.

60 T. C. Barker and J. R. Harris, *A Merseyside Town in the Industrial Revolution,* Liverpool, 1954, p. 455.

61 Klapper, pp. 49, 222–3; Johnstone and Hume, pp. 127–9.

62 John F. Ede, *History of Wednesbury,* Wednesbury, 1962, p. 329.

63 Klapper, p. 47.

64 Sam B. Warner, *Streetcar Suburbs,* Cambridge, Mass., 1962; Charles W. Cheape, *Moving the Masses: Urban Public Transport in New York, Boston and Philadelphia, 1880–1912,* Cambridge, Mass., 1980.

65 A. Reckenzaun, commenting on Edward Hopkinson's paper, 'Electrical railways: The City & South London Railway', *Proceedings of the*

Institution of Civil Engineers, 112, 1893, p. 235.
  66 Barker and Robbins, II, pp. 16–19.
  67 *Ibid.,* pp. 21–2.
  68 Klapper, pp. 87–8, 211–12; Johnstone and Hume, pp. 109–13.
  69 Redford, III, pp. 43–6, ch. XXXIV; A. D. Keate, *Passenger Transport in Manchester, 1914–1939,* M.Sc. Report, LSE Economic History Department, pp. 6–13.
  70 Alan A. Jackson, *Semi-Detached London,* 1973, pp. 54–5; Barker and Robbins, II, pp. 91–101.
  71 *Ibid.,* II, pp. 94–5, 99.
  72 Quoted in Lucy Masterman, *C.F.G. Masterman,* 1939, pp. 82–3.
  73 D. L. Munby, *Inland Transport Statistics. Great Britain 1900–1970,* I, Oxford 1978, pp. 296–7; R. C. K. Ensor, *England 1870–1914,* Oxford, 1936, pp. 509–10; Nicholas Owen, *History of the British Trolley Bus,* Newton Abbot, 1974, ch. 1.
  74 Barker and Robbins, II, p. 149. This paragraph, the preceding and suceeding one are based upon this source unless otherwise stated.
  75 Munby, p. 537.
  76 *Ibid.*
  77 Simmons, p. 116. See also R. J. Irving, *The North Eastern Railway Company, 1870–1914. An Economic History,* Leicester, 1976, pp. 257–8.
  78 Theo Barker (ed.), *The Economic and Social Effect of the Spread of Motor Vehicles,* 1987, ch. 1.
  79 Barker and Robbins, II, ch. 6.
  80 John Hibbs, *The History of British Bus Services,* Newton Abbot, 1968, pp. 47–8, 64.
  81 Barker and Robbins, II, pp. 167–70, 182; *Commercial Motor,* XVI, 10 October 1912, pp. 105–14.
  82 Barker and Robbins, II, p. 185.
  83 Hibbs, pp. 59 ff.
  84 Keate, p. 13.
  85 Redford, III, p. 282.
  86 Hibbs, p. 65; Jenson, p. 146.
  87 Hibbs, p. 64.
  88 Munby, p. 226.
  89 Return of Motor Cars, *British Parliamentary Papers,* 1904 [292], LXXXIX.
  90 B. R. Mitchell and Phyllis Deane, *Abstract of British Historical Statistics,* Cambridge, 1962, p. 230.
  91 Barker and Robbins, II, p. 329.
  92 *Ibid.,* p. 190.
  93 Turnbull, p. 50.
  94 *Ibid.,* pp. 151, 153.
  95 Munby, pp. 83, 100.
  96 Mitchell and Deane, p. 230.
  97 Edwin A. Pratt, *A History of Inland Transport and Communication,* 1912; repr. Newton Abbot, 1970, p. 484.
  98 Thompson, *Victorian England,* p. 10.

99 Anthony Edward Harrison, 'Growth, Entrepreneurship and Capital Formation in the United Kingdom Cycle and Related Industries, 1870–1914' University of York Ph.D., 1977, p. 307. Professor Feinstein has published an article based on the late Dr Harrison's work (A. E. Harrison, 'The origins and growth of the UK cycle industry to 1900', *Journal of Transport History*, 3rd ser., VI, 1, March 1985, pp. 41–70).

Coastal shipping

The growth of British coastal shipping

The years between the accession of Queen Victoria in 1837 and the outbreak of the First World War in 1914 may be considered as the Golden Age of British coastal shipping. The tonnage of shipping engaged in the coastal trade very nearly trebled in this period. W. G. Hoffman found that 'coastal shipping expanded in a surprisingly steady manner right up to . . . 1914'.[1] This impressive performance is summarised in table 5.

Whether the British economy was booming – as was the case for much of the period 1850–75 – or was experiencing depression – as in most of the years 1875–95 – the tonnage of ships engaged in the coastal trade grew by just over 1½ per cent annually. This broadly corresponded with the rate of growth of the population of Great Britain, but was below that of the economy which expanded in the order of 3 to 3½ per cent per annum up to 1872, declining to about 2 per cent for the remainder of the century.

Table 5 shows that at the beginning of Victoria's reign the tonnage of sailing vessels engaged in the coastwise freight trade was three-and-a-quarter times the tonnage of the steam vessels similarly engaged. By the later 1860s, however, the steam tonnage was the greater and by 1912–13 it was twelve times that of the sailing vessels. The dominance of the steamship, with its greater average tonnage, larger freight-carrying capacity, and quicker turn-around times, was a key factor in the continuing importance of the coastal trade. By the outbreak of the First World War there was a fairly clear division of labour between steamers and sailing vessels in the coastwise trade. The steamers dominated bulk trade between the large ports where there were adequate docking facilities for loading and unloading cargoes. For this trade the tendency was for the size of the vessels to

Table 5 *Vessels entering UK ports in the coastal trade with cargoes, (five-yearly averages)*

Years	No. (000)		Tonnage (000)		Total	
	Sail	Steam	Sail	Steam	No. (000)	Tonnage (000)
1837–41	132	15	9,424	2,876	147	12,300
1842–46	138	16	9,946	3,405	154	13,351
1847–51	139	19	10,300	4,309	158	14,609
1852–56	129	22	9,873	5,363	151	15,236
1857–61	123	29	9,403	7,157	152	16,560
1862–66	120	32	9,150	8,821	152	17,971
1867–71	105	37	8,171	10,107	142	18,278
1872–76[a]	125	50	8,455	13,308	175	21,763
1877–81	131	64	8,805	16,848	195	25,653
1882–86	121	78	8,090	18,865	199	26,955
1887–91	116	93	7,388	21,407	209	28,795
1892–96	107	103	6,368	24,669	210	31,037
1897–1901[b]	69	116	4,477	26,776	185	31,253
1902–06	55	127	3,653	28,605	182	32,258
1907–11	46	120	3,026	28,547	166	31,573
1912–13	39	129	2,610	31,347	168	33,957

Notes:

[a] In 1873 the basis for recording vessels changed. Before that date vessels with certain low-value cargoes, such as manure, flints and chalk, were not recorded. After 1873 they were recorded.

[b] From 1898 trade within the Thames estuary (generously defined to include Rochester, Faversham and Colchester) ceased to count as 'trade by sea', so the figures for these ports dropped quite significantly.

These figures do not include ships carrying passengers only, e.g. ferries, which were recorded as 'in ballast' if they neither loaded nor discharged cargo.

Sources: B.P.P., Annual Statements of Navigation and Shipping.

increase. It rose from an average of 191.7 tons in 1837–41 to 243 tons in 1912–13. Sailing vessels survived for services to the smaller ports, where docking facilities were inadequate for the larger capacity steamers and where protracted time was needed to load and unload specialised cargoes such as Portmadoc slates or Portland stone. In contrast with the growing size of steamships, sailing vessels declined in average size from 71.4 tons in 1837–41 to 66.9 tons in 1912–13.[2] By and large steam vessels predominated in the liner trades, engaged on a regular pattern of routes, for example, the Aberdeen–London meat trade and the coal trade between Newcastle and London (at least in the later nineteenth century and after), while the sailing vessels were more generally employed in the tramp trade on varied and irregular routes.

For three-quarters of the period from 1837 to 1914 the tonnage of vessels with cargoes entering ports in the coastal trade exceeded that of vessels coming from abroad. It was not until the 1890s that the 'foreign and colonial' shipping entries exceeded in register tonnage the entries in the domestic trade, though by 1914 they had forged ahead and were one-and-a-half times as great. The importance of coastal shipping should not be exaggerated in comparison with the overseas trade. Since the ships entering British ports from abroad generally had much longer voyages they docked in Britain less frequently; but the work they performed, measured in ton-miles, was substantially greater throughout the period.

Coastal shipping's contribution to transport provision

The years before 1914 are frequently referred to as 'the Age of the Railway'. One social historian wrote of the railway's 'unchallenged supremacy in every major field of transport'.[3] While this latter statement is broadly true in respect of long-distance passenger travel it misrepresents the situation in freight transport. With few exceptions,[4] transport historians have either ignored coastal shipping[5] or given it very scant coverage.[6] For these reasons the attempt has been made elsewhere to calculate the share of coastal shipping in the total provision of freight transport in Britain and to compare its contribution to that of the canals and railways.[7] In that article the shortcomings of the official statistics, which are most imperfect for the coastal trade, were explained, and reasons given as to why total ton-milage worked is the most appropriate measure to show relative shares of different transport modes. The statistics available for 1910 show that the three forms of transport aimed at different segments of the market, so avoiding head-on competition. The canals, by the early twentieth century, had been relegated to short hauls – 17.5 miles on average – and a total tonnage of nearly forty million tons, so that the total non-mileage worked out at about 690 million. The railway system carried a vastly greater tonnage, more than 330 million tons, a longer average haul, perhaps forty miles, so that their ton-mileage worked was approximately thirteen billion, over eighteen times as much as the canals. The coasters had the longest haul of the three modes, 251 miles, greatly in excess of both the canal and the railway. The tonnage of goods coastal shipping carried was just under seventy-five million tons, twice the tonnage carried by the canals but less than one-quarter of that of the railways. However, when the total ton-mileage of the coaster is calculated, by multiplying the average haul by the total tonnage, it works out at over eighteen billion ton-miles, greater than the railways and canals added together. It may, therefore, be concluded that in 1910 coastal shipping provided the lion's share – nearly 60 per cent – of freight transport compared with the railways' 40 per cent, when measured in ton-miles. The canals contributed an insignificant 2 per cent to total ton-mileage, but a rather more respectable 9 per cent in total tonnage carried. The railway network carried more tonnage, 75 per cent of total, than the two water-based modes added together, with the coaster carrying about 16 per cent. Quite obviously the coastal ship achieved its dominance in ton-mileage terms by the great length of haul it carried its cargoes. It carved out for itself this long-haul segment of the market. In the paper already cited reference was made to ships engaged in long hauls. Given the importance of this aspect of coastal trade to the case for the coaster's contribution to overall transport provision, it may not be inappropriate to reinforce this view. The Coppack family of Connah's Quay in Flint were coasting-ship owners from before the 1880s to the Second World War. Their main trade between 1900 and 1914 was carrying bricks from ports in their home river, the Dee, to London, South Wales and Ireland,[8] respectively 650, 220–280 and 100-plus nautical miles. Where individual voyages are known they are all well over 100 nautical miles, with cargoes of cement from London to the River Dee, pitch from Queensferry to Cardiff and Swansea, bricks and tiles from Connah's Quay to Dublin with malt as a return cargo, flour from Hull to Shoreham, and bricks from Connah's Quay to Swansea, Rochester, Dungarvon and Youghal.[9] The average, of eighteen separate voyages where both ports and the cargo are given, is 281 nautical miles, equal to about 323 land miles, well above our national average. The cargoes carried also confirm our characterisation of typical coastal commodites: bulky, low-value products not requiring rapid transit, e.g. bricks, tiles, coal, pitch, cement, steel ingots, hides, malt and flour.[10]

The choice of the year 1910 for making this comparison of the contributions made by the three principal modes of transport was deliberate. If earlier dates, say 1875 or 1850, had been chosen, it might have been argued that the railways had not reached their full potential in competition with coastal shipping. By 1910, however, the rail network was virtually complete, the organisation of the freight traffic and links with the ports was far more advanced than it had been in earlier years, and the railway companies were more favourably placed to provide a comprehensive service than they had been at any time since the accession of Queen Victoria in 1837. However, the average railway haul would have been longer but for some railways possessing their own docks. Because long-distance through traffic involved the wagons running over other companies' lines with little financial reward to the originating company, some railways preferred to route such freight a short haul over their own lines to their company-owned port facilities, then to cover the bulk of the journey by sea and complete it by yet another short rail journey from the port of arrival to the final destination. This may have maximised the individual railway company's income but not the haul on the railway system.[11]

The regional distribution of coastal trade

How was this remarkably large volume of coastal trade distributed between the ports? Table 6 gives the register tonnage of ships (*not* the tonnage of goods carried) entering and clearing the ten busiest ports in coastwise traffic in the years 1841, 1855, 1876, 1896 and 1912. The figures are for ships carrying cargoes, and do not include those entering or clearing in ballast. Ships engaged in the Irish trade are included, though Irish ports have been omitted from the tables, despite the fact that a number of them would qualify for inclusion in the 'top ten'. (Dublin and Belfast were among the top receiving and despatching ports in each year. Cork makes an occasional appearance in the 'entries' table.)

As was the case as far back as the sixteenth century, London was the greatest centre of conspicuous consumption in the country, having a population more than four times that of the next largest conurbation. It is not surprising, therefore, that London heads all five tables of the number and tonnage of vessels entering in the coastwise trade. The explanation of the decline in both number and tonnage of ships entering between 1896 and 1912 lies in the strike of 100,000 London dockers between May and August 1912 when the

Table 6 *The top ten coastal ports, by tonnage of entries and clearances, in 1841, 1855, 1876, 1896 and 1912*

	Vessels inwards			Vessels outwards	
Port	Number	Tons	Port	Number	Tons
1841					
London	22,726	3,030,713	Newcastle	14,120	1,990,144
Liverpool	9,208	1,021,833	London	11,832	1,081,530
Glasgow	3,731	396,580	Stockton	7,614	1,020,591
Bristol	5,114	310,876	Liverpool	8,204	910,026
Leith	3,432	280,844	Sunderland	4,460	664,931
Newcastle	3,035	278,416	Newport	8,707	471,313
Swansea	3,940	239,531	Glasgow	4,384	426,547
Lynn	2,229	208,137	Swansea	6,636	396,725
Yarmouth	2,577	193,480	Whitehaven	4,570	377,506
Goole	3,249	181,001	Bristol	3,723	257,523
1855					
London	19,040	2,852,223	Newcastle	10,679	1,498,682
Liverpool	8,434	1,336,106	Sunderland	11,098	1,374,697
Glasgow	3,217	516,466	Liverpool	9,032	1,277,565
Bristol	5,210	400,587	London	8,483	878,182
Plymouth	3,320	361,982	Hartlepool	5,680	763,627
Swansea	4,043	292,045	Glasgow	4,245	551,194
Beaumaris	2,246	282,091	Swansea	7,036	485,354
Newcastle	2,335	259,134	Newport	7,050	423,340
Leith	1,610	238,728	Cardiff	5,662	415,781
Sunderland	1,401	234,756	Bristol	3,969	339,991

	Vessels inwards			Vessels outwards	
Port	Number	Tons	Port	Number	Tons
1876					
London	32,282	3,872,087	Tyne[a]	6,812	1,885,935
Liverpool	7,987	1,901,042	Liverpool	7,172	1,637,516
Glasgow	4,500	1,027,554	Sunderland	6,588	1,379,891
Greenock	4,263	937,760	London	9,611	1,369,148
Tyne[a]	3,657	659,030	Glasgow	5,164	995,023
Bristol	7,765	619,811	Cardiff	6,675	578,743
Beaumaris	2,291	599,520	Beaumaris	2,201	559,213
Plymouth	2,874	500,656	Newport	7,252	536,566
Rochester	3,901	403,383	Swansea	4,530	460,624
Aberdeen	1,702	370,678	Hartlepool	3,333	447,126
1896					
London	38,641	6,160,610	Tyne[a]	7,581	3,016,044
Liverpool	12,280	2,267,197	Liverpool	12,998	2,327,708
Glasgow	7,903	1,599,795	London	17,601	2,330,362
Greenock	7,690	1,376,663	Sunderland	5,323	1,525,394
Aberdeen	2,823	765,023	Greenock	7,422	1,508,174
Southampton	4,886	762,160	Glasgow	7,679	1,381,030
Bristol	6,448	651,113	Cardiff	6,491	1,253,146
Tyne[a]	3,249	638,725	Beaumaris	4,626	713,158
Plymouth	2,537	635,138	Newport	5,924	614,371
Rochester	6,440	531,861	Leith	2,113	524,548

Vessels inwards			Vessels outwards		
Port	Number	Tons	Port	Number	Tons
1912					
London	11,135	5,147,284	Liverpool	13,085	2,367,241
Liverpool	11,437	2,118,676	Tyne^[a]	4,128	2,228,704
Glasgow	7,395	1,440,752	London	9,321	2,120,447
Beaumaris^[b]	2,883	1,028,550	Cardiff	5,012	1,431,310
Southampton	4,814	851,252	Glasgow	7,740	1,385,448
Portsmouth	7,212	848,716	Beaumaris^[b]	5,276	1,280,304
Cowes^[c]	12,506	833,495	Sunderland	2,676	1,052,171
Aberdeen	2,685	796,261	Hull	3,477	847,079
Plymouth	2,186	793,451	Cowes^[c]	9,164	755,655
Bristol	6,222	707,363	Cardigan^[d]	1,317	655,298

Notes:
[a] Tyne includes Newcastle, North Shields and South Shields.
[b] Beaumaris includes Holyhead.
[c] Cowes includes the whole coast of the Isle of Wight.
[d] Cardigan includes Fishguard and Goodwick.

Sources: B.P.P., 1842, XXXIX, pp. 624–5; *B.P.P.*, 1856, LVI, pp. 384–5; *B.P.P.*, 1877, LXXX, pp. 436–41; *B.P.P.*, LXXXVII, pp. 706–14; *B.P.P.*, 1913, LXI, pp. 764–85.
Sources: As Table 6.

port was generally at its busiest.[12] The prominence of ports such as Glasgow, Leith, Liverpool, Bristol and Newcastle in the 'entries' tables is partly explained by the fact that the population of their hinterlands was growing at a faster rate than the general rise in population in the UK, and that the demand for building materials, coal, food and drink was buoyant. Industrial development contributed to the inward traffic of Liverpool, through which passed the china clay from Cornwall for the Staffordshire potteries, and of Swansea, which handled imports of iron ore from the Cumberland ports. In 1912 the southern ports of Southampton, Portsmouth and Cowes appeared in the 'vessels inward table'. Southampton had risen to pre-eminence in the Atlantic passenger trade with liners of unprecedented tonnage requiring large supplies of coal, food and equipment, all shipped coastwise. Portsmouth's coastal trade was benefiting from the naval race with the Kaiser's Germany[13] and Cowes was the focus of imports into the Isle of Wight, whose population grew from 57,697 in 1871 to 88,186 in 1911, largely on account of its development as a holiday resort. Rochester, which appeared in both the 1876 and 1896 tables, but not in that of 1912, owes its disappearance from the table to a change in the method of classifying coastal trade. From 1895 onwards trade within the Thames estuary ceased to count as coastal trade and Rochester 'lost' about half its tonnage.[14]

The coal trade dominates coastal clearances. In each of the first four tables, five of the ports are essentially coal-shippers: Newcastle, Sunderland, Newport, Cardiff and Swansea. Some of the other ports, such as Glasgow and Liverpool, also 'exported' coastwise large quantities of coal. At least three ports, London, Glasgow and Bristol, had a large entrepôt function, i.e. they redistributed imports from overseas to the other ports in the British Isles. Some ports such as Glasgow, Liverpool, Bristol and Beaumaris, but particularly the last named, secured a place in the tables at least in part because of the large volume of business conducted with Ireland.

In the Victorian and Edwardian era the coastal trade of Great Britain became less concentrated in the larger ports and, instead, became more evenly distributed between the ports of less pre-eminence. Table 7 illustrates this decline of concentration of coastal ships in the largest ports. Between 1841 and 1912 the proportion of tonnage entering the top three ports fell by nine percentage points. Although the decline in percentage tonnage of the ships in the top five

Table 7 *The proportion of total coastal tonnage entering the top ports, 1841–1912 (%)*

Year	Top three ports	Top five ports	Top ten ports
1841	35·3	40·0	48·8
1855	31·6	36·7	45·5
1876	28·2	34·9	45·2
1896	31·2	37·8	47·8
1912	26·3	31·9	43·9

Note: This is based on entrances with cargoes only, and does not include ships in ballast.
Sources: As table 6.

and the top ten ports was less dramatic, the shift in shipping to the medium-sized ports was unmistakable. Coastal ships were concentrating on medium to small ports where there was less direct railway competition. In part this was caused by the great increase in foreign trade which crowded out the coastal craft. Ships trading overseas were larger and had more exotic cargoes, thus they paid more revenue to the port authorities who were, understandably, quicker to accommodate them and keep the coaster waiting for a berth. In addition, for some coastal towns the quantity of traffic generated was insufficient to justify the fixed capital expenditure of railway connection, and the coaster continued to provide the main flow of goods.

Although some coastal vessels such as the collier brigs used in the coal trade from the ports of the North-East, the china clay boats plying between such Cornish ports as Charlestown and Newquay and the Mersey estuary, and the iron-ore freighters linking the Cumbrian ports with Swansea, were used exclusively for freight transport, the masters of many cargo vessels were willing to carry passengers and the owners of passenger vessels were happy to augment their revenues by carrying goods. In the late 1840s the steamship *Cornwall*, which plied regularly between Hoyle and Bristol, always carried goods, principally vegetables and fish, besides a large number of passengers. One Friday in mid-March 1848 the passage was so stormy and the ship so long delayed at sea that the ship's captain sold the bacon and other provisions, intended for Bristol shopkeepers, to those passengers still well enough to be hungry.[15] The practice of mixing passenger and freight traffic continued right up to 1914. From Newcastle a new passenger steamer, the *Stephen Furness* of the Tyne–Tees Shipping Company, sailed to London via Middlesbrough in July 1910 with forty-six first-class and twenty-two second-class passengers and 'half cargo consisting of steel rails shipped at Middlesborough and a miscellaneous Newcastle cargo'.[16]

Freight traffic: railway and coaster competition

In the early years of Queen Victoria's reign, when there was a more comprehensive network of coastal steamship services than there was of railways, many merchants and traders used water transport not only for the carriage of bulky freights of low value but also for high-value goods. In 1840 Captain Laws, General Manager of the Manchester and Leeds Railway, sent a vast quantity of textiles for the London market first to Hull over his company's lines and then by steamboat to the Thames. The whole journey was completed in thirty-six hours, compared with the five days taken by canal, and the cost was '100 per cent less than the railways' were charging from Manchester to London.[17] Five years later Lawrence Wylder, a grocer of Grantham, had two-thirds of his supplies from London sent by coastal steamer at a cost of 30s a ton, including 5s insurance, and the remaining third, presumably goods of a more perishable kind, mostly by railway at 55s a ton.[18]

By the later 1840s, however, the situation was beginning to change. With over 5,000 miles of railway now open to traffic, the direct rail route for the movement of freight became more frequently advantageous. Between 1847 and 1850 the Goods Committee of the Railway Clearing House removed many of the obstacles, such as variations in goods classification and ton mileage charges, which had hindered the through passage of freight over the lines of more than one company.[19] Although the London & North Western Railway in the late 1850s found that vigorous coaster competition affected its traffic in ale and iron from the Midlands to Scotland,[20] where the railway route was decidedly shorter than that by sea the railways were generally able to capture high-value traffic from the coasters. Thus, before the railway reached Poole in 1847, sixty-four vessels were regularly engaged in bringing groceries to the town. However, railway competition from then on was so effective that the coastwise grocery trade had completely collapsed by 1852. It was the same story with Bridport, further down the coast. The products of the town's rope works and net works, formerly dispatched by sea, were all sent by freight train after 1857, when the town's railway link was established.[21] The peak of coastal shipping activity based on Teignmouth came in 1854 when there were 399 vessels operating from the port. From then onwards the railways captured a considerable proportion of the coastwise trade, especially that in groceries, manufactures and other goods of high value for bulk.[22] In most cases, once through rail communication was established between the place of supply and the market, the coastal trade was largely confined to the carriage of low-value commodities for which speed and regularity of transit were not essential.

The existence of competition from other forms of transport helped to keep down freight rates. In the second quarter of the nineteenth century coastal steamships were often able to charge high rates because of the ineffectiveness or absence of alternative rail transport. For fully fifty years before 1886, when the railway reached the quarrying districts of Portland, the charge for carrying the famous stone to London by coaster was from 4s 6d to 5s a ton. By the early years of the twentieth century, as a result of a price war between the GWR and the owners of the coasters, freight rates came down to one-third of their former level.[23] In later years the existence of alternative water-borne transport often obliged railway companies to bring down their charges, as Cain has cogently argued for agricultural produce.[24] But it was not confined to this sector. Mr Clark, a manufacturer of chemicals, told a public meeting in Liverpool on 2 March 1865 that the railways charged him more than 2½d per ton-mile for carrying his consignments between Liverpool and Wakefield, where there was no coastal shipping competition, and only ¾d per ton-mile between Newcastle and Hull where he had the alternative of sending the freight by sea.[25] In the mid-1870s the West Coast Conference of the railway companies at several of its meetings discussed the loss of goods traffic between Liverpool, Dundee and Aberdeen to the steamships which were using the Caledonian Canal. On 31 October 1874 'a large falling off in traffic' on the rail route was noted and on 20 January 1875 it was resolved that 'the rates for traffic from Liverpool by rail to Dundee and Aberdeen . . . be reduced to such as will secure the traffic from Liverpool by rail'. The reduction was to 20s a ton, until Messrs Langland, their shipping competitors, brought down their freights from 16s 8d to 12s 6d per ton. This obliged the railway companies to reduce their rates a second time to 15*s*, in a determined effort to regain their lost traffic.[26] The above were not isolated examples. In 1872 the Select Committee on Railway Companies' Amalgamation reported that coastal shipping competition with the railways affected not merely those towns directly, but 'the charges for the use of the railway that leads to the ports', and it drew attention to the view of 'a very competent witness', Mr C. H. Parkes, who estimated that water transport competition 'affected the rate for goods at three-fifths of all railway stations in the United Kingdom'.[27] The opening of the Manchester Ship Canal on 1 January 1894 posed further problems for the railways. A meeting of the West Coast Conference on 6 March 1896 was presented with figures showing a sharp decline in freight traffic in the heartland of Britain's textile industry over the previous four years. There was complaint that the 'steamship companies were conveying the traffic at such low rates as to make it impossible for the railway companies to compete successfully'.[28] As late as 16 June 1904 'water competition' was being blamed for loss of railway traffic, 'principally in fine goods' between England and Scotland.[29]

Coal trade

A statistician writing in 1846 declared that the 'coasting trade in coal constitutes about seven-ninths of the whole coasting trade by sailing vessels and it forms . . . nearly seven-twelfths of the entire coasting trade of Great Britain'.[30] This view may be exaggerated. However, throughout the period before the First World War, London dominated the coastwise coal trade. In 1839 the quantity entering the Thames was 2,625,000 tons, or just under a third of the total of 7,223,000 tons of coal carried round the coast of Great Britain.[31] By 1910 the quantity coming by sea to the capital had risen to nearly nine million tons, a figure which was almost two-fifths of the total coastwise trade in coal.[32] Figure 18 indicates the importance of London in receiving coastal coal in 1910. It took more coal than the next ten ports added together. Before 1844 the task of bringing coal to London was shared between the canal barges and the seagoing colliers, though even in 1840 the proportion of the total trade going by canal was less than 2 per cent and by the early 1850s it had fallen to under one per cent.[33] From the time the

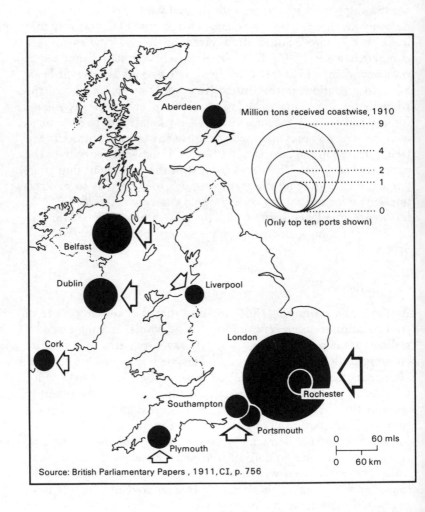

Million tons received coastwise, 1910

Only top ten ports shown

Source: British Parliamentary Papers , 1911, CI, p. 756

18   Coal received coastwise, 1910

first substantial consignments of coal were brought into London by train in 1844 until the outbreak of war seventy years later, there was fierce competition between the railway companies and the coasters to gain the lion's share of the transport of the huge consignments from the north-east coalfields which had a near monopoly of the London market.[34] Figure 19 shows how the east coast dominated this trade, six of the top ten ports sending coal by coaster in 1910 were so located. Only the Welsh ports of Newport and Cardiff, with their steam coal, and Liverpool, by virtue of its Irish trade, break this pattern. The story of the struggle between railway and coaster is summarised in table 8. The editor of *Herapath's Railway Journal* in 1853 pointed out that there was 'immense scope for the Great Northern and other railway companies to enlarge their coal traffic', and he went on to prophesy 'that in the course of time there will not be a ton of coal conveyed by water'.[35] In 1867, when for the first time the tonnage of coal brought into London by rail exceeded that carried by the coasters, his prophecy seemed to be coming true. By the late 1870s the sea-borne tonnage had fallen to little more than half that brought in by rail. Yet by the mid-1890s the coal brought coastwise again exceeded the quantities brought in by rail.

The buoyant performance of the coasting trade in coal to London was due to the greater willingness of its entrepreneurs to accept innovation in coal handling and movement. The railway companies,

Table 8 *Quantity of coal brought into London by coaster, in tons and as a proportion of the total (selected years)*

Year	Tons (000)	% of total
1845	3,403	100
1854	3,400	78
1864	3,117	57
1874	2,728	37
1884	4,294	38
1890	5,262	41
1898	7,337	51
1904	8,285	54
1911	9,147	53

Sources: 1844–74: B. R. Mitchell and P. Deane, *Abstract of British Historical Statistics*, Cambridge, 1962, p. 113; 1884 and 1890: *B.P.P.*, Annual Reports of the Commissioners of Mines and Quarries; 1898–1911: *The Coal Merchant and Shipper*, XXVI, 1913, p. 111.

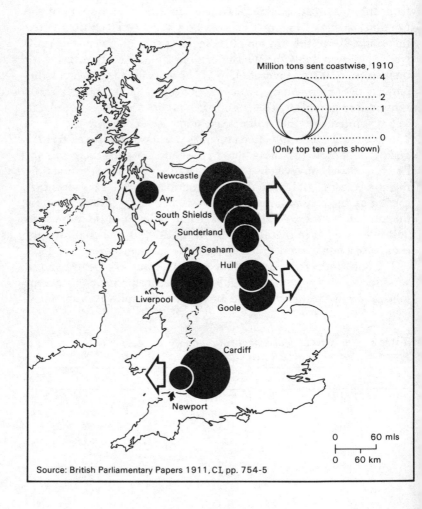

19 Coal sent coastwise, 1910

by contrast, persisted in their use of uneconomic ten-ton waggons. Their coal trains were not fitted with continuous brakes and their handbrakes were of a bewildering variety which endangered the life and limb of the shunters. The NER pioneered the use of twenty-ton waggons after the appointment of George S. Gibb as General Manager in 1902, but the large majority of his contemporaries failed to follow his example.[36]

The most dramatic innovation in the sea coal trade was the introduction of the screw collier. The first of this class of vessel to appear was the *QED,* launched on the Tyne in 1844, which had a double bottom to enable her to take in water ballast. Better known, because of the early work of the *QED* in France, was the *John Bowes,* launched at Jarrow in 1852 and capable of carrying 650 tons of coal, well over double the weight of cargo of a typical collier brig. Employed on the east-coast route, she steamed from Newcastle to London and back in five days, including the time taken in discharging her cargo. Thus she accomplished the amount of work it would have taken two average-sized collier brigs a month to perform.[37] By 1854 thirty-six screw colliers brought 202,607 tons of coal to London in 348 voyages.[38] In the early 1850s (apart from the period of inflated prices in the Crimean War) the cost of a screw collier capable of carrying 600 tons of coal was £12,000. For this price a shipowner could have bought eight second-hand collier brigs capable of carrying about 300 tons each. Because of the very high initial capital cost of the screw colliers their owners were under the imperative necessity of securing a quick turn-round time when docked.[39] For this reason William Cory, who owned the largest coal-merchanting business in London, acquired at a knock-down price in 1861 a 250-foot long floating derrick and fitted it with six hydraulic cranes which discharged the colliers direct into lighters. The collier brig's cargo was discharged into lighters by eight-man teams of whippers who could unload between fifty and sixty tons of coal in a day. Cory's *Atlas* derrick cranes could clear 1,200 tons of coal in ten hours.[40]

Given the seemingly overwhelming advantages, in economies of scale, speed and reliability, of the screw colliers over the collier brigs, it is remarkable that in 1863, eleven years after the first commercial voyage of the *John Bowes,* three-quarters of the coal entering the Pool of London came in sailing vessels.[41] It was not until the mid-1870s that the large majority of the water-borne tonnage of coal supplied to the capital came by steamship.[42] Many circumstances combined to keep the sailing colliers in business long after the technological superiority of the steamers had been demonstrated. In July 1844 Gideon Smales, a shipowner of Whitby, blamed the low freight rates prevailing in the Baltic trade for the glut of ships on England's east coasts. 'The freights in the Baltic have been so reduced', he said, 'that ships cannot live in it, and it has driven them out of that trade into the coasting trade.'[43] To make a living in the coastwise coal trade the brig owners were obliged to make operational economies. On the Tyne, staiths were built downriver, where there was deeper water, so that the brigs could be loaded direct by means of 'spouts' rather than by the expensive and time-consuming labour of keelmen. At Gosforth in 1841 keelmen loaded nearly 4,000 chaldrons of coal: eight years later their share had fallen to 648 chaldrons, while 31,004 chaldrons passed through the spouts.[44] In the early nineteenth century the brigs were laid up during the months of January and February when the east-coast storms were generally at their fiercest. By mid-century this practice had largely ceased. In 1844 Robert Anderson, a shipowner, said that brigs were making more voyages to London in a year than had been the case a quarter of a century earlier: 'the owners, I think, are trying by increasing activity to make up for their differences in profits'.[45]

Briefly, during the years of the Crimean War (1854–56) the owners of the brigs were able to charge higher freights, but when the screw colliers returned from war service the competition between the two types of vessels intensified. The historian of the Gas, Light and Coke Company summed up what he described as the 'catastrophe' of the collier brigs: 'Freight charges fell rapidly; expenses were cut; ships were overloaded, so that the company had to issue express instructions that no vessels in their service might sail with a deck cargo of coal. What had always been a hazardous service increased in danger.'[46]

Despite these continuing difficulties the brig owners continued in the trade with which they were so familiar and so reluctant to abandon. With a number of vessels it was generally assumed that insurance was unnecessary, for in the case of an accident disabling one, or even two, brigs, the delivery of coals would only be interrupted or delayed, whereas the consequences could be disastrous if a shipowner's entire resources were invested in a screw collier which subsequently foundered. There was an additional advantage to the brig owner that he could more easily divert his vessel into other trades if coal freights were exceptionally low, whereas the owner of the screw collier had more resources tied up in a specialised vessel and often its loading and unloading equipment as well.[47]

If the sailors on the collier brigs – and there were at least 12,000 of them at mid-century – had been well organised in a trade union they might have been able to prevent the deterioration of their working conditions. As it was there were only very brief periods of successful organisation, as in 1857 on the east-coast ports, particularly Great Yarmouth and Ipswich, and in 1887–90 and 1911–13. Because coal freights by sea were low and their seamen at best sporadically organised, collier brigs were undermanned and overloaded and their sailors poorly paid. It was the general rule that the screw colliers' freight rates were kept 6d under the rate of the sailing vessels for the east-coast run.[48] The guideline for the manning of sailing ships which merchant seamen considered reasonable in the 1840s was that for every 100 tons of the ship's register five men and one boy should be employed. Under the pressure of low coal freights and the competition of the screw colliers, manning levels were reduced. In 1867 sailors from the county of Durham petitioned for the restoration of the old manning levels, since the number of hands had been gradually lowered, with consequent considerable loss of human life.[49] This concern was echoed in 1896 when W. J. Howell, of the Board of Trade Marine Department, declared that undermanning was 'a serious cause of loss of life'.[50] The *Economist* in the summer of 1911 commented that 'money wages of seamen in many ports had not risen for twenty or thirty years'.[51] Had trade unionism been strong in the merchant marine, and had better manning scales and higher wages been enforced, there would have been an earlier ascendancy of the screw collier and a quicker demise of the collier brigs which would have been uneconomic to run.

The sea traders, for the above and for other reasons, were able to substantially underquote the railway companies. Though the cost of coal freight by ordinary collier brig varied according to the supply of shipping, in the later 1850s and early 1860s it averaged 6s 6d. When local dues and city dues were added, the total cost, Newcastle–London, came to around 10s per ton, whereas the cost via the Great Northern Railway was 13s 9½d per ton.[52] By the early twentieth century, as a result of continual competition, the cost of freighting coal from the Tyne to the Thames had fallen further and lay within the range 2s 3d to 5s 6d.[53] By then there was a clearly marked division of labour between the railways and the sea traders. The railway companies concentrated on the supply of coal for domestic use and they established 155 local depots in London to further this end: the now predominant screw colliers supplied the gasworks, electricity generating plants and industrial sites, many of which had been established on the banks of the Thames. To expand the river-side deliveries H. C. Petty started building screw colliers (later known as 'flatirons') specially designed to pass under low river bridges. The London gas companies chartered these vessels in large numbers and in so doing ensured that sea-borne deliveries of coal to London once more exceeded the quantity of coal brought to the capital by rail.[54]

Coal figured largely in the coastal trade of many other British ports besides London and the ports of the Tyne, Wear and Tees. Coming second only to Newcastle in the domestic coal trade was Cardiff, whose exports of coal coastwise soared upwards from a quarter of a million tons in 1858 to over three million tons in 1913.[55] The Welsh coal was particularly prized for its high thermal qualities, and it was the main source of supply of bunkers for the rapidly expanding tonnage of British steam shipping. A lot of coal also passed through Liverpool in the coastwise trade. The port's Bills of Entry reveal that a total of 322,844 tons were cleared in coasters in 1875, three-fifths of the total being sent to Irish ports in exchange for food grains and livestock. By 1910 Liverpool's coastwise clearances of coal had shot up to 1,807,924 tons, most of which, as in 1875, went to Irish ports. Other towns and cities were completely dependent on coastwise imports of coal for their economic and social well-being. As early as 1845 the city of Aberdeen imported 132,518 tons of coal, a larger quantity than all the other merchandise brought in by coasters.[56] The coal exported coastwise from the Scottish port of Grangemouth in 1910 was 222,652 tons.[57]

Other bulk trades

There are no comprehensive figures in this period for the coastal shipment of grain. However, evidence is available from Bills of Entry and other sources at different dates. Records of coastal imports of grain into London in the four years 1880, 1885, 1890 and 1895 show variations between 30,312 and 54,244 tons, with Ipswich being the most important regular supplier, although in 1890, exceptionally, Aberdeen supplied over 25,000 tons of oats.[58] Figure 20 demonstrates how the London coastal trade was mainly served by east-coast ports of which the rich east Anglian farmlands predominated. Glasgow's grain imports by coaster in 1850 were nearly 52,000 tons, coming from over fifty ports in Scotland, England and Ireland. Bristol's coastwise grain imports in 1849 amounted to 33,434 tons, derived from Ireland, Wales and the West Country. In 1875 Liverpool's imports coastwise of 27,970 tons of grain of all kinds came almost exclusively from Irish ports.

Because of their bulky character, large quantities of iron goods were sent to their destinations by coaster rather than by rail. The twin thousand-ton bascules of London's Tower Bridge raised for the first time in 1894 were brought to locations north and south of the river by coastal steamer, and the cast iron 'tubes' of London's underground were also brought to the capital by sea.[59] Some statistics exist for the coastwise trade in iron. The impressive total of 158,974 tons of iron products of all kinds was despatched from Workington in 1910, over half the total being in the form of steel rails, while most of the remainder was of pig-iron or ferromanganese.[60] In the same year pig-iron provided nearly three-quarters of the coastwise imports of Port Glasgow, while Grangemouth imported nearly 480,000 tons of pig-iron, most of it from Teesside ports, and Harrington sent coastwise 102,410 tons of ferrous goods, roughly equally divided between pig-iron and rails. Iron products were an essential component of coastal trade throughout the Victorian era. In 1850 Glasgow exported by coastal ship nearly 110,000 tons of iron products, the bulk being pig-iron; in 1875 Newcastle received nearly 60,000 tons of iron and by 1881 this had risen to over 75,000 tons; as Vamplew points out: 'Turning to the ferrous industries we find that throughout the nineteenth century coastal shipping carried most of the Anglo-Scottish traffic.'[61]

The nineteenth-century coastal trade was characterised by great regional variations dependent on topography, geology and the proximity to markets. Because of shortage of space it is only possible to cite a few examples of this diversity. The development of the china clay trade between Cornwall and Runcorn for the Potteries and Gloucester (for the Worcester factories) was heavily dependent on the construction of adequate harbours at key points on the rugged Cornish coast. A four-acre harbour, able to accommodate ships of

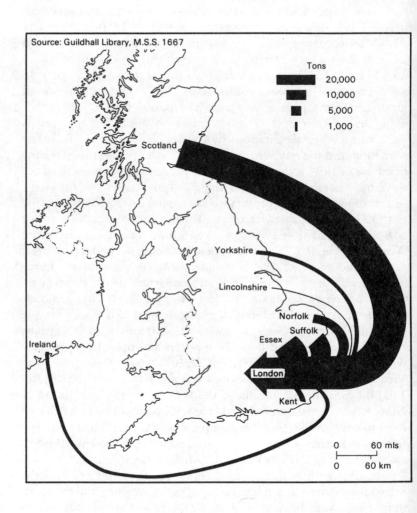

Source: Guildhall Library, M.S.S. 1667

Tons
20,000
10,000
5,000
1,000

Scotland

Yorkshire

Lincolnshire

Norfolk

Suffolk

Essex

Ireland

London

Kent

0   60 mls
0   60 km

20   Grain shipped coastwise into London, 1880

700 tons burden, was opened at Newquay in 1833, followed shortly afterwards by the opening of the new harbour at Par. By far the most impressive of the new ports was that at Charlestown with a 1,200-foot breakwater and a 35-acre harbour.[62] The result of these improvements was that the amount of china clay and china stone shipped at Charlestown rose from 20,784 in 1838 to 582,445 in 1904. Shipments coastwise were often three times the tonnage of those sent abroad.[63] The success of the pottery industry in Staffordshire and Worcestershire was dependent on both coastal shipping and canal transport, since from Runcorn and Gloucester a short haul by inland waterways followed the long haul by coaster. In 1875 Runcorn's bills of entry record nearly 100,000 tons of china clay and stone entering from Cornwall.

In 1819 there was neither a town nor a port on the site which subsequently became Portmadoc. However, the completion of a harbour in 1824, the abolition of the *ad valorem* tax on slates carried coastwise in 1831 and the establishment of the Steam Tugboat Company in 1862, with widely subscribed local capital, to help the sailing vessels' departure from port, combined to bring prosperity to the slate-quarrying industry. The quarrying firms had every encouragement to send their slates coastwise to the London market, as well as to other expanding urban areas, for the cost of sending slates to London, as a percentage of their value at the port of landing, fell from 61 per cent in 1790 to 12 per cent in 1880. So the output of Festiniog slates rose from 20,000 tons in 1835 to 114,000 tons in 1867. The London building boom of the early 1870s helped to boost shipments to their maximum in 1873, as did the growth of other urban centres. In 1875 the bills of entry for Garston and Runcorn show over 26,000 tons of Welsh slates coming into the Merseyside area. By the early 1890s the decline of Portmadoc's sea trade, due largely to railway competition, was apparent.[64] For the shipowners, returns were uncertain. The schooner *William* of Portmadoc carried many consignments of slates to the pool of London between the years 1844 and 1854 with freights per ton varying from 9s to 11s 6d, depending on the fluctuations in house-building activity and the quality of the slates themselves.[65]

Coastal shipping carried a wide range of other bulk freights. Goods such as salt were regular cargoes. For example, in 1875 Liverpool sent over 100,000 tons of salt coastwise, about a third to Newcastle and a quarter to Leith, probably for use in the chemical industry.[66] Bulk chemicals regularly moved by coaster; in 1875 Newcastle despatched 62,000 tons, mainly soda crystals and alkali, and by 1881 this had risen to 89,000 tons.[67] Building requisites such as bricks, tiles and cement were normal loads for the coaster, as were ores of all sorts. In 1875 Newcastle received 171,000 tons of iron ore coastwise and in 1881 167,000 tons plus a further 28,000 tons of pyrites. Runcorn in the former year received 28,000 tons of various ores, about half of it from Irish ports.[68]

Coastal shipping played a leading part in the expansion of the livestock industry in Victoria's reign, particularly in the growth of the Anglo-Irish trade.[69] It was also important in the sale of Scottish beef cattle in the London market. Through the agency of the Aberdeen Steam Navigation Company, an organisation formed through the amalgamation of two earlier companies in 1835, the cattle trade with ports to the south, but particularly with London, flourished until the arrival of the Scottish North Eastern Railway in Aberdeen in 1850. A few years of reduced activity and earnings followed. But by an energetic policy of chartering its surplus vessels to other traders, and reaching agreement on the division of traffic with the railway in 1856, the company achieved further expansion of its business in the 1860s and 1870s.[70] Part of the success of the company arose from its ability to secure return cargoes. The East Coast Conference of the Railway Companies, meeting on 15 February 1865, regretted the fact that 'the principal goods traffic from Newcastle to Aberdeen, consisting of soda, soda ash, soap, paints, oil, dyewood, white lead, pig lead, sheet lead, iron, anchors and chains, went by water'.[71]

The minutes of an earlier meeting of the same conference reveal that in 1854, 200 tons of the 300 tons of Dundee jute and hemp goods sent to London each week went by coast. Nor was the rail share of the traffic increasing. In the six months ending 31 March 1857 steamers and smacks carried 6,250 tons of Dundee's traffic to London, whereas the railways' share was only 1,222 tons.[72] From 1 January 1870 the Dundee, Perth and London Shipping Company operated a five-year agreement with the railway companies in the English and Scottish Traffic Rates Conference, that the shipping company should carry nine-tenths of the Dundee traffic, other than that in cattle, and the railway companies should carry the remaining one-tenth. In each of the six-month periods up to 31 December 1874 the shipping company paid the railway company compensation because it had carried traffic in excess of its quota.[73] The agreement was renewed in 1875 at the request of the shipping company. Under this second five-year agreement, which expired on 31 December 1879 and was not renewed, the shipping company agreed to reduce its proportion of the traffic from nine-tenths to seven-eighths, so that it might have more of a free hand to develop its trade with Hamburg. Coastal shipping's dominance of the trade between Dundee and London was partly due to the sea route being shorter than that by rail. In consequence the shipping company's charges were 25s per ton, whereas the charge by the railway was 41s 8d per ton.[74] The fact that the rail traffic had to pass over the lines of several companies on its journey to London, while the sea traffic was in the hands of a single organisation, must also have contributed to the ascendancy of the coasters.

The growing number of published business histories provide further evidence of manufacturers making use of coastal shipping for the distribution of their products well into the railway age. Thus Huntley and Palmers of Reading used the railway for the first stage in the distribution of its biscuits, but then used hoys which sailed from Hambro's wharf in London to the Medway towns, Faversham and other places on the Kent coast. From Bristol steamships served ports as far apart as Hale and Penzance in Cornwall and Neath in South Wales.[75] In the 1880s William H. Lever (later Lord Leverhulme), founder of the firm of Lever Brothers, established at Bromborough Pool on the banks of the Mersey, out of the reach of Liverpool Dock and Harbour dues, an anchorage from which he could load his cargoes before despatching them down the Mersey to all parts by sea, entirely independent of the railways.[76]

Some coastal trade – whose quantity cannot be measured – may well have escaped being recorded in port offices or customs houses. The 'puffer' ships, which carried stone from the quarries of J. & A. Garland & Co in Scotland, often pulled up on beaches rather than alongside harbour quays and thus avoided paying port dues. To the extent that such practices prevailed in the transport of bulky commodities, the volume of coastal trade was greater than published figures might suggest.[77]

Passenger traffic

In the first decade of Queen Victoria's reign coastwise steam-packet services expanded rapidly. By the mid-1840s virtually all the major British ports had reliable, frequent and fast services provided by purpose-built vessels and organised on a liner basis, i.e. with regular advertised dates of sailing. Travel by coastal steamship was generally faster and certainly much cheaper than by stage-coach, especially where the route by sea was shorter than that by land. Although Britain possessed a skeleton network of main-line railways by the early 1840s, it was not until the later years of that decade that many of the obstacles to long-distance rail travel over several companies' lines had been overcome.

Before railway links were extensive, businessmen frequently used steamships as the best available means of transport. When Barclay Fox, the Quaker shipowner and ironmaster, attended yearly meetings in London in the 1830s and 1840s he travelled from his home town, Falmouth, by the *Sir Francis Drake* as far as Plymouth where he changed into another steamer, the *Brunswick,* which took him to Portsmouth. The last stage of his journey was completed by coach. When he visited his ironworks he took the steamer *Bristol* from Ilfracombe or Hale to Cardiff, before proceeding to Swansea by road.[78] In the 1840s Liverpool businessmen could travel by steamboat to Glasgow, Annan, Lancaster, Beaumaris, Whitehaven, Belfast, Cork and Londonderry. From these destinations they could change vessels to join other steamship routes.[79] Although there was a less ample choice of domestic steamship routes from ports on the south coast, since the railway reached Southampton as early as 1840 and the journey by sea to London was generally substantially longer than that by rail, the examples of coastal steamship operations given above could be repeated for many other ports.

Different reasons explain the large volume of passenger traffic between London and the Kentish seaside resorts. Before the days of steam the sailing hoys took middle-class holidaymakers and the convalescent to Margate and the other coastal towns. The steamboats took over this business and greatly expanded it. The railway did not reach Dover until 1843. Estimates of the number of passengers carried by the steamboats varied greatly. According to one witness in 1836 75,000 people visited either Margate or Ramsgate by steam packet while 12,480 persons travelled to Dover by the same means.[80] One published account, on the other hand, gives the number of passengers to Margate only as 40,000 in 1830.[81]

The estuaries of the Clyde, Forth, Humber, Thames and Severn were still swarming with passenger steamboats in the late 1830s and early 1840s. In 1839 thirty-one passenger steamboats linked Glasgow with towns further down the Clyde and some of the islands of the Inner Hebrides. Speeds did not exceed an average of ten miles per hour, but these were marginally faster than the coaches, and with cabin fares averaging less than a penny a mile (e.g. 2s for the thirty-two miles to Dunoon) the steamboats had a decided cost advantage.[82] Competition was intense between the steamboat owners before the railway between Glasgow and Greenock opened in 1841, after which competition between the coasters and the railway was more formidable than anything experienced by the steamers among themselves.[83] What enabled coastal passenger steamboats to stay in business after the arrival of railway competition was their ability to cut fares in order to increase their cost advantage, and their success in persuading large numbers of travellers that steamship travel was more commodious and comfortable than that by rail. One of the best examples of fare cutting was that of the London & Edinburgh Steam Packet Company. In 1826 the fares charged for conveying passengers between the two capital cities were £5 for cabin and £2 10s 6d for steerage accommodation. In 1846, two years after the railway reached Edinburgh, the steamship fares were down to £3 and £1 15s. Three years later cabin passengers were charged £2 10s with meals provided or £2 without meals, and the steerage fare was £1 2s 6d. After the railway races to the north had cut rail journey times, the steamboat fares were once more reduced, in 1885, when 'chief cabin' passengers could make the journey for 22s, or 34s return, and 'second cabin' accommodation was offered for only 16s or 24s 6d return.[84] Services three times a week in each direction were still being advertised on this route in 1908.[85] Thus cheap fares were part of the explanation why in 1849, when the railway link to London had been opened seven years, only 5,792 persons took the rail route while 11,584 opted for the Leith–London steamship.[86]

According to Professor Simmons, 'a Mid Victorian (rail) journey from London to Wales could still be a formidably unpleasant business in winter'. Primitive footwarmers were available in some first-class railway carriages from the mid-1850s. It was not until twenty years later that steam heating of carriages was introduced, and then only for Pullman cars, which were in limited supply.[87] By contrast, cabin passengers travelling in coastal steamships from the 1820s

onwards were warmed by coal fires.[88] Glasgow and Liverpool were
linked by rail, via Beattock and Carlisle, from 1848, and yet a large
majority of travellers fifteen years later preferred to take the
16½-hour sea route on vessels 'of a superior class' with heated
cabins and a chance to stretch their legs rather than to pay more to
travel cooped up in an unheated railway compartment for fourteen
and a half hours. From 1860–63 inclusive passengers travelling
between the two cities by steamboat numbered 128,877 while only
57,033 preferred the train.[89] Only with the opening of the Carlisle–
Settle line in 1876, giving the rail route a decisive time advantage, did
passengers desert the steamboats.

Glaswegians and Liverpudlians had a choice of means of transport. For the inhabitants of the Inner and Outer Hebrides and the
Orkney and Shetland Islands there was no choice but to use water
transport. Moreover, populations were so thinly scattered that the
provision of a packet service was rarely economic. The peoples of
these islands were therefore dependent on the Post Office, the Scottish Office or the Treasury's Highlands and Islands vote to subsidise
their sea link with the Scottish mainland. It was not until the winter
of 1850–51 that the Aberdeen, Leith & Tay Shipping Company's
steamship *Sovereign* provided the first regular winter service to the
Orkneys.[90] For the Hebrideans, who had as prolonged a struggle to
achieve satisfactory services to their islands as did the Orcadians,
some success was achieved in 1871 when a contract was signed
between the Post Office and the Dingwall & Skye Railway Company
by which the company's steamer *Cardan* was to provide a service six
times a week in summer and three in winter for an annual payment of
£1,250.[91] By 1891 six routes to the northern and western isles were
subsidised at a total cost of £8,755, borne by the Post Office vote.[92]
As Lord Dunmore of Harris wrote in a letter to the Postmaster-
General in 1911, 'the whole prosperity of the people was dependent
on good communication'.[93]

By the closing years of the nineteenth century the superior speed
and more comprehensive services of the railways had greatly reduced
the role of coastal shipping in the provision of passenger transport.
However, to offset shrinking business on their old established routes
the steamship companies began to exploit opportunities in the growing holiday trade. A rising standard of living, bank holidays, and a
more tolerant attitude towards recreational activities on Sundays fed
the demand for day cruises. In the second half of the nineteenth

century a rapidly growing number of middle-class families spent holidays by the seaside. From the 1830s there were regular steamship crossings from the mainland ports to the Isle of Wight, but these had been heavily dependent on Post Office subsidies. Tourist traffic provided an enormous boost to passenger revenues. In 1861 the 224,000 passengers carried on the Southampton–Cowes route were three times as numerous as the total of passengers on all three routes to the island in 1831.[94] As late as the 1880s (as shown for the Bristol Channel in fig. 21) there was a substantial network of passenger carrying steamboat services.

Post Office contracts were also important for the provision of regular steamship services to the Isle of Man and the development of the island as a holiday resort. From 1833 the Isle of Man Steam Packet Company secured the Post Office contract for the carriage of the mails in return for an annual payment of £850. However, as the island was more densely populated and more easily accessible to industrial England's holidaymakers than are most of Scotland's islands to their nearest populous areas, the postal revenue soon exceeded the payment to the packet company.[95] Swollen by the contribution of Wakes Weeks, the number of summer visitors to the island reached an all-time peak of 634,572 in 1913.[96]

The provision of capital

The capital required for the building and servicing of ships employed in the coastal trade was supplied principally through two types of organisation: the joint-stock company and private ownership where the value of the ship was divided into sixty-fourths. Generally it was the larger concerns, often owning fleets of steamships, which were joint-stock companies and the single sailing vessels that were owned in sixty-fourths. It was usual for the ships belonging to the companies to be engaged in liner trades carrying passengers and freight between a regular pattern of ports. Thus the principal activity of the Aberdeen Steam Navigation Company was to carry livestock, meat, and passengers to London and general freight and passengers on the return journey to Aberdeen. The vessel owned in sixty-fourths was frequently engaged in tramping – calling at a variety of ports with no fixed schedule of services. Thus in 1851 the *Star* smack of Pwllheli whose master, Watkin Perry, owned some of the sixty-fourths shares of the ship he managed, at different times took coal, slates and china

21 Bristol Channel steamer services in the 1880s

Source: The White Funnel Handbook

Chepstow
Bristol
Clevedon
Weston-super-Mare
Cardiff
Barry
Minehead
Port Talbot
Porthcawl
Lynmouth
Swansea
Mumbles
Ilfracombe
Bideford
Clovelly
BRISTOL
CHANNEL
Tenby
To Stack
Rocks
Lundy Island

10 mls
10 km
0

clay to a variety of ports including Portsmouth, Falmouth, Aberystwyth and Runcorn.[97]

The dead company files in the Public Record Office reveal details of a number of companies which were formed to operate in the coastal trade. Appendix 1 gives their names and information about their share ownership at various dates: column 1 in the classification gives the percentage of the shareholders living the cities or towns directly served by the company, and the percentage of the shares these people held. Column 2 includes all shareholders living within twenty miles of the principal centres served and shows what proportion of the company's shares they held. The third column includes all shareholders living outside the areas included in columns 1 and 2. A glance down column 1(a) reveals that, with few exceptions, the majority of shareholders lived within the 'home port' of the company. If the percentages in 1(a) and 2(a) are added together then it is seen that in every case, with the single exception of the North Devon Shipping Company in 1856, shareholders living within a radius of twenty miles of the ship's main trading port, or ports, formed a very large majority of the total. Columns 1(b) and 2(b) reveal that only in the cases of the North Devon Shipping Company and the Cambrian Steam Packet Company – in the one year 1867 – were the majority of the shares held by persons living outside the twenty-mile radius. In the case of the railway companies a 'Lancashire party' purchased railway stocks *as investments* in all parts of the country.[98] There was no parallel development to this in the case of the capital for coastal shipping, which was mainly owned by persons living in the area most likely to have direct benefit from the services the shipping company was designed to provide. This mirrors Ward's findings on the sources of finance for canals: 'Canals were generally financed by persons resident in the localities which they served.'[99]

Particulars of the ships owned in sixty-fourths are obtainable from the shipping registers in the custom ports. To determine the pattern of ownership of these vessels the registers were examined for three sample years: 1850, 1875 and 1910. The number of ports where records survive for all three of the sample years was limited, but information is available for Ipswich, Glasgow, Whitehaven and Liverpool. These four ports gave a sample of 370 ships with an aggregate of 42,953 tons. Table 9 shows the areas of residence of the shareholders of these ships at the three dates and table 10

Table 9 *Residences of coastal shipowners in ships' registers (%)*

Category		1850	1875	1910
Glasgow	1	74	60	96
	2	10	5	1
	3	14	32	3
Ipswich	1	94	89	78
	2	3	8	16
	3	2	3	3
Liverpool	1	70	57	82
	2	14	3	18
	3	16	40	0
Whitehaven	1	88	81	65
	2	6	8	32
	3	5	10	3

Notes:
Category 1 Those living in the port of registry.
Category 2 Those living outside the port of registry but within a twenty-mile radius of it.
Category 3 Those living more than twenty miles from the port of registry.

Table 10 *Occupations of coastal shipowners in ships' registers (%)*

Category		1850	1875	1910
Glasgow	1	75	66	3
	2	19	12	1
	3	4	4	3
	4	1	19	93
Ipswich	1	46	46	82
	2	23	28	7
	3	17	2	4
	4	10	25	7
Liverpool	1	49	42	14
	2	21	10	29
	3	18	6	0
	4	11	42	57
Whitehaven	1	39	32	40
	2	26	25	4
	3	24	22	2
	4	9	21	54

Notes:
Category 1 Those who would benefit from improved transport because they had goods to move.
Category 2 Those who might gain indirectly through employment or providing a service to the ship.
Category 3 Those who had nothing to gain, other than distributed profits.
Category 4 Those who described themselves as 'shipowners'.

summarises the occupational groups to which they belonged. The classifications for areas of residence are the same as in appendix 1. The occupational classification, group 1, includes all those who were likely to have gained 'external economies' through the operation of the boat in which they invested. They include all kinds of shopkeepers, merchants, manufacturers or farmers who hoped either to buy or to sell their wares or produce more extensively or cheaply than would have been the case without the boat's services. Group 2 includes all those whose employment opportunities would be enhanced through the sailing of the ship, i.e. mariners, master mariners, wharfingers, rope-makers, solicitors and bankers. In the third group were persons who put money in the ship as an investment only, expecting a money income in return, and they included spinsters, widows, teachers and 'gentlemen', among others. The fourth group, coded 'SO' are those describing themselves simply as shipowners.

Allowing for the fact that the place of residence of the owners of 1,443 tons out of 42,953 tons is unknown, it remains true that the owners of 80 per cent of the tonnage lived within the port of registry. If the owners who lived within a radius of twenty miles of the port of registry are included then 88 per cent of the tonnage was owned by persons living within the port or nearby. The preponderance of local owners was greatest in Ipswich, where 94 per cent of the tonnage was owned by those living in the port and 97 per cent within a radius of twenty miles from the dockside in 1850. 'Outside' ownership was greatest in the case of Liverpool, where as much as 40 per cent of the tonnage was owned by persons living more than twenty miles from the port, a situation which is explained by Liverpool's importance in the 'liner' trades with Scottish and Irish ports, and with London.

Examination of the occupations of the owners of sixty-fourth shares shows that the overwhelming majority had a direct trading or occupational benefit from their share ownership. As merchants or shopkeepers they anticipated more reliable and prompt delivery or dispatch of their stocks. As craftsmen they hoped to obtain orders for the equipment of the ship and as bankers and solicitors they anticipated that their professional services would be needed. The percentage of the shares of ships held simply as an investment, by widows, spinsters or gentlemen, was very small. The greatest involvement of this class of shipowner was in Whitehaven, where they owned over 20 per cent of the tonnage in both 1875 and 1910;

they were least involved in the case of Glasgow. The proportion of individuals describing themselves as 'shipowners' rises over time in all cases except Ipswich, to the extent that it comprises over half the total in 1910 in Liverpool and Whitehaven and nearly all in Glasgow. This reinforces the suggestion of Davis and Cottrell that professional shipowning was 'not . . . by any means common until the mid-nineteenth century'.[100] Our findings are not directly comparable with those of Ward for the canal system as his categories vary from ours: for instance, merchants and bankers are placed in the same category by him but are separated in our schema. However our group three, the *rentiers*, contributed 17 per cent, or 35 per cent if landed gentlemen are included, to canal funding.[101] This is much higher than the equivalent group's participation in coastal shipping and may in part be explained by the later date of the coastal shipping investment. Ward's data end in 1815 whereas the shipping data is for the mid to late-nineteenth century. By this time merchant and manufacturing wealth in the country increased markedly, and landed wealth declined proportionately. Thus peers and landed gentlemen were much less apparent in coastal ship funding.

The register of ships at Fowey in Cornwall in 1850 exemplifies the diversity of ownership so typical of coastal shipping. The 110-ton schooner *East Cornwall* was in every respect a community enterprise, as were many ships from small ports throughout Great Britain. It had no less than twenty-four different owners, including merchants, corn dealers, ironmongers, shipbuilders, mariners, a doctor, a solicitor, an innkeeper, a draper, a wharfinger, a cashier, a painter and a 'domestic'.

Insurance

When severe storms swept the British coasts, for example on 20–21 February 1862, it was not unusual for Lloyds to report over one hundred ships wrecked or damaged.[102] As outlined in the authors' earlier work,[103] there were three main ways in which shipowners endeavoured to prevent or mitigate disasters. The individual investor could spread his risks by buying shares in a number of vessels, so that if one was wrecked the others would continue to bring in some return. Joint-stock shipping companies often established their own reserve funds, finding this method less expensive than paying premiums to the marine department of an established insurance company. The third method was to form a non profit-making mutual insurance society among shipowners of a single port or very limited geographical area. The division of a ship's capital into sixty-fourth parts greatly encouraged the first method of risk spreading. The Aberdeen Steam Navigation Company provided an example of the second method when in March 1836 it decided not to insure some of its vessels but instead 'to open an account and debit it with what it would have cost to insure them'.[104] The mutual insurance societies of the North-East, pioneered by the owners of the collier brigs in the late eighteenth-century, multiplied rapidly in the early Victorian era. By 1848 North Shields had eighteen of them and South Shields eleven. In 1837 the Committee of the Shields Insurance Clubs established the South Shields Coasting Board which examined ships' masters and pilots and issued certificates to those who passed its tests in navigation and allied subjects, in the belief that properly qualified and sober sailors were more likely to bring their ships safely to harbour. When the Board of Trade became the examining board for the issue of masters' and pilots certificates under the provisions of the Merchant Marine Act, 1850, it followed closely the procedures already followed by the South Shields Coasting Board.[105]

Although the mutual insurance societies were most numerous in the North-East they were to be found all round Britain's coasts, but especially in Devon and Cornwall, Wales and the North-West. The first society in North Wales, the Portmadoc Mutual Ship Insurance Society, was formed as early as 1841. Despite suggestions that many of the clubs were closed down in the 1860s,[106] they continued to play an important role in the coasting trade. In the 1870s many Cornish ships insured with the Newquay Maritime Association.[107] In 1893 the schooner in which David Roberts was employed as mate was damaged in the winter gales. In Roberts's memoirs he notes that the ship was insured with the Bangor Insurance Society who sent a surveyor to inspect the damage.[108] The Dee Shipowners Mutual Insurance Association, formed in 1880, provided insurance for a large proportion of the sailing ships whose base was the Dee estuary.[109] Slade's father belonged to 'an insurance society of Braunton' in the 1900s.[110] It proved possible to run these clubs very economically. The vessels were generally owned locally and were subject to strict inspection by a surveyor. No premiums were paid; but a small initial sum was contributed by the members to meet running expenses and a guarantee was given that if an insured vessel was damaged each member would pay a contribution towards the cost of repair. In the case of the Portmadoc vessels their practice of trading in 'packs' was an additional form of insurance.[111]

Changes in technology

Technological changes in British coastal shipping contributed greatly to the improvement of British marine transport as a whole. They were responsible for substantial reductions in transport costs. The *Rainbow,* launched in Birkenhead in 1837 for the General Steam Navigation Company's London–Margate station, was the first iron vessel to be navigated in British seas. Those owners of coastal vessels who were keen to acquire more cargo space amidships were delighted when screw-propelled ships such as the *Archimedes,* launched at Millwall in 1838 for the coastal trade, proved the soundness of the new principle. It was in coastal vessels that the first experiments were made in replacing the old box-shaped boilers by cylindrical ones which had a longer life because they were easier to maintain and did not silt up so easily. Most important was the discovery that by working steam expansively, i.e. by filling the cylinders to the extent of only a quarter of their capacity, more work was performed by the engine at considerably less cost in the consumption of coal. It was by innovations such as these, together with the later introduction of the compound engine, that it proved possible to use steamships for long ocean voyages, something that had previously proved uneconomic because of the huge quantity of bunker coal the ship needed to carry. As the railway network spread, coastal steamers needed to achieve greater speeds if they were to retain their passenger traffic. This was the great incentive for the introduction of forced draught boilers, which consumed more coal but made possible speeds of twenty knots for vessels such as those that served the Clydeside towns.[112]

The requirements of coastal vessels engaged in the transport of bulk cargoes led to changes in ship design. In the coal trade, as we have noted above, the most dramatic innovations were the introduction of the screw collier – one of which could achieve in five days the amount of work it would take two collier brigs a month to perform – the use of large riverside derricks to speed the discharge of cargoes, the substitution of water for gravel in ballasting, thus making it possible to dispense with the labour of ballast heavers, and the construction of the 'flatiron' type of vessel which enabled supplies of coal to be brought under Thames (and other) river bridges direct to gasworks and electricity power stations. Around 1900 cantilevered brackets replaced pillars within the hold to increase ease of access to the cargo and speed loading and unloading. This 'opening up' of holds made possible the carriage coastwise of large machinery, steel plates and other awkwardly shaped objects which it would have been difficult, if not impossible, to carry by rail.[113]

The adaptation of smaller sailing vessels to the particular needs of the estuaries and stretches of coast which they served was a much slower process, but one which produced a fascinating variety of types of craft. For the east-coast trade there were by 1860 three main types of sailing barges: the 'topsails', 'stumpies' and 'boomies', so called because of their differences in rigging and construction. For the important trade of transporting hay from the harbours of Essex and Suffolk to London, 'stackies' carried cargoes which resembled floating haystacks, but with a low profile to enable them to pass under Thames bridges. They were a familiar sight on the river until the outbreak of the Second World War. There were numerous other types of sailing vessels. The 'Billyboys' of the Humber, with their shallow draught and stout build, were designed both to penetrate far inland up the rivers Trent and Ouse and to withstand the treacherous east-coast gales. The 'trows', with their double-ended open decks and single square sails, were designed to serve the upper reaches of the Severn. The Mersey flats gradually changed their structure in the course of the nineteenth century to enable them to extend their range of operations from the Mersey and its tributaries to coastal work.[114]

Conclusions

It has already been observed that coastal shipping has received scant attention from transport historians. At the time, and subsequently, 'coastal trade . . . was never regarded as anything other than inferior to "real trade" '.[115] Foreign trade was exotic, dealt in higher-value commodities, involved much longer ocean voyages, and was better recorded because it bore the bulk of port dues and all tariffs making it a greater source of concern to government. Similarly, railways and canals have received much more attention from historians, perhaps because they were perceived as more of a discontinuity in the historical process than the coaster. The coastal sailing ship went back to prehistoric times, whereas the canals and railways, with their impressive civil engineering achievements, their large and unruly gangs of 'navigators' and their need for Parliamentary approval to compel the sale of land and protect their investors by corporate form, seemed a radical departure from the past with highly visible physical and political manifestations. Because of the obvious newness of their technology, their sheer size and the power of their steam locomotives, railways also acquired an aura of glamour which attracted an enthusiastic following down to the present day.

In an age of small firms, owned and managed by a couple of partners or one family, railways and canals had hundreds of shareholders, a board of directors or trustees, and employed thousands when the average firm employed less than fifty. This meant the creation of a bureaucratic organisation, which created and maintained extensive records to keep its shareholders informed and fulfil the terms of its act of incorporation. In addition, by virtue of their large boards of directors, the railways were able to muster a significant number of friendly Members of Parliament who promoted railway interests and ensured it had a high visible presence.[116] Debates, select committees, and royal commissions on railway matters abounded, and created a further body of archival material which latter-day historians might utilise. Coastal shipping could boast no similar devotees and was the subject of no such Parliamentary investigations. The small scale of operations of coastal ships meant there was little need to create records, as most owners could keep in touch less formally, and they lacked the institutionalised longevity of joint-stock companies, so that where records were created they were fragmentary and scattered and unlikely to survive the destructive influences which afflict such fragile material – salvage drives, fire and flood.

The task of analysing the role of coastal shipping in the Victorian economy is therefore more difficult than for the railways or canals because there is no large body of records to draw on. Instead there are numerous small-scale references scattered among a variety of locations and types of source – newspaper advertisements, port records, ships' logs, odd passing references in many business papers, diaries, and local histories. Where there is a significant amount of material on the coastal trade in one source – the bills of entry – they are exasperatingly incomplete, inconsistent and tedious to use.

That said, some conclusions can be drawn. Coastal shipping in the

Victorian era was more important as a provider of freight transport than for passenger traffic. In terms of the work done, measured in ton-miles of freight carried, coasters did a larger job than the railways throughout the period and incomparably more than the canals. They achieved this by responding to railway competition most effectively. Whereas in the early years of Victoria's reign they carried a whole range of commodities from high-value, low-bulk products like tobacco or tea, through to the high-bulk, low-value products such as stone and sand, by the later nineteenth century they were carrying low-value, high-bulk products almost exclusively. The railways on many routes could offer a faster service than the coaster. For high-value goods the cost of the capital tied up in a large cargo could outweigh the extra cost of rail freight, so making the more expensive form of transport cheaper overall. For perishable goods too, high speeds were crucial. However for bulky, low-value, non-perishable goods such as coal, ores, or even pig-iron, time was less crucial and the coaster could offer a cheap mobile warehouse for long hauls. Externalities were as important to the coaster as its own operating efficiency. Steam, iron and later steel hulls, screw propulsion, more efficient rigs to allow lower manning, all improved the coastal ship's cost profile, but just as important were port improvements in allowing ease of berthing and fast turn-round times through use of cranes, and other mechanical devices. As railways improved their access to the larger ports the coasters put more effort into the medium to small ports where there was less competition from rail. By concentrating on bulky, long-haul, low-value products the coasters carved out a niche in the market from which the railways could not easily dislodge them.

It is surprising how long coastal passenger traffic survived in competition with the new technology of the railways in some areas. Where the steamship route was more direct than the rail, the east coast for example, the coaster could offer a cheaper and as rapid service, with greater comfort in good weather, and the salubrious effects of an ocean trip. Where the route by rail was more direct, for example Bristol to London, the railway had a decisive advantage. In some areas, such as the Scottish islands or the Isle of Wight, coastal shipping was vital to the economic survival and growth of the region. Although business travel declined in the later nineteenth century the converse was true of pleasure sailings: 'The excursion business reached its zenith in the years immediately before and after the dawn of the twentieth century. These were the years when every resort of any size was served by an excursion steamer . . . and when nearly two hundred paddle steamers operated along the south coast alone.'[117] Thus the coastal steamer serviced the birth of a leisure industry.

Investment in coastal shipping was undertaken principally by persons living in the areas to be served by a liner trade or the home port of a general trader. The investors usually anticipated a dual return. They hoped to be provided either with external economies via a cheaper transport service or additional employment prospects as well as a steady return on surplus capital. Competition among steamers, particularly in estuarial waters, and later between steamer and railway, prompted innovation in all aspects of steam navigation, and these improvements led the way for the eventual domination by the steamship on all maritime routes and the parallel expansion of British overseas trade.

To date the role of coastal shipping has been severely underestimated, as much because of the nature of ownership and scale of operations as by the lack of any substantial, easily accessible body of records. This chapter has shown that, like road freight transport in our own time, it was ubiquitous, extensive and performed a vast and vital service to the Victorian economy.

Appendix I   *The location of shareholders in coastal shipping companies*

Company	Year	1		2		3	
		(a)	(b)	(a)	(b)	(a)	(b)
1 Aberystwyth & Aberdovey Steam Packet Co	1910	77	51	8	5	16	43
2 Aberystwyth & Cardigan Bay Steam Packet Co. Ltd	1864	88	85	2	1	9	14
	1869	74	72	3	3	18	18
	1874	67	67	4	3	24	26
	1879	64	61	8	9	22	24
3 Bristol General Steam Navigation Co	1853	77	79	7	4	15	17
	1856	77	81	7	3	16	17
	1860	80	83	6	5	14	13
4 Cambrian Steam Packet Co. Ltd	1856	83	67	—	—	12	35
	1862	90	54	—	—	8	43
	1867	84	29	—	—	10	69
5 Cardiff & Penarth Steam Ferry Co	1858	83	65	12	35	4	1
6 Cardiff Steam Navigation Co	1850	78	68	14	18	1	<
	1856	53	48	36	36	<	<
	1858	52	48	36	36	<	<
	1862	52	49	35	36	3	4
	1866	50	49	35	35	3	4

Company	Year	1		2		3	
		(a)	*(b)*	*(a)*	*(b)*	*(a)*	*(b)*
7 Dartmouth Steam Packet Co. Ltd	1859	29	10	71	90	—	—
	1860	70	24	19	69	8	8
	1862	71	24	19	69	8	8
	1863	76	46	15	50	7	4
	1864	70	56	19	34	11	11
	1869	55	31	27	42	19	28
	1871	53	25	29	46	18	30
	1876	49	23	30	48	21	30
8 Devon & Cornwall Tamar Steam Packet Co. Ltd	1858	88	88	—	—	8	10
	1859	81	77	—	—	7	10
9 Dublin & Liverpool Steam Ship Co	1845	87	89	—	—	10	10
	1846	87	89	—	—	11	9
10 Galloway Saloon Steam Packet Co	1893	67	79	16	1	16	20
11 Hayle & Bristol Steam Packet Co. Ltd	1858	32	44	47	31	19	24
	1859	34	44	51	34	15	21
	1860	34	40	52	39	14	22
	1861	34	40	52	39	14	22
12 Hull, Ferriby Sluice & Brigg Steam Packet Co. Ltd	1858	19	19	77	80	<	<
	1863	16	15	81	84	<	<
	1870	15	10	79	86	<	<
13 Isle of Wight Packet Co. Ltd	1863	57	56	14	11	28	33
14 Lancaster Steam Navigation & Shipping Co. Ltd	1857	94	96	6	3	—	—
	1859	87	94	13	5	—	—
	1861	87	94	13	5	—	—
	1864	87	94	13	5	—	—
15 Larne & Stranraer Steam Boat Co. Ltd	1871	20	15	80	85	—	—
	1885	44	57	42	28	13	14
16 Maryport, Carlisle, Liverpool & Belfast Screw Steam Navigation Co	1852	74	NG	16	NG	7	NG
	1853	65	58	26	23	7	17
	1856	65	63	23	19	8	13
17 North Devon Shipping Co	1852	49	32	9	11	42	57
	1853	52	33	7	10	41	56
	1854	56	34	6	6	37	59
	1856	42	32	7	2	49	67
	1860	50	40	8	2	42	57
18 Poole, Isle of Purbeck, Isle of Wight & Portsmouth Steam Packet Co	1845	88	94	5	3	5	2
	1846	84	89	8	7	4	2
	1847	84	90	7	6	4	2
19 Port of Hartlepool & London Screw Steam Ship Co	1858	65	50	16	41	19	9
	1859	48	26	29	66	24	8
	1860	48	26	24	66	24	8
20 Port of Portsmouth & Ryde United Steam Packet Co. Ltd	1851	91	70	6	26	3	5
	1856	74	55	17	27	9	16
	1859	72	56	18	26	9	16
	1862	68	58	22	24	11	18
21 Portsea, Portsmouth, Gosport & Isle of Wight New Steam Packet Co	1850	95	92	4	6	2	3
22 Ramsey, Isle of Man Steam Packet Co	ND	100	100	—	—	—	—
23 Saltash & St. Germans Steam Packet Co. Ltd	1859	96	98	—	—	4	2
	1866	94	90	—	—	6	10
	1872	97	93	—	—	3	7
	1875	98	93	—	—	2	7

Company	Year	1 (a)	1 (b)	2 (a)	2 (b)	3 (a)	3 (b)
	1876	98	93	—	—	2	7
24 Southampton, Isle of Wight & Ports-	1861	55	48	19	28	17	17
mouth Improved Steamboat Co. Ltd	1862	60	58	20	21	19	20
25 Stockton & London Screw Steam	1856	40	40	44	43	16	18
Shipping Co	1857	40	38	41	40	18	21
	1862	38	32	42	42	20	26
	1867	35	30	44	43	21	26
	1869	35	29	43	43	22	26
	1871	36	30	42	42	22	26
26 Sunderland & London Steam	1844	43	NG	57	NG	—	NG
Navigation Co							
27 Tamar Steam Navigation Co. Ltd	1857	75	81	17	4	4	2
	1859	75	81	17	4	4	2
28 West of Ireland Steam Navigation Co.	1859	71	33	—	—	29	67
Ltd	1860	62	33	—	—	37	67

Key:
1. Living within the boundaries of the city, or cities from which, or between which, the service is plying.
2. Living within a twenty-mile radius of 1 above, but not included in that category.
3. Living outside the areas defined in 1 and 2.
(a) Number of shareholders expressed as a percentage of all shareholders.
(b) Shares held expressed as a percentage of the total number of shares.
ND = no data
NG = not given
< = less than 1%
Sources: P.R.O., dead company files, BT31 & BT41; National Library of Wales, Mss. 5431E; Scottish Record Office BR/GSP/2/1 and BR/LSS/4/1; Manx Museum B159 1x.

Notes

The authors are grateful to the SSRC for funding some of the research on which this chapter is based, to Giles Harrison for references to the railway companies' regional conferences under the aegis of the Railway Clearing House, and to Jim Bailey for the dates of opening of some railway services.

1 W. G. Hoffman, *British Industry 1700–1950,* trans. by W. O. Henderson and W. H. Chaloner, Oxford, 1955, p. 47.
2 R. Craig, *Steam Tramps and Cargo Liners,* vol. 5 of the National Maritime Museum series 'The Ship', HMSO, 1950, p. 45. The size of ships can be calculated from the Trade and Navigation Accounts published annually in Parliamentary Papers.
3 H. Perkin, *The Age of the Railway,* 1970, p. 283.
4 P. S. Bagwell, *The Transport Revolution from 1770,* 1974, devotes ch. 3 to coastal shipping.
5 C. I. Savage in both editions of his *An Economic History of Transport,*

1959 and 1966. In a further, major, revision of this book, published in 1974, the earlier omission of coastal transport was partly made good by T. C. Barker.

6   H. J. Dyos and D. H. Aldcroft, *British Transport*, Leicester, 1969, devoted two pages to the subject though they did acknowledge that coastal shipping played an important part in freight transport.

7   J. Armstrong, 'The role of coastal shipping in UK transport: an estimate of comparative traffic movements in 1910', *Journal of Transport History*, 3rd ser., VIII, 1987.

8   T. Coppack, *A Lifetime with Ships*, Prescot, 1973, p. 31.

9   *Ibid.*, pp. 24, 31, 33, 34, 37, 41, 45, 48, 49, 51, 53, 63, 65, 68.

10   *Ibid.*

11   P. J. Cain, 'Private enterprise or public utility? Output, pricing and investment on English and Welsh railways, 1870–1914', *Journal of Transport History*, 3rd ser., I, 1980, p. 14; P. J. Cain, 'Railways and price discrimination: the case of agriculture, 1880–1914', *Business History*, XVIII, 1976, p. 191.

12   H. A. Clegg, *A History of British Trade Unions since 1889 Vol. 2 1911–1933*, Oxford, 1985, p. 26.

13   R. C. Riley, 'The industries of Portsmouth in the nineteenth century', *Portsmouth Papers*, XXV, 1976, pp. 10–12.

14   *B.P.P.*, 1899, XCVI, p. vi.

15   *West Briton*, 17 March 1848.

16   *Newcastle Daily Chronicle*, 18 July 1910.

17   SC on Railways, *B.P.P.*, 1840, XIII, Q 4427.

18   HLRO, SC on the York and North Midland Railway Bill, Minutes of Evidence 9 May 1845, p. 171 ff.

19   P. S. Bagwell, *The Railway Clearing House in the British Economy, 1842–1922*, 1968, ch. 4 *passim*.

20   T. R. Gourvish, *Mark Huish and the London and North Western Railway: A Study of Management*, Leicester, 1972, p. 231.

21   P. J. Perry, 'Return cargoes and small port survival: two Dorset examples', Dorset Natural History and Archeological Society, *Proceedings*, LXXXIX, 1968, p. 314.

22   E. A. G. Clark, *The Ports of the Exe Estuary, 1660–1890*, Exeter, 1960, p. 170.

23   Perry, 'Return cargoes', p. 320.

24   Cain, 'Railways and price discrimination', pp. 190–201.

25   *Report of the Proceedings of a Public Meeting of Industrialists of the Borough of Liverpool held in the Corn Exchange, Brunswick Street on 2 March 1865*, p. 7.

26   PRO Rail 727/1 London and North Western and Caledonian Railways: *West Coast Conference Minutes*. Minute 1317, 31 October 1874; Minute 1333, 20 January 1875.

27   SC on Railway Companies' Amalgamations, *B.P.P.*, 1872, XIII, *Report*, p. xix, and Minutes of Evidence, Q 3696.

28   PRO Rail 727/2 *West Coast Conference Minutes*, Minute 2671 of 4 March 1896.

29   *Ibid.*, Minute 3020 of 16 June 1904.

30   Anon., *Ships and Railways*, 1846, p. 15.

31   S. Salt, *Statistics and Calculations*, 1845, p. 70.

32   B. R. Mitchell and P. Deane, *Abstract of British Historical Statistics*, Cambridge, 1962, p. 113.

33   *Herapath's Railway Journal*, 20 January 1855, p. 69.

34   M. W. Flinn, *The History of the British Coal Industry*, Vol. 2, Oxford, 1984, p. 216, wrote that in 1830 96 per cent of London's requirements for coal came from the North-East.

35   *Herapath's Railway Journal*, 19 November 1853, p. 1239.

36   R. J. Irving, *The North Eastern Railway Company, 1870–1914*, Leicester, 1976, pp. 213–27.

37   W. H. White, 'Steam colliers', Institute of Civil Engineers, *Proceedings*, CLV, 1904, p. 106; W. S. Lindsay, *History of Merchant Shipping*, Vol. 4, 1876, p. 546.

38   R. Smith, *Sea Coal for London*, 1961, p. 284.

39   E. E. Allen, 'On the comparative cost of transport by steam and sailing colliers and on the different modes of ballasting', Institute of Civil Engineers, *Proceedings*, XIV, 1854–55, p. 318.

40   Smith, *Sea Coal*, p. 291.

41   *Ibid.*, p. 292.

42   *Ibid.*, p. 276.

43   SC on British Shipping, Minutes of Evidence, *B.P.P.*, 1844, VIII, Qs 1407, 1410.

44   *Newcastle Courant*, 1 March 1850.

45   SC on British Shipping, Minutes of Evidence, *B.P.P.*, 1844, VIII, Q 2094.

46   S. Everard, *History of the Gas, Light and Coke Company*, 1949, p. 196.

47   Allen, 'Comparative cost of transit', p. 327.

48   C. Capper, *The Port and Trade of London*, 1862, p. 476.

49   Papers relating to the Accommodation of Seamen in Merchant Ships, *B.P.P.*, 1867, LXIII, p. 340.

50   SC on Manning of Merchant Ships, Minutes of Evidence, *B.P.P.*, 1896, XL, Q 53.

51   *Economist*, 29 July 1911.

52   Capper, *Port and Trade of London*, p. 473. Letter dated 16 August 1853 from Seymour Clarke, General Manager of the Great Northern Railway, to A. C. Sheriff, regarding the supply of 50,000 tons of coal a year for three years to the Imperial Gas Company, London, from Johnassen and Elliot of Sunderland, PRO Rail GNI/275.

53   E. A. V. Angier, *Fifty Year's Freight, 1869–1919*, 1920, pp. 106–31.

54   Smith, *Sea Coal*, p. 338.

55   'Various well-known experts', *The Industrial Rivers of England*, 1891, pp. 137–8; Cardiff Chamber of Commerce, *Annual Reports*.

56   HLRO, SC on the Aberdeen Railway Bill, 1845, Vol. 1, Evidence of William Marshall, 30 May 1845.

57   The figures for Liverpool and Grangemouth are calculated from

these ports' Bills of Entry.
58 Guildhall Record Office, London, Ms 1667.
59 J. E. Tuit, *The Tower Bridge,* 1894, p. 70; J. R. Day, *The Story of London's Underground,* 1969, p. 52.
60 Workington Iron Returns, Customs 83/7 in Customs and Excise Records Office, London.
61 Glasgow bills of entry 1850 and 1910; Customs 83/7, Workington iron returns; Newcastle Central Library (NCL), River Tyne Improvement Commission; W. Vamplew, 'Railways and the transformation of the Scottish economy', *Economic History Review,* 2nd ser., XXIV, 1971, p. 49.
62 R. M. Barton, *A History of the Cornish China Clay Industry,* Truro, 1971, pp. 75–6; R. Pearse, *The Ports and Harbours of Cornwall,* St Austell, 1963, *passim.*
63 *V.C.H. Cornwall,* I, 1906, p. 577; K. Hudson, *The History of English China Clays,* Newton Abbot, 1969, pp. 24, 29.
64 H. Hughes, *Immortal Sails,* Prescot, 1969, pp. ix, xi, 26, 31, 69; J. Lindsay, *A History of the North Wales Slate Industry,* Newton Abbot, 1974, p. 185.
65 National Library of Wales, Ms 12108D.
66 Liverpool bill of entry, 1910.
67 NCL, River Tyne Improvement Commission.
68 *Ibid.;* Runcorn bill of entry, 1875.
69 J. O'Donovan, *The Economic History of Livestock in Ireland,* Cork, 1940.
70 G. Channon, 'The Aberdeenshire beef trade with London: a study in steamship and railway competition, 1850–69,' *Transport History,* II, 1969, p. 9; C. H. Lee, 'Some aspects of the coastal shipping trade: the Aberdeen Steam Navigation Company, 1835–80', *Journal of Transport History,* III, 1975, pp. 94–107.
71 PRO Rail/172/1 Minutes of the East Coast Conference as to Scottish traffic, 15 February 1865, Minute 69.
72 *Ibid.,* Minute 8 of meeting on 15 August 1854 and Minute 243 of meeting on 22 April 1857.
73 PRO RCH/1/511 English and Scottish Traffic Rate Conference, Minutes of meeting on 18 December 1875, Minute 3088.
74 *Ibid.,* Minutes 3155 and 3182 of 12 March 1875 and 28 April. Minute 4211 of 24 October 1879.
75 T. A. B. Corley, *Quaker Enterprise in Biscuits: Huntley and Palmer of Reading 1822–1972,* 1972, p. 63.
76 C. Wilson, *The History of Unilever,* Vol. 1, 1954, pp. 34–5.
77 J. Armstrong's interview with A. J. Struthers, a 'puffer' master of J. & A. Gardner & Company, 30 March 1970.
78 R. L. Brett, *Barclay Fox's Journal,* 1979, pp. 36, 186, 189.
79 *Gore's Liverpool Directory,* 1841.
80 HLRO SC on the South Eastern Railway Bill, Minutes of Evidence, Vol. 36, Appendix AA.
81 W. Camden, *The Steam Boat Pocket Book: a descriptive guide from London Bridge to Gravesend, Southend, the Nore, Herne Bay, Margate and*

Ramsgate, n.d.

82   HLRO SC on the Glasgow, Paisley, Kilmarnock and Ayr Railway, Minutes of Evidence, Capt. J. Hunter, pp. 78–83.

83   J. Williamson, *The Clyde Passenger Steamer: its Rise and Progress during the Nineteenth Century,* Glasgow, 1904, p. 82.

84   *Edinburgh Evening Courant,* 25 March 1826, 3 March 1846 and 1 January 1849. *Edinburgh Courant,* 1 January 1885.

85   Advertisement in Ward Lock Guide, *The Peak District,* 1908 edn.

86   J. Thomas, *The North British Railway,* Vol. 1, Newton Abbot, 1969, p. 43.

87   J. Simmons, *The Railways of Britain,* 1962, pp. 145–6.

88   B. Greenhill and A. Gifford, *Travelling by Sea in the Nineteenth Century,* 1972, p. 44.

89   PRO Rail 727/1, London & North Western Railway and Caledonian Railway, West Coast Conference, Minute 256 of 13 April 1864, 'Abstract of Passengers Carried'.

90   A. and A. Cormack, *Days of Orkney Steam,* Kirkwall, 1971, p. 13.

91   P.O. Records, Scot 1015/1871.

92   P.O. Records, Post 12/26. Report of the Inter-Departmental Committee appointed by the Postmaster-General to enquire into the Mail Steamer Services on the North and West Coasts of Scotland, January 1898, App. C. Mail Steamer Services to Scotland and Islands of West Coast before May 1891.

93   P.O. Records, Scot 1303/1912 File II.

94   G. W. O'Connor, *Southampton, Isle of Wight and South of England Royal Mail Steam Packet Company: the first hundred years,* Southampton, 1962, p. 30.

95   P.O. Records, 4474/1860, Report of the Committee on Contract Packets, 1853.

96   *Manx Year Book and Directory,* 1971, p. 75.

97   National Library of Wales, Ms 12105(1) B.

98   S. A. Broadbridge, 'The sources of railway share capital' in M. C. Reed (ed.), *Railways in the Victorian Economy,* Newton Abbot, 1977, pp. 209–10.

99   J. R. Ward, *The Finance of Canal Building,* Oxford, 1974, p. 79.

100   P. L. Cottrell, 'The steamship on the Mersey, 1815–80: investment and ownership', in P. L. Cottrell and D. H. Aldcroft (eds.), *Shipping, Trade and Commerce: Essays in Memory of Ralph Davis,* Leicester, 1981, p. 156; R. Davis, 'Maritime history: progress and problems' in S. Marriner (ed.), *Business and Businessmen: Studies in Business, Economic and Accounting History,* Liverpool, 1978, p. 171.

101   Ward, *The Finance of Canal Building,* pp. 18, 22, 74.

102   R. Larn, *Devon Shipwrecks,* Newton Abbot, 1974, pp. 190–219, lists over 1,200 nineteenth and twentieth-century wrecks on the coasts of Devon.

103   J. Armstrong and P. S. Bagwell, 'Coastal shipping', in D. Aldcroft and M. Freeman, *Transport in the Industrial Revolution,* Manchester, 1983, pp. 167–8.

104 Aberdeen Steam Navigation Company, Ms 2479/1, 21 March 1836.

105 G. B. Hodgson, *The Borough of South Shields,* Newcastle upon Tyne, 1903, p. 305.

106 H. A. L. Cockerell and E. Green, *The British Insurance Business, 1593–1970,* 1976, p. 6.

107 R. Pearce, *The Ports and Harbours of Cornwall,* St Austell, 1963, p. 127.

108 *Memoirs of Captain David Roberts,* Bangor Ms 11540.

109 T. Coppack, *op. cit.,* p. 37.

110 Slade, *Out of Appledore,* pp. 16–17.

111 Hughes, *op. cit.,* pp. 53, 56. M. Hughes, 'The Historical Geography of the Sea Faring Industry of the Coast of Cardigan Bay during the eighteenth and nineteenth Centuries', University of Wales Ph.D., 1962, p. 296.

112 W. H. White, 'Progress in shipbuilding and marine engineering since 1859', Institution of Civil Engineers, *Proceedings,* CLV, 1903, p. 38. W. H. Macfarland, 'The growth of economy in marine engineering', *Engineering Magazine,* XXII, May 1902, pp. 208–15.

113 J. C. Robertson and H. H. Hagan, 'A century of coaster design and operation', *Transactions of the Institute of Engineers and Shipbuilders in Scotland,* 1953, p. 213.

114 F. G. G. Carr, *Sailing Barges,* 2nd edn., 1951, p. 71. M. K. Stammers, *West Coast Shipping,* Haverfordwest, 1976, pp. 20–2.

115 G. Jackson, 'The ports', in Aldcroft and Freeman, *op. cit.,* p. 181.

116 P. S. Bagwell, 'The railway interest: its organization and influence, 1839–1914', *Journal of Transport History,* VII, 1965; G. Alderman, *The Railway Interest,* Leicester, 1973.

117 G. Body, *British Paddle Steamers,* Newton Abbot, 1971, p. 154.

The ports

The nineteenth century was the greatest period in the history of British ports. There was more romance, perhaps, in the half-forgotten ports of the Middle Ages, more fumbling responses to booming trade in the eighteenth century, and spectacular activity in modern ports where single ships brought more tonnage in a day than most ports had experienced in a year. But the nineteenth century was special. Never before had there been so much physical expansion, engineering splendour, capital investment or human endeavour. Strident demand was answered with confidence and the ports – or at least the major ones – became huge, wealthy, and proud. London was the pivot of world trade; Liverpool the hub of the Atlantic; Glasgow the 'Second City of the Empire'; Hull the industrial gateway to Europe; and Newcastle and Cardiff were colliers supreme.

The ascendancy of these and other ports was founded on the unprecedented growth in volume and variety of trade during the eighteenth century, which favoured estuaries having the best communications with the interior. Initially there had been much encouragement of the eastern ports importing northern European manufactures and raw materials, with a subsidiary benefit for south-western ports trading to southern Europe. Then a more dynamic influence was felt by certain western ports, as new-found colonies sent produce from which extra wealth could be squeezed through entrepôt dealing into Europe, advancing them more than their own hinterlands, before cotton transformed Lanarkshire and Lancashire, to the profit of Glasgow and Liverpool.

However, despite industrialisation providing northern ports with a new range of exciting exports, at the end of the century London was still completely dominant as the country's leading port because her geographical position, her own economy and the East India monopoly enabled her to trade efficiently in all directions and to act as general entrepôt for Europe as well as the coastal trade. Her tonnage of foreign clearances was almost equal to that of Glasgow, Liverpool, Bristol, Leith and Hull combined, though her lead in exports was less commanding because she exported no coal (see table 19).

Growth in the early nineteenth century

The order of magnitude of the growth of trade, and the overall demands made on ports facilities in the years following the Napoleonic War, can best be illustrated by the tonnage of vessels entering and clearing the country (see table 11). Entries were growing between 1820/24 and 1850/54 at an accelerating rate of around 24, 36, 57, and 73 per cent per decade. Clearances grew even faster, by 22, 46, 62 and 75 per cent. Until the early 1830s the superior volume of imports represents the large amount of raw materials, foodstuffs and manufactures brought into the country, while the superior volume of clearances thereafter represents the continued popularity in Europe of colonial and oriental goods, the growth of manufactured exports and the rise − though initially slow − of the coal trade. Table 19 contains tonnage with cargo only, in order to show the position of ports more clearly as importers and exporters of goods.

Although there was some locally important activity in smaller places (table 19), many of the ancient, well-known ports were handling only a few thousand tons of shipping in 1841, when the leaders were handling nearer a million. The only ports which made notable advances in entries and clearances between 1791 and 1841 were the coal ports of Cardiff, Newcastle, Newport, Stockton, Sunderland and Swansea; the packet ports − Dover, Plymouth, Southampton; and the general ports − Hull, Liverpool, London, Aberdeen, Dundee, Glasgow and Leith. Gloucester, Goole and Grimsby were new ports which showed great promise but had achieved little by 1841. It is apparent from table 11 that the so-called principal ports (the official list also includes three Irish ports of no great size) maintained their share of entries and clearances at over 70 per cent during the first half of the century, and the discrepancy between major and minor ports was accentuated. London, Liverpool, Newcastle and

Table 11 Foreign-going vessels entering and clearing principal ports in the UK, cargo and ballast, 1820/24–1850/54 (five-yearly averages, '000 tons)

	1820–24		1830–34		1840–44		1850–54	
Entries	Tons	%	Tons	%	Tons	%	Tons	%
UK total	2,225.2		3,017.0		4,741.4		8,192.8	
London	779.2	35.0	920.6	30.5	1,313.6	27.7	2,299.4	28.1
Liverpool	444.2	20.0	660.8	21.9	1,053.0	22.2	1,882.2	23.0
Hull	160.8	7.2	221.2	7.3	335.0	7.1	449.4	6.1
Bristol	63.2	2.8	65.2	2.2	82.8	1.7	150.2	1.8
Newcastle	56.6	2.5	106.8	3.5	326.0	6.9	372.2	4.5
Leith	47.4	2.1	51.4	1.7	83.0	1.8	132.5	1.6
Southampton	26.4	1.2	33.6	1.1	119.4	2.5	215.8	2.6
Greenock	44.8	2.0	67.4	2.2	72.0	1.5	111.2	1.4
Glasgow	4.4	0.2	11.2	0.4	50.8	1.1	126.8	1.5
Clearances								
UK total	2,073.4		3,017.8		4,889.8		8,542.0	
London	626.8	30.2	811.6	26.9	1,073.8	22.0	1,748.0	20.5
Liverpool	469.6	22.6	708.0	23.5	1,129.0	23.1	1,951.0	22.8
Hull	131.0	6.3	178.8	5.9	262.4	5.4	384.8	4.5
Bristol	56.0	2.7	61.0	2.0	69.0	1.4	91.2	1.1
Newcastle	155.0	7.5	227.0	7.5	580.8	11.9	930.2	10.9
Leith	37.4	1.8	38.8	1.3	42.4	0.9	65.5	0.8
Southampton	23.4	1.1	30.2	1.0	119.2	2.4	223.4	2.6
Greenock	53.2	2.6	75.4	2.5	73.6	1.5	66.2	0.8
Glasgow	6.0	0.3	11.0	0.4	92.8	1.9	227.4	2.7

Sources:
Total: 1820–40: B.P.P., 1847 (588), LX, 142; 1850–52: 1852/53 (318), LVII, 199; 1853–54: 1954/55 (133), XLVI, 283.
Ports: 1820–50: 1851 (656), LII, 213; 1851–53: 1854 (390), LX, 241; 1854: 1854/55 (326), XLVI, 287.

Hull combined accounted for well over 60 per cent of ships' operations until mid-century, when their clearances slipped to 59 per cent under comparative pressure from the new coal ports. Hull advanced least because she had little part in the transatlantic trade, and her coal trade had not yet developed. At the top, two notable developments took place: Liverpool's inexorable rise took her ahead of London in export tonnage by the early 1840s; and, under competition from the northern industrial ports and the rising coal ports, London lost something of her commanding lead while still enjoying huge increments in activity. In general, then, the vast majority of general European trade continued to enter the Forth, Humber and Thames; transatlantic traffic still went through the Clyde, Mersey and Severn; and the coal trade remained concentrated on the Tyne, Wear and Tees, though there were 'new' Scottish and Welsh ports, some of which, for sheer tonnage of shipping, would eventually rival the largest general ports. The coastal trade, though more generously distributed than foreign trade, also remained firmly fixed on the major ports (see table 20). Its volume exceeded that of the foreign trade, but in minor ports it was not usually a problem fitting tiny coasters into natural harbours, and in major ports they could still be accommodated in facilities no longer good enough for foreign traders. In any case, coasters accumulated a large tonnage by rapid movement, so that quite small harbours could build up a respectable tonnage that would have been difficult in foreign trade.

Growth of this order had long placed a great strain on port facilities and encouraged the perfection of engineering skills in the eighteenth century which produced many piers, a number of substantial harbours, and the first generation of wet docks in Liverpool, Hull, London, Bristol and Leith. Around the turn of the century there was sufficient accommodation existing or proposed in the major ports to offset any tendency for the real cost of using them to rise above what their trade could bear, and further increases were accommodated in relatively simple fashion by additions to their first generation of docks and harbour works. On the Clyde, for instance, improvements were chiefly a matter of harbour-building in Greenock (East India Harbour, 1809), and the gradual deepening of the river, which resulted in Glasgow itself becoming a legal port in 1812, though Greenock remained the chief landing place, by tonnage, until the 1840s.[1] Liverpool's booming trade relied on a progression of new docks built in the two decades following the war (Union 1816,

Princes 1821, Clarence 1830, Brunswick 1832, Waterloo 1836, Trafalgar 1836 and Victoria 1837). At a more modest level, in Hull, where the bulky Baltic and north European trade had brought excessive congestion because the local private dock company refused for some time to extend its facilities, a second (Humber) dock was opened in 1809 and a third (Junction) in 1829.

London was also facing pressure, but unfortunately the absence of a single dock authority thwarted coherent development: the specialist dock companies did not respond readily to generalised demand. A new company stole a march – literally – on the others by building St Katharine's Dock (1828) next to the Tower, and ended up with a hugely expensive dock, too far up-river, that contributed little to the real needs of the port in the 1830s and 1840s. More, perhaps, was gained from the London Dock Company's counter-attack with its East Dock, opened in the same year, while the growing portion of goods that did not require warehousing were better catered for by the West India Company's timber dock (1829) and the extensive accommodation provided by the new Surrey Commercial Company's works south of the river.

Criticism of St Katharine's Dock springs from its awkward water space, constricted land site and fortress warehouses, which looked to the past rather than to the future. It would, however, be wrong to give the impression that the first generation of docks were inadequate. They were sound in engineering, once teething troubles had been ironed out by John Rennie, Thomas Telford and others; and though they might be congested, they continued to cater for the sort of ships and trades for which they were designed. The problem was that even before the 1830s they could no longer accommodate new trades and new ships which required a second generation of docks designed for their specific characteristics.

Pressures for change: steamships and railways

Of the pressures from commodities, the most widely disruptive was not coal, as might be imagined, but wood, with which all ports, large, small and decayed, were involved to some extent. Every house, factory and mine used imported wood, and in the eastern ports (and some western ones) vast amounts of Baltic deals were landed for storage and seasoning in raff yards that had to be adjacent to docks to save labour. In London new docks had been required because the original ones had little quay space and no cheap land nearby. However, no sooner had ports equipped themselves to deal with raff than the introduction of powered sawmills in Britain created the unsawn timber trade, which brought a different sort of pressure: 'timber' went overside into the water. During the season, from July to October, ships often could not move for logs in the worst afflicted docks, and one of the aims of new dock building in the 1830s was to get rid of them, though because timber ships were usually quite small this usually meant more dock and quay space, or adjacent timber ponds, rather than 'improved' facilities.

It was steam power that brought the first great qualitative changes to ports; the demand for space and facilities was no longer for 'more of the same'. Paddle-steamers came before trains, in the second decade of the century, but were slow to establish themselves. They quickly conquered – or created – the distribution trade from the Clyde to the Highlands and Islands of the West of Scotland; they were active between the ports of the Forth; they penetrated the middle reaches of the Humber and its tributaries; and, of course, they soon began their runs on the Thames. There were over a hundred of them active in Britain by 1823,[2] but their limited role was revealed in their owners, who were victuallers, vintners, brewers and drapers,[3] and if port authorities were reluctant to admit such fire hazards, their owners were equally anxious to avoid the loss of time and convenience involved in passing locks and traversing docks. They preferred river quays and piers, so for a time – which in some cases stretched into the 1850s – ports were able to accommodate an increased trade without a corresponding increase in dock space.

Rapid and precise turn-round was even more in demand when steamers ventured coastwise. 'If they use the Docks they will be great losers', Aberdeen owners alleged in opposing a dock in 1839, and drew support from an earlier form of power: 'For one class of horse you want a particular sort of stable; you do not put a cart horse where you put a racer . . . those who want to get quick in and out will not use the Docks.'[4] In fact entry to 'old' docks was soon not an option. By 1830 the largest steamers were bigger than 'typical' 300-ton sailing ships for which the early locks were planned, and with paddle-boxes increasing their breadth by another ten feet, they required four times as much water space in which to lie and manoeuvre.[5] Many were already too wide to pass the locks, and Goole, Hull and Bristol shipowners were probably not alone in negligently commissioning steamers which could not enter their docks.[6] Yet widening a lock was perhaps the most difficult and expensive improvement undertaken in the early nineteenth century, since it involved the compete closure of a dock, and it is not surprising that the first reaction of several dock companies was to insist that steamers had no right to enter their works.[7]

The ensuing argument on a matter of principle recurred each time technical change took the most advanced vessels beyond the capacity of existing docks. Aberdeen steam owners feared that port charges would fund an expensive dock which they did not wish to enter. Elsewhere sailing owners resisted the cost of wider locks needed *only* for a small number of paddle-steamers which did not actually pay dues on the tonnage of the paddle-boxes for which the new locks were required, or, indeed, on the engine-room which powered them. The argument reached its height towards the end of the century, over accommodation for grand liners which demanded vast docks but paid dues on little more than 60 per cent of their gross measured tonnage.[8]

Whatever sailing owners thought, there was no choice for ports benefiting from regular and rapid accumulation of tonnage by paddlers: they must provide suitable facilities or risk losing them. Liverpool was probably the first port to provide a specific steamship dock, and other ports followed rather fitfully over the next two or three decades to provide the bigger 'second generation' locks and docks designed specifically for steamships.

This tardy provision of steamer docks reflects the long gestation of the seagoing paddler, which was still on trial in the 1830s. It also reflects, to some extent, its ability to work faster than sailing vessels, so that a greater tonnage of ships or goods could be accommodated without enlarging the dock space. Indeed, steamers came and went with such relentless precision that goods could not be brought to or removed from the quays with the necessary speed. They generated a bottleneck in land transport that had to be removed before they could operate effectively. The advantages for national trade derived from steamships and railways were therefore interdependent, though this was not clearly understood in the early days, to the long-term cost of those ports where docks were built either for railways or steamers, but not for both.

Railways took longer than steamers to penetrate the major dock systems, where shippers were still mesmerised by the productivity of overside working between ship and barge. Indeed, the infancy of railways actually witnessed the pinnacle of achievement in the building of *canal* ports.[9] Gloucester (1827) was linked to the Severn for 300-ton ships by the Gloucester & Berkeley Company's ship canal;[10] Goole (1828) was built by the Aire & Calder Navigation Company to divert traffic from Hull;[11] Grangemouth ('Old Dock', 1843), at the eastern end of the Forth & Clyde Canal, was intended to divert transhipment trade from Bo'ness;[12] and Runcorn was developed with such success by the Bridgewater Trustees that it became an independent port (from Liverpool) in 1847.[13] Goole in particular had an excellent dock system and an extensive hinterland, and made a significant bid for a direct share of British trade. The very success of shallow-draughted river steamers inhibited railway building in some estuaries: the Leeds–Hull section of the Liverpool–Hull railway was delayed for a decade by their great success on the Ouse,[14] and their activity on the Trent encouraged the establishment of the port of Gainsborough in 1841,[15] though the superiority of rail over river was by then established, and the marriage of railways and ports seen as vital for the future welfare of both.

Railways were as demanding of new facilities as steamers, not least because of topographical problems. Since ports were devoted to water-borne traffic they formed tight semi-circles round harbours or docks, with scant regard for land access. Rails along waterfronts would damage water access, while an approach from the landward side would demolish valuable warehouses as well as housing. Moreover, open space for railway working was difficult to create around existing basins, and Liverpool, Hull and Bristol, for instance, could only bring rails to the early docks down public streets. The problem was worst in London, where docks had been built to keep landsmen out, and had little space for railways. Nonetheless, St Katharine's Dock, opened after the Stockton–Darlington Railway, illustrates the point that docks could still afford to ignore the latest form of transport: old forms still continued, especially in the voluminous coastal trade, and were served adequately by 'old' facilities.

Outside London the availability of rail transport also brought problems in the shape of larger, heavier goods such as railway engines themselves, and agricultural machinery for export, and these again required open quays and, incidentally, powered lifting devices. The same was true of coal, which was entering more strongly into foreign trade with the spread of steam power. In sum, quite apart from any shortcomings of locks for steamships, the first generation of 'town centre' docks were out of date by the late 1830s.

Although most ports were eventually linked to railways, the long-term results were not always what had been expected or desired. Railways which could service hinterlands efficiently and cheaply could also shift the balance between ports, by the interpenetration of 'private' hinterlands created by rivers and canals. In Scotland, for instance, Dundee benefited from railways to Arbroath (1849) and Perth (1847), but was then one of the few ports to lose overall, by railways to Glasgow and Leith (1848).[16]

In England the four major commercial ports stood at the corners of the country's heartland, but neither London nor Bristol had adequate communications with a substantial industrial hinterland,[17] and competition was largely between Liverpool in the west and Hull in the east, with Liverpool endeavouring to attract some of the trade between Lancashire and Europe, and Hull touting for trade between Yorkshire and the USA. The Manchester–Liverpool railway pulled trade westwards, while the Manchester–Grimsby railway pulled some of it eastwards though not – to the chagrin of its commercial community – to Hull. The Leeds–Hull railway redressed the balance somewhat, but Hull probably suffered more than most ports from the rise of alternative rail-borne traffic flows, culminating in the attempts of the North Eastern Railway to divert trade from Hull to Hartlepool in order to save expenditure on the Humber section of its overloaded metals. The resultant frustration was such that while many railway companies built ports, Hull appears to have been the only port which built a major railway (the Hull & Barnsley) in self-defence.

'Second generation' steamer docks

The combined influence of railways, steamships, and increasing trade brought a handful of improved harbours and a large number of more advanced docks between *c.* 1830 and 1870. In the early stages places such as Bristol seemed specially favoured, since the extensive facilities created at the beginning of the century apparently catered for a comparatively lethargic trade growth after Brunel designed a new – and novel – lock in the 1840s and new wharves (Princes and Bathurst) were built in the 1860s. However, in Bristol's case there was danger in opting to maintain an up-river site which would hardly serve the ships attempting to use it by the 1860s:[18] large ships were excluded by the great tidal range and the Avon Gorge, which could hardly be blasted away with the same determination with which Newcastle approached the massive dredging of the Tyne in the 1860s, and Glasgow blew out the bottom of the Clyde in its determination to create an up-river port for the largest transatlantic steamers.[19]

For most ports there was no question of improving harbours: steamship docks were the only way forward. Liverpool led the way under the guidance of Jesse Hartley, one of the greatest Victorian engineers, who hit upon the happy expedient of filling the Mersey shore with a string of linked small docks of great variety that were easy to construct, finance and match to the pattern of growing demand. Clarence Dock (1830) was the first built specifically for steamers, well away from other docks for fear of fire, and three more followed in the mid-1830s (Waterloo, Victoria and Trafalgar). After a brief diversion to produce Albert Dock (1845) for the warehouse trades, and three little ones (Salisbury, Collingwood and Stanley) as a new terminus for the Leeds–Liverpool canal, five more open docks (Nelson, Bramley Moore, Wellington, Sandon and Huskisson), were constructed by 1852. This phase of Liverpool's titanic activity was brought to a close with Canada Dock, opened in 1859 for the very largest oceanic steamers. The changing needs of the long-haul steamers even within this short period of time are clearly seen in the steady rise in the width of entrance locks: forty-five feet for the earliest, sixty for Collingwood, eighty for Huskisson and 100 for Canada.[20]

London had little opportunity for further dock building after the opening of St Katharine's in 1828. The London Dock Company had opposed the new dock by denying that 'any additional docks were required by the state of the commerce of the Port',[21] and any initiative was inhibited by the financial troubles of the dock companies. The East and West India companies amalgamated for self-preservation and rationalisation in 1838, but it was left to the two great railway contractors, Peto and Brassey, to work out how to bring London into the railway age with Victoria Dock, opened in 1855 with the latest facilities for rail and steamer access.[22]

Victoria Dock, though rather late on the scene as a steam dock, marks an important shift in gear. At 100 acres it was the first of the very large rectangular docks that would mark the way ahead wherever large volumes of shipping were concentrated, not least because dock space was easier and cheaper to build than were locks. There was, however, a major drawback to large docks at this time. While a dead water area had obvious advantages for working with barges, or turning steamers, it was wasteful for working small ships at quays, for which the most advantageous formula was the highest ratio of quay length to water area. The answer was to build piers inside the dock to give the maximum quay length within a given impounded area, and this was to be the pattern within docks until very large steamers demanded their replacement by simple lineal quayage towards the end of the century.[23]

A second important feature of Victoria Dock also set a useful precedent. Because it was served by railways it could move down-river to cheaper land and deeper water. It could therefore undercut the older docks companies, and attracted sufficient shipping to frighten them. Additional competition from river wharves, following changes in customs regulations after 1854, drove the dock companies towards bankruptcy, and in 1864 the London, St Katharine's and Victoria Dock companies amalgamated as the London & St Katharine's Company and the Commercial and Grand Surrey companies amalgamated as the Surrey Commercial Dock Company. Nevertheless, the amalgamations did not produce companies able to add to the modern facilities of the port, and the second large railway dock was constructed by yet another new company, the Millwall Dock Company, which opened in 1868. Other extensions in the port (Canada, 1876, and South-West India docks) served their purpose – especially the timber trade – but were unable to accept the largest ships.

If the difficulties of the London dock companies raised doubts as to the wisdom of leaving port facilities in the hands of competing private enterprise, the situation in Hull called into question the existence of private dock companies of any sort. Hull's monopoly had no desire to spend money on modern docks, and demands for facilities for railways, steamers and huge quantities of floating timber were resisted until, with ill grace and confused planning, a tiny railway dock was provided within the existing old-fashioned dock system and the 'modern' Victoria Dock was constructed on the other side of the port without proper rail access.[24] Paddle-steamers were expected to use the entrance piers of the latter, and the connection between steamers and railway was made by barges. The Dock

Company performed no better when next they fought off rivals and extended their facilities: Albert Dock (1869) was so narrow that passage along it was frequently impossible, and it was so unfortunately sited that the large steamers for which it was theoretically intended could enter only stern first and on the ebb tide until the entrance was changed in 1889.[25] It is well to note that not all nineteenth-century engineering was sound or sensible.

Railway ports

Railways were undoubtedly more dynamic than ports burdened with assets designed for a previous age, and for many promoters the simplest thing was to take the most advantageous route to a suitable part of the coastline and there build on a clear site, where the latest organisation and machinery could be introduced without upsetting vested interests or traditional working patterns. Railways were created in the first place to get coal to ports, but while many snaked their way across County Durham to the Tyne, the first steam railway, from Darlington to Stockton, ignored the quays of the latter and established its staiths at 'Port Darlington' on the Tees. By 1834 rival coal railways had established Port Clarence (on the Tees) and Hartlepool, where Victoria Dock was opened in 1840. Middlesbrough followed in 1842 (receiving a powerful boost after 1851 from the iron trade), and Seaham in 1844 for the collieries of Lord Londonderry. Blyth, opened in the mid-1850s, was the last of the staith ports which supplemented but never came anywhere near to replacing the traditional coal ports, where railways also encouraged improvements. As well as river works, the Tyne Commissioners built Northumberland Dock (1857), while the North Eastern Railway built Jarrow Dock (1859), for 500 colliers, on the Tyne, and Hudson Dock (1850/55) and Hendon Dock (1868) in Sunderland.[26]

Railway/mineral ports came more slowly to the North-West, where competing coal interests brought railways into the old port of Whitehaven, whose excellent harbour, now devoted to coastal exports, was augmented by a small dock in 1876. Maryport also expanded its capacity rapidly with the building of Elizabeth Dock in 1867 and Senhouse Dock in 1884. Neighbouring Harrington and Workington were developed for the iron trade, and, further south, ironstone was shipped at a primitive 'port' called Borthwick Rails before the Furness Railway Company established Barrow in the

1860s. It was grandly conceived, with Devonshire and Buccleuch Docks together forming over sixty acres, and Ramsden Dock added in the 1870s; but foreign trade was scarce, and the docks became, more or less, part of the Vickers shipbuilding enterprise.[27]

In Scotland, several of the smaller western ports owed their success to railway penetration of the Ayrshire coalfield. At various dates facilities ranging from minor piers to elaborate docks were built by railway companies at Largs, Irvine, Troon, Ayr and Girvan, and by a consortium of interests in Ardrossan, chiefly to assist the transportation of coal to Ireland and foodstuffs from Ireland. On the east coast direct coal–railway participation in ports came somewhat later, with developments by the North British Railway Company at Burntisland after 1876 and the more important Methil (originally privately owned) after 1889.

The most important of all the 'new' mineral ports were those of South Wales, where Newport, Cardiff, Penarth, and Llanelli all thrived on coal or the interrelated metal trades. It was Cardiff, originally an iron port, which went ahead most rapidly with the building of West Bute Dock (1839) and the Taff Valley Railway. By the time East Bute Dock was opened in 1855 Cardiff had risen from fourth to first coal exporter on that coast, and there was enough encouragement to provoke a rival dock at Penarth (1863).[38] Swansea (which followed Bristol's pattern of creating a floating harbour in 1852) and Port Talbot did not have a suitable hinterland to maintain an early boom in coal exports, and became principally copper ports.

Minerals also provided the basis for much of the trade of the south-western ports, and indeed there were enough railways carrying ore, clay, coal and granite to the coast to justify an enthusiasts' book about them.[29] Hayle, Portreath and Devoran were leading copper ports; St Austell, Par, Newquay and Fowey shipped china clay; Wadebridge and Watchet exported a variety of things. But while these and other places owed their origin or growth to railways (and some to earlier granite ways) only Falmouth, Plymouth and Exeter were of any significance in national trade. The rest were coastal ports or shipping places with unsophisticated harbours built out of local stone or cliff face.

A railway-inspired coal port was simply a matter of engineering and money: it could hardly fail. A new general port was quite a different matter, and in fact there were only two of consequence in the whole country: Birkenhead and Grimsby. Both were on ambitious lines and both, significantly, tried to duplicate major ports. The Birkenhead, Lancashire & Cheshire Railway sought to divert southern traffic from Liverpool, but two preliminary docks (Morpeth and Edgerton, 1847) absorbed the funds, and humiliating failure was avoided only because the 'Great Float' was taken on, for sentimental reasons, by Thomas Brassey, the railway-builder, who was born in Birkenhead.[30] When Brassey in turn failed to complete the port, its subsequent sale to Liverpool Corporation defeated the object of its creation. The Mersey Docks and Harbour Board was created in 1858 to run both sides of the Mersey as a single port, in which Birkenhead was a collection of subsidiary docks rather than a commercial centre. It failed partly because its engineer, Rendel, neglected coaling equipment and effective communications with the Lancashire coalfield, which were, instead, created by the St Helen's Canal & Railway Company, whose two docks (1853, 1875) at Garston eventually took away half Liverpool's coal trade.[31]

Grimsby, also designed by Rendel, was more immediately successful than Birkenhead and must rank as the leading general railway port. Built by the Manchester, Sheffield & Lincolnshire Railway Company (the Great Central) to divert traffic from Hull by its superb inland connections, it was soon importing large quantities of Continental foodstuffs and exporting enough manufactures to make it the fifth port, by value, for a time in the late 1860s. Moreover, the expanding South Yorkshire and Midlands coalfields found a natural outlet there, soon amply justifying the magnificent dock which, in the provision for shipping and the level of its hydraulic equipment, must rank as the first of the truly modern docks.[32]

Railway-inspired ports were not all giants of the coal – or any other – trade. Many small places gained disproportionately from the addition of railway traffic, and sometimes pushed their way to ease pressure on congested rails to larger ports. Goole received a great addition to its canal-borne traffic when the Lancashire & Yorkshire Railway established its railhead there in 1848, though Railway Dock was built by the Aire & Calder Navigation, which retained control of the port.[33] The trade of Grangemouth soared after its acquisition by the Caledonian Railway brought Stirlingshire coal;[34] and later provisions at Leith (Edinburgh Dock, 1881, and Imperial Dock, 1902) were chiefly for rail-borne coal from the Lothians. Boston regained minor port status when it was linked to the Derbyshire coalfield in

1884.[35] King's Lynn's small Alexandra Dock attracted Midlands coal in sufficient quantity for Bentinck Dock to be opened in 1883. Ipswich, an important agricultural and machinery centre, was greatly strengthened by a 33-acre dock opened there in 1841 and linked to the national rail network in 1846.[36]

Creating ports was, however, a risky business outside the coal trade, and there are several examples of wasted investment where neither railway nor dock achieved the desired objective. At Silloth, the Carlisle & Silloth Bay Railway & Dock Company failed to produce the coal traffic to justify their ambitious Marshall Dock (1859), with facilities rivalling Grimsby and Swansea, but used principally by the biscuit firm, Carr's of Carlisle.[37] Preston was a little – but not much – more successful in its grand design to divert trade from Liverpool, despite one of the largest single docks in Britain (Albert Edward was over forty acres).[38]

There is no denying the combined influence of railways and steamers on the trade in materials, but in the long term it was the trade in people which made the most intensive demands on ports. Foreign travel of every sort was fostered. Oceanic business rocketed as emigrants flooded out to the USA and the British Dominions, with surges in 1847–54, 1863–74, 1880–93 and 1900–13. Though emigration in rough sailing ships and worn-out steamers continued for decades, the luxury liners catering for businessmen and wealthy tourists, with emigrants in 'steerage', grew rapidly in size and fixed the passenger trade in the few ports which could provide the elaborate accommodation required. Liverpool's response was to revert to river steamer days: a floating iron pontoon was anchored off

Table 12 *Passengers between Britain and non-European ports (five-yearly averages)*

Years	Outwards	Inwards	Years	Outwards	Inwards
1820–24	19	—	1870–74	271	64
1830–34	76	—	1880–84	368	90
1840–44	93	—	1890–94	301	156
1850–54	328	—	1900–04	378	191
1860–64	155	—	1910–13	650	341

Note: There are no accurate records of passengers inwards before 1870. The difference between passengers outwards and inwards gives a net migration figure.

Source: B. R. Mitchell and P. Deane, *British Historical Statistics*, pp. 47–9.

George's Dock wall (1848), and extended in the following decade as oceanic liners grew in size and number. However, the luxury end of the trade was fixed in the south-east of England, and since London itself was unsuitable (because of excessive voyage time compared with railway time) there was renewed pressure for a southern port closer to the capital than Liverpool. The old colonial packet port at Falmouth was dimissed out of hand as too far away, and the Great Western Railway's claims for Plymouth were no more successful than Brunel's attempt to make Bristol the 'Western Gateway'.[39]

In fact the nearest place to London with a suitable water site was the decayed port of Southampton, and it was here, at what Capper called 'almost an outport of the Port of London',[40] that the London & Southampton Railway built its packet station in 1840, and opened 'Outer' Dock in 1842.[41] P&O and Royal Mail quickly established a base there, and it was also a natural port of call for shipping between the major American and European ports. As early as 1841 Southampton was the third port in terms of *steam* tonnage entering and clearing, though its sailing tonnage was negligible.

Table 13   *Steamers clearing in foreign trade, 1841*

	No.	Tonnage	% of total	Average (tons)
London	646	154,470	40·4	239
Bristol	5	3,395	0·9	679
Dover	1,294	86,096	22·5	67
Falmouth	1	494	0·1	494
Hull	183	41,537	10·9	227
Liverpool	72	24,293	6·4	337
Shoreham	41	5,829	1·5	142
Southampton	238	66,194	17·3	278

Source: B.P.P., 1842 (409), xxxix, 630.

The leading packet port was clearly Dover which, even before the railway arrived, in 1844, had the second largest tonnage of steamers clearing in foreign trade. Their diminutive size indicates their role as passenger and postal vessels. Massive port developments (Wellington Dock and the great Admiralty Pier, building between 1847 and 1871) never attracted heavy goods traffic, though the easy Channel crossing raised the tonnage using the port fivefold between 1840 and

1880, by which time Dover could be included with confidence among the major ports.[42]

The remaining southern packet ports enjoyed mixed fortunes. Southampton's rise more or less ruined the old Channel Islands' packet port of Weymouth, from which the postal service was withdrawn to Southampton in 1845.[43] Not until the late 1880s did the Great Western Railway make serious efforts to revive Weymouth as an importation point for Channel Islands produce destined for the west of England.[44] Railway interest was crucial. Shoreham's inclusion among the steamer ports in 1841 resulted from the opening of the London and Brighton railway in that year, and its rapid demise from the London & Brighton's decision to compete with Dover through the better port of Newhaven, where the Dieppe steamer service was opened in 1849 and improved following the deepening of the harbour in the 1870s.[45] Newhaven was also ideally placed for the French and Channel Islands fruit and vegetable trades, and the diminutive port of Littlehampton was also developed for the same purpose in the 1860s. The nearest rival to Dover was actually Folkestone, on the same railway, which began a ferry service to Boulogne in the late 1840s. In practice the harbour was much inferior to Dover's, and Folkestone did not develop much until the present century.

Another old packet station that lost its post to Dover, in 1836, was Harwich, which, with no railway, also looked like losing its passenger trade to Ipswich. Although the railway arrived in 1854, local problems inhibited development and it was not until the 1880s that the Great Eastern abandoned the port and built a large deep-water quay at 'Parkestone', following the opening of Rotterdam's new channel to the sea and in preparation for the opening of the Harwich–Hoek van Holland run in 1893. Harwich's importance was far greater than her passenger role; by the end of the century imported luxuries for the South Midlands and London pushed Harwich (and Dover) ahead of Grimsby as one of the major importation ports (see table 18).

Major ports and deep docks

The combined effects of railways, steamers, new docks and new trades was to raise the tonnage of shipping clearing British ports from *c*. 8.5 million in the early 1850s to 21.3 million in the early 1870s. Allowing for errors, double counting and changes in measurement, this still represents the largest rise in any twenty-year period between 1800 and 1914. It depended on an increase in shipping of all sorts and sizes. Although the sailing fleet included many small vessels plying their humble way around Europe (or round the coast), the average tonnage of long-haul sailers rose significantly around mid-century. So far as steamers were concerned the more influential of their two 'new' characteristics was probably their greater efficiency rather than their greater size, which was still limited in the 1850s by the physical constraints of wooden construction and paddle power. The evolution of the iron screw-steamer led to larger vessels, but in 1870 the average foreign-going steamer was still only 813 tons, and even the grandest could be accommodated in the second generation of docks in the major ports. Thereafter the ports were faced with three factors demanding urgent attention: the continued rise in aggregate tonnage; the evolution of a more modern steamer; and the growth of coal exports.

In absolute terms the pressure of shipping on the port system as a whole reached its climax on the eve of the Great War. The tonnage clearing in foreign trade with cargo and in ballast more than trebled between 1870–74 and 1911–14, from twenty-one to seventy-four million, and to this must be added a smaller but nevertheless substantial rise in the tonnage of coastal trade, with cargo and ballast, from thirty-one to sixty-three million. The pattern of this growth after *c.* 1870 was somewhat different from that in the earlier period. In particular, the rise in foreign-going tonnage was slowing down after the initial railway/steamer boom, and reached a low point of only a 23 per cent increment between 1880/84 and 1890/94. It is tempting

Table 14 *Shipping clearing foreign and entering coastwise at British ports, cargo and ballast, 1870–74 to 1910–13 (five-yearly averages; million tons)*

| Years | Clearing foreign | | Entering coastwise | |
	Cargo	Cargo and ballast	Cargo	Cargo and ballast
1870–74	18·8	21·3	19·6	31·2
1880–84	27·7	31·1	26·3	42·1
1890–94	34·1	38·4	29·6	51·2
1900–04	43·1	50·8	31·2	57·4
1910–13	61·6	74·0	32·9	62·9

Source: Annual Statements of Navigation and Shipping.

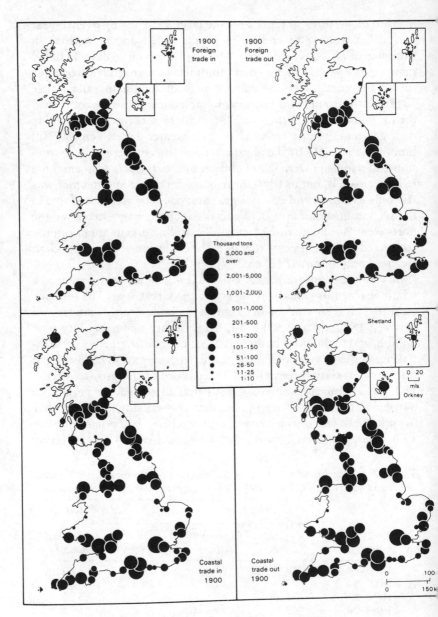

22   Trade by port, 1900 (from G. Jackson in J. Langton and R. J. Morris (eds.), *Atlas of Industrializing Britain*, Methuen, 1986, p. 99)

to assume that some of this variation in growth rate of foreign trade was caused by an increased tendency to clear ships in ballast, but a careful comparison of tonnage in cargo and in ballast reveals a constancy of *c.* 89 per cent cargo until the 1890s, when it began to fall slowly to around 83 per cent on the eve of the war. There was a greater tonnage in ballast inwards in foreign trade and outwards in coastal trade, but the purpose here is to assess the total activity within ports, and that is represented by ships passing locks and occupying quays, whether or not they carried cargo in both directions. (A ship entering in ballast is, of course, as vital to the nation's trade as when it leaves with cargo.)

This slowing down in growth rate may also reflect the rise in manufactures compared with bulk trades: industrial products were greatly in demand throughout the world, while the major consumers of shipping space, in particular corn and coal, came rather late in the century and would explain the faster growth in tonnage from the 1890s.

So long as they had space available, port authorities could cope with marginal increases in total shipping better than they could cope with increases in the size of individual ships. Unfortunately for them, the demise of the paddlers and early iron steamers, for which all recent docks had been designed, led to the most serious challenge in the last quarter of the century from the new multi-decked steel ships: the long-distance tea and corn clippers, and the fuel-efficient compound-engined steamers.

Though a great deal of the increased trade towards the end of the century, especially on the coast and within Europe, was still carried by small vessels, the burgeoning imperial and intercontinental trades of Glasgow, Liverpool, Southampton and, eventually, London and Hull favoured large ships; many ports had a tramp trade in largish vessels with various parts of the world; and even the European trade, which had grown so much that Germany, Holland, Belgium and France sent almost half the tonnage arriving in Britain in 1910–13, involved large regular steamers as well as diminutive sailers. The net result was a rise in the average tonnage of foreign-going sailers to 1,568 by 1913, and of steamers to no less than 2,500. At the turn of the century there were already 4,442 ships engaged in foreign trade that exceeded 1,000 tons net, with dimensions of approximately 250 feet by 30 feet. The typical tonnage of a large ship was then 3,000–4,000, and there were 623 over 5,000 tons, with the largest,

Celtic, over 20,000 (gross).[46]

Since a 3,000-tonner required thirty feet of water, the implications for port authorities were severe. None of the mid-nineteenth-century docks, and very few harbours, could take them, and ports wishing to remain in the long-haul, bulk and passenger trades were forced to build deep docks, which in turn secured their command of the superior end of the nation's foreign transport system.

Table 15   *Average net tonnage of British shipping employed in foreign trade*

Year	Sail	Steam	Year	Sail	Steam
1870	513	813	1895	1,264	1,497
1875	586	1,003	1900	1,395	1,838
1880	647	998	1905	1,460	2,087
1885	816	1,133	1910	1,548	2,298
1890	988	1,267	1913	1,568	2,500

Source: Annual Statements of Trade and Navigation.

The third formative influence on the nineteenth-century port system was coal. It scarcely figured in foreign trade in the 1850s, rose to prominence in the 1890s, and became the chief employer of shipping and port facilities in the first decade of this century. If we exclude London and Liverpool, which lost something of their old predominance precisely because they were not involved in the coal trade, most shipowners and merchants arguing for large deep docks were planning to move coal before all other commodities. On the basis of their coal trade, Cardiff and Newcastle were by the end of the century the first and third port in terms of tonnage clearing. They, and other coal ports, dominated whole areas of British trade.[47] While London, Grimsby and Leith were the chief recipients of tonnage from Germany, Newcastle had twice London's tonnage

Table 16   *Tonnage of exported coal from Britain, 1850/54–1910/13 ('000 tons)*

Years	Tons	Years	Tons
1850/54	3,574	1890/94	29,341
1860/64	7,833	1900/04	44,066
1870/74	12,308	1910/13	66,132
1880/84	20,120		

Source: Based on Mitchell and Deane, *British Historical Statistics*, p. 121.

clearing to Germany, and Sunderland and Methil both had more than Grimsby. The Dutch and Belgian trades were firmly in the hands of east-coast general ports, but coal ports accounted for *c.* 40 per cent of the tonnage clearing to France. They figured largely in trade with Portugal, Spain, Italy, Greece, Algeria, Egypt, and most of Latin America. Tonnage from Cardiff to Argentina, for instance, was ten times that from Liverpool, and perhaps indicates why Cardiff was one of the leading importers of meat.

The role of the coal ports in the growth of national trade can hardly be exaggerated. Cardiff and Newcastle, together with Newport, Port Talbot, Sunderland, Swansea, the Fife ports, Goole, Grimsby, Hartlepool and Leith (which were more concerned with coal than anything else), accounted for over half the increase in national tonnage after 1870. If Hull and Glasgow are added (since much of their growth was actually in coal exports, and they shipped a tenth of the nation's coal), the percentage attributable to 'coal' ports rises to 63, although obviously a certain amount of confusion between coal ports and general ports had taken place. If London, Liverpool, Southampton and the packet ports are added to this, it will be readily appreciated that most of the remaining ports played little part in the growth of trade and shipping during this crucial period in port development.

The course of the revolution in port facilities in England and Wales is reflected in the pattern of investment of some £159 million between 1850 and 1914: approximately £34 million up to 1870, when the 'second generation' docks were still being constructed; £76 million between 1870 and 1900, when the transition to deep docks was being made; and no less than £52 million between 1900 and 1913, when work began on the deep docks.[48]

The largest portion of this investment was, as always, in Liverpool, where Langton (1879), Alexandra (1881) and Hornby (1883) docks brought the total water space to around 450 acres. Even these were soon too small, and since New York was a pier port unconstrained by docks or locks, Rotterdam had acquired its Nieuwe Waterweg to the sea, and Southampton was wooing liners with its unenclosed deep water, the Mersey Docks and Harbour Board decided in 1890 in favour of yet more elaborate work. The better docks were refurbished; Prince's Landing Stage was rebuilt for the largest vessels; and to provide the necessary dry-docking facilities Gladstone Dock (1913) was constructed as a single-ship wet or dry

Table 17 *Average tonnage of vessels entering and clearing principal ports in the UK with cargo and in ballast, 1870/74–1910/13*

	1870/74 Tons	%	1880/84 Tons	%	1890/94 Tons	%	1900/04 Tons	%	1910/13 Tons	%
Entries										
UK total	20,768		30,141		37,666		50,581		73,541	
London	4,410	21·2	6,254	20·7	7,860	20·9	10,300	20·4	13,284	18·1
Liverpool	4,043	19·5	5,139	17·0	5,661	15·0	7,023	13·9	11,569	15·7
Hull	1,258	6·1	1,600	5·3	2,077	5·5	2,588	5·1	4,360	5·9
Bristol	382	1·8	509	1·7	636	1·7	793	1·6	1,453	2·0
Cardiff	884	4·3	2,248	7·5	3,466	9·2	4,738	9·4	6,719	9·1
Newcastle[a]	1,867	9·0	2,710	9·0	3,341	8·9	4,711	9·3	8,450	11·5
Leith	480	2·3	621	2·1	800	2·1	1,024	2·0	1,640	2·2
Southampton	729	3·5	963	3·2	1,010	2·7	1,820	3·6	5,740	7·8
Greenock	281	1·4	298	1·0	224	0·6	131	0·3	1,105	1·5
Glasgow	416	2·0	843	2·8	1,091	2·9	1,551	3·1	3,271	4·4
Clearances										
UK total	21,343		31,141		38,361		50,803		74,012	
London	3,459	16·2	4,708	15·1	5,876	15·3	7,549	14·9	11,244	15·2
Liverpool	3,969	18·6	4,912	15·8	5,034	13·1	6,313	12·4	10,617	14·3
Hull	1,095	5·1	1,329	4·3	1,646	4·3	2,069	4·1	3,944	5·3
Bristol	137	0·6	215	0·7	275	0·7	478	0·9	1,093	1·5
Cardiff	1,872	8·8	3,971	12·8	6,107	15·9	7,568	14·8	9,431	12·7
Newcastle[a]	2,870	13·4	4,079	13·1	4,952	12·9	6,441	12·7	10,122	13·7
Leith	389	1·8	478	1·5	692	1·8	945	1·9	1,599	2·2
Southampton	658	3·1	861	2·8	919	2·4	1,600	3·1	5,632	7·6
Greenock	203	1·0	207	0·7	199	0·5	106	0·2	1,024	1·4
Glasgow	670	3·1	1,286	4·1	1,694	4·4	2,503	4·9	4,032	5·4

Note:
[a] Includes Blyth.

dock. (Its modern extended form was a creation of the 1920s.)

Extended and improved facilities enabled shipping entering Liverpool and Birkenhead in cargo and in ballast to rise from four million tons in 1870–74 to 11.6 million in 1910–13. This might have been forecast. More surprising was the great revival of London, which at mid-century was in decline relative in the northern industrial ports. The rise in overseas shipping entering the capital, from 4.4 million tons in 1870–74 to 13.3 in 1910–13, represents the great surge of European trade towards the end of the century, and the rise of London's passenger and cargo liner traffic with the empire and the Orient in general. It also reflects the ample provision of deep-water docks, though the circumstances surrounding their construction was, even more than in Hull, a presage of the evils that would shortly overtake the port industry as a whole. The London & St Katharine's Company added the vast Royal Albert to its modernised Royal Victoria in 1880; the India Company endeavoured to siphon off traffic from the Royals by siting its Tilbury Dock (1886) down-river where access was easier, and Continental liners more likely to call; the London Company retaliated with a new lock for the Royals (1886); and the Surrey Commercial Company followed with its Greenland Dock (1894).[49] But the chief element in competition was a rate war which ruined all the companies (including Millwall, which had not extended its facilities), and cast doubts on the ability of the port to provide further deep water when the need arose. Joint working appeared the only solution, and following a Royal Commission investigation, the Port of London Authority was established in 1909 to take over the private companies for the public good. One of the PLA's first acts was to commission the third Royal dock which was now long overdue, but as with many of the last deep water docks, it was unfinished when war started in 1914. The structural chaos and related labour problems would eventually destroy the port of London, but it must be admitted that at least until the Great War, and probably later, these same factors made London a cheap and attractive port.

Southampton in particular had cause for alarm at London's revival as liner companies threatened to move to Tilbury. However, its natural deep water enabled it to provide adequate quays by dredging the Test and Itchen (1889–1913), and British and Continental liner companies began using the port extensively in the 1890s, pushing the tonnage entering from one million in 1890–94 to 5.7 million in

23   Liverpool docks, 1900 (from H. J. Dyos and D. H. Aldcroft, *British Transport*, Leicester University Press, 1969, p. 252)

1910–13. This was done comparatively cheaply, since open, single-sided quays cost a fraction of enclosed dock quays,[50] but even so the local dock company ran into difficulty and was forced to sell out to the London & South Western Railway.

Southampton was especially favoured by nature. Most major ports on ancient sites were searching for deep water, Tilbury-fashion. Bristol was severely affected by the inadequacy of the Avon, and only survived as a port for oceanic trade because a private company built a railway-linked dock at Avonmouth (1877), which was greatly improved by the opening of a modern dock – the Royal Edward – in 1908.[51] (The rival development at Portishead (1879) was not a deep dock.) Grimsby and Hull were also both on the move, partly to service the Yorkshire, Nottinghamshire and Derbyshire coalfields. Grimby's fifty-acre Alexandra Dock was built (1880) to export coal and import timber, but the increased size of ships required the next dock to be built several miles up the coast, at Immingham (1913), where the deep-water channel of the Humber touches Lincolnshire. For the same reason Hull moved down the coast when local shipowners, in competition with the Hull Dock Company, formed the Hull & Barnsley Railway and Dock Company to acquire exportable coal to balance import trades, and build 'Deepdock, Hull' – to quote the telegraphic address of their Alexandra Dock – the deepest, in its day (1888), on the east coast.[52] For the Aire & Calder Navigation Company a move down-river would have ended the *raison d'être* of Goole and was therefore out of the question, with the result that Goole could not enter the ranks of the deep-water ports. Nevertheless, abandoning hope of attracting the largest ships, the Company aimed at medium steamers of *c.* 2,000 tons by reversing the process and constructing the 'Ouse Seaway' (1894).[53] In the north, those responsible for training the rivers Tyne, Wear and Tees were more successful in serving the ports of Newcastle, Sunderland and Middlesbrough; nobody, however, came near to rivalling the Clyde Navigation Trust, which spent some £8 million deepening the river to the 206-acre Glasgow Harbour which, with elaborations called Queen's Dock (1880) and Prince's Dock (1892/7), had something of the order of eleven miles of quays by 1914.[54] Strenuous attempts by Greenock to deflect shipping into its deeper James Watt 'Dock' (1886) came to nothing because, as was the case with Tilbury, it takes more than a superior water site to make a port.

The deep docks owed a great deal to advances in civil engineering, especially in the handling of concrete and the sinking of deep foundations. Given enough money and nerve there was almost nothing that could not have been done to rationalise overseas transportation. In fact there was only one serious attempt to disturb the status quo, and that looked backwards rather than forwards. The Manchester Ship Canal aimed to seize Lancashire trade from what was regarded as the over-priced port of Liverpool, and after a faltering start (1894) it was successful in bringing large ships to the heart of the city. So valuable was locally generated trade that Manchester was the fourth port (after London, Liverpool and Hull) on the eve of the war, though its tonnage was small, and half of it carried coal.[55]

The value of trade was not necessarily related to its tonnage, as can be seen from the tiny share of national trade enjoyed by Newcastle and Cardiff (table 18). The supremacy of the major ports is apparent, with London and Liverpool holding over half the value of imports and exports, and three-quarters of re-exports; and London,

Table 18   *The value of trade at certain major ports, 1913*

Port	Imports £m	Imports %	Exports £m	Exports %	Re-exports £m	Re-exports %	Total £m	Total %
Bristol	18·02	2·4	3·96	0·8	0·08	0·1	22·06	1·6
Cardiff	6·70	0·9	17·18	3·3	0·03	0·0	23·92	1·7
Dover [a]	24·36	3·2	6·73	1·3	4·15	3·8	35·24	2·6
Goole	8·44	1·1	10·32	2·0	0·09	0·1	18·84	1·4
Grimsby	15·85	2·1	21·87	4·2	0·13	0·0	37·85	2·7
Harwich	25·64	3·4	5·98	1·1	2·68	2·5	34·30	2·5
Hull	49·84	6·6	29·22	5·6	5·54	5·1	84·60	6·1
Liverpool	175·49	23·4	170·10	32·4	25·18	23·3	370·78	26·8
London	253·88	33·8	99·11	18·9	58·81	54·4	411·79	29·8
Manchester[b]	35·29	4·7	20·63	3·9	0·38	0·4	56·30	4·1
Newcastle	11·35	1·5	13·19	2·5	0·03	0·0	24·57	1·8
Newhaven	13·48	1·8	5·01	1·0	2·49	2·3	20·98	1·5
Southampton	25·49	3·4	20·67	3·9	7·41	6·9	53·57	3·9
Glasgow	18·49	2·5	35·92	6·9	0·35	0·3	54·76	4·0
Leith	15·75	2·1	6·89	1·3	0·35	0·3	22·98	1·7
Others	55·34	7·4	57·75	11·0	0·48	0·4	111·57	8·0
TOTAL	751·40		524·52		108·18		1384·10	

Notes:
[a] Includes Folkestone.
[b] Includes Runcorn.
Source: Annual Statement of Navigation.

Liverpool, Manchester, the Humber ports and Glasgow between them had 74 per cent of all imports and exports and 84 per cent of re-exports. The most important feature towards the end of the century was the growing share of valuable trade flowing through the southern packet ports, including Newhaven, whose trade was almost as valuable as that of Cardiff and Bristol on the eve of the war.

By 1914 the British ports as a group had reached the peak of their performance. In association with industrial development and population growth, the railways had opened a great flood of internal transport that raised all the large ports and many small ports to ever greater levels of activity, and steam-shipping served the same purpose for external traffic. Although there were changes in the method of calculating tonnage, it is not unreasonable to assert that entries and clearances at British ports rose from an average of *c.* two million per annum in 1820–24 to *c.* seventy-four million by 1910–14. At the same time coastal traffic grew from *c.* eight million to *c.* sixty-three million, and this was of special significance because of the increasing tendency for large foreign traders to go coastwise in search of export coal or bunkers.

Faced with such pressure the ports responded with a vast amount of physical construction in three distinct, though overlapping phases: larger harbours or simple docks for sailing ships; larger and slightly deeper docks, with hydraulic power and coal hoists, for early steamers and railway access; and extensive deep docks for the modern cargo and passenger liners. Such activity was not spread evenly around the ports. The commercial giants had prospered in their enjoyment of the oceanic trades and their superiority in the European connection. Railway influence had created a number of new leading ports and encouraged many minor ports. The coal ports had contributed a huge amount of effort to the growth of the port and shipping industries. On the other hand, a range of small ports did not share in the expansion of overseas trade, though most of them continued, in varying degrees, to find employment in the coastal trade, which was still exceedingly important. There were, in truth, few places that were not better off in 1913 than they had been in 1815.

The enthusiasm with which ports invested in their future and expressed their confidence in magnificent port offices was, however, based on a fundamental misconception. It was assumed that trade would continue to grow along established routes. So far as the

Table 19 Tonnage of foreign-going vessels entering and clearing British ports, 1791, 1841 and 1900 (nearest '000 tons)

Port	1791 in	1791 out	1841 in	1841 out	1900 in	1900 out
Aberystwyth	1	2	2	2	2	0
Barnstaple	3	2	1	0	1	0
Barrow	—	—	—	—	199	32
Beaumaris	1	4	8	7	11	2
Berwick	4	0	8	3	16	0
Bideford	1	1	4	3	?	0
Blyth	—	—	—	—	10	1,513
Boston	3	0	5	1	93	72
Bridgwater	1	1	6	3	14	2
Bristol	79	71	75	70	719	302
Caernarvon	—	—	—	—	4	13
Cardiff	0	1	16	30	1,399	7,072
Cardigan	0	4	2	1	0	0
Carlisle	2	0	3	3	11	0
Chester	17	14	5	5	20	2
Colchester	3	0	4	2	5	0
Cowes	4	2	2	2	2	1
Dartmouth	11	9	5	15	3	0
Dover	55	58	91	92	663	677
Exeter	9	8	8	7	11	1
Falmouth	14	13	11	8	83	59
Faversham	5	0	2	1	8	0
Fleetwood	—	—	6	3	136	21
Folkestone	—	—	—	—	357	202
Fowey	4	4	9	6	9	103
Gainsborough			3	2		

Port	1791 in	1791 out	1841 in	1841 out	1900 in	1900 out
Portsmouth	11	1	17	14	51	6
Preston	3	1	0	0	55	10
Ramsgate	—	—	4	0	11	0
Rochester	11	0	26	8	47	1
Runcorn	—	—	—	5	72	18
St. Ives	2	1	4	—	0	0
Scarborough	3	5	5	1	3	0
Shoreham	4	2	12	11	30	3
Southampton	18	14	116	118	1,559	1,285
Stockton	6	4	62	125	122	18
Sunderland	97	117	188	303	189	1,089
Swansea	3	36	49	48	412	1,404
Teignmouth	—	—	13	—	10	13
Truro	3	5	13	11	0	0
Weymouth	1	2	4	1	112	102
Whitby	9	8	5	1	0	7
Whitehaven	40	212	23	28	46	34
Wisbech	2	0	5	1	36	2
Yarmouth	13	26	17	8	63	16
London	547	397	1,316	1,064	9,381	5,863
SCOTLAND						
Aberdeen	7	4	25	33	141	27
Alloa	3	8	2	13	86	154
Arbroath	—	—	—	—	7	0
Ardrossan	0	0	0	0	200	106

Port						
Gloucester	—	—	29	20	228	36
Goole	—	—	6	9	469	584
Grimsby	—	—	11	7	687	911
Hartlepool	—	0	—	5	489	336
Harwich	2	2	2	5	709	556
Hull	115	53	342	256	2,357	2,048
Ipswich	3	0	7	6	69	8
Lancaster	11	9	9	5	10	1
Littlehampton	5	7	13	11	7	0
Liverpool	268	275	995	1,029	5,897	5,167
Llanelli	—	—	—	—	8	88
Lowestoft	—	—	—	—	42	14
Lynn	20	4	29	6	138	80
Malden	3	0	5	2	0	0
Manchester	—	—	—	—	781	441
Maryport	—	—	—	—	292	72
Middlesbrough	—	—	—	—	767	783
Milford	2	10	9	4	4	1
Newcastle	35	100	299	594	1,232	4,638
Newhaven	2	0	6	6	296	243
Newport	—	—	17	48	451	1,467
Padstow	0	1	3	3	0	0
Penzance	3	2	6	6	11	8
Plymouth	10	4	47	46	230	33
Poole	15	14	12	13	21	17
Ayr	15	18	3	3	65	19
Banff	—	12	5	5	3	2
Bo'ness	26	2	4	41	154	336
Campbeltown	3	1	1	0	2	0
Dumfries	1	1	5	3	1	0
Dundee	11	1	57	50	232	29
Fraserburgh	—	—	—	—	6	8
Glasgow	65	64	48	90	1,347	2,098
Grangemouth	—	—	18	15	339	929
Granton	—	—	—	—	131	115
Greenock	1	32	91	89	120	38
Inverness	27	14	1	1	12	3
Irvine	9	12	5	26	3	6
Kirkcaldy	36	1	12	18	83	1,251
Leith	0	3	101	48	940	878
Lerwick	6	0	0	1	16	26
Montrose	3	—	18	22	24	2
Perth	3	—	4	0	0	0
Peterhead	—	9	—	6	6	4
Port Glasgow	—	—	31	26	0	0
Port Patrick	38	—	—	0	0	0
Stornoway	0	—	1	0	2	4
Troon	—	—	—	—	61	76
Wick	—	—	3	6	8	4

Note: The following ports had an average tonnage entering and clearing of 1,000 tons or less in the three sample years: Aldeburgh, Arundel, Blakeney, Bridlington, Bridport, Caernarvon, Chepstow, Chichester, Deal, Gweek, Ilfracombe, Looe, Lyme, Minehead, Penrhyn, Rye, Sandwich, Scilly, Southwold, Wells, Woodbridge, Anstruther, Dunbar, Fort William, Kirkcudbright, Kirkwall, Oban, Prestonpans, Rothesay, Stranraer and Wigtown.

Source: 1791, Customs 17/13; 1841, *B.P.P.*, 1842 (259), xxxix, p. 626; 1900, *Annual Statement of Navigation.*

Table 20 Tonnage of vessels entering and clearing British ports coastwise, with cargo, 1791, 1841 and 1900 (nearest '000 tons)

Port	1791 in	1791 out	1841 in	1841 out	1900 in	1900 out
Aberystwyth	6	5	13	9	23	14
Aldeburgh	7	8	12	8	0	0
Arundel	7	11	20	9	0	0
Barnstaple	11	4	39	20	115	70
Barrow	—	—	—	—	196	310
Beaumaris	44	43	106	44	506	654
Berwick	16	22	39	44	14	12
Bideford	9	6	31	14	0	0
Blakeney	11	17	18	10	0	0
Blyth	—	—	—	—	13	229
Boston	43	21	73	35	21	51
Bridgewater	24	12	138	45	135	35
Bridlington	7	4	10	6	0	0
Bridport	—	—	15	5	0	0
Bristol	103	68	311	258	644	485
Caernarvon	—	—	—	—	53	93
Cardiff	12	11	49	176	435	1,327
Cardigan	4	3	21	2	13	5
Carlisle	3	2	49	74	101	100
Chepstow	17	26	12	15	0	0
Chester	17	24	49	115	62	111
Chichester	12	14	25	10	0	0
Colchester	22	29	57	27	31	5
Cowes	10	10	50	21	258	159
Dartmouth	18	6	74	25	118	15
Dover	15	7	44	13	126	40
Exeter	41	18	95	43	37	14
Falmouth	14	7	60	33	265	215
Poole	18	29	36	46	69	41
Portsmouth	69	17	88	44	493	284
Preston	11	11	—	0	90	48
Ramsgate	—	—	80	17	61	11
Rochester	76	29	162	31	317	105
Runcorn	—	—	—	—	153	103
Rye	9	4	39	14	0	0
St. Ives	19	19	79	72	0	0
Sandwich	10	8	0	0	0	0
Scarborough	17	4	21	3	27	22
Scilly	1	1	3	1	16	16
Shoreham	8	6	72	7	75	7
Southampton	48	19	150	86	742	500
Southwold	17	6	12	5	0	0
Stockton	10	10	68		84	64
Sunderland	44	517	73	665	173	1,343
Swansea	70	91	240	397	283	442
Teignmouth	—	—	—	—	83	80
Truro	25	30	45	46	0	0
Wells	11	14	17	12	0	0
Weymouth	13	22	39	11	60	17
Whitby	57	9	29	12	10	96
Whitehaven	20	28	68	377	65	111
Wisbech	23	6	62	40	10	7
Woodbridge	11	10	20	16	0	0
Yarmouth	86	56	193	111	100	51
London	1,011	1,010	3,031	1,082	5,543	2,259

Port						
Fowey	12	4	43	52	80	145
Gainsborough	—	—	22	37	—	—
Gloucester	45	60	60	100	65	231
Goole	—	—	181	187	137	326
Grimsby	—	—	1	2	19	148
Hartlepool	—	—	—	—	115	285
Harwich	23	21	40	28	30	38
Hull	124	93	185	184	390	543
Ipswich	26	24	95	64	141	73
Lancaster	14	6	62	46	104	71
Littlehampton	—	—	—	—	24	8
Llanelli	9	26	49	130	66	78
Liverpool	116	129	1,022	910	2,302	2,310
Lowestoft	—	—	—	—	64	15
Lynn	84	46	208	69	57	57
Malden	31	48	90	61	0	0
Manchester	—	—	—	—	335	367
Maryport	—	—	—	—	59	297
Middlesbrough	—	—	—	—	120	284
Milford	9	63	45	66	259	245
Newcastle	115	760	278	1,990	640	2,751
Newhaven	9	3	29	8	112	57
Newport	—	—	77	471	179	440
Padstow	6	12	30	9	24	10
Penzance	8	3	57	17	201	124
Plymouth	46	10	246	94	638	441

Port						
Ardrossan	4	—	17	3	304	318
Ayr	—	119	32	69	131	222
Banff	119	26	14	81	29	22
Bo'ness	8	9	34	23	28	59
Campbeltown	7	6	116	58	79	70
Dumfries	41	20	167	91	20	10
Dundee	—	—	116	58	225	204
Fraserburgh	—	—	—	—	22	19
Glasgow	43	48	397	427	1,671	1,435
Grangemouth	—	—	34	31	216	118
Granton	—	—	141	25	72	71
Greenock	18	14	64	67	1,672	1,730
Inverness	4	3	15	134	401	356
Irvine	7	9	38	64	39	54
Kirkcaldy	3	4	13	14	43	121
Kirkwall	2	1	14	15	219	205
Leith	86	37	281	252	551	541
Lerwick	35	85	41	23	98	76
Montrose	—	—	31	37	23	13
Perth	—	—	2	2	—	—
Peterhead	5	3	20	13	31	21
Stornoway	—	—	—	—	245	238
Stranraer	—	—	31	37	172	166
Troon	—	—	—	—	33	88
Wick	—	—	—	—	92	93

Note: The following ports had an average entering and clearing of 5,000 tons or less in the sample years: Deal, Gweek, Ilfracombe, Littlehampton, Looe, Lyme, Minehead, Penrhyn, Anstruther, Dunbar, Fort William, Isle Martin, Kirkcudbright, Port Patrick.

Source: 1791, Customs 17/13; 1841, B.P.P., 1842 (259), xxxix, p. 626; 1900, Annual Statement of Navigation.

transatlantic ports were concerned it did, but those places relying on extensive European connections were hard hit, if not devastated, by the Great War. More seriously, the collapse of the coal trade left many of the once most flourishing ports, so far as sheer tonnage was concerned, in a desperate situation: the new docks at Methil, Cardiff, Hull and Grimsby, for example, were white elephants for decades. The smaller railway ports turned out to be less necessary than had been thought. And many of the smallest ports lost what little trade they had retained as the coastal trade went into inexorable decline. The large-scale building and investment in the decades before the war produced an oversupply in port facilities outside London and Liverpool, and the provincial part of the port system began to wind down or collapse, depending on the health of the dominant local trades. The great period of extensive activity, between 1870 and 1913, had turned out to be a passing phase in the history of the British ports.

Notes

1 J. F. Riddell, *Clyde Navigation: a History of the Development and Deepening of the River Clyde,* 1979, chs. 6, 10; G. Jackson, *The History und Archaeology of Ports,* 1983, p. 64.

2 *Evidence & Proceedings in the Committee of the House of Commons in regard to the Aberdeen Habour Bill,* Aberdeen, 1839, speeches of Mr Merewether, pp. lxxv–vi, and Mr Talbot, pp. 307–8.

3 *B.P.P.,* 1837/8 (137), XLVII, p. 60.

4 Glasgow Shipping Registers, Custom House, Glasgow.

5 *House of Commons Committee on the Hull Dock Bill, 15 June 1850,* evidence of James Walker.

6 Two vessels purchased by the Goole Steamship Company had to be sold because they could not pass the lock; and a Hull steamer rebuilt within the docks had to be dismantled when it stuck in the lock. For a similar case in Bristol, see D. Large, *The Port of Bristol,* 1984, p. 50.

7 Hull owners were told to build ships to fit the lock.

8 Tonnage dues were payable on external measurements less engine and crew space: but it was external measurements which occupied docks.

9 For details, see J. D. Porteous, *Canal Ports,* 1977, *passim.*

10 C. Hadfield, *Canals of South and Southeast England,* 1969, p. 348.

11 B. F. Duckham, *The Yorkshire Ouse,* 1969, pp. 86–92.

12 B. Lenman, *From Esk to Tweed,* 1975, pp. 104–8.

13 H. F. Starkey, *Schooner Port,* 1983, chs. 3–5.

14 B. F. Duckham, 'Selby and the Aire & Calder Navigation, 1774–1826', *Journal of Transport History,* VII, 1965.

15 I. S. Beckwith, 'The river port of Gainsborough, 1550–1850', *Lincolnshire History and Archaeology,* 2, 1967. Gainsborough ceased to be a

port in 1881.

16 Lenman, *op. cit.*, pp. 112–13.

17 Large, *op. cit.*, p. ix.

18 *Ibid.*, pp. 48–53.

19 The very great importance of the development of modern dredging is discussed in J. Guthrie, *The River Tyne, its History and Resources*, 1880, *passim*, and Riddell, *Clyde Navigation*, chs. 14, 15.

20 F. E. Hyde, *Liverpool and the Mersey*, 1971, ch. 5.

21 Quoted in C. Capper, *The Port and Trade of London*, 1862, p. 156.

22 *Ibid.*, p. 161.

23 J. G. Broodbank, *History of the Port of London*, 1921, II, p. 194.

24 The inadequacy of these works was revealed in *Minutes of evidence to the Select Committee on the Hull Docks Bill, 1859*, when the Dock Company Secretary (W. H. Huffman) asserted that 17,000 vessels per annum passed the Humber Lock.

25 *Minutes of Parliamentary Committee on Hull & Barnsley Railway and Dock Bill*, QQ. 5792–5805.

26 For a brief survey of north-eastern ports, see Jackson, *op. cit.*, pp. 83–7.

27 *Ibid.*, pp. 87–8.

28 M. Daunton, *Coal Metropolis: Cardiff, 1870–1914*, 1977, p. 4.

29 T. Fairclough and E. Shepherd, *The Mineral Railways of the West Country*, 1975.

30 For a brief survey of Birkenhead, see F. E. Hyde, *op. cit.*, pp. 83–8.

31 *Ibid.*, pp. 133–4.

32 G. Dow, *Great Central*, 1959, I, ch. xiii.

33 Duckham, *op. cit.*, *Yorkshire Ouse*, pp. 101–6.

34 Lenman, *op. cit.*, pp. 106–7.

35 Jackson, *op. cit.*, p. 137.

36 Details of railway activity in the East Anglican ports from W. J. Wren, *The Ports of the Eastern Counties*, 1976, *passim*.

37 J. Marshall and J. K. Walton, *The Lakeland Counties*, 1981, pp. 34–5.

38 Details of Preston's growth are contained in J. Barron, *A History of the Ribble Navigation*, 1938, *passim*.

39 Plymouth did in fact experience considerable growth at the end of the period, largely because changes in customs regulations required the counting of vessels 'calling off' Plymouth to send telegraphic messages or disembark some of the passengers. The same was true of Cowes.

40 Capper, *op. cit.*, p. 167.

41 D. J. Rowe, 'Southampton and the railway mania', *Transport History*, iv, 1969; A. Temple Patterson, *A History of Southampton*, 1975, III, chs. 1, 6.

42 Jackson, *op. cit.*, pp. 92–4.

43 A. G. Jamieson (ed.), *A People of the Sea: a Maritime History of the Channel Islands*, 1986, p. 450.

44 *Ibid.*, p. 455; P. J. Perry, 'The development of cross-Channel trade at Weymouth', *Transport History*, II, 1969.

45   J. H. Farrant, *The Harbours of Sussex, 1700–1914*, 1976, p. 25; D. W. Gibbs, 'The rise of the port of Newhaven, 1850–1914', *Transport History*, III, 1970, p. 261.

46   Details of ships from *Annual Statements of Navigation*. The growth of the large ships is shown in diagramatic form in A. Kirkaldy, *British Shipping*, 1913, fig. XVII.

47   'Vessels from and to principal countries at principal ports', *Annual Statement of Navigation, B.P.P.*, 1914, LXXXII, 46–60.

48   A. G. Kenwood, 'Port investment in England and Wales, 1851–1913', *Yorkshire Bulletin of Economic and Social Research*, XVII, 1965.

49   J. Pudney, *London's Docks*, 1975, chs. 10–11.

50   F. M. Du-Plat-Taylor, *The Design, Construction and Maintenance of Docks Wharves and Piers*, 3rd edn, 1949, p. 46.

51   Large, *op. cit.*, introduction and pp. 157 ff.; J. Bird, *The Major Seaports of the United Kingdom*, 1963, ch. 7.

52   Jackson, *op. cit.*, pp. 126–8.

53   Duckham, *op. cit.*, ch. 7.

54   Riddell, *op. cit.*, chs. 11–12.

55   D. Farnie, *The Manchester Ship Canal and the rise of the port of Manchester*, 1980, pp. 1–29, 92.

The shipping industry

At the end of the eighteenth century British ships were, by later standards, few in number and small in size. Although there had been recent substantial gains, the first stage of industrialisation was served by a remarkably small tonnage of vessels. In 1790 England owned 9,603 ships of native build, with an aggregate tonnage of only 1,040,000. There were also fifty-seven ships (19,461 tons) of foreign build and, since this was a time of recurrent warfare, another 453 'Prizes made Free' which added 74,470 tons to the fleet. Scottish ports owned a further 2,013 ships (151,032 tons) between them, and Irish ports considerably less.[1]

This fleet consisted of a number of different types of vessels, their size, broadly speaking, proportional to the distance or danger of their usual voyages. The grandest were those of the East India Company, up to 1,400 tons, and lately built in the East, of teak. They were used in what – ton for ton – were probably the richest of all trades: the importation of Chinese tea, silk and porcelain, and South-East Asian and Indian spices, coffee, drugs and dyestuffs. They represented wealth rather than industry, for there was almost no export of manufactures to the East at this time. The profitable operation of these huge vessels was protected by legal monopoly preventing other ships rounding the Capes, and, significantly, the ending of the Indian monopoly in 1813 reduced the average vessel to a more manageable and competitive 500 tons, and allowed it to be used for the export eastwards of new British industrial products.

Apart from Indiamen, 'big' ships had for generations been around 300 tons, serving the long-distance food and raw material trades. From the northern and eastern Baltic they brought the wood and bar iron on which industrialisation depended; the flax, hemp and naval stores which kept the merchant marine and navy afloat; corn – when the 'Corn Law' allowed – to feed the rising population; and seeds for the oil mills. In the Arctic the law as well as expediency required them for the subsidised search for whale oil, for lighting and industrial purposes, in the last quarter of the century.[2]

Vessels of this sort were also in demand for the flourishing North American and hugely valuable West Indian colonial trades, exporting manufactures in return for tobacco, rice, sugar, coffee, spices, rum and, latterly, raw cotton. Others carried dried codfish from Newfoundland to the slaves of Brazil and the West Indies and to the Catholics of southern Europe. There can be no doubt about the immense value of these colonial trades as generators of national wealth and stimulators of national industry. By the 1790s Asia and the Americas were providing 55 per cent of British imports by value and, perhaps more importantly, absorbing no less than 62 per cent of exports.[3] But in volume, and employment of shipping, they were less important. In the early 1790s colonial traders accounted for only about a quarter of total tonnage entering and a third of that clearing the country.

The great bulk of trade was, therefore, European, and – excepting the larger vessels mentioned above – merchants preferred the more adaptable ship of something over 100 tons, which was also handy for coastal trade, could enter most ports, was easily filled and sailed well. In the late eighteenth and early nineteenth centuries western Europe was still the source of a vast range of manufactured goods, chemicals, wine, fruit and luxury foodstuffs, though the net flow of manufactures had already been reversed on Britain's favour.[4] But for most goods, especially on short routes, smaller ships sufficed to the point where progress was heroic if not horrific: eighty-tonners occasionally sailed for Newfoundland, sixty-tonners for Prussia, forty-tonners for the West Indies, and thirty-tonners for Holland. France and the Channel Islands could be served by cockle-shells: two from Rye together contributed twenty-two tons to national trade in 1790. The average ship was then no more than 102 tons, though this was rising under a variety of opportunities and pressures on both the demand and supply side. The ease and speed of filling large ships was increased through timetabled sailings; insurance and wet docks reduced risks; and the Transport Service and American, whaling and cod-fishing trades, which favoured large ships, grew during the Napoleonic War. Trades most seriously disrupted were those employing the smallest ships.

The problem during the war was how to get ships rather than how to use them. The Inspector General of Customs reported in 1798 that in colonial trade, confined to British shipping, 'we find the merchants complaining of the great inconveniences they labour under from the scarcity of shipping and the high price of freights'. He advised against relaxing the Navigation Laws, 'by which this country has been gradually raised to the present exalted state of naval power and commercial wealth', but, since colonial trade was growing faster than British-built shipping, owners must be allowed to buy or employ foreign ships.[5] The latter course was preferred because excess shipping was expected when Transports returned to mercantile use, and foreign rather than British owners would become the marginal casualties of peace. In the meantime merchants in restricted trades continued to complain, and the rest relied on 'the vast increase of Foreign Tonnage employed in our carrying trade'.[6]

The war did not, then, reduce the overall demand for shipping: industrialisation continued to require materials and serve markets. But protective duties, and shipping restrictions in northern Europe, produced the first major switch in a bulk trade when Canadian timber was substituted for Russian and Scandinavian. In consequence the British fleet expanded quite rapidly, from 1.457 million tons average in 1795–99 to 1.886 million in 1800–04. Thereafter it moved steadily to 2.504 million by 1816; and, since that was the highest point for some decades to come, it might be assumed that native building and war prizes together caught up with the physical expansion of trade. It could also be argued that regular sailers were more intensively used, and that some trades – along the coast and with nearby Europe – were inherently able to carry larger volumes of goods in relatively smaller increments of vessels because they involved fewer ton-miles in which a fleet's workload is more properly expressed. The growth of the eastern Baltic and Atlantic trades put the greatest strain on resources because individual vessels performed fewer voyages in the year. Unfortunately there is no way of assessing capacities, usage and load factors in this period.

Rising demand for shipping in the peculiar conditions of war accelerated a most important change: shipping was becoming a capitalist industry in its own right as opposed to an ancillary of merchanting. Merchants for whom ships were a necessity rather than an investment spread risks by owning shares in various vessels which carried their goods. However, the growing volume and complexity of trade demanded ships in a hurry, and consequent higher returns attracted 'outside' capital assembled by managing owners devoted fully to the disposition of ships to earn maximum freight from various combinations of trades, ports and cargoes. Dr Ville has recently shown the importance of this attention to detail in active as opposed to passive shipowning in his examination of one of the first large shipowners, Joseph Henley & Son of London,[7] though in their case, expansion depended on reinvested profits rather than introduced capital. Collier and whaler owners were prominent among specialist shipowners, along with 'merchants', master mariners, shipbrokers and shipbuilders.[8]

Specialist enterprise and initiative was all the more necessary as export merchants were eclipsed by shipping agents acting for inland manufacturers. But it was probably the exceptional profits to be gained from war conditions – through scarcity of shipping and higher load factors – that provided the major encouragement to specialisation: there was money to be made by leasing vessels to the Transport Service or adventuring them on novel trades when conditions in European waters or ports became too difficult. Owners pursuing lucrative freights may have started as merchants, but their reaction to perceived opportunities, and necessary attention to operational detail, made them professionals – or bankrupts. There was also a new and interesting possibility: owning ships that were not used within British trade at all. In the 1780s, for instance, two-thirds of the bulk trade of the USA was transported in British-owned ships, whether or not their cargoes were destined for Britain,[9] and the business of operating ships chiefly abroad grew noticeably during the nineteenth century.

The benefits of war – for those who enjoyed them – could not last for ever, and peace which relieved merchants threatened upstart shipowners. Transports and impressed seamen were returned to service, and wages and operating costs fell, but profits were diminished through intensified competition for freights which failed to boom as envisaged. Continuing difficulties and protectionism in Europe, and fluctuations in the American market, depressed trade in the post-war decade, in the early 1830s and the early 1840s, sufficiently so for Parliamentary enquiries into the state of shipping to be held in 1833 and 1844. The British fleet had declined steadily after 1816 to a low point in 1827 (table 21),[10] and the tonnage of ships built and first registered in British ports reached its lowest level since records began, at 51,000, in 1822. Not until the late 1830s did any noticeable buoyancy occur. However, the exploration of alternative distant markets (particularly for cottons, in Latin America and the East) did offer some stimulus to shipowners, and apart from one or two years of actual decline, there was in fact a steady growth in the tonnage of ships entering and clearing Britain throughout the period of 'stagnation' (table 22). Unfortunately some of that increase consisted of more British ships entering in ballast (3 per cent in 1825/29 and 16 per cent in 1840/44), though this was still little more than half the tonnage clearing in ballast, which was traditionally greater.

Table 21 *Tonnage of ships owned and built in Britain, 1790/4–1845/9 (five-yearly averages: '000 tons)*

| Years | Tonnage | | Years | Tonnage | |
	Owned	Built		Owned	Built
1790–94	1,428·8	60·8	1820–24	2,352·4	66·0
1795–99	1,457·2	78·0	1825–29	2,262·4	99·9
1800–04	1,886·0	n.a.	1830–34	2,254·2	87·8
1805–09	2,113·4	n.a.	1835–39	2,407·2	134·6
1810–14	2,296·8	n.a.	1840–44	2,959·2	135·8
1815–19	2,461·6	88·9	1845–49	3,303·6	127·0

Sources: Tonnage owned, Mitchell and Deane, *British Historical Statistics*, pp. 217–18; tonnage built, Customs 17 *passim* and *ibid.*, 220–1.

Table 22 *Tonnage of British and foreign shipping entering and clearing, 1820/24–1845/49 (five yearly averages; '000 tons)*

| | Cargo and ballast | | | | Cargo only | | | |
| | Entering | | Clearing | | Entering | | Clearing | |
Years	Brit.	F'gn	Brit.	F'gn	Brit.	F'gn	Brit.	F'gn
1820–24	1,694	531	1,557	517	n.a.	n.a.	n.a.	n.a.
1825–29	2,092	750	1,898	741	2,029	659	1,327	406
1830–34	2,243	774	2,234	783	2,059	672	1,569	506
1835–39	2,690	1,081	2,694	1,120	2,405	947	1,938	752
1840–44	3,409	1,332	3,517	1,373	2,879	1,101	2,620	992
1845–49	4,600	1,958	4,581	2,077	3,988	1,571	3,312	1,484

Sources: Cargo and ballast from *B.P.P.*, 1847 (588) lx, 142 and 1852/3 (318) lvii, 199; cargo only from *B.P.P.*, 1852/3 (318), lvii, 200.

This growth was provided for in a number of ways. Britain had long made use of ships built in North America, and in 1816–17 they were almost half as numerous as home-built ones. Encouraged by duties on Baltic timber, New Brunswick and Nova Scotia built many – perhaps most – of the largest ships registered in Britain in the first half of the century. By the 1840s and 1850s these exceeded 1,000 tons in size, about as large as wooden sailing ships could be safely – or economically – operated. Their chief advantages were speed of delivery and low prime cost, though this was offset by a shorter A1 classification at Lloyds.[11] Their chief purchasers were the long-haul shipowners of London, Liverpool and Glasgow; and Pollok, Gilmour & Company of Glasgow and Canada were doubtless not alone in combining timber-importing, shipbuilding and shipowning in their highly successful enterprise.[12]

An abundance of sturdy colonial vessels sustained the British fleet at a time when the prohibition on cheap foreign-built ships could have been devastating. The fleet began to grow again in the 1830s, and more vigorously in the 1840s, at the start of a great expansion lasting until the Great War. But this British fleet was not used uniformly across the whole spectrum of British trade or, more accurately, the accumulated number of ships trading differed widely from trade to trade (table 23). By far the greatest activity was coastal trade in which some 130,000 ships entered and 140,000 cleared British ports in 1841, aggregating approximately eleven million tons. Its reservation to British shipping until 1849 necessitated the investment of much British capital in a relatively unrewarding area (compared with overseas earnings), but one in which valuable experiments in shipowning and shipbuilding occurred during the quarter century after the war. By comparison shipping employed in the lucrative and protected colonial trade was slight, at around 6,000 entries grossing 1.35 million tons in 1841. There was, of course, a great discrepancy between typical ships employed in the two areas of protected trade: coasters averaged eighty-three tons, colonial traders 225.

The critical area for industrialisation was foreign trade, and in value terms the gains in imports were almost entirely outside Europe as North America came to provide a quarter of total imports and South America, Africa and Australia were brought within Britain's trading orbit. Huge quantities of raw cotton arrived from the USA, timber from Canada, and tea and silk from Asia. These gains outside

Table 23 The deployment of shipping in British trade, 1841 ('000 tons)

| | | All ships | | | | Foreign ships | | | |
| | | Entering | | Clearing | | Entering | | Clearing | |
Trade		No.	Tons	No.	Tons	No.	Tons	No.	Tons
Coastal	Sail	116,382	8,425	128,556	9,424	—	—	—	—
	Steam	12,709	2,333	12,104	2,092	—	—	—	—
	Total	129,091	10,758	140,560	11,516	—	—	—	—
Colonial	Total	5,975	1,346	5,933	1,357	—	—	—	—
Foreign	Sail	18,305	2,583	19,417	2,812	8,818	1,206	9,709	1,249
	Steam	2,415	379	2,480	382	478	56	498	60
	Total	20,720	3,062	21,897	3,195	9,296	1,261	10,208	1,309
% foreign ships		—	—	—	—	44·9	41·2	46·6	41·0

Source: B.P.P., 1842 (409), xxxix, 624.

Europe were, however, offset to some extent by the absolute decline in the value of imports from the West Indies, which had been the most valuable source of imports at the end of the war. On the export side Europe and the Near East were actually growing significantly in importance as exports to the USA and West Indies declined relatively. Only South America showed any significant overall growth since the beginning of the century, though the most important of all potential changes was in the export of cottons to the East, which was only beginning in the 1840s (table 24).

So far as *tonnage* of trade is concerned, the rising share of America and the relative decline of Europe are both of great significance because of the disproportionate demands of long-haul trades on available shipping. However, the truth is that British shipping was not coping with all the potential demands of trade. Around 11,500 ships and 1.8 million tons of native shipping were employed in foreign trade in 1841, but its current volume was more than marginally dependent on 10,000 ships and 1.3 million tons that were foreign owned (table 23). By mid-century foreign ships made up around 40 per cent of tonnage entering and clearing in foreign trade. The myth of the permanent superiority of the British marine cannot be sustained, but the chagrin of British shipowners is understood.

Where was all this foreign tonnage employed? The United States' fleet had continued to grow after independence to rival the British by the 1840s, and Europe was coming on apace. By 1845, around two-thirds of ships and tonnage trading with the USA, Sweden, Norway, Denmark, Prussia, Germany and Belgium were foreign-owned, reflecting to some extent the availability of cheap timber.[13] Not surprisingly, trade with Russia, Holland, France and Italy was very firmly in British ships, while in the remainder of world trade they were completely dominant. The argument that Britain 'could not compete' with American and northern European shipowners may have some economic justification, but it is based largely on an unwarranted assumption that a Norwegian ship carrying Norwegian wood to Britain must in some way represent the failure of a British shipowner. Contrary to a popular misunderstanding of the Navigation Laws, foreign ships had never been excluded from trading with Britain, and British merchants had for centuries been happy to leave some – often less remunerative – trades in the capable hands of owners in developed countries, while they got on with the business of pushing trade with undeveloped regions unlikely to produce their

Table 24 *Value of trade and tonnage of shipping by region (%)*

	Imports						Exports and re-exports					
	1790/96[a]		1844/46[b]		1900		1790/96[a]		1844/46[b]		1900	
Region	Val.	Tons	Val.	Tons	Val.	Tons	Val.	Tons	Val.	Tons	Val.	Tons
Europe/Near East	45	75	39	53	46	69	39	66	49	55	47	65
N. America	7	10	24	29	31	19	28	13	17	27	13	16
West Indies	25	10	7	5	0	0	18	12	6	6	1	1
S. America	1	0	6	3	5	4	0	3	9	3	7	5
Africa	1	1	4	6	2	3	3	3	3	3	6	6
Asia	21	2	17	5	9	3	13	2	15	7	16	4
Australasia	0	0	3	0	7	2	0	0	2	0	8	2
Fisheries	0	3	0	0	0	0	0	4	0	0	0	0

Notes:
[a] Value 1794/96, tonnage 1790; whaling was counted for tonnage only.
[b] Value 1844/46, tonnage 1845.

Sources: Values, 1794/96 and 1844/46 from R. Davis, *The Industrial Revolution and British Overseas Trade,* 1979; 1900 from *Annual Statement of Trade*; volumes, 1790 from P.R.O. Customs 17, 1845 and 1900 from *Annual Statement of Navigation.*

own oceanic shipping. The abolition of the Navigation Laws opened *all* British trade to foreign shipping at a time of rapid expansion when it needed every ton it could get, and a flow of foreign capital to support the lower end of the industry was by no means unwelcome to many sections of the mercantile community, or, indeed, to Britain's industrial capitalists.

A second reason for the tonnage of British shipping lagging behind the volume of trade lay in its more efficient use. Although the number and tonnage of ships over fifty tons clearing more than doubled between 1790 and 1841, the total tonnage registered grew by only 55 per cent and the number barely changed, while the clearances per ship rose from 5.5 to 12.1 per annum and the number of clearances per ton rose from 3.9 to 6.0 times.[14] Whatever the shortcomings of these figures, they indicate a notable rise in productivity. Again, this is partly owing to substantial growth in coastal trade where vessels did more work; but it also reflects their more efficient use.[15] The predominant colliers gave up wintering, and turned round faster with the aid of new docks, cranes and coal hoists. Larger vessels carried more coal for (within reason) the same amount of manoeuvring in ports and the same labour costs. The price of freight could fall – and so encourage more business – without denying the capitalists the profits on which further investment in shipping depended.

The greatest advance in productivity came, as might be expected, from a crucial change in technology: sail made way for steam, and steamers did more work per ton per annum than sailers could ever do. In 1841 registered steamers over fifty tons (ignoring tugs and 'luggage boats') numbered only 793 (96,000 tons) but were 9 per cent of coasters trading, and 22 per cent and 18 per cent respectively of tonnage entering and clearing coastwise. In foreign trade, just under 2,000 steamers entering and clearing accounted for 18 per cent and 17 per cent respectively of the tonnage of *British* ships trading (table 23).

For an innovation that transformed world trade, the steamship was a long time on the drawing board. It emerged before the steam train because it was easier and cheaper to build: it required no permanent way, and other capital costs such as piers could be shifted on to the public purse. Engines and paddles were relatively simple additions to a vehicle whose structure and operation were well understood, but they were only justified if novel working methods repaid heavy additional expense. In trades depending on the cheapness of sea transport, low cost remained for some decades more desirable than high speed: for some bulk goods it remained so until the end of the century.

The first vessels 'constructed to row with wheels or paddles wrought by a steam engine'[16] were introduced on the Clyde to serve Glasgow's distribution trade, and until 1817 Scotland had more than England. They spread fairly rapidly to the Humber, Mersey and Thames, but the first important breakthrough came when more efficient engines and larger paddles allowed them to venture along the coast, where they improved rapidly under competition for the most lucrative freights between major ports. Thus, after a slow start, numbers grew rapidly in the early 1820s and again in the 1830s (table 25). The apparent stagnation in size after 1820, at around 100 tons, does not indicate the typical steamer. There remained many small river boats and tugs, but steamers moving into European and American trade in the 1840s (and heavily concentrated in Glasgow, Hull and London), grew rapidly in size. Hull already had many engaged in Baltic and North European runs that were over 600 tons, with the largest over 1,000. Glasgow (where the average steamer over fifty tons rose from 182 to 236 tons between 1842 and 1850) had sixteen over 600 tons, of which nine exceeded 1,000 and averaged 1,510 tons.[17] Liverpool was not yet much interested in steam, because it remained inappropriate for many of her trades.

Steamers had important characteristics that revolutionised sea transport. By generating their own power they ran to timetable in most parts of the world, irrespective of 'trade winds' constraining sail voyages; their superior speed offered notable gains on both long and short routes; and their high capital cost forced owners to reduce time in port and press for improved dock facilities which enabled them to work even more efficiently. But these advantages were not fully realised in the wooden paddle steamer. Three major advances were required to make the fullest use of the potential of steam.

Firstly, the experimental application of iron plates to hull construction, in the 1840s, brought a greater strength that encouraged a more seaworthy and economical shape. Large ships could now be long and narrow, presenting relatively less resistance to water without fear of breaking their back; they could have larger deck hatches for speedy cargo handling with cranes; and they enjoyed a distinct weight advantage (metal ships weighed considerably less than wooden ones of equal tonnage) which reduced fuel consumption.

Table 25 Steamers belonging to Scotland and England, 1815–36

Year	No.	Tons	Year	No.	Tons	Year	No.	Tons
1814	1	69	1821	59	6,051	1828	272	29,010
1815	8	638	1822	85	8,457	1829	287	29,501
1816	12	947	1823	101	10,361	1830	295	30,009
1817	14	1,039	1824	114	11,733	1831	320	32,262
1818	19	2,332	1825	151	15,764	1832	348	35,238
1819	24	2,548	1826	228	24,186	1833	382	38,122
1820	34	3,018	1827	253	27,318	1834	424	43,429
						1835	497	52,767

Source: B.P.P., 1837–8 (137), xlvii, 60.

Moreover, greater strength and size permitted much larger engines without vibration weakening the hull, or engine and fuel taking up too much potential cargo space.

Equally important was the use of iron plates in boiler-making, permitting steam pressure to rise from 6 p.s.i. in the early days to 60 p.s.i. by mid-century, when it could be used to work compound engines with two cylinders. Fuel consumption fell from 10lb of coal per HP per hour to 3.5lb, and consequent savings produced lower freight rates, larger engines, longer journeys between coal depots, or a mixture of the three.

The third advance replaced the paddle by the screw, which was more effective when ships rolled or faced into heavy seas. The removal of external paddle boxes was particularly important, since they had greatly increased the cost of locks and dock space per ton of cargo space, and prevented larger steamers from entering existing docks. Moreover, steamers could now lie directly alongside quays and benefit from hydraulic cranes (introduced in the 1850s) which facil-itated the rapid movement of heavy goods such as railway engines, and of coal hoists which revolutionised the loading of coal. Iron screw steamers and hydraulic power were interdependent: wider, deeper, straight-sided vessels carried far more cargo per lineal foot of ship (and quay) and could only load and unload economically with the new equipment.

The inexorable growth in the size of steamers was the chief and best known feature of late nineteenth-century shipping, but before examining the changing technology involved it is important to note the emergence of a more dynamic system of shipowning. The chief movement in sailing-ship owning in the early nineteenth century had been towards specialisation of function and sole or partner-ownership. The early steamers, which were not involved in orthodox trade, reversed this trend. The first, on the Clyde, were built by very large companies of 'metropolis' tradesmen: bakers, tobacconists, brewers, tailors, and manufacturers of a wide range of household goods found on board. There were twenty-four such companies by 1820. Significantly, while their numbers remained high, the primary occupation of shareholders changed dramatically once vessels ven-tured beyond the Clyde, and though they remained predominantly local men, some capital was already being attracted from London and the English manufacturing towns.[18] Between them these joint-stock companies were operating fifty-seven steamers 'in the trade of the Clyde' by 1840.[19] On the Mersey twenty-one companies, owning twenty-nine steamers, were founded between 1821 and 1833, chiefly engaged on the Mersey itself and the Irish runs.[20] So far as London, the principal steam port, is concerned, 214 of the 334 steamers on the register in 1852 were owned by joint-stock companies.[21] By contrast, Hull had only two joint-stock companies in the experimental period: the Hull Steam Packet Company and the Humber Union Steam Packet Company, both started, like the Clyde companies, by river men rather than merchants.[22] When steam traffic expanded rapidly on the short run to the Continent, the local initiative was seized and retained by individuals and family partnerships, which in many cases had been involved earlier in sailing-ship owning.

There were countervailing tendencies around mid-century which inhibit generalisations about the way shipowning was developing. The Clyde, Mersey, Thames and Humber Registers show large groups of steamship shareholders giving way to smaller groups and single owners as expertise and enterprise were rewarded with generous profits from which capital was readily accumulated. This process was assisted by the introduction of mortgages, which facilitated purchase out of operating profits, but commonly on the security of a whole ship rather than ship shares. On average 525 ships (83,650 tons) per annum were fully and 244 (50,928 tons) part-mortgaged in the years 1840–44.[23] Significantly, an analysis of mortgages on the Thames shows a preponderance of local merchant–gentlemen, shipbrokers and others who would have been found among ship part-owners: their money now came by a different route, taking a fixed percentage on capital rather than a share of profit and loss. Steamship builders and engineers also assisted specialised owners by retaining shares or acting as mortgagees for all or part of a vessel, though this may have been more common on the Clyde and Humber than the Thames, where few builders were found among mortgagees in the sample years analysed by Dr Palmer.[24]

It follows that the mortgage was most useful during periods of expansion when new ships were required in a hurry, and especially in new ventures where experience was not available or existing owners established. The mortgage was particularly desirable if very rapid profits were expected to flow from novel trading enterprises, and for that reason disruptions to trade flows caused by the Crimean War and American Civil War were an added inducement to gamble with mortgages. The problem was that over-generous mortgages created excess shipping which reduced the freight rates which had made them attractive in the first place, while ill-considered mortgages placed large resources in the hands of men with limited capital who, though doubtless enterprising and resourceful, had little to fall back on in case of misjudgement or misfortune. 'Sometimes', it was said in defence of Z. C. Pearson at his bankruptcy hearing, 'men are weak in prosperity and accordingly are tempted into deep waters'.[25]

While many steamers were owned by small partnerships or single individuals, at the other end of the scale there was, again around mid-century, a move towards much bigger organisations in order to seize advantages accruing to multi-ship companies. Whatever the size of vessels, a regular, timetabled operation, connecting with railways, minimising demurrage and encouraging customer loyalty against rivals, was part of the new system. Since the first days of coastal rivalry, passengers had been wooed by speed and luxury, with 'floating palaces' ruining owners, who sought solvency through working agreements which experience showed were rarely lasting. An alternative was common ownership of vessels on popular routes, doubly attractive because the only way a Free Trade State could subsidise initially – or permanently – unremunerative services was through Post Office monopoly mail contracts which required sufficient vessels to sail regularly, loaded or not.

A further powerful influence in favour of big companies emerged when larger, fuel-efficient, iron screw steamers fostered rapid oceanic travel. Their success on the Atlantic in particular was a powerful stimulant to investment because this route enjoyed the most lucrative of freights: the first-class passenger. But it had to be investment on a scale beyond small companies of the sort already operating steamers on the North Sea, and, with considerable risks to capital in such unprecedented enterprise, prudence suggested joint-stock rather than private ownership. A combination of these factors produced the most famous shipping organisations in the mid to late nineteenth century: the great liner companies on the Cunard model.

Samuel Cunard came from a timber and shipbuilding background in Halifax, Nova Scotia (the terminus for Atlantic packets), and was well established in American coastal trade and general agency work when the Admiralty invited postal tenders in 1838. He had been involved in abortive auxiliary steam crossings in 1833,[26] and had a plan of operations awaiting suitable ships and subsidies. Since exemplary ships had been built by John Wood and engined by Robert

Napier for the City of Glasgow Steam Packet Company, it was to Glasgow that Cunard took his proposals for a steamer fleet to outclass any rivals for the £55,000 per annum subsidy. The City of Glasgow Company was enthusiastic, as was the Glasgow & Liverpool S.S. Company, which would operate the British feeder services. Twenty-eight Glasgow shipowners and merchants contributed the bulk of the £300,000 capital, while G. & J. Burns (of the Glasgow & Liverpool) handled the Glasgow office and D. & C. MacIver (of the City of Glasgow) the Liverpool office. Others from Clyde Steam Navigation Company and North British Steam Navigation Company were drawn in to form the British & North American Royal Mail Steam Packet Company, which purchased the Glasgow & Liverpool's 649–ton *Unicorn* and ordered four sister ships – *Britannia, Arcadia, Caledonia* and *Columbia,* of 1,136 to 1,176 tons gross – from Clyde yards.[27] Thus it fell to the *Unicorn* to begin the most famous line in the world, initially with economy fittings and plenty of space for emigrants who, it was hoped, would contribute more than cargo in those less lucrative portions of the ships where 'passengers' could not be accommodated.

The new service was successful, and inevitably drew competitors on the same or adjacent routes as transatlantic traffic began to build up. Cunard was followed across the Atlantic by the Inman (*c.* 1850), National (1863), White Star (1867/70), Guion (1866) and Leyland (1873) lines. Lamport & Holt sent their first steamer to South America in 1857, Booth opened up the Amazon in 1866, and the Pacific Steam Navigation Company, which took the mails round to Chile by sail in 1840, was one of the largest – if not the largest – steamship companies in the world by the 1870s. Improvements to both hull and engine stimulated by the Atlantic 'race' opened up greater possibilities for mixed passenger/cargo liners to Africa and Asia where (since the eastern monopoly of the East India Company was abolished only in 1833) the liners became pioneers of direct trade. Here the Cunard Company's activities were mirrored to some lesser degree by the Glasgow-based City, Anchor and Glen lines, the British & Africa Steam Navigation Company and British India Steam Navigation Company; by the Liverpool-based Africa Steamship Company, Guinea, Blue Funnel, Bibby, White Star and Castle Lines; and by the great Peninsula & Orient (P&O) line which evolved in 1840 from the huge Dublin Steam Packet Company to enjoy the eastern mail contracts, and Royal Mail which grew prosperous on the South-American contract.[28]

The prosperity of the successful lines was based chiefly on a rapid expansion of economic activity in the temperate grasslands of both hemispheres, and in the desire to speed up and regularise trade with the Orient. If trade followed the flag, it was most likely the house flag of a shipping line seeking goods to fill its vessels, striving to beat off ruinous competition and justify a mail contract. In the process of opening the Far East to Western enterprise men such as Alfred Holt (Ocean Steamship Company – Blue Funnel Line) and John Swire (Butterfield & Swire and China Navigation Company) made their own fortune while serving their European customers and introducing a new and dynamic element to the economies of their chosen region.[29] Direct, fast and regular steamer lines soon acquired the sanctity of institutions and, in particular, were associated with the administration of a rapidly expanding empire depending on the transmission of messages, migrants, officials and troops. Even on the Atlantic the Cunard subsidy (£180,000 per annum by 1857) could be justified on the grounds that 'keeping the superiority of the British lines appears to My Lords [of the Admiralty] to be of national importance'.[30] South America was also an area of national trading and financial interest, with British shipping heavily involved, and some of it heavily subsidised (to the annoyance of unsubsidised owners). However, accusations that major lines used their strength and Conference agreements to raise freights against the interest of South-American economies are difficult to justify.[31]

In some 'new' areas of the world, especially Africa, it is possible to see shipping lines in the vanguard of international competition for annexation of potential ports and hinterlands. Dr Davies has described in great detail the activities of the Liverpool 'trade makers' in West Africa,[32] and even more direct than the influence of the 'imperialist' Sir Alfred Jones of Elder Dempster was that of Sir William MacKinnon, whose desire to open up a circular India Ocean service for his British India Steam Navigation Company led to the formation of the Imperial East Africa Company to establish the hinterland for necessary bases in Africa and justify an East-African mail contract.[33] Such activity was, of course, largely dependent on the opening in 1869 of the Suez Canal, which cut almost 4,000 miles off the route from Britain to Calcutta.

International competition was not of great significance east of Suez or the Cape. Far-East routes were dominated by British capital, which also exercised so powerful an influence on the China Seas and Yangtze river that American competition – chiefly Russell & Company – withdrew. Singapore and Hong Kong became the chief entrepôts; Shanghai was largely a British port; and British officials created and ran the Chinese Customs Service.[34] Once British shipping was deeply involved in Asiatic trade it was difficult to dislodge, and its profitability was assured through various Conference agreements from 1879, which raised freight rates but ensured regularity.[35]

More serious rivalry was always to be found on the North Atlantic, and here the worst excesses of competition between British lines were avoided by the Liverpool North Atlantic Conference formed in 1874.[36] In the early days of oceanic steam (when American shipping was in considerable disarray) the only serious contender was the Collins Line, with bigger, more luxurious ships and, from 1847, a Congressional subsidy. 'We shall also have national prejudice to contend with', said Samuel Cunard when considering the quality of Collins ships, and the two lines secretly fixed rates and pooled earnings until disasters and uneconomic ships drove Collins to bankruptcy in 1858.[37]

Eventually the most threatening 'national prejudice' came from European countries, whose nationals made up a large portion of emigrants in steerage. Although Germany had few ports and no great mercantile marine (much of her overseas trade passing through Rotterdam), merchants in Hamburg and Bremen anxious to engage in oceanic trade created a handful of very strong lines to attack the most lucrative routes. North German Lloyd and Hamburg–America were the most formidable operators, who by 1883 had 30 per cent of steerage passengers westwards, and in 1886 North German Lloyd even secured a mail contract from Southampton. The Continental operators guarded their backs with a Conference agreement which endeavoured to keep British liners out of Continental ports, and British operators were sufficiently worried for the British and Continental Conferences to come together in 1886.[38]

Such Conferences failed to achieve a permanent division of passengers or income because companies deserted when it suited them to undertake 'rate wars'. Their main economic consequence was excessive liner tonnage on the North Atlantic, while competition encouraged an endless search for speed and comfort through technical superiority. The size, performance, equipment and efficiency of liners were enhanced in ways unforeseen in the 1830s or 1840s. In 1914 Adam Kirkaldy indicated four stages in his famous 'Diagram showing the evolution of the Atlantic Liner':[39] rapid enlargement of wooden paddlers in the 1840s; a plateau in the 1850s and 1860s as iron screw vessels rose in number more than size; a slight growth in the 1870s as ships were made longer; and a revolutionary advance in the 1880s when triple compound engines facilitated longer, broader and deeper vessels. Ships trebled in tonnage between 1848 and 1888, while their length roughly doubled and their indicated horse power rose from a little over 1,000 to around 17,000. Nevertheless, these were still not the great liners of popular legend, which originated in the intense national rivalries in the period 1890–1914. *Celtic* exceeded 20,000 tons in 1901, *Mauretania* 30,000 in 1907, and *Aquitania* reached 47,000 tons in 1914. The latter's new turbine engines were 150 times as powerful as those of paddlers crossing in 1838 (table 26).

Giant liners increased the large companies' hold on the industry.[40] A sample of twenty-four companies taken in 1912 shows total capital, debentures and debts of £50 million, and fleets worth £46.7 million, consisting of 884 vessels and 4,182,828 tons gross (they also had other assets of £14 million). There were enough companies in the sample to illustrate their diversity, with vessels ranging from average Cunarders at 10,000 tons to the 4,000–5,000 tonners of the Eastern trade; from extravagant transatlantic liners to utilitarian passenger/cargo vessels serving the empire. In terms of capital and debentures Cunard and P&O were well in the lead with over £5 million, Royal Mail with almost £4 million and Leyland with £3 million (table 27). The Oceanic Steam Navigation Company (Blue Funnel) had the most valuable fleet, worth £8 million; Cunard's was worth £5.6 million, and P&O's only £3.3 million, though it did have various other assets worth £4.8 million. In terms of tonnage, three companies had well over 400,000, one had over 350,000, and at least sixteen had more than 100,000 (table 27).

Big companies were created by men themselves larger than life. There were grand fortunes to be made by aggressive enterprise in good times, and even in bad times falling freight rates were offset by a secular decline in the unit costs of shipping. There were many paper millionaires by the end of the century, and not a few lived in a style commensurate with their knighthoods or peerages.

Some of these men started 'at the bottom' – often in sail – licking

Table 26 *Specifications of sample transatlantic liners, 1838–1914*

Ship	Date	Material	Propulsion	Engines	Tonnage	Indicated H.P.	Length (ft.)	Beam (ft.)
Great Western	1838	wood	paddle	single	1,340	440	236	36
Great Britain	1843	wood	paddle	single	3,270	1,000	303	51
Persia	1855	iron	paddle	single	3,300	3,600	376	45
Oceanic	1871	iron	screw	compound	3,800	3,000	420	41
Servia	1881	steel	screw	compound	7,391	9,900	515	52
City of Paris	1888	steel	2xscrew	3x compd	10,669	18,000	528	63
Celtic	1901	steel	2xscrew	4x compd	20,907	n.a.	681	75
Mauretania	1907	steel	4xscrew	turbines	31,938	70,000	762	88
Aquitania	1914	steel	4xscrew	turbines	47,000	60,000	901	97

Source: Kirkaldy, appendix xviii.

Table 27 *Sample passenger liner companies, 1912 (£'000 and '000 tons gross)*

Company	Paid-up capital	Other funds	Fleet bk val.	Other assets	Fleet No.	Fleet Tons	Dividends (%)
British India	1,657	1,671	3,384	900	108	458·6	6·4
Clan Line	500	993	1,996	27	53	223·0	6·0
Cunard	1,600	4,077	5,571	1,176	26	267·0	6·0
Ellerman	1,400	888	2,163	243	87	335·8	7·0
Leyland	2,614	527	2,167	798	41	251·2	0·0
Oceanic	750	4,804	8,137	1,161	43	425·6	60·0
Pacific	1,477	285	1,486	738	35	167·8	6·0
P & O	3,500	2,828	3,297	4,793	89	447·4	8·3
Royal Mail	1,700	3,447	4,875	817	59	237·5	5·0

Source: Kirkaldy, *British Shipping*, appendix xxiii.

stamps, as they liked to boast. Some, such as Alfred Jones (of Elder Dempster) entered small firms as clerks and rose with the firm through ability in operating ships. More began by purchasing ships for existing trading activities: Thomas Wilson (Thos. Wilson & Sons) in Swedish iron, Charles Booth (Booth Line) (of London Survey fame) in corn, and Christopher Furness (Furness, Withy & Company) in provisions. A few were 'outsiders'. J. R. Ellerman, richest of all shipowners, was a successful accountant who secured control of Leyland Line after the death of its founder in 1892.

Success was partly luck: being in the right place with the right ships at the right time. But there must also be a huge capacity for hard work and grasp of detail, a clear understanding of the movement of markets and freight rates, a thorough acquaintance with the operational requirements of ships, and an opportunist approach to new trades and technology. It was also a matter of nerve, perhaps a gamble: William Burrell, a tramp owner whose art collection has become Scotland's major tourist attraction, made his money buying and selling ships at appropriate times, and Christopher Furness established his fortune in the same way in the 1880s. Above all, these men were financiers, augmenting personal funds with public share issues and debentures while keeping control firmly in their own hands. There were, of course, those who did not speculate with others' capital: the Wilson brothers, for instance, made so much profit in their inherited business that they reputedly had the largest private fleet in the world by the end of the century.[41] Whatever their funding, all of them were absorbed by the interplay of their multifarious interests, some intimately connected with shipping, and some completely independent of it. They bought collieries, shipyards and tugs for obvious reasons, but Jones also bought bananas, Ellerman breweries, Charles Wilson trawlers and Phillips orange squash. Ellerman's success has been attributed to 'dedication, added to a genuine love of business or the satisfaction of a well planned and accurately timed deal', and Jones' dedication to 'his joy in the exercise of power'.[42] Certainly shipowners did not retire happily to their imitation châteaux.

Eventually the founding fathers relaxed their grip and companies amalgamated, not least because of the predatory activities of men such as John Ellerman, and the more potent threat from J. P. Morgan's International Mercantile Marine Company.[43] Union and Castle lines came together in 1900, Blue Funnel and China Mutual in

1902. In the following year, Owen Phillips, with almost no capital of his own, miraculously secured control of the weakly managed Royal Mail and proceeded, by manipulating non-voting capital in a ruthless fashion, to seize control of Elder-Dempster, Pacific Steam Navigation, Union-Castle and other lines to make himself the leading 'shipowner' in Britain and his group one of the biggest companies, certainly the biggest ever to collapse, when his capital manipulations ran ahead of real business and the law caught up with his nefarious practices.

There is danger of too much attention to passenger liners distorting the image of British shipping in the late nineteenth century. The sample companies chosen by *Fairplay* in 1912 owned only about a quarter of the *gross* tonnage of British shipping, and a smaller share of *net* tonnage. It is necessary also to emphasise the continued importance of sailing ships after 1850, and the increasing role of the cargo steamer.

For a long time the economics of steam discouraged the long-haul carriage of cheap bulk goods, and the increasing supplies of tea, grain and raw materials coming to Europe from the Far East and the north-west coast of America were carried in sailing ships which had themselves undergone important technical changes since the ending of the East India company's China monopoly in 1833. Adventurous hulls – 'Aberdeen bow' and 'Greenock model' – and expansive sails permitted the clipper races with new season tea. But with the opening of Suez, in 1869, steamers halved the time of the China run, forcing clippers into other trades where medium speed was acceptable if cheap: coal exports to the Far East, and oil and corn from the USA. As the historian of ship design noted, 'in the battle between sail and steam the sailing ship had to progress and develop to survive at all'.[44] Steel hulls and masts were an important improvement, but the survival of the sailing ship was largely a matter of steamship economics, as Harley has shown.[45] Humble sailing ships held their own where cheap freight was essential to commodities such as Baltic timber, but where speed offset higher freight rates steamers became economically suitable for longer distances with each improvement in propulsion or hull design, especially after the opening of the Suez and Panama canals. On costs alone sail was superior in some trades until *c.* 1890,[46] but it was disappearing rapidly from most routes. The tonnage of British steamers passed that of sail in 1883, and a very marked decline in sail occurred from *c.* 1890, with the perfection of the cheaper triple expansion-engined vessels, and steamers accounted for 58.6 per cent of total British ships in 1910–14 and for no less than 91.9 per cent of their tonnage (table 29).

It is impossible to exaggerate the importance of cargo steamers to Britain's economic performance after *c.* 1870, as Kipling suggested in *The Seven Seas*:

The Liner she's a lady by the paint upon 'er face,
An' if she meets an accident they count it sore disgrace:
The Man-o'-War's 'er 'usband, and 'e's always 'andy by,
But, oh, the little cargo boats! they've got to load or die.

The Liner she's a lady, but if she wasn't made,
There still would be the cargo-boats for 'ome an' foreign trade.
The Man-o'-War's 'er 'usband, but if we wasn't 'ere,
'E wouldn't have to fight at all for 'ome an' friends so dear.

The development of liner traffic with Africa, India, the Far East and South America is obviously important, with new specialised tonnage such as Houlder's introduced for the meat trade. So too is the passenger liner trade with North America. But having recognised the new corn trade and the booming cotton trade, the fact remains that the *relative* share of exports to North America fell drastically in value and tonnage, and though imports of foodstuffs and machinery increased relatively in value their tonnage did not (table 24). Nor were the exotic trades able to fill the gap. The bulk of shipping was employed in European trade, which returned to the dominance evident at the start of the century. The enthusiasm for empire and memory of Cunarders must not obscure Britain's growing reliance on both foodstuffs and manufactures from Europe, while in return went huge quantities of coal which, foreign and coastwise, employed about 60 per cent of British shipping by 1900.

Cargo boats were owned by companies which could not match the wealth and dignity of the liner companies, but nevertheless included some important accumulations of capital and expertise. In some regards it was a more complicated and exacting business to send steamers tramping in search of freights, but this was a necessary part of world trade, and many smaller companies engaged in it. Larger companies endeavoured to copy passenger lines and employ vessels on regular voyages between specific ports, and since it was not easy to attract shipping lines to small or new ports some companies were established for specific local needs: Goole & West

Riding S.S. Company, West Hartlepool S.N. Company and Manchester Liners are obvious examples.

Cargo companies varied greatly in size, depending on their interests. A sample of 100 taken in 1912 shows thirty-four with paid-up capital over £100,000, though the smallest was £9,760 and the largest group fell between £10,000 and £20,000[47] (table 28). An analysis of the companies' holding of ships further illustrates the relatively small size of most cargo companies, with 25 per cent owning one ship and 72 per cent owning between one and five. The single ship companies were generally engaged in tramping, and their growth was an interesting feature of the late nineteenth century when opportunities abroad – especially in exporting coal – were buoyant.[48] Their success was owing not least to the long-term secular decline in freight rates,[49] which the most famous estimated index (1869=100) puts at 107 for 1870–74, sixty-eight for 1885–89 and fifty for 1902–06 (avoiding the Boer War).[50] This represents a possible attack on income, but declining costs enabled shipowners to survive while providing the cheap incentive for a much more active international trade.

Table 28   *Frequency distribution of 100 sample cargo companies, 1912*

Paid-up capital	Number of companies	Number of ships	Number of companies	
£9,000+	22	1	25	
£25,000+	18	2	13	
£50,000+	18	3	9	
£75,000+	8	4	12	
£100,000+	11	5	7	72%
£150,000+	4	6	6	
£200,000+	7	7	1	
£250,000+	5	8	2	
£300,000+	1	9	6	
£350,000+	2	10	4	19%
£400,000+	1	11–14	7	
£450,000+	2	15–19	4	
£500,000+	1	20–24	3	
		31	1	15%

Source: A Kirkaldy, appendix viii.

Measured in terms of growth in tonnage and activity in trade, British steam shipping must be seen as one of the most phenomenally successful industries of the late nineteenth century. The fleet doubled in tonnage between 1870–74 and 1910–14, while a reduction in the number of ships, from 25,800 to 21,000, represents the expected advance in average size. As noted above, the contraction of the sailing fleet was very noticeable from 1880, with a virtual collapse in the present century, while steam shipping rose steadily by over one million tons per decade, from 1.5 million in 1870–74 to 10.9 million in 1910–14 (table 29).

Table 29 *Net tonnage of British-owned shipping, 1870/74–1910/14 (five-yearly averages, '000 ships and tons)*

Years	Sail		Steam		Total		% steam	
	No.	Tons	No.	Tons	No.	Tons	No.	Tons
1870–74	22·2	4,273	3·6	1,511	25·8	5,784	14·0	26·1
1875–79	21·0	4,207	4·6	2,184	25·6	6,390	18·0	34·2
1880–84	18·9	3,628	5·9	3,347	24·8	6,975	23·8	48·0
1885–89	15·7	3,252	6·8	4,218	22·5	7,470	30·2	56·5
1890–94	13·6	3,003	7·9	5,525	21·4	8,527	36·9	64·8
1895–99	11·9	2,565	8·7	6,460	20·6	9,026	42·2	71·6
1900–04	10·5	1,942	9·8	8,016	20·3	9,958	48·3	80·5
1905–09	9·7	1,478	11·2	9,825	20·9	11,303	53·6	86·9
1910–14	8·7	961	12·3	10,857	21·0	11,818	58·6	91·9

Source: Annual Statements of Navigation and Shipping.

If one turns to the use to which the fleet was put it is immediately evident from official calculations of the tonnage of registered ships employed in the home (coastal and nearby Europe), foreign, and 'mixed' (home and foreign) trades, that by 1910 some portion of the sailing fleet was either working entirely abroad or not working at all: the tonnage 'registered' as employed in foreign trade (629,000, table 30a) was almost double the tonnage of sailing ships clearing from British ports (324,000, table 30b). It is also noticeable that throughout the period from 1880 the proportion of steamers wholly devoted to foreign trade was vastly greater than the tonnage engaged in the home trade: only about a tenth of steamer tonnage (and half the sail tonnage) was devoted to it.

It follows that the largest overall gain in productivity flowing from the change from sail to steam was in the rapid turn-round home

Table 30a *Tonnage of British ships employed in home, foreign and mixed trade, 1880–1910 ('000 tons)*

Year	Home[a]		Mixed[b]		Foreign	
	Sail	Steam	Sail	Steam	Sail	Steam
1880	694	236	133	69	2924	2289
1890	575	325	51	134	2267	4563
1900	379	508	16	202	1595	6696
1910	295	658	6	518	629	9233

Notes:
[a] Home = coastal and nearby Europe.
[b] Mixed = home and foreign employment.

Table 30b *Tonnage owned and clearing, 1870–1910 (with cargoes only; '000 tons)*

Year	Registered tonnage		Coastal clearances		Foreign clearances			
					British ships		Foreign ships	
	Sail	Steam	Sail	Steam	Sail	Steam	Sail	Steam
1870	4,578	1,113	8,091	10,072	5,502	6,432	3,967	813
1880	3,851	2,723	8,265	16,299	4,282	14,586	3,983	2,835
1890	2,936	5,043	5,785	21,502	2,252	23,015	2,819	5,771
1900	2,096	7,208	3,576	26,535	1,029	26,877	1,976	13,790
1910	1,113	10,443	2,768	28,655	324	35,914	1,238	19,851

Source: Annual Statements of Navigation.

trade. Indeed, steam tonnage clearing coastwise was not overtaken by *British* tonnage clearing foreign until the 1890s. In fact between 1880 and 1910 steamers clearing foreign rose by 145 per cent (from 14.6 million to 35.9 million tons) and the tonnage of steamers devoted to the trade rose by 300 per cent from 2.3 million to 9.2 million. But in the same period coastal steam clearances rose by 76 per cent from 16.3 million to 28.7 million tons while the tonnage of shipping devoted to home trade rose by 178 per cent, so there is really little to choose between the two discrete areas of trade. But one thing is clear. Ignoring growth rates, in 1910 some 28.7 million tons of *coastal* steam clearances were being accounted for by an estimated 658,000 tons of 'home' and 518,000 tons of 'mixed' steamer, i.e. a maximum of 1.2 million (and 'home' implied a great deal more than coastal). At the same time 9.2 million tons of foreign traders accounted for only 35.9 million tons of steam trade.

One result of Britain's early start in steam was a flourishing industry which owners were reluctant to see dissipated through the intrusion of foreign 'flags'. It mattered little that by 1890 there was more foreign than British sail tonnage engaged in foreign trade, and that by 1910 there were 1.2 million tons of foreign against 0.3 million of British sail clearing British ports (table 30b). But shipowners and nationalists alike were greatly worried by the volume of foreign steamer tonnage in overseas trade: 5.8 million tons in 1890, 13.8 million in 1900 and 19.9 million in 1910, when it was 45 per cent of the total clearing. Moreover, it was not so much over colliers as over ocean liners that sentiment developed. One can hint at, without being able to measure, the long-term damage done to Britain by the fostering of a popular antipathy to Germany as a threat to British shipping, shipping routes and, by extrapolation, to the British empire. There is no real evidence that German shipowners were more efficient, enterprising or obliging (though they spent less on wages and provision for crews). If they competed effectively it was more likely to be for the simple reason that it was convenient for German emigrants to board German ships in Hamburg. There was still plenty of room left for British companies, but that escaped the fevered imaginings of those such as J. A. Cramb, who in *Germany and England* (1914) taught that Germany's destiny required 'the destruction of England's supremacy at sea'.[51]

Shipping, like land transport, changed out of all recognition between 1814 and 1914. It started with small wooden sailing vessels variously owned, and moved through specialist ownership to company ownership to 'group' ownership of highly sophisticated steel steamers. Quite apart from its function as carrier of foodstuffs, material and manufactures, shipping was also, like railways, an immense influence on other industries. A large amount of coal produced in Britain was used to drive ships, as was an unknown but considerable amount of that exported. In reverse, over half the tonnage of shipping leaving Britain by 1910 was involved in the coal trade. The shipbuilding industry was obviously dependent on it: in the 1890s the annual net tonnage of steamers built in Britain was moving upwards from around half a million to around three-quarters of a million by 1900, reaching its peak, at 950,000 tons, in 1913.[52] The demand for new tonnage was fairly volatile, following fluctuations in world trade and freight rates, and it is impossible to generalise about investment over time. Nevertheless Feinstein has estimated capital formation in gross mercantile shipbuilding at around £4.5 million per annum in the late 1850s, £12 million in the late 1870s and 1880s, £17 million after the turn of the century and rising to £25 million in 1913.[53] Such investment linked back into steelworks, paintworks and the like, creating large-scale employment and large shipbuilding centres such as Belfast, Birkenhead, the Clyde, Tyne and Tees and others.

Shipowners were used to fighting each other with a make-or-break ruthlessness, and it is not surprising that they are not renowned for their generosity to labour, which was one area where they could reduce costs. Various Acts of Parliament were required to regulate conditions for both emigrants and crewmen, especially when steamers were developed and there was room for doubt as to both manning levels and crew accommodation. Nevertheless there can be no doubting the role of shipping as a large direct employer of labour. Ton for ton, sailing vessels and steamers employed roughly the same number of seamen in the 1880s, when there were approximately 200,000 employed in British ships, including about 20,000 Lascars. By 1913 this had risen to 292,000 including 32,639 foreigners and 64,848 Lascars. Unionisation had always been difficult, and seamen suffered with dock workers from the strength of the Shipping Federation during the troubles of the early 1890s.

On the eve of war in 1914 shipowners were riding proud and confident on the crest of a wave. They had grown rich by servicing the international economy which their economical ships and efficient management had done much to create. But in the process they had moved towards the over-provision of ships. They were vulnerable as other countries endeavoured to create their own fleets, and when trade faltered, as it did most noticeably in the mid 1880s and around 1908. In particular their future prosperity rested on the continuation of the old relationships between Europe and the periphery, on the continued prosperity of Europe, and on the continued popularity of British coal. In all these things they were to be disappointed as shipping fell under influences after 1914 which were increasingly beyond their control. However, the supremacy of British shipping had lasted for a century, and it is more sensible to praise its achievements than to bemoan its future after the First World War.

Notes

1 Based on PRO, Customs 17/12.

2 The best survey of British trade in the early nineteenth century is R. Davis, *The Industrial Revolution and British Overseas Trade*, 1979, pp. 13–52; for whaling vessels see G. Jackson, *The British Whaling Trade*, 1978, pp. 68, n. 2, 75–6.

3 Davis, p. 93.

4 For a detailed analysis of European trade goods see G. Jackson, *Hull in the Eighteenth Century*, 1972, ch. 3.

5 PRO, Customs 17/20, Report of Inspector-General of Customs, 1798.

6 PRO, Customs 17/21, Report of Inspector-General, 1799.

7 S. Ville, *English Shipowning during the Industrial Revolution: Michael Henley & Son, London Shipowners, 1770–1830*, 1987, ch. 3.

8 For the background to shipping in one provincial port, see Jackson, *Hull*, ch. 6.

9 PRO, BT 6/20, ff. 291–8, Council for Trade and Plantations: Queries regarding . . . tonnage duties levied by U.S. States on British Ships, Dec. 1789.

10 Since the tonnage in that year was depressed by around 150,000 tons, through the sudden removal of vessels hitherto lost but not deregistered, the earlier 'high' figures obviously exaggerate the size of the post-war fleet.

11 D. MacGregor, *Merchant Sailing Ships, 1815–50*, 1984, p. 13.

12 *Ibid.*, pp. 111–12; Glasgow Shipping Registers.

13 Based on figures in *B.P.P.*, 1847 (588), LX, 313.

14 Figures for 1790 calculated from PRO, Customs 17/12, ff. 21, 32; 1841 from *B.P.P.*, 1842 (409), XXXIX, 624. (The difference between the participation of numbers and tonnage is a result of the concentration on coastal trade, in which average size was 67.7 tons in 1791 compared with 111.9 tons in foreign trade.)

15 S. Ville, 'Total factor productivity in the English shipping industry: the North East coal trade, 1700–1850', *Economic History Review*, XXXIX, 3, 1986.

16 *S.S. Thames*, Glasgow Shipping Registers, 4/1815.

17 Glasgow Shipping Registers, *passim*.

18 The Clyde Shipping Company included one banker and 151 'merchants', among them some of Glasgow's foremost names; the Clyde & Liverpool Shipping Company had shareholders in Leeds, Huddersfield, Rochdale, Manchester, London and Liverpool; Glasgow Shipping Registers, *passim*.

19 *Glasgow Directory, 1840*, appendix, p. 46.

20 The two most important of the early companies trading in Liverpool – the St George's Steam Packet Company (1821) and the City of Dublin Steam Packet Company (1824) – were in fact Irish; P. L. Cottrell, 'The steamship on the Mersey 1850–1880; investment and ownership', in Cottrell and D. H. Aldcroft (eds.), *Shipping, Trade and Commerce*, 1981,

pp. 146–7.

21   S. R. Palmer, 'Investors in London shipping 1820–50', *Maritime History*, 2, 1973, p. 46.

22   G. Jackson, 'Port competition on the Humber: docks, railways and steamships in the nineteenth century', in E. M. Sigsworth, *Ports and Resorts in the Regions*, 1980, p. 45.

23   Palmer, p. 60; *B.P.P.*, 1847 (719) LX, 161.

24   Palmer, 'Investors in London shipping', p. 64.

25   Pearson's temptation had been to purchase part or all of seven sailing vessels and thirteen steamers, principally for American trade and very largely on mortgage. But profits expected from blockade running during the American Civil War were wiped out by heavy loss of vessels, and Pearson, who placed £1.2 million through his bank account in his last year, and had £400,000 in Bill transactions, was bankrupted for less than £50,000. *Z. C. Pearson in Bankruptcy, 11 March 1864, before Mr. Commissioner Goulburn*, pp. 16–17, pamphlet, copy in Hull Central Library, Local History Dept.; Hull Shipping Registers.

26   F. E. Hyde, *Cunard and the North Atlantic Crossing*, 1975, p. 3.

27   *Ibid.*, p. 15; Glasgow Shipping Registers.

28   Details of Liverpool and other lines from G. Chandler, *Liverpool Shipping*, 1960, *passim*.

29   F. E. Hyde, *Far Eastern Trade, 1860–1914*, 1973, chs. 1, 10.

30   Quoted in Hyde, *Cunard*, pp. 35–6.

31   B. Greenhill, 'Shipping 1850–1914', in D. C. M. Platt (ed.), *Business Imperialism 1840–1930: an inquiry based on British experience in Latin America*, 1977, pp. 147–55.

32   P. Davies, *The Trade Makers: Elder Dempster in West Africa*, 1973.

33   F. Munro, 'Shipping subsidies and railway guarantees: William Mackinnon, Eastern Africa and the Indian Ocean, 1860–93', *Journal of African History*, 28, 1987, pp. 209–30.

34   The best summary of the relationship between shipping and the opening of the east is Hyde, *Far Eastern Trade, passim*. British shipping in Chinese waters is examined by Dr A. Blue in two unpublished theses: 'British Ships and West China, 1875–1941, with special reference to the Upper Yangtze', B.Phil, Open University, 1978 and 'The China Coast: a Study of British Shipping in Chinese Waters, 1842–1914', Ph.D, University of Strathclyde, 1982.

35   Hyde, *Far Eastern Trade*, pp. 26–41.

36   Hyde, *Cunard*, p. 93.

37   *Ibid.*, pp. 25, 39–45.

38   *Ibid.*, p. 105; D. H. Aldcroft, 'The mercantile marine', in D. H. Aldcroft (ed.), *The Development of British Industry and Foreign Competition, 1875–1914*, 1968; H. J. Dyos and D. H. Aldcroft, *British Transport*, 1969, pp. 289–96.

39   A. Kirkaldy, *British Shipping*, 1914, appendix xviii.

40   *Ibid.*, appendix xxiii.

41   P. Davies, *Sir Alfred Jones*, 1978, p. 118.

42   For Kylsant, see E. Green and M. Moss, *A Business of National*

Importance, The Royal Mail Shipping Group, 1902–1927, 1982, *passim*. For Wilsons, see G. Jackson, 'Wilson, C. H.' and 'Wilson, A.' in *Dictionary of Business Biography*, 1986.

43 V. Vale, *The American Peril: challenge to Britain on the North Atlantic, 1901–4*, 1984, pp. 32–61. Ellerman had acquired the Leyland Line, started a joint American line with Wilsons and approached Cunard before negotiating with American interests: J. Taylor, *Ellermans, a Wealth of Shipping*, 1976, *passim*. He reputedly died the richest man in Britain (1933) in terms of liquid assets.

44 D. MacGregor, *The Tea Clippers: their History and Development, 1833–75*, 1983, p. 211.

45 C. K. Harley, 'The shift from sailing ships to steam ships, 1850–90: a study in technological change and its diffusion', in D. N. McCloskey (ed.), *Essays on a Mature Economy: Britain after 1840*, 1971.

46 *Ibid.*, p. 227.

47 Kirkaldy, appendix viii.

48 A. G. Course, *The Deep Sea Tramp*, 1960.

49 D. C. North, 'Ocean freight rates and economic development, 1750–1913', *Journal of Economic History*, 18, 1958; E. A. V. Angier, *Fifty Years of Freight, 1869–1919*, 1920.

50 L. Isserlis, 'Tramp shipping cargoes and freights', *Journal of the Royal Statistical Society*, 101, 1938, table reprinted in B. R. Mitchell and P. Deane, *Abstract of British Historical Statistics*, p. 224.

51 P. Cramb, p. 71, quoting the views of Treitschke.

52 Mitchell and Deane, *Abstract*, p. 222.

53 *Ibid.*, p. 375.

Bibliography

Railways 1830–70

There is an immense literature on railways in this period, a great deal of it nostalgic in character. The main bibliographical guide is G. Ottley, *A Bibliography of British Railway History* (2nd edn, 1983). A second volume is promised. One or two contemporary works retain their usefulness. H. G. Lewin's *Early British Railways* (1925) and *The Railway Mania and its Aftermath* (1936) chart the progress of railway building to 1852, D. Morier Evans, *Facts, Failures and Frauds* (1859; modern reprint, 1969) deals with the seamier side of railway fianance, while R. D. Baxter, 'Railway expansion and its results', *Journal of the Statistical Society,* XXIX (1866), reprinted in E. M. Carus-Wilson (ed.), *Essays in Economic History,* Vol. III (1962), and D. Lardner, *Railway Economy* (1850; reprint of 1855 edn, 1968) are key sources for the economic impact of the new technology. There are a number of tried and tested modern introductions to the subject: P. S. Bagwell, *The Transport Revolution from 1700* (1974); T. C. Barker and C. I. Savage, *An Economic History of Transport in Britain* (1974); H. J. Dyos and D. H. Aldcroft, *British Transport* (Leicester, 1969; Penguin edn, 1974); T. R. Gourvish, *Railways and the British Economy 1830–1914* (1980), and see also his 'Railway enterprise', in R. A. Church (ed.), *The Dynamics of Victorian Business* (1980); and H. Pollins, *Britain's Railways* (Newton Abbot, 1971). Still of value is J. Simmons, *The Railways of Britain* (2nd edn, 1968), but it is being superseded by his ambitious four-volume work on *The Railway in England and Wales 1830–1914*. Vol. I (Leicester, 1978) and Vol. II (Newton Abbot, 1986) have appeared. An important visual representation of the period is provided by M. Freeman and D. H. Aldcroft, *The Atlas of British Railway History* (1985).

On the railways' economic impact, the seminal work is B. R. Mitchell, 'The coming of the railway and United Kingdom economic growth', *Journal of Economic History,* XXIV (1964); this, and others of the more pertinent articles on the subject, were collected in M. C. Reed (ed.), *Railways in the Victorian Economy* (Newton Abbot, 1969). Reed's book, together with Gary Hawke's path-breaking application of the social saving approach, *Railways and Economic Growth in England and Wales 1840–1870* (Oxford, 1970), remain essential reading. Scholars have devoted considerable attention to railway investment. The principal sources for data are Mitchell (*q.v.* above) and G. R. Hawke and M. C. Reed, 'Railway capital in the United Kingdom in the nineteenth century', *Economic History Review,* 2nd ser., XXII (1969). The latter is critically reviewed, in the course of an investigation of high capitalisation, by R. J. Irving, 'The capitalisation of Britain's railways, 1830–1914', *Journal of Transport History,* 3rd ser., V (March 1984). The implications of spending levels, in macro-economic terms, are examined by, *inter alia,* R. C. O. Matthews, *A Study in Trade Cycle History* (Cambridge, 1954), J. R. T. Hughes, *Fluctuations in Trade, Industry and Finance,* (Oxford, 1960), S. Broadbridge, *Studies in Expansion and the Capital Market in England 1825–1873* (1970), and M. C. Reed, *Investment in Railways in Britain 1820–1844* (Oxford, 1975). The last two contributions also devote much space to the character of the railway investors themselves. The more speculative circumstances of the post-1860 period have been explored by H. Pollins, 'Railway contractors and the finance of railway development in Britain', *Journal of Transport History,* III (1957–58), also in Reed, *op. cit.* (1969), P. L. Cottrell, 'Railway finance and the crisis of 1866', *Journal of Transport History,* new ser., III (1976). For institutional effects see Reed's work, W. A. Thomas, *The Provincial Stock Exchanges* (1973), and, more recently, T. R. Gourvish, 'The performance of British railway management after 1860', *Business History,* XX (July 1978), and R. C. Michie, *Money, Mania and Markets* (Edinburgh, 1981). The railways' impact on company law remains a controversial question: cf. H. A. Shannon, 'The coming of general limited liability', *Economic History,* II (1931), in E. M. Carus-Wilson (ed.), *Essays in Economic History,* I (1954), and P. L. Cottrell, *Industrial Finance 1830–1914* (1980).

Information on the constructional effects of railways must be unearthed from a wide variety of sources, although Mitchell, *loc. cit.*

gives a basic survey, and Hawke, *op. cit.* (1970) extends the debate
on iron and steel, along with Gourvish, *op. cit.* (1980) and D.
Brooke, 'The advent of the steel rail, 1857–1914', *Journal of Transport History*, 3rd ser., VII (March 1986). We now know a little more
about the railways' demand for coal, thanks to B. R. Mitchell,
Economic Development of the British Coal Industry 1800–1914
(Cambridge, 1984), and R. A. Church, *The History of the British
Coal Industry. Volume 3. 1830–1913* (Oxford, 1986). Recent work
on the railways' impact on employment includes D. Brooke, *The
Railway Navvy* (Newton Abbot, 1983), E. Jones, *Accountancy and
the British Economy* (1981), and T. R. Gourvish, 'The rise of the
professions', in T. R. Gourvish and Alan O'Day (eds.), *Later
Victorian Britain 1867–1900* (1988). For railways' urban effects the
standard work is J. R. Kellett, *The Impact of Railways on Victorian
Cities* (1969).

The consequences of railway operation have not inspired so much
academic effort. Among the more important works are W. T. Jackson, *The Development of Transport in Modern England*, II (1916;
new edn, 1962), T. R. Gourvish, *Mark Huish and the London and
North Western Railway* (Leicester, 1972), and R. J. Irving, *The
North Eastern Railway Company 1870–1914* (Leicester, 1976). The
social savings approach has been brought to a wider audience by the
short surveys in R. Floud and D. McCloskey (eds.), *The Economic
History of Britain Since 1900. I: 1700–1860* (Cambridge, 1981),
and P. O'Brien (ed.), *Railways and the Economic Development of
Western Europe 1830–1914* (1983). The interpretation of the
results is still a matter for debate: cf. F. Crouzet, *The Victorian
Economy* (1982). The neglected area of management and corporate
development is taken up by T. R. Gourvish, 'The railways and the
development of managerial enterprise in Britain, 1850–1939', in K.
Kobayashi and H. Morikawa (eds.), *Development of Managerial
Enterprise* (Tokyo, 1986).
T. R. Gourvish

Railways 1870–1914

Bibliographical guides
(a) *General histories.* The indispensable guide is G. Ottley, *A
Bibliography of British Railway History* (1966) which can now be
supplemented by J. Butt, 'Achievement and prospect: transport

history in the 1970s and 1980s', *Journal of Transport History*, 3rd ser., II (1981). The *JTH* also issues a biannual survey of transport history articles appearing in scholarly periodicals. The best introduction to railways history in this period are probably J. Simmonds, *The Railway in England and Wales 1830–1914. The System and its Working* (1978) and H. Pollins, *Britain's Railways. An Industrial History* (1971). There are also good chapters on railways in P. Bagwell, *The Transport Revolution, 1770–1970* (1974) and in T. C. Barker and C. Savage, *An Economic History of Transport* (1975). Among general histories those with the best coverage on railways in this period are W. Ashworth, *An Economic History of England 1870–1939* (1960), and F. Crouzet, *The Victorian Economy* (1982).

(b) *Statistical sources.* The basic source is the annual government publication *Returns of Capital, Traffic, Receipts and Working Expenditure etc. of the Railway Companies of the United Kingdom.* Many of the major series are reprinted in B. R. Mitchell and P. Deane, *Abstract of British Historical Statistics* (1962). Additional material of importance for the Edwardian period can be found in D. L. Munby and A. H. Watson, *Inland Transport Statistics, Great Britain 1900–1970* (1970). Estimates of ton-mileages for English and Welsh railways have recently been attempted by P. J. Cain in 'Private enterprise or public utility? Output, pricing and investment on English and Welsh railways, 1870–1914', *Journal of Transport History*, 3rd ser., 1 (1980). Series for railway capital expenditure which distinguish 'real' and 'nominal' capital are G. Hawke and M. C. Reed, 'Railway capital in the United Kingdom in the nineteenth century', *Economic History Review*, 2nd ser., XXII (1969), and R. J. Irving, 'The capitalization of British railways, 1830–1914', *Journal of Transport History*, 3rd ser., V (1984). On railways as investments the best sources for this period are R. C. Michie, 'Income, expenditure and investment of a Victorian millionaire: Lord Overstone, 1823–83', *Bulletin of the Institute of Historical Research*, LVIII (1985) and S. W. Martins, *A Great Estate at Work. The Holkham Estate and Its Inhabitants in the 19th Century* (1980). Some reasons for the decline of interest in railway securities after 1900 are given in A. Stockbroker, 'The depreciation of British home investments', *Economic Journal*, XXII (1912) and R. J. Irving, 'British railway investment and investors 1900–1914. An analysis with special reference to the North Eastern and London and North Western

Companies', *Business History,* XIII (1971).

(c) *Company histories.*   Good, scholarly histories of railway companies are hard to find. The best by far is R. Irving, *The North
Eastern Railway Company. An Economic History* (1976). G. Dow's
second volume of *The Great Central* (1962) is also useful as are one
or two of the older histories, especially E. T. McDermott's *History of
the Great Western Railway II: 1863–1921* (1964 edn, rev. C. R.
Clinker) and W. W. Tomlinson, *The North Eastern Railway,* (1915).
E. G. Barnes, *The Midland Main Line 1875–1922* (1969) has some
vivid detail but lacks the coherence of the other works cited. On
smaller companies the pick of the bunch is clearly C. L. Mowat's *The
Golden Valley Railway* (1964).

(d) *Network extensions.*   E. Carter, *An Historical Geography of the
Railways of the British Isles* (1959) is a year-by-year guide to lines
planned and opened. Further details can be found in the various
volumes of the *Regional History of the Railways of Great Britain.* A
graphic account of one famous extension is P. E. Baughan, *North of
Leeds. The Leeds–Settle–Carlisle Line and its Branches* (1966).
Dow's *Great Central* has a splendid account of the building of the last
main line to London.

(e) *Railway traffic.*   On the freight side, only the London coal traffic
has received any serious treatment, by R. Smith, *Sea-Coal for
London. History of the Coal Factors in the London Market,* though
there are some useful general remarks in Bagwell's *The Transport
Revolution.* Freight rates have been recently studied by P. J. Cain in
'The British railway rates problem 1894–1913', *Business History,*
XX (1978). The development of surburban and cheap passenger
travel has, however had extensive treatment most comprehensively
by J. R. Kellett in *Railways and Victorian Cities* (1969) and by H.
Perkin, *The Age of the Railway* (1971). An outstanding regional
study is T. C. Barker and R. M. Robbins, *A History of London
Transport,* Vol. II (1974). There is some useful information for
Scotland in J. R. Hume, 'Transport and towns in Victorian
Scotland', in G. Gordon and B. Dicks (eds.), *Scottish Urban History*
(1983).

(f) *Railways and economic development.*   The most wide-ranging general survey is J. Simmons, *The Railway in Town and Country, 1830–1914* (1986) and there is some information to be gleaned from P. J. Waller, *Town City and Nation. England 1850–1914*. The railways' influence on engineering is best explored via S. B. Saul, 'The market and the development of mechanical engineering industries in Britain, 1870–1914', *Economic History Review*, 2nd ser., XX (1967). Railway towns are the theme of D. E. C. Eversley, 'Engineering and railway works', *V. C. H. Wilts.*, Vol. 4, which deals with Swindon, and W. H. Chaloner in *Social and Economic Development of Crewe 1780–1923* (1950). B. J. Turton, 'The railway towns of southern England', *Transport History*, 2 (1969) is also extremely useful. On agriculture see C. Hallas, 'The social and economic impact of a rural railway: the Wensleydale Line', *Agricultural History Review*, 34 (1986) and P. J. Atkins, 'The growth of London's milk trade, *c.* 1845–1914', *Journal of Transport History*, new ser., IV (1977–78). D. W. Howell, *Land and People in Nineteenth Century Wales* (1977) also has a short section on the railways's impact. Agricultural traffic and rates are also the theme of P. J. Cain, 'Railways and price discrimination. The case of agriculture 1880–1914', *Business History*, XVIII (1976). Studies of the impact of the railway on particular businesses are few, but one of especial interest is C. Wilson, *First With The News. The History of W. H. Smith's 1792–1972* (1985). On the railways and resort development, Simmonds and Waller can be amplified by Perkin's *Age of the Railway* and J. K. Walton's books, *The Blackpool Landlady* (1978) and *The English Sea-side Resort. A Social History 1750–1914* (1983).

(g) *Railways as business concerns.* The pioneering works here are by Ashworth in the *Economic History of England* and D. H. Aldcroft, *Studies in British Transport History, 1870–1970* (1974), ch. 2. Criticisms and new departures can be found in: R. J. Irving 'The profitability and performance of British railways, 1870–1914', *Economic History Review*, 2nd ser., XXXI (1978); T. R. Gourvish, 'The performance of railway management after 1860: the railways of Watkins and Forbes', *Business History*, XX (1978); P. J. Cain, 'Private enterprise or public utility?', *op. cit.*; and Pollins, *British Railways*. An older but still useful study is D. E. C. Eversley, 'The Great Western Railway in the Great Depression', in G. Hawke and M. C. Reed, *Railways in the Victorian Economy* (1969).

(h) *Railways and government.* The 'railway interest' in Parliament is the subject of G. J. Alderman, *The Railway Interest 1870–1913* (1973). On pricing legislation and combination see P. J. Cain, 'Railway combination and government 1900–14', *Economic History Review,* 2nd ser., XXV (1972), and the articles by Cain referred to above. The survival of nationalisation as an issue before 1914 is discussed in E. Eldon Barry, *Nationalization in British Politics. The Historical Background* (1965).
P. J. Cain

Urban transport

Study of this subject from the point of view of British urban development, as distinct from particular rail, tram or bus services, is quite recent. The larger the town, the more it depended upon transport for its continued outward growth. London, the largest metropolitan centre in the world in the Victorian period, has been studied from this broader point of view in T. C. Barker and Michael Robbins, *A History of London Transport* (Allen & Unwin, I, 1963, covering the nineteenth century, and II, 1974, the twentieth; both volumes were issued in paperback in 1976). Theo Barker, 'Towards an historical classification of urban development from the eighteenth century', *Journal of Transport History,* 3rd ser., I (September 1980), which included new material not published in the fuller *History,* was written in the hope of encouraging others to apply this broad treatment to other towns; but so far without any published result.

The growing importance of horse-drawn transport until the beginning of the twentieth century is stressed in F. M. L. Thompson, 'Nineteenth-century horse sense', *Economic History Review,* 2nd ser., XXIX (February 1976), which should be on everybody's reading list, as should Alan Everitt's work on country carriers, 'Town and country in Victorian Leicestershire: the role of the village carrier' in Alan Everitt (ed.), *Perspectives in English Urban History* (Macmillan 1973) and 'Country carriers in the nineteenth century', *Journal of Transport History,* 2nd ser., III (February 1976).

Alan A. Jackson's *Semi-Detached London* (Allen & Unwin, 1973) is strongly to be recommended, a model deserving of emulation for other cities and other parts of London. His *London's Metropolitan Railway* (David & Charles, 1986) also contains relevant information and ideas. So does R. H. G. Thomas, *London's First Railway*

(Batsford, 1972; paperback 1986). Jack Simmons, *The Railway in Town and Country* (David & Charles, 1986) should also be read carefully. It is the second volume in a series he is writing on Britain's railways between 1830 and 1914, and to be published, under different publishers' imprints.

H. J. Dyos, *Victorian Suburb. A Study of the Growth of Camberwell* (Leicester University Press, 1961) is a classic and lasting memorial to the scholar and academic entrepreneur who endeavoured to make urban history a separate, definable discipline in Britain.
T. C. Barker

Coastal shipping

Guides to source material
Although there is some overlapping of the information provided, the following are all useful: R. C. Jarvis, 'Sources for the history of ships and shipping', *Journal of Transport History*, 3, 4 (1958), pp. 212–34; R. S. Craig, 'Shipping Records of the nineteenth and twentieth centuries', *Archives*, Vol. 7, No. 36 (1966), pp. 39–68, and R. J. B. Knight (ed.), *Guide to the Manuscripts of the National Maritime Museum, Vol. 2, Public records, Business Records and Artificial Collections* (Mansell, 1980). P. Mathias and A. W. H. Pearsall, *Shipping: a Survey of Historical Records* (David & Charles, Newton Abbot, 1971) include information on the location and availability of the records of some companies, such as the Bristol Steam Navigation Company, which participated in the coastal trade.

Primary sources
In the Parliamentary Papers, the *Trade and Navigation Accounts* record the tonnage of shipping engaged in coastwise services. The bills of entry in the Custom House Library, London, are an exasperating source – partial, inconsistent, and erratic – but they do contain much information on coastal freight carriage. The manuscript minutes of evidence of contested railway, harbour and pier bills, in the House of Lords Record Office, provide information on passenger and freight traffic going by sea. The records of the West Coast Conference and the English and Scotch Traffic Committee of the Railway Clearing House throw light on the competition between railways and coastal shipping and on the volume of freight and the number of passengers carried by each transport mode. For the

important links between mainland Britain and the Western Isles, Orkney and Shetland, the Isle of Man and the Isle of Wight, the Post Office Records, 23 Glasshill St., London SE1, are essential reading for the terms agreed with shipping contractors and the revenue produced from the provision of passenger and freight services.

Literary. R. L. Brett (ed.), *Barclay Fox's Journal* (Bell & Hyman, 1979), reveals the importance of steam packet services to business and other travellers in early Victorian England. H. V. Moffat's *From Ship's Boy to Skipper with Variations* (Simpkin, Marshall, Hamilton, Kent & Co., 1910), is a first-hand account of life in the east coast coal trade. E. Eglinton, *The Last of the Sailing Coasters* (HMSO, 1982), was written by a sailor engaged in the West Country coasting trade in the early years of the present century.

Freight transport
The growth of the tonnage of ships employed in coastal trade is mentioned in W. G. Hoffman, *British Industry 1750–1950* (Basil Blackwell, Oxford, 1955), p. 47. R. Craig, *Steam Tramps and Cargo Liners* (HMSO, 1980), includes a useful section on the coastal freight trade. Reasons for the predominance of steam shipping in coastwise traffic are considered in B. F. Duckham, 'The decline of coastal sail: a review article', *Transport History*, 2, 1 (1969). The competition between coasters and railways is examined in P. J. Perry, 'Return cargoes and small port survival: two Dorset examples', Dorset Natural History and Archeological Society, *Proclamations*, 89, (1967), pp. 314–17; in T. R. Gourvish, 'The railways and steamboat competition in early Victorian Britain', *Transport History*, 4 (1971), pp. 1–22 and in G. Channon, 'The Aberdeen beef trade with London, a study in steamship and railway competition', *Transport History*, 2, 1 (1969). Useful as illustrating the flexibility of the tramping coaster is B. Greenhill, 'The Mary of Truro: the life story of a coasting smack', *Mariners Mirror*, 46, 2 (1960), pp. 81–7. 'Coastwise lines of Great Britain' in *The Times Shipping Number*, 1913, gives a summary of the situation in the last year of peace. *The Coastwise Trade of the UK Past and Present and Its Possibilities*, anonymously authored (George Thompson, 1925), although written just after the war, gives a good view of the variety of freight services provided by coasters in the early twentieth century.

Coal trade
Still very useful is R. Smith, *Sea Coal for London* (Longman, 1961). R. Finch, *Coal from Newcastle* (Lavenham, 1973), includes many illustrations of the type of ships employed in carrying coal and maps showing the links with rivers and canals for its inland distribution. W. Runciman, *Collier Brigs and their Sailors* (Conway Maritime Press, 1971), gives a first hand account of the principal vessels employed in the east-coast coal trade.

Other main cargoes
Some specialised studies include: P. H. Stanier, 'The copper ore trade of south-west England in the nineteenth century', *Journal of Transport History,* new ser., V, 1 (1979); J. Lindsay, *A History of the North Wales Slate Industry* (David & Charles, Newton Abbot, 1974); E. Hughes and A. Eames, *Portmadoc Ships* (Gwynedd Archive Service, Caernarvon, 1975); R. M. Barton, *A History of the Cornish China Clay Industry* (Bradford Barton, Truro, 1971); L. T. C. Rolt, *The Potters Field: A History of the South Devon Ball Clay Industry* (David & Charles, Newton Abbot, 1984); and K. Hudson, *The History of English China Clays* (David & Charles, Newton Abbot, 1969).

Regional studies
Among the more valuable of these are H. C. Brookfield, 'Three Sussex ports, 1850–1959', *Journal of Transport History,* 2, 1 (1955); H. E. S. Fisher (ed.), *Ports and Shipping of the South West* (University of Exeter, 1970); W. J. Slade, *Out of Appledore* (Percival Marshall & Co., 1959); G. Farr, *Ships and Harbours of Exmoor* (Exmoor Press, Williton, 1974); A. Eames, *et al.* (eds.), *Maritime Wales* (Gwynedd Archives Service, 1976); H. F. Starkey, *Schooner Port: Two Centuries of Mersey Sail,* (G. W. and A. Hesketh, Ormskirk, 1983); A. Eames, *Ships and Seamen of Anglesey* (Llangefni, 1973); M. B. Wray, 'The Ramsay Steam Ship Company Ltd', *Maritime History,* III, 2 (1973); C. H. Lee, 'Some aspects of the coastal shipping trade: the Aberdeen Steam Navigation Company 1835–80', *Journal of Transport History,* new ser., 3, 2 (1975); A. M. Northway, 'The Tyne Steam Shipping Company: a late nineteenth-century shipping line', *Maritime History,* 2, 1 (1972). P. T. Wheeler, 'The development of shipping services on the East Coast of Scotland', *Journal of Transport History,* 6, 2 (1963); R. Simper, *East*

Coast Sail: Working Sail, 1850–1979 (David & Charles, Newton Abbot, 1972) and C. Capper, *The Port and Trade of London,* (Smith, Elder & Co, 1862). A fictional but broadly accurate account of a Clyde-based 'puffer' is to be found in Neil Munro's *Parahandy Tales* (Pan, 1969).

Passenger transport
Many of the published works on passenger steamships serve an antiquarian, rather than a transport history interest. Of the many books appearing in recent years the following are among the most useful: G. Donaldson, *Northwards by Sea* (Paul Harris Publishing, Edinburgh, 1978); Ken Davies, *Solent Passages and their Steamers, 1820–1981* (Isle of Wight County Press, Newport, 1982); A. and A. Cormack, *Days of Orkney Steam* (Kirkwall Press, Kirkwall, 1971); A. J. S. Paterson, *The Victorian Summer of the Clyde Steamers, 1864–1888* (David & Charles, Newton Abbot, 1972); A. Eames, *Ships and Seamen of Anglesey* (Anglesey Antiquarian Society, Llangefni, 1973); G. Farr, *West Country Passenger Steamers* (T. Stephenson, Prescot, 2nd edn., 1967) and *The Centenary of the Isle of Man Steam Packet Company 1830–1930* (published by the Company, Douglas, 1930). For the railway companies' participation in steamship services, B. F. Duckham's 'Railway steamship enterprise, the Lancashire and Yorkshire Railway's east coast fleet, 1904–14', *Business History,* 10, 1 (1968), should be consulted.

The provision of capital
A good introduction to the privately-owned ships is to be found in R. C. Jarvis, 'Fractional shareholding in British merchant ships, with special respect to the sixty-fourths', *Mariner's Mirror,* 45, 4 (1959). This should be followed by an examination of the *Shipping Registers* in the custom ports. G. E. Farr's *Chepstow Ships* (Chepstow, 1954), is invaluable for the area it covers. S. Palmer's 'Investors in London shipping, 1820–50', *Maritime History,* 2, 1 (1972), reveals the pattern of ownership in the most important maritime centre in Britain in early Victorian years. For shipping companies engaged in the coastal trade the Return: *Companies Formed under the Joint Stock Companies Act 1856, 1857 and 1862* (P.P., 1864, Vol. XVIII, p. 298), and subsequent dates and the Dead Company's Register, in the P.R.O., London, provide some essential information.

Insurance

In H. A. L. Cockrell and E. Green, *The British Insurance Business, 1593–1970*, (Heinemann, 1979), pp. 6, 10 and 14–15 and in Insurance Institute of London, *Shipping and Insurance Sketches* (the Institute, 1867 (reprinted 1967)) p. 70, essential information is provided about the mutual insurance clubs which insured much of coastal shipping. H. Hughes, *Immortal Sails* (R. Ross & Co., 1969), records the insurance arrangements made in the Welsh ports.

Technology

Technological developments in coastal shipping have been the subject of more intensive study than have commercial and business developments. J. G. Bruce's 'The contribution of cross channel and coastal vessels to the development of marine practice', *Journal of Transport History*, 4, 2 (1959), provides a good starting point. This may be followed by C. K. Harley's chapter 'The shift from sailing ships to steamships, 1850–1890: a study of technological change and diffusion', in D. N. McClosky (ed.), *Esssays in a Mature Economy: Britain after 1840* (Methuen, 1971). J. C. Robertson and H. H. Hagan's *A Century of Coaster Design and Operation*, (Institute of Engineers and Shipbuilders of Scotland, Glasgow, 1953), reveals how the design of ships was altered to meet the changing character of coastal trade. Two exceptionally good contemporary accounts are: E. E. Allen, 'On the comparative cost of transport by steam and sailing colliers and on the different modes of ballasting', Institution of Civil Engineers, *Proceedings*, XIV (1854–55), p. 318 ff, and L. Barnet, 'Description of a cargo carrying coastal steamship with detailed investigation as to its efficiency', Institution of Civil Engineers, *Proceedings*, LXVI (1881), p. 263 ff.

P. S. Bagwell and J. Armstrong

Ports

The only modern survey of port development is G. Jackson, *The History and Archaeology of Ports* (1983). J. Bird, *The Major Seaports of the U.K.* (1963) deals with the geographical side of the larger ports. Older surveys, such as D. Owen, *Ports and Docks* (1904) and W. French, *The Scottish Ports: Handbook of Rates, Charges and General Information* (1938), contain some useful information but little history.

The movement of trade and shipping at individual ports was recorded by the Customs Service, published as Parliamentary Papers and summarised in the *Annual Statement of Trade and Navigation*. Moreover, since major harbour and dock work was undertaken by authority of Parliament, Select Committee Reports offering a detailed examination of local history and current conditions are to be found indexed under the name of the port concerned.

Apart from J. D. Porteous, *Canal Ports* (1977), there has been no serious attempt to examine groups of ports according to economic or organisational types, and little attempt even to set ports in either local or national context. As a result the bibliography is largely a list of studies of individual ports, grouped by region for convenience.

There are many old and some new histories of individual ports, though there is a tendency to regard ports as physical rather than economic entities. In the North-East the rise and heyday of the coal ports is summarised in W. W. Tomlinson, *North Eastern Railway* (1915) and detailed in J. Guthrie, *The River, its History and Resources* (1880); C. Sharp, *History of Hartlepool* (1851); and P. Barton, 'The port of Stockton-on-Tees and its creeks, 1825–61', *Maritime History,* 1 (1971). R. Weatherhill, *The Ancient Port of Whitby and its Shipping* (1908) is completely overshadowed by S. Jones, 'A Maritime History of the Port of Whitby' (unpublished Ph.D., University of London, 1983). The best sources for Hull are K. J. Allison, *A History of the County of York: East Riding, 1: The History of Kingston upon Hull* (1969), pp. 215–86, J. M. Bellamy, *The Trade and Shipping of Nineteenth-Century Hull* (1971), and E. Gillett and K. Macmahon, *A History of Hull* (1980). Hull's role as a coal port is revealed in K. Hoole (ed.), *The Hull & Barnsley Railway* (1972) and H. E. C. Newham (ed.), *Hull as a Coal Port* (1913). Goole is covered by B. Duckham, *The Yorkshire Ouse* (1967), and Grimsby by G. Dow, *Great Central* (2 vols., 1959), G. Jackson, *Grimsby and the Haven Company, 1796–1846* (1971) and E. Gillett, *A History of Grimsby* (1970). The smaller places in the South-East are the subject of W. J. Wren, *The Ports of the Eastern Counties* (1976).

The history of London is the subject of a major research exercise which may take decades to complete. In the meantime J. G. Broodbank's old-fashioned and inadequate *History of the Port of London* (2 vols., 1921) remains the source on which are based recent accounts such as R. D. Brown, *The Port of London* (1978) and J.

Pudney, *London's Docks* (1975). C. Capper, *The Port and Trade of London* (1862) is a mine of information for the middle of the century, and this period is beautifully illustrated in G. Doré and B. Jerrold, *London* (1872). Since docks tend to dominate the story, a useful corrective is A. Ellis, *Three Hundred Years on London River: The Hay's Wharf Story* (1952).

One of the best introductions to the Channel Ports is still W. C. Russell, *English Channel Ports* (1884). Subsequent local studies include H. C. Brookfield, 'Three Sussex ports', *Journal of Transport History*, 2 (1955); J. H. Farrant, *The Harbours of Sussex, 1700–1914* (1976), and 'The seaborne trade of Sussex', *Sussex Arhaeological Collections*, 114 (1976); D. W. Gibb, 'The rise of the port of Newhaven, 1850–1914', *Transport History*, 3 (1970); P. J. Perry, 'The development of cross channel trade at Weymouth, 1794–1914', *Transport History*, 2 (1969). The standard history of Southampton is A. Temple Patterson, *A History of Southampton, 1700–1914* (3 vols., 1975), while the role of railway companies is brought out in D. J. Rowe, 'Southampton and the "railway mania", 1844–7', in *Transport History*, 2 (1969).

The best sources for south western ports are E. A. G. Clark, *The Ports of the Exe Estuary, 1660–1860: a Study in Historical Geography* (1960); H. E. S. Fisher (ed.), *Ports and Shipping in the South West* (1971); and R. Pearse, *Ports and Harbours of Cornwall* (1963). C. Wells, *A Short History of the Port of Bristol* (1909) is unfortunately still the only full-scale work on Bristol, though many aspects of port development and operation are revealed in the records of the dock authority edited in David Large, *The Port of Bristol, 1848–84* (1984).

The South Wales ports are covered by R. S. Craig, 'Ports and shipping, 1750–1914', in *Glamorgan County History*, Vol. 5 (1980), and individually by E. L. Chappel, *History of the Port of Cardiff* (1939), M. Daunton, *Coal Metropolis: Cardiff, 1870–1914* (1977) and W. H. Jones, *History of the Port of Swansea* (1922).

The best source for Liverpool and Birkenhead is F. E. Hyde, *Liverpool and the Mersey* (1971). The operation of the Mersey Docks and Harbour Board is recounted by S. Mountfield, *Western Gateway* (1965); the success of a minor upriver port (Runcorn) in H. F. Starkey, *Schooner Port: Two Centuries of Upper Mersey Sail* (1983); and of a major rival in D. Farnie, *The Manchester Ship Canal and the Rise of the Port of Manchester, 1894–1975* (1980).

Attempts to establish rival port at Preston are discussed in P. N. Davies, *Henry Tyrer, a Liverpool Shipping Agent and his Enterprise, 1879–1979* (1979). The old and new Cumbrian ports are discussed in J. Marshall and J. K. Walton, *The Lakeland Counties* (1981), J. D. Marshall and S. Pollard, 'The Furness Railway and the growth of Barrow', *Journal of Transport History,* 1 (1953), and S. Pollard, 'Barrow-in-Furness and the 7th Duke of Devonshire', *Economic History Review,* 8 (1956).

The Scottish Ports have been well served in recent years. B. Lenman, *From Esk to Tweed* (1975) examines the major eastern ports, while A. R. Buchan, *The Port of Peterhead* (1980) is a specialist study by an engineer. The smaller places are covered in J. R. Hume, *Industrial Archaeology of Scotland* (2 vols., 1976), and I. Donnachie, *The Industrial Archaeology of Galloway* (1971). There is, unfortunately, no satisfactory economic study of Glasgow, though a major research project is under way. J. D. Marwick, *The River Clyde and the Clyde Burghs* (1909) and W. F. MacArthur, *History of the Port of Glasgow* (1932) are useful, but the outstanding work, dealing with the physical structure of the port, is J. F. Riddell, *Clyde Navigation: a History of the Development and Deepening of the River Clyde* (1979).

The docks and engineering side of ports can be followed in F. M. Du Plat Taylor, *The Design, Construction and Maintenance of Docks, Wharves and Piers* (3rd edn, 1949); L. F. V. Harcourt, *Harbours and Docks* (2 vols., 1885); J. Rennie, *The Theory, Formation and Construction of British and Foreign Harbours* (1858); and T. Stevenson, *Design and Construction of Harbours* (1874). J. Glynn's *Rudimentary Treatise on the Construction of Cranes* (1854) introduces the significant changes around mid-century which are amplified and continued in I. McNeil, *Hydraulic Power* (1972). Coal loading machinery is described in detail in G. Head, *A Home Tour through the Manufacturing Districts* (1835) and in the works of Guthrie, Sharp, *supra*. Most of the major construction works were the subjects of papers delivered to the Institution of Civil Engineers, and may be found in their *Proceedings,* complete with diagrams. The men who worked the machinery are dealt with in two admirable local studies: J. Lovell, *Stevedores and Dockers: a Study of Trade Unionism in the Port of London, 1870–1914* (1969); and R. Brown, *Waterfront Organisation in Hull, 1880–1900* (1972).

Shipping

Because of their importance to national revenue and security, a huge volume of statistics and reports covering every aspect of trade and shipping is contained in Parliamentary Papers and summarised in *Annual Statements of Trade and Navigation*. This material is, however, so obscure and difficult to analyse that it is rarely used by inexperienced students, though abstracts of some of it are to be found in B. R. Mitchell and P. Deane, *Abstract of British Historical Statistics* (1962). Partly because of this overabundance of information there is still no adequate general survey of British trade or shipping in the nineteenth century. In the 1930s W. Schlote attempted a commentary on statistics in his *British Overseas Trade from 1700 to the 1930's* (1952), which is widely quoted but must be used with care. There are, however, two superb studies of certain aspects of trade for limited periods: R. Davis, *The Industrial Revolution and British Overseas Trade* (1979) and S. B. Saul, *Studies in British Overseas Trade 1870–1914* (1960). The vexed question of Britain's failure to compete towards the end of the period is dealt with in R. J. S. Hoffman, *Great Britain and the German Trade Rivalry, 1875–1914* (1933).

There is a growing body of literature examining the importance of British trade and shipping in opening up specific areas of the world, of which the following are excellent examples: D. C. M. Platt, *Latin America and British Trade, 1806–1914* (1972); F. E. Hyde, *Far Eastern Trade* (1973); G. C. Allen and A. G. Donnithorne, *Western Enterprise in Far Eastern Economic Development: China and Japan* (1954); M. Greenberg, *British Trade and the Opening of China, 1800–42* (1951); and P. N. Davies, *The Trade Makers: Elder Dempster in West Africa, 1852–1972* (1973). The role of the overseas agency system for encouraging trade and production in America and the Far East is revealed in S. Marriner, *Rathbones of Liverpool, 1845–73* (1961). The importance of Suez to the establishing of an international economy is discussed in M. E. Fletcher, 'The Suez Canal and world shipping, 1869–1914', *Journal of Economic History*, 18 (1958), and, in great detail, in D. Farnie, *East and West of Suez: the Suez Canal in History* (1969).

The best general survey of nineteenth-century shipping is still W. Kirkaldy, *British Shipping: its History, Organisation and Importance* (1914, reprinted 1970). The more recent R. H. Thornton,

British Shipping (1939) is a reasonable but old-fashioned introduction to the subject. A good modern summary is H. J. Dyos and D. H. Aldcroft, British Transport: an Economic Survey from the C16th to the C20th (1969), chs. 8–9.

The evolution of the shipowner is examined in S. P. Ville's important study of English Shipowning during the Industrial Revolution: Michael Henley & Son, London Shipowners, 1770–1830 (1987). The development of the 'shipping empires' at the end of the century is best followed in E. Green and M. Moss's examination of the activities of Lord Kylsant in A Business of National Importance (1985) and in books on individual lines, managers and owners, of which the following are the most satisfactory: G. Blakc, The Ben Line (1956); P. N. Davies, 'The African Steam Ship Company', in J. R. Harris (ed.), Liverpool and Merseyside (1969); P. N. Davies, Sir Alfred Jones: Shipping Entrepreneur par excellence (1978); P. N. Davies, Henry Tyrer: A Liverpool Shipping Agent and his Enterprise, 1879–1979 (1979); F. E. Hyde and J. R. Harris, Blue Funnel: a History of Alfred Holt & Co., 1865–1914 (1956); F. E. Hyde, Cunard and the North Atlantic, 1840–1973 (1975); A. H. John, A Liverpool Merchant House, being the History of Alfred Booth & Co., 1863–1958 (1959); F. E. Hyde, Shipping Enterprise and Management, 1830–1939: Harrisons of Liverpool (1967); S. Marriner and F. E. Hyde, The Senior: John Swire, 1825–1898 (1967); J. Orbell, E. Green and M. Moss, From Cape to Cape: the History of Lyle Shipping Company (1978); and J. Taylor, Ellermans, a Wealth of Shipping (1976). Brief bibliographies of a number of important men are contained in C. Jones, Pioneer Shipowners (1934), and potted histories of lines out of Liverpool, with some reference to other ports, are in G. Chandler, Liverpool Shipping: a Short History (1960).

Developments in early nineteenth-century shipping in specific ports are studied in: F. Neal, 'Liverpool shipping in the early nineteenth century', in J. R. Harris (ed.), Liverpool and Merseyside (1969); P. L. Cottrell, 'The steamship on the Mersey, 1850–80: investment and ownership', in Cottrell and Aldcroft (eds.), Shipping, Trade and Commerce (1981); G. Jackson, 'Port competition on the Humber: docks, railways and steamships in the nineteenth century', in E. M. Sigworth (ed.), Ports and Resorts in the Regions (1980); and S. R. Palmer, 'Investors in London shipping, 1820–50', in Maritime History, 2 (1973).

The technical changes occurring within shipping are covered best in: E. C. Smith, *A Short History of Naval and Marine Engineering* (1937); D. R. MacGregor, *Merchant Sailing Ships, 1815–50* (1984); D. R. MacGregor, *The Tea Clippers: their History and Development, 1833–75* (2nd expanded edn. 1983); G. S. Graham, 'The ascendancy of the sailing ship, 1850–85', in *Economic History Review*, IX (1956); and C. K. Harley, 'The shift from sailing ships to steam ships, 1850–90: a study in technological change and its diffusion', in D. N. McCloskey (ed.), *Essays on a Mature Economy: Britain after 1840* (1971).

Fluctuations and profitability in shipping have been little studied, but one minor line is discussed in national context in T. E. Milne, 'British shipping in the nineteenth century: a study of the Ben Line papers', in P. L. Payne (ed.), *Studies in Scottish Business History* (1967). The relationship between freight rates and activity is discussed in D. C. North, 'Ocean freight rates and economic development, 1750–1913; in *Journal of Economic History*, 18 (1958), L. Isserlis, 'Tramp shipping cargoes and freights', in *Journal of the Royal Statistical Society*, 101 (1938), and E. A. V. Angier, *Fifty Years of Freight, 1869–1919* (1920).

The role of shipping in imperialism is discussed in A. J. H. Latham, *The International Economy and the Undeveloped World, 1865–1914* (1978); R. Greenhill, 'Shipping, 1850–1914', in D. C. M. Platt (ed.), *Business Imperialism, 1840–1930: An inquiry based on British experience in Latin America* (1977), pp. 119–55; and F. Munro, 'Shipping subsidies and railway guarantees: William Mackinnon, East Africa and the Indian Ocean, 1860–93', in *Journal of African History*, 28 (1987).

The difficulties for shipping building up in the years before 1914 are analysed in E. S. Gregg, 'Vicissitudes in the shipping trade, 1870–1920', in *Quarterly Journal of Economics* (1921) and D. H. Aldcroft, 'The depression in British Shipping, 1901–11', *Journal of Transport History*, VII (1965). The growth of competition is examined in Aldcroft, 'The mercantile marine', in D. H. Aldcroft (ed.), *The Development of British Industry and Foreign Competition, 1875–1914* (1968), and more extensively in V. Vale, *The American Peril: Challenge to Britain on the North Atlantic, 1901–4* (1984) and S. G. Sturmey, *British Shipping and World Competition* (1962). The question of subsidies is dealt with from the American perspective in R. Meeker, *History of Shipping Subsidies* (1905) and more recently from the British side in L. Saletan, *State Subsidies to the British Merchant Marine, 1900–50* (1954). Protective Conferences are surveyed in B. M. Deakin, *Shipping Conferences: a Study of their Origins, Development and Economic Practices* (1973), and more particularly in Hyde's *Cunard*.

G. Jackson

Index